THE AMERICAN LAWYER

The AMERICAN LAWYER

A Summary of the Survey of the Legal Profession

By

ALBERT P. BLAUSTEIN

and

CHARLES O. PORTER

With CHARLES T. DUNCAN

Foreword by

REGINALD HEBER SMITH

Director, Survey of the Legal Profession

GREENWOOD PRESS, PUBLISHERS

WESTPORT, CONNECTICUT

Library of Congress Cataloging in Publication Data

Blaustein, Albert P 1921-
The American Lawyer.

Bibliography: p.
1. Lawyers--United States. I. Porter, Charles Orlando, 1919- joint author. II. Survey of the Legal Profession. III. Title.
[KF301.B5 1972] 340'.023 72-5452
ISBN 0-8371-6438-9

Originally published in 1954 by The University of Chicago Press, Chicago

Reprinted with the permission of Albert P. Blaustein

Reprinted in 1972 by Greenwood Press, Inc.
51 Riverside Avenue, Westport, CT 06880

Library of Congress catalog card number 72-5452
ISBN 0-8371-6438-9

Printed in the United States of America

10 9 8 7 6 5 4 3 2

Foreword

This book is designed to make available to leaders of public opinion—business executives, economists, editors, journalists, labor leaders, clergymen, scholars, social workers, sociologists, teachers, and vocational guidance counselors—as well as to members of the public generally and to members of the bar a *summary* of the facts, cognate material, and recommendations assembled by the Survey of the Legal Profession during the last seven years. These materials were published in approximately 175 separate reports written by the "Survey team" of over four hundred men and women, more than 90 per cent of whom were volunteers and devoted hours of labor to their assigned subjects because of their love for their profession and their country.

Of these many reports, twelve are in book form, six statistical tomes are in IBM typed form, and the rest have been printed as articles in various periodicals—mostly bar journals and law reviews. Although some few libraries have complete sets, the scattered Survey reports are virtually inaccessible to the busy reader, writer, lawyer, or scholar. It is hoped that they may all be published as a complete set by the American Bar Foundation, so that they may be readily available at least in all law libraries, court libraries, and state libraries.

Even if easily available, the aggregate bulk of all this material would dismay most potential readers and impose an intolerable burden on their limited time.

When the University of Chicago Press first suggested the idea of a summary volume, there at once occurred to me two analogous situations in my own experience which, I am sure, have been shared by many others.

Never have I had the time to read the twelve volumes by Sir James George Frazer, but I have read his one-volume condensation of *The Golden Bough*. Nor have I read the six volumes of Arnold J. Toynbee's *A Study of History*, but I have read the one-volume abridgment by D. C. Somervell. These two summaries have been a blessing to many persons because they have opened doors to important knowledge that otherwise would have been locked.

For those who may be hearing for the first time of the Survey of the Legal Profession, it is appropriate to tell the nature of this Survey, its origin, its organization, and its financing.

The Survey of the Legal Profession is a broad study of the functioning of lawyers in a free society.

Under a government of laws the lives, the fortunes, and the freedom of the people are wholly dependent upon the enforcement of their constitutional rights by an independent judiciary and an independent bar.

The legal profession is a public profession. Lawyers are public servants. They are the stewards of all the legal rights and obligations of all the citizens. It is incumbent on stewards, if they are to be faithful to their trust, to render an accounting from time to time.

This Survey is an honest effort to make a complete audit and report for submission to the American people.

When World War II was drawing to its close and the thoughts of men were turning again to the future, the American Bar Association's Section of Legal Education and Admissions to the Bar proposed a study of those subjects for the purpose of improving professional standards.

It soon became apparent that a worth-while study of the proper objectives of legal education involved the much wider problem of finding out what lawyers actually do in present-day society and whether they are adequately meeting the needs of the public.

This broader plan was approved by the House of Delegates in 1944. Under this authority, the project was carefully developed until it was in the blueprint stage.

By 1947 financial support for the undertaking had been secured. The Carnegie Corporation of New York made a grant of $100,000. The American Bar Association appropriated $50,000, payable over a five-year term, and authorized its president to select a group of lawyers and laymen who would constitute an independent Council having complete charge of the undertaking.

In 1951 supplemental grants were made—$75,000 by the Carnegie Corporation, $20,000 by the American Bar Association, and

$30,000 by the American Bar Association Endowment. All officers of the Survey, the members of its Council, and its two directors have served without compensation.

Early in 1947 President Carl B. Rix had recruited the original personnel of the Council, and the group at once went to work to organize the Survey.

From the moment of its inception, the Council has been independent, autonomous, and self-perpetuating, with its own constitution, its own officers, and its own treasury.

This cardinal fact cannot be emphasized too much or stated too often. It has been expressed most clearly by the late Judge William L. Ransom, editor-in-chief of the *American Bar Association Journal,* in its issue of May, 1947:

> The Survey will be conducted as an independent project in the interests of the profession and the public by the Director and the staff which he selects, and will go forward with the advice of the Council.
>
> The relationship of our Association is that it perceived the need for finding out the facts about our profession, arranged for the financing of the Survey jointly by the Carnegie Corporation and the Association, sponsored the selection of the Council from among lawyers and non-lawyers with outstanding qualifications, and committed the project to the independent judgment of this distinguished body and the Director chosen by it. With these steps of organization completed in April, the Survey and its results are completely in the hands of the Director and Council.

As an independent entity the Council chose its own officers and elected the following: chairman, Judge Orie L. Phillips, of Denver, chief judge of the United States Court of Appeals for the Tenth Circuit; secretary, Dean Albert J. Harno, of the University of Illinois College of Law; and treasurer, Judge Walter M. Bastian, of Washington, D.C., judge of the United States District Court for the District of Columbia.

In addition to the officers, the members of the Council have been: Howard L. Barkdull, James E. Brenner, Herbert W. Clark, Charles P. Curtis, John W. Davis, John S. Dickey, Charles E. Dunbar, Jr., Albert J. Harno, Paul G. Hoffman (a member until his appointment as ECA Director), Devereux C. Josephs, William Clarke Mason, Philbrick McCoy, Harold G. Moulton, Orie L. Phillips, Carrol M. Shanks, Reginald Heber Smith, Robert G. Storey, and Arthur T. Vanderbilt; and ex officio: Cody Fowler, Harold J.

Gallagher, Tappan Gregory, Frank E. Holman, William J. Jameson, and Carl B. Rix.

The first Director of the Survey was Arthur T. Vanderbilt, who resigned late in 1947 when he was appointed chief justice of the Supreme Court of New Jersey. His successor is the undersigned.

In a sincere effort to secure objectivity, the Council created an Advisory Committee of Laymen which has met regularly, which has been given access to all material and furnished with all reports, and which has the right at any time to speak its own mind. This Advisory Committee has itself supervised the preparation of the Survey Report entitled "Complaints against Lawyers."

The members of that Advisory Committee of Laymen have been: Theodore C. Briggs, J. Frank Dobie, Wallace B. Donham, Rev. Frederick M. Eliot, Channing Frothingham, George C. Hull, Louis M. Lyons, The Most Reverend Eric F. MacKenzie, William Miller, Sumner Welles, and Laurence L. Winship.

Just as objectivity was the Survey's first great problem, so ultimate control of and responsibility for all the Survey work, reports, and findings became its second. This is the age-old problem of censorship.

Inasmuch as there were no strings on the grants of money by the Carnegie Corporation, the American Bar Association, or the American Bar Association Endowment, they had no power of censorship. The issue, if it ever arose, would be between the Council and the Director.

At its organization meeting, Mr. Hoffman explained to the Council the principles involved and illustrated them out of his experience as chairman of the Committee on Economic Development. On the one hand, no self-respecting person will give years of his life to an undertaking if, at the end, his report is to be suppressed or thrown away. On the other hand, self-respecting persons cannot afford to serve on a Council if, at the end, they are to be held publicly responsible for proposals which they believe to be evil.

The only tolerable solution was written into the Survey's constitution and provides:

> The Director of the Survey shall have academic freedom to determine the scope of the various divisions of the Survey, the selection of the staff to conduct the work of the Survey and the order of conducting the same.

The Director shall make report to the Council from time to time of the conduct and progress of the Survey and, as and when the divisions of the Survey shall in the judgment of the Director be concluded to the point of forming a basis for publication, shall make report to the Council before actual publication thereof shall be made. Matters concerning publications may, by the Council, be referred to its Committee on Publications.

The Council shall consider with the Director all matters with respect to the Survey intended for publication and, in the event that there may be disagreement between the Director and a majority of the Council with regard to conclusions based upon recorded facts, the Council shall record its conclusions and they shall be published simultaneously with the report of the Director.

This academic freedom accorded to the Director has in practice also been extended to the writers of Survey reports after their selection by the Director and approval by the Council.

For the arduous and responsible task of abridging thousands of printed pages into a one-volume summary and doing it so impartially and without distortion of undue emphasis, it would have been difficult to have found two men better qualified than Mr. Blaustein and Mr. Porter.

Both joined the "Survey team" at an early date; both worked hard and became my first lieutenants; both have seen the Survey intimately, at close range, and from the inside. They have shared in the joy of having splendid reports come in, and they are aware of our disappointments and failures. Both are now in independent practice, and neither is beholden to me or to the Survey.

Although this volume is entirely a project of the University of Chicago Press and is wholly independent of the Survey, I have been glad to co-operate whenever possible along the way; and so I have been close enough to the work to assure the reader that Mr. Blaustin and Mr. Porter have written their summary in all good faith. The recommendations herein set forth are those of the Survey report-writers themselves; they are not personal editorial opinions smuggled into this text.

Because the need for a summary of this sort is so obvious, I have set great store by this project. Those of us who have devoted years to the Survey of the Legal Profession are interested only in concrete results. The organized bar today is ready to make an enormous contribution toward a better administration of justice, a finer national life, and a more peaceful world. Although lawyers see the evils and the dangers quite clearly and have positive ideas as to sound remedies, all reform and all improvement must wait upon the understanding, approval, and support of public opinion.

It must be an informed public opinion, and the information must come from those to whom the public naturally and properly looks for guidance and leadership. In a complex society the people need many leaders. I have ventured to suggest many of them in the first paragraph of this Foreword.

To them I affirm that I believe they can rely on this volume as an honest summary of the Survey reports which, in turn, had been accepted by the Survey as the best that could be obtained under limitations of time and of resources. A glance at the Bibliography shows how many men, universally respected and regarded as authorities in their several fields, wrote or participated in the Survey reports.

Inasmuch as I hope and have faith that this volume will be widely used, three more things should be said in the interests of clarity and complete understanding.

First, when Mr. Blaustein and Mr. Porter did their writing, two major Survey reports were not available to them. "Bar Association Organization and Activities," by Glenn R. Winters, was published in book form in May, 1954. "Law Schools in the United States" will be published in book form in 1955.

Second, after these last reports have been issued and a reasonable time for criticism and correction has elapsed, it will be my duty as Director of the Survey to write a final report which will not be in the nature of a summary but will be, God willing, a synthesis of all the Survey reports and material, together with an integrated plan for improving our administration of justice, for making the legal profession a stronger force for the public good and a more splendid instrumentality to serve our national welfare.

Finally, when my report is out of the way, a layman will have the final say. For this task the Survey Council in 1951 selected Mr. George Waverley Briggs, of Dallas, Texas. Since that time he has received all Survey reports, has been given access to all Survey files, and has been free to ask any questions of the Director or members of the Survey Council.

It is true that the members of the "Survey team" have been predominantly lawyers. If we lawyers have had blind spots, if we have not been harsh enough in self-criticism, if we have failed in impartiality or objectivity, at least we have lived up to the finest traditions of the legal profession, because we have selected an honest and upright judge who will render his final verdict upon us and our work in the court of public opinion.

REGINALD HEBER SMITH

BOSTON, MASSACHUSETTS

Contents

CHAPTER I

The Legal Profession: Status in Society

WHO IS THE AMERICAN LAWYER?

From all outward appearances the American lawyer is much like everybody else. He is dressed no better than representatives of other occupations or businesses requiring contact with the public: the salesman, the teacher, the doctor. Certainly he possesses neither the home nor the car which corresponds to the income that others may think he earns, based upon his many years of education and the hours he devotes to his profession.

He is generally well known in his community, partly because of his leadership in politics and worth-while communal activities, partly because of his constant service to those in need. In the time and effort he devotes to his neighbors' problems, without compensation, he more closely resembles the clergyman than he does the member of any other calling. Yet he is surprisingly unpopular. He has been unhappily described as one who gets two other men to strip for a fight and then takes their clothes. And the cause he serves with such diligence is constantly met with carping criticism and complaint.

His standards are high; and it must be said to his great credit that the standards are self-imposed. Not only must he meet the rigid character and educational barriers set by his brethren for admission to the trade but, once a member of the profession, he is required to conform to their—and his—rigorous code of principles and practice.

He is a good citizen. While his income places him squarely within the great American middle class, he seldom finds himself in the financial straits which beset other members of that class. Few of his fellow-practitioners ever go into bankruptcy, for example. He is a good credit risk and a good insurance risk. He is also a good joiner and a good neighbor. And, if he beats his wife with a stick no thicker than his thumb, he does so in accordance with personal tastes and habits common to all men—and without any exceptional motivation based on his special knowledge of the common law.

Statistically speaking, he was born in the decade 1905–14 and is now between thirty-seven and forty-six years of age. The chances are better than four to one that he attended college, but there is more than a 50 per cent possibility that he did not receive a college degree. There is more than a 93 per cent probability that he attended law school, and the odds are four to one that he received a law degree. He is probably a solo practitioner, possessing neither partners nor associates, and it is likely that he practices his profession in one of the big cities—one with a population of more than 200,000. He now numbers more than 200,000, or approximately 1 to every 740 persons in the United States.

He is the American lawyer.

And this is his story—a story told through the medium of the 12 volumes and 158 special articles and reports written for the Survey of the Legal Profession—a story which encompasses his professional and public services, his education and his economics, his standards and his ideals, and his activities as a member of the organized bar.

When research for the Survey of the Legal Profession was begun in 1947, it was found, to the astonishment of the researchers, that comparatively little was really known about the American lawyer. Despite the profusion of legal literature, little or nothing had been written about what lawyers actually *do* in present-day society and about the accomplishments of the profession in striving to meet the needs of the public. Not even the number of lawyers in the United States was a known quantity.

HOW MANY LAWYERS ARE THERE?

Lawyer-population studies were among the first jobs on the Survey agenda, and through the co-operation of Martindale-Hubbell, Inc., publishers of the nation's largest legal directory, the figures began to take shape. Four mammoth statistical reports were prepared by James V. Martindale, Edward J. Nofer, and William Hildebrand, Jr., based upon information contained in the 1949 and 1952 directories, and eight additional studies were submitted outlining and analyzing the Martindale-Hubbell figures.

The only preliminary data on the subject were contained in the Census reports of 1940, listing a total of 180,483 lawyers and judges in the United States. And since the Survey began its studies, the Bureau of the Census has reported on a legal population of 181,226 as a result of its 1950 tabulations.

These statistics are totally inadequate for any comprehensive analysis. To begin with, there is a serious question as to their accuracy: the census-taker accepts any person's statement as to his occupation, and there is no provision for a check on the answers. How much this makes the count inadequate it is impossible to say. Further, a lawyer is listed by the Census according to the state in which he lives rather than the state in which he practices. This prevents the figures from giving any clear picture of the availability of legal services. Finally, the Census failed to provide any of the supplementary data desired by the bar, relating to such matters as status in practice, education, and the number of lawyers in public office.

Accordingly, the Survey turned to Martindale-Hubbell for assistance. Three of the four reports which were prepared were based upon information compiled as of September, 1948, for the *Directory* of 1949; the fourth contains data as of September, 1951, on the members of the bar whose names appeared in the 1952 edition. Of the eight analytical studies, seven were predicated on the 1948 compilations—going into the details of lawyers at work, America's women lawyers, legal education, and the special figures gathered for New York State and New York City. The legal education reports are considered in chapter vi below; the other 1948 figures are presented merely as supplementary information to the 1951 population summary.

Unfortunately, from the statistical point of view, there is no one individual figure which can be used to indicate the total active membership of the American bar. Martindale-Hubbell records reveal a total of 221,605 "lawyers accounted for," but 19,568 of that number were not included in the 1952 *Directory,* since they failed to complete the forms necessary for listing. Those who failed to return questionnaires include members of the bar who never entered practice, who have discontinued practice, or who, for business or personal reasons, were not interested in being identified as lawyers. Thus, while the 221,605 figure is accurate, it is by no means the best or the most useful one to reflect the number of attorneys whose services are available to those seeking legal guidance.

Subtracting 19,568 from 221,605 leaves the total of 202,037 attorneys whose names have been listed by Martindale-Hubbell—1 lawyer for every 746 men, women, and children in the United States. This total, however, could not be used for the statistical breakdowns. Some members of the bar maintain two offices, and, as a result, the 1952 *Directory* actually contained 204,111 entries—a figure which could not be corrected in the individual state totals, since many attorneys with more than one place of business maintain their second offices in other states. Consequently, it is the uncorrected figure which was used in collating the data on age, education, status in practice, etc., and in comparing state and national totals.

The fourth important total used by the Survey refers to the number of lawyers in private practice—176,995, or 1 lawyer to every 851 members of the national population. This figure reflects those attorneys whose legal services are available to private citizens and corporations and excludes the listings for government service, judicial office, salaried positions, and those lawyers who are inactive or retired.

Of the 204,111 "lawyers' listings," 107,151 (52.5 per cent) are in cities with populations in excess of 200,000, while 96,960 (47.5 per cent) are in the smaller communities.

New York State has by far the greatest total number of lawyers and, with the exception of the District of Columbia (which has been classified as a "state" for statistical purposes) the highest concentration of the legal profession. One out of every six attorneys in America has his law office in the Empire State, and there are more lawyers in New York than in the twenty-six smallest states combined. Nearly 12 per cent of the nation's lawyer population is located in New York City alone, and the city's figure is actually larger than the total for twenty-three of the small-population states combined. There are 33,206 lawyers listed for the state, 16.26 per cent of the 204,111 Martindale-Hubbell entries.

Illinois has the second largest number of lawyers, 15,643 (7.66 per cent), followed by California with 14,577 (7.14 per cent), Ohio with 11,020 (5.39 per cent), Texas with 9,997 (4.90 per cent), and

TABLE 1

Comparison of Lawyer Population and General Population, by States

Total population, continental United States, 1950 Census	150,697,361
Total number lawyers accounted for	221,605
Total number lawyers' listings	204,111
Total number lawyers listed (corrected figure based on allowance for multiple listings)	202,037

State	1950 Population Rank	1951 Lawyer Rank	No. of Lawyers' Listings	Per Cent of Total Lawyers' Listings
Alabama	17	29	2,098	1.03
Arizona	38	37	865	0.42
Arkansas	30	32	1,628	0.80
California	2	3	14,577	7.14
Colorado	34	28	2,122	1.04
Connecticut	28	26	2,515	1.23
Delaware	47	48	316	0.15
District of Columbia	36	9	6,637	3.25
Florida	20	13	4,165	2.04
Georgia	13	16	3,636	1.78
Idaho	44	43	579	0.28
Illinois	4	2	15,643	7.66
Indiana	12	14	4,119	2.02
Iowa	22	21	3,261	1.60
Kansas	31	27	2,220	1.09
Kentucky	19	22	3,009	1.47
Louisiana	21	24	2,730	1.34
Maine	35	36	887	0.43
Maryland	24	19	3,320	1.63
Massachusetts	9	7	7,788	3.82
Michigan	7	10	6,561	3.21
Minnesota	18	18	3,500	1.71
Mississippi	26	34	1,606	0.79
Missouri	11	11	5,802	2.84
Montana	43	40	794	0.39
Nebraska	33	30	2,079	1.02
Nevada	49	49	313	0.15
New Hampshire	45	45	492	0.24
New Jersey	8	8	7,042	3.45
New Mexico	40	42	617	0.30
New York	1	1	33,206	16.26
North Carolina	10	25	2,714	1.33
North Dakota	42	44	563	0.27
Ohio	5	4	11,020	5.39
Oklahoma	25	15	3,740	1.83
Oregon	32	31	1,922	0.94
Pennsylvania	3	6	9,526	4.67
Rhode Island	37	39	800	0.39
South Carolina	27	35	1,399	0.69
South Dakota	41	41	740	0.36
Tennessee	16	20	3,284	1.61
Texas	6	5	9,997	4.90
Utah	39	38	838	0.41
Vermont	46	46	383	0.19
Virginia	15	17	3,515	1.72
Washington	23	23	2,967	1.45
West Virginia	29	33	1,622	0.79
Wisconsin	14	12	4,215	2.07
Wyoming	48	47	380	0.19
Alaska			94	0.05
Hawaii			265	0.13
Total			204.111	99.94*

* 0.06 per cent lost in computing to nearest hundredth.

Pennsylvania with 9,526 (4.67 per cent). The smallest numbers of lawyers are in Nevada, 313 (0.15 per cent), Delaware, 316 (0.15 per cent), Wyoming, 380 (0.19 per cent), and Vermont, 383 (0.19 per cent). These figures, based on a report by Blaustein, are detailed in Table 1.

Chicago is the city with the second greatest number of lawyers, 11,187, and the Washington, D.C., bar numbers 6,637. There are 5,299 lawyers in Los Angeles, 4,548 in Boston, 3,635 in Detroit, 3,482 in Philadelphia, and 3,098 in Cleveland.

The greatest lawyer concentration by state is in the District of Columbia, with 1 lawyer for every 121 persons. New York State is second, with 1 lawyer for every 447; followed by Nevada, with 1 for every 511; Illinois, with 1 for every 557; Oklahoma, with 1 for every 597; and Massachusetts, with 1 for every 602 persons. States with relatively small numbers of lawyers are South Carolina (1 to 1,513), North Carolina (1 to 1,497), Alabama (1 to 1,459), and Mississippi (1 to 1,357). The median state is Kansas, where there is 1 lawyer for every 858 persons; half the states have more lawyers in proportion to the population than Kansas, and half the states have less.

Chart I shows the number of persons per lawyer in each state.

Generally speaking, the states with the highest percentages of lawyers are those with the greatest populations. And industrial states are relatively richer in lawyers than the farming communities. But this is not the whole story. Some of the figures fail to fit any pattern. It is certainly easy enough to understand the high lawyer concentration in the District of Columbia, in the highly industrialized states of New York, Illinois, and Massachusetts, and in the "divorce" state of Nevada. But why the unusually high percentage of lawyers in Oklahoma (1 to 597) and Colorado (1 to 624)? Do the oil and mining industries require unusually large numbers of attorneys? Are the people of those states unusually prone to legal argument? Or is it possible that they have been educated, more than the populations of other states, to see their lawyers first and avoid legal difficulties?

And why so small a lawyer count in North Carolina (1 to 1,497)? North Carolina is tenth in state populations and twenty-fifth in state lawyer rankings—and forty-eighth in the lawyer-concentration

CHART I

NUMBER OF PERSONS PER LAWYER IN EACH STATE IN 1951

(The average for the United States is 739.6 persons per lawyer. The median number by states is 858 persons per lawyer. Kansas is the median state.)

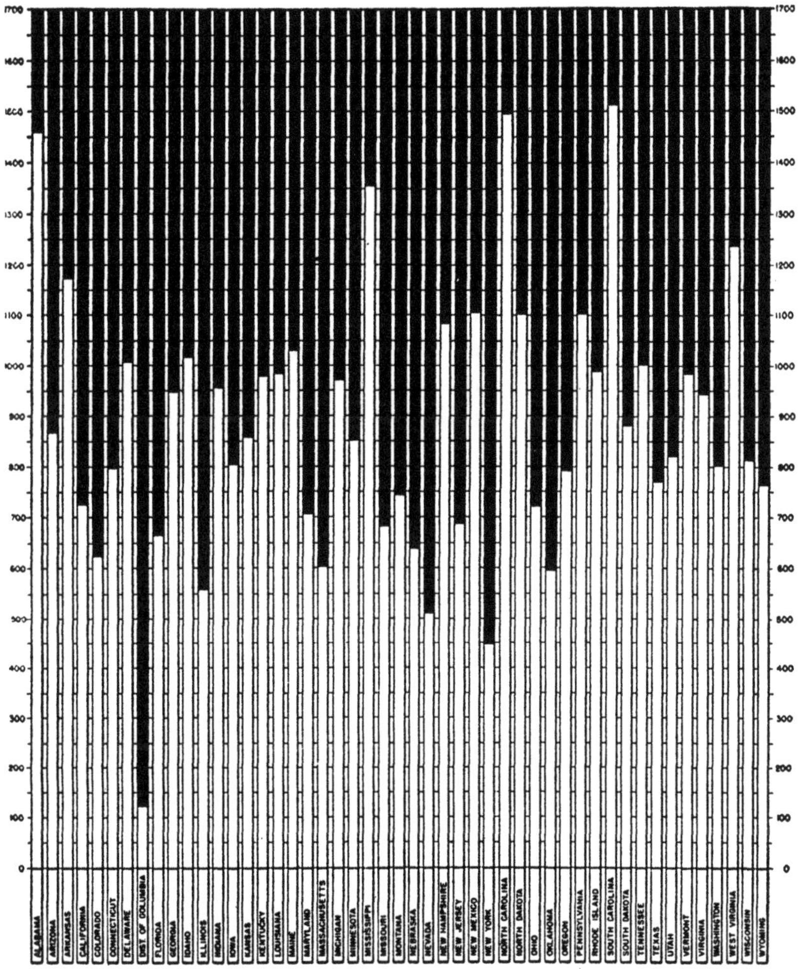

figures. Does this mean that North Carolinians are particularly adept at solving their disputes without recourse to counsel or the courts? Is the nature of the busines in that state such that few lawyers are required? Or is it possible that the state can now offer great opportunities for lawyers seeking a place to practice? These are some of the questions raised by the Survey findings that are as yet unanswered. Further study is being made by the organized bar.

WITH WHOM DO LAWYERS WORK?

The story of the working habits of the American lawyer also can be read in the statistical data. Here the Survey based its studies on 224,347 entries, 20,236 more than the total of 204,111 lawyers' listings. The reason for this larger number lies in the fact that many attorneys are classified in more than one category or subcategory. For example, a partner in a law firm who has been elected to the state legislature has been tabulated under both the subdivision "state" in the "government service" division and under the subdivision "partner" in the "private practice" division.

Most lawyers, of course (78.89 per cent), are in private practice, and, of the 176,995 members of the bar in this category, 90,959 are located in cities with more than 200,000 population, and 86,036 are in the smaller communities. The total number of practicing attorneys in the continental United States is 176,680. Of this number, 120,123 (67.99 per cent) are individual practitioners, performing their professional duties with neither partners nor associates. A total of 47,224 (26.73 per cent) are partners in law firms, and 9,333 (5.28 per cent) are associates, that is, employees of an individual practitioner or of a law firm.

The remaining 47,352 entries—lawyers not exclusively engaged in private practice—are set forth in Chart II.

Private industry claims 11,274 of the 12,997 "salaried" American lawyers, including those serving in corporate legal departments and those employed by business concerns in a nonlegal capacity. The majority of the 1,213 attorneys in educational institutions are professors of law, but the number also includes teachers of commercial law in business schools, law librarians, and administrative officials. Most of the lawyers classified under "other private employment" are employees of professional and trade associations and re-

CHART II

Lawyers Not Exclusively Engaged in Private Practice

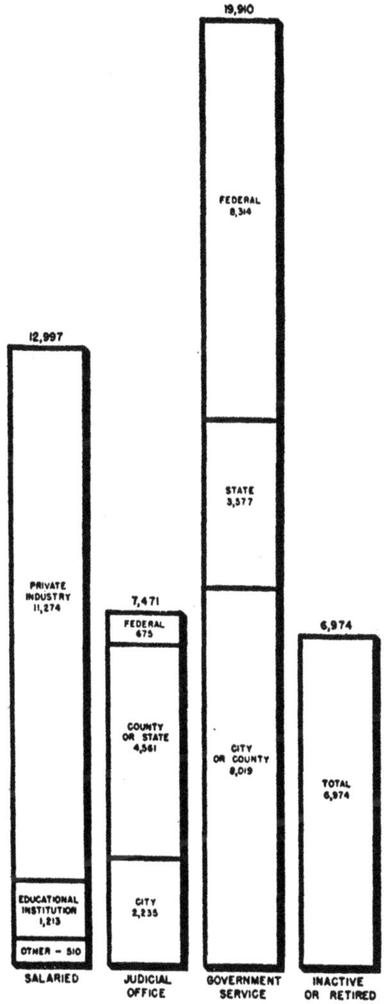

ligious and other charitable organizations. The 7,471 attorneys in judicial office include not only judges but justices of the peace, city police magistrates, circuit-court commissioners, and United States commissioners and referees in bankruptcy.

"Government service"—in all three of its subdivisions—refers to all government officials and employees with the exception of judicial officers. The group includes cabinet members, governors and other state and federal executive officers, members of Congress and of the state legislatures, district attorneys and their staffs, and representatives of the various "alphabetical agencies." Also included are members of the armed forces.

Of the 19,910 members of the bar in this category, 8,314 are in federal service, 3,577 are in the state governments, and 8,019 are city or county employees.

Detailing the figures on the 176,680 lawyers in private practice in the continental United States, the Survey found, as was expected, that the number of "associates" was far greater in the centers of population than in the smaller cities and towns. However, despite the existence of so many of the so-called "law factories" in New York, Washington, Chicago, Los Angeles, and Boston, there were more law-firm *partners* (as against "associates") in the smaller communities than in the large metropolitan areas.

In New York State, for example, 70.85 per cent of the members of the bar in active practice are solo practitioners, as compared with 24.76 per cent who are partners in law firms and 4.39 per cent "associates." And, of the lawyers practicing in the crowded boroughs of Manhattan and the Bronx in New York City, 70.04 per cent are in private practice without partners. States with the highest percentages in the solo-practice category are Wyoming, 77.09 per cent; Maryland, 77.02 per cent; New Jersey, 76.52 per cent; Maine, 75.37 per cent; and Massachusetts, 74.90 per cent.

The highest percentages of partners are in Iowa, 39.93 per cent; Louisiana, 36.20 per cent; Kansas, 35.83 per cent; and Arizona, 35.38 per cent. As far as "associates" are concerned, Delaware heads the list with 14.83 per cent, followed by Rhode Island, with 8.28 per cent; the District of Columbia, with 7.95 per cent; and Missouri, with 7.58 per cent.

Status-in-practice figures are of particular significance in view of the lawyer-income studies prepared in co-operation with the Survey by the Office of Business Economics of the United States Department of Commerce. The Commerce report for 1948, which showed an average net income of $8,315 and a median net income of $6,336, also revealed that partners and members of law firms have, in general, much greater earnings than do solo practitioners. Individual earnings of attorneys are much greater in the large law firms than in the smaller legal associations. The figures are striking (Table 2).

TABLE 2

AVERAGE AND MEDIAN NET INCOME OF ATTORNEYS BY SIZE OF LAW FIRM

Size of Law Firm (Members)	Per Cent of Lawyers in Firm of Specified Size	Average Net Income	Median Net Income
1	73.6	$ 5,759	$ 4,275
2	14.8	8,030	6,500
3	4.9	12,821	9,477
4	2.1	16,614	12,500
5–8	3.4	20,467	16,833
9 or more	1.3	27,246	21,500

Further and more detailed data on the economics of the legal profession were prepared for the Survey by Robert M. Segal, of the Boston bar, and Dr. John Fei. Their report, which followed a pilot study on the economic factors affecting the lawyers of Massachusetts, also covers and interprets the significant findings of the Department of Commerce.

IS THE BAR AN OVERCROWDED PROFESSION?

Although no general conclusions could be drawn as to whether the American bar was an overcrowded profession or was, in fact, understaffed, the economics studies did point up the fallacy of analyzing the need for lawyers' services in terms of population alone. During the last one hundred years the proportionate increase in the total number of lawyers has greatly exceeded the rise in population. In 1850 there was 1 attorney for every 969 persons in the country; in 1920 there was 1 attorney for every 863 persons; and by 1951, roughly comparable figures showed 1 attorney for every 746 persons.

Statistics like these have led vocational guidance counselors to theorize that the profession is becoming increasingly overcrowded and have resulted in advice to stay away from the law as a lucrative career. That such an analysis is faulty is to say the very least. Further, it is impossible to reach any general conclusions on "overcrowding" in the absence of some knowledge as to the adequacy of legal services in 1850, 1900, or 1920. And, still further, the population figures fail to take into account the degree to which legal services are interwoven with developments in business—apart from the additional business which naturally flows from an increase in population.

The number of lawyers has increased approximately in proportion to the growth of American business, as measured by such factors as the number of retail, wholesale, service, and manufacturing firms and their sales. A close relationship has been found between the level of economic activities of each state and the demand for lawyers and their services. Furthermore, there is a close relationship between the incomes of lawyers, by state, and the incomes after taxes of the corporations of the corresponding states.

Human population, however, cannot be discounted as a source of business affecting the number of lawyers. The Department of Commerce study showed that nonsalaried (i.e., self-employed) and part-salaried lawyers receive 47.9 per cent of their total gross incomes from services to business; 52.1 per cent from services to individuals. Thus it is no surprise to see that New York leads the nation in population, number of lawyers, and (with the exception of the District of Columbia) lawyer concentration. California, second in population, ranks third in number of lawyers; Pennsylvania, third in population, is sixth in lawyer rank; Illinois, fourth in population, is second in lawyer rank; and Ohio, fifth in population, is fourth in lawyer rank.

At the other end of the list are Nevada, forty-ninth in both population and proportion of lawyers; Wyoming, forty-eighth in population and forty-seventh in proportion of lawyers; and Delaware, forty-seventh in population and forty-eighth in proportion of lawyers. The complete comparison of the percentage of lawyers by state and the nation's population showed them to move closely together.

A far closer relationship was found in comparing the percentage of lawyers with the percentage of economic activity in each state. The size of the bar is best reflected in the proportionate wholesale sales by state. High agreement was found between lawyer populations and the number of manufacturing establishments, the number of service establishments, the number of corporations, retail sales volume, the number of retail trade establishments, and the size of service and trade sales.

Even the statistics reflecting business activity, however, fail to tell the whole story. Four states (Arkansas, Kentucky, Nebraska, and Oklahoma) and the District of Columbia have a far greater percentage of lawyers than their respective degrees of economic activity would indicate. Oklahoma's 1.83 per cent of the nation's legal talent is well in excess of its wholesale sales percentages. Connecticut, Michigan, New York, and Pennsylvania have relatively large numbers of lawyers but far fewer than an analysis of the wholesale sales, corporate incomes, and number of corporations in those states might be expected to show.

Virtually no state-by-state relation exists between lawyer earnings and income per person. Nor is there any definite relationship between the figures for lawyer incomes and the statistics on state population. On the other hand, the Survey's analysis of state-wide net corporate income per lawyer was in direct proportion to the earnings of attorneys. (The figure for state-wide net corporate income per lawyer was reached by totaling the after-tax incomes of all corporations in each state and dividing that total by the number of lawyers in the state.)

HOW MUCH DO LAWYERS MAKE?

Recent, complete, and comprehensive tabulations were not available on lawyer earnings, nor were the comparative figures on the incomes of lawyers, doctors, and dentists. Most of the data was based on 1947 tabulations, then already seven years old. So far as could be determined, however, there is no great divergence between the 1947 studies and more recent data; thus the earlier statistics are still valid for comparative purposes.

The 1948 Department of Commerce reports showed an average net income for lawyers of $8,315 and a median net income of $6,336 (half the lawyers received more than this amount and half received less). By 1951 their average net income had risen to $9,375 and the median figure to $6,956. These statistics can be further detailed as shown in Table 3.

Probably the most important of these figures are those relating to nonsalaried practitioners, since that category represents the income received directly from clients. Those whose major income is from independent sources include salary incomes as well as legal

TABLE 3

AVERAGE NET INCOMES OF LAWYERS, 1951

	Average	Median
All lawyers	$ 9,375	$6,956
Major part of income from independent sources	8,936	6,766
Major part of income from salaries	10,197	7,100
No income from salaries	8,730	6,307
All income from salaries	10,339	7,811

fees. The nonsalaried statistics have additional meaning since it was only for this classification that the incomes of lawyers, doctors, and dentists could be compared. The year 1951 was the most recent in which such a comparison was made.

Since 1929, lawyers in nonsalaried practice have increased their average net incomes by 58 per cent, as compared with 83 per cent for nonsalaried dentists and 157 per cent for nonsalaried physicians. To keep these figures in perspective, it should be noted that the average earnings of all nonfarm entrepreneurs rose 144 per cent over this period.

In 1929 lawyer net incomes exceeded those of doctors and dentists. By 1951 the physicians had far outstripped the members of the bar, and the dentists were rapidly catching up. These average figures are set forth in Table 4, together with information on gross earnings which help give a picture of the cost of practicing the various professions of law, medicine, and dentistry.

Comparative data on state-by-state lawyer incomes were prepared on the basis of the more detailed 1947 tabulations. Generally speaking, the incomes of lawyers in the Middle East and Far West sections of the country were uniformly and markedly higher than those in any other region, whether all lawyers, independent lawyers, or salaried lawyers were considered and whether the mean or median figure was used. With $7,532 as the nation-wide average net income for all lawyers, state-based average incomes ranged from a low of $4,824 in Iowa to a high of $9,910 in the District of Columbia. Other high averages were found in California, New York, and Pennsylvania, and low average earnings were recorded in Kentucky, Virginia, and Minnesota. In the median net income category, California and Pennsylvania led with $7,313 and $7,017, respectively, while Oklahoma and Iowa were at the bottom, with median net incomes of $3,896 and $4,120.

TABLE 4

GROSS AND NET INCOMES OF LAWYERS, PHYSICIANS, AND DENTISTS

YEAR	LAWYERS		PHYSICIANS		DENTISTS	
	Gross	Net	Gross	Net	Gross	Net
1929	$ 7,997	$5,534	$ 8,567	$ 5,224	$ 7,112	$4,267
1940	6,747	4,507	7,632	4,441	6,592	3,314
1947	11,498	7,437	17,742	10,726	12,032	6,610
1951	14,171	8,730	22,298	13,432	14,085	7,820

Details of the income figures by state are given in Table 5.

There proved to be a close relation between lawyer income and net corporate income per lawyer (even closer if the District of Columbia is excluded). Here, again, significant variations were found. The Washington, D.C., bar and the bars of California and Georgia showed far higher incomes than might be expected from the analysis of corporate net profits; and Iowa, Virginia, Minnesota, Wisconsin, and Michigan have smaller lawyer incomes than would be predicted on the basis of such agreement between the two on the national level.

Other factors also play a large part in determining lawyer income. As previously noted, earnings will vary according to the

TABLE 5

NET INCOME OF LAWYERS, BY MAJOR SOURCE OF LEGAL INCOME, BY REGIONS AND FOR SELECTED STATES, 1947

Region and State*	All Lawyers			Major Independent		Major Salaried	
	Per Cent in Each Region	Mean Net Income	Median Net Income	Mean Net Income	Median Net Income	Mean Net Income	Median Net Income
New England	6.5	$6,981	$5,240	$ 7,064	$5,150	$ 6,830	$5,594
Connecticut	....	8,532	6,250	*	*	*	*
Massachusetts	....	6,942	4,933	7,159	3,812	6,641	5,438
Middle East	30.0	8,779	6,566	8,948	6,246	8,546	6,910
District of Columbia	....	9,910	7,000	14,317	7,375	7,350	6,625
Maryland	....	7,074	5,909	6,871	5,389	*	*
New Jersey	....	6,930	5,667	6,246	6,021	*	*
New York	....	9,024	6,632	9,357	6,224	8,608	7,068
Pennsylvania	....	8,731	7,017	7,995	6,156	10,443	8,688
Southeast	13.5	6,566	5,201	6,617	4,647	6,375	5,906
Alabama	....	5,532	5,208	*	*	*	*
Arkansas	....	5,756	4,313	5,772	3,250	*	*
Florida	....	6,755	4,857	6,824	4,679	*	*
Georgia	....	8,619	6,313	9,102	6,450	*	*
Kentucky	....	5,190	4,375	4,705	3,607	*	*
Louisiana	....	7,976	6,063	*	*	*	*
North Carolina	....	8,093	5,700	7,625	4,500	*	*
Tennessee	....	7,230	6,083	7,816	6,833	*	*
Virginia	....	5,359	4,214	5,059	3,979	*	*
Southwest	7.2	6,177	4,660	6,137	3,976	6,254	5,224
Oklahoma	....	5,314	3,896	4,801	3,125	6,095	5,281
Texas	....	6,289	4,690	6,241	3,925	6,374	5,156
Central	28.7	7,040	5,391	6,854	5,033	7,380	6,022
Illinois	....	8,326	6,134	7,842	5,462	8,915	6,450
Indiana	....	6,100	5,400	6,062	5,556	*	*
Iowa	....	4,824	4,120	4,767	3,977	*	*
Michigan	....	8,306	6,594	8,914	6,500	7,514	6,650
Minnesota	....	5,369	4,500	5,297	4,442	*	*
Missouri	....	6,856	5,219	7,208	5,500	6,440	5,125
Ohio	....	7,442	5,342	7,359	5,309	7,632	5,385
Wisconsin	....	6,033	5,092	5,899	4,625	6,362	5,453
Northwest	4.8	5,933	4,790	6,032	4,656	5,638	5,021
Colorado	....	5,785	4,643	5,776	4,125	*	*
Kansas	....	6,369	4,850	*	*	*	*
Nebraska	....	5,757	4,667	*	*	*	*
Far West	9.3	8,679	6,608	9,259	7,039	7,549	6,089
California	....	9,752	7,313	10,487	7,562	8,446	6,812
Oregon	....	6,427	5,167	*	*	*	*
Washington	....	6,294	5,450	6,869	6,000	*	*
United States	100.0	$7,532	$5,698	$ 7,517	$5,303	$ 7,560	$6,134

* States with too few cases to yield reliable results are included in regional data but are not shown separately. In addition to the states listed above, the regions include the following states: New England—Maine, New Hampshire, Rhode Island, Vermont; Middle East—Delaware, West Virginia; Southeast—Mississippi, South Carolina; Southwest—Arizona, New Mexico; Central—None; Northwest—Idaho, Montana, North Dakota, South Dakota, Utah, Wyoming; Far West—Nevada.

size of law firms, and the Survey also found a significant differential depending upon size of community. Lawyers in cities with more than one million population, for example, have more than twice the incomes of those in localities with fewer than a thousand inhabitants.

A lawyer's age and number of years in practice are additional—and important—considerations affecting his income. As in most professional pursuits, the age-income pattern reflects low earnings during the early years, a steady income rise until a peak is reached somewhere between fifty and fifty-four years of age, and then a gradual decline with advancing years.

Data on the age of 197,708 members of the bar are based on the 1952 Martindale-Hubbell report. These statistics reveal that fully 25 per cent of the members of the bar are fifty-seven years of age and older and that more than 10 per cent of the counselors-at-law have passed the social security retirement age of sixty-five.

How good a life insurance risk the lawyer is can be determined by comparing these figures with those for the population as a whole. Only 17 per cent of the people of the United States are fifty-five years of age and older. Only 8.2 per cent have reached sixty-five. Considering that 97.5 per cent of lawyers are males and that the average life-span of the American female is more than four years greater than that of the male, the figures on lawyer longevity are striking. A scant 7.7 per cent of the total male population is sixty-five years of age or older, compared with 8.4 per cent for the women.

Lawyers from thirty-seven to fifty-six (those with the greatest earnings) are more likely to be found in cities with a population of more than 200,000 than in the smaller towns. On the other hand, both the oldest and the youngest groups of lawyers seem to prefer the smaller communities. Whether lawyers live longer away from the hustle and bustle of metropolitan practice, or whether many lawyers desert the cities for a quieter practice after reaching the riper age brackets, it is impossible to say. But it does appear that the younger attorneys generally find the small-population areas better for starting the practice of law. They move on to the bigger cities—and, presumably, the bigger clients—after making their marks in the country.

Breakdowns on the age of the American bar in 1951 are set forth in Table 6.

Table 7 gives statistics showing the earnings of the American lawyer by age groups in 1947.

There is agreement between these figures and the statistics on years in practice, although the relationship has probably been somewhat blurred as a result of the extensive war service of lawyers in nonlegal work. Most lawyers become members of the bar at approximately age twenty-five. It would be expected, therefore, that their peak median net incomes would be attained after twenty-

TABLE 6

AGE OF LAWYERS, 1951

Year Born	Age in 1951	Age					
		Nation		Cities with More than 200,000 Population		Cities with Less than 200,000 Population	
		No.	Per Cent	No.	Per Cent	No.	Per Cent
Before 1875...	Over 76	5,858	2.96	2,322	2.28	3,536	3.69
1875–84.......	76–67	15,486	7.83	6,846	6.71	8,640	9.03
1885–94.......	66–57	27,299	13.81	14,003	13.73	13,296	13.89
1895–1904.....	56–47	43,190	21.85	24,307	23.83	18,883	19.73
1905–14.......	46–37	56,909	28.78	31,093	30.49	25,816	26.97
After 1914.....	Under 37	48,966	24.77	23,414	22.96	25,552	26.69
Total.....	....	197,708	100.00	101,985	100.00	95,723	100.00

TABLE 7

EARNINGS OF LAWYERS BY AGE GROUPS, 1947

Age in 1947	Per Cent of Lawyers in Each Group	Average Net Income	Median Net Income
25–29........	2.8	$ 3,527	$3,398
30–34.........	14.9	5,139	4,490
35–39.........	18.9	6,874	5,761
40–44.........	18.7	7,854	6,322
45–49.........	11.9	8,818	6,835
50–54.........	9.3	10,034	7,304
55–59.........	7.6	8,951	6,807
60–64.........	5.7	8,835	5,833
65 and over...	10.3	7,231	3,750

five to twenty-nine years in practice, and so it works out (Table 8).

These are the statistics; their value in understanding the economics of the legal profession cannot be doubted. Over a long period a good estimate as to the comparative numbers and incomes of lawyers in each state can be obtained from an analysis of the economic activity in the state. In the short run, however, any conclusions as to the economic status of any lawyer or group of lawyers requires the additional analyses of many variables, some not readily subject to statistical evaluation. Age of lawyers, size of law firms, etc., have already been mentioned in this connection. Lawyer

TABLE 8

RELATIONSHIP OF YEARS IN PRACTICE TO MEDIAN NET INCOME

Years in Practice	Per Cent in Each Group	Median Net Income
Less than 5	10.1	$3,354
5–9	12.8	4,754
10–14	17.9	5,784
15–19	17.7	6,476
20–24	12.9	7,394
25–29	8.5	7,813
30–34	6.5	6,750
35–39	5.0	6,313
40–44	3.9	5,273
45 or more	4.6	3,988

population and earnings are also affected by changing political and social forces, which have a varying impact on the demand for legal services. And the nature of clients, or even one client, may make a big difference in patterns and norms. The aged solo practitioner in an Iowa town with less than 1,000 population, for example, may have an unusually high income as the counsel for the one big company in that town—despite all the statistics. And the size and wealth of the lawyer population in any one particular state might conceivably represent the result of restrictions on admissions to the bar in that state.

Notwithstanding all the economic trials and tribulations of the legal profession in regard to income, professional opportunities, office organization, social security, and retirement, the lawyer has apparently succeeded in the great American game of making ends meet. Despite his familiarity with the law and legal procedures, the attorney is seldom in court with his own financial affairs. And, despite the fact that every lawyer has at least some knowledge of bankruptcy, the knowledge is virtually never used to solve his own economic ills.

In the twenty-one-month period from July 1, 1947, through March 31, 1949, a Survey report by Porter showed, 36,894 bankruptcy proceedings were filed in the United States. Of that number, only fifteen were filed on behalf of lawyers. And, of the fifteen lawyers, ten went bankrupt as a result of business interests outside their professional activities. The other five, all of whom were solo practitioners, went into bankruptcy because their personal obligations exceeded their incomes from the practice of law. One of the five managed to pay his creditors in full.

Two of the four lawyer bankrupts who were unable to meet creditors' demands owed less than $2,000. In one of those cases the attorney had incurred nearly $1,500 in medical expenses following an automobile accident and was unable to continue practice in the face of his obligations; in the other case, where less than $2,000 was owed, the lawyer left the profession to take a salaried position in a corporation and apparently desired to start his new post without debts. The third attorney, according to a local observer, went bankrupt because of "illness and domestic difficulties." The fourth, a practitioner who had spent nearly fifty years at the bar, owed $13,384.77, of which $9,000 was his law-office rent from 1929 to 1939. None of the lawyer bankrupts, on the record, was liable for malfeasance or a misappropriation of funds.

These facts are not in accordance with the impression of the legal profession held by a number of persons, including some lawyers. If many lawyers are slipshod in their business dealings and quick to find a legal way out from under their responsibilities, the evidence does not lie in the bankruptcy records kept in our federal district courts. The statistics are readily available: 1 out of every 740 persons in the United States is a lawyer, but fewer than 1 in every 7,400 bankrupts during the test period was a member of the bar who was unable to meet financial obligations incurred in the practice of law.

WHAT DOES IT COST TO RUN A LAW OFFICE?

One other factor in the income field which warrants special consideration is law-office organization. It is readily apparent that mean and median *net* incomes might be higher or lower, depending upon the business efficiency of the practitioner as well as upon such abstract elements as "net corporate income per lawyer." A comprehensive Survey report was prepared on this subject by Eugene C. Gerhart, of the New York bar, analyzing a 1949 sample of the estimated 115,000 law officers in the United States.

Highly important to lawyer economics was this question: "What percentage of your annual gross income is spent on your annual office overhead?" The responses ranged all the way from 10 per cent to 100 per cent, and a large number of firms reflected their careful accounting systems with answers of 21.50 per cent, 24.14 per cent, or 41.57 per cent. The average overhead cost was 31.06 per cent.

What comprises this lawyer overhead? The biggest item, of course, is personnel. Depending upon the size of the firm, there might be as many as sixty-five lawyer-employees and a hundred and forty-five nonlegal professional, clerical, and other office workers. Or there might be a single part-time secretary. Salaries of stenographers and secretaries ranged from $20.00 and $25.00 per week to $94.32. Law-office bookkeepers earned between $32.50 and $112.50; file clerks and telephone operators, from $31.25 to $87.50; receptionists, from $29.99 to $58.75; and messenger–office boys, from $20.00 to $65.00. Some law firms have office managers receiving as much as $550 a month and accounting managers earning $100 weekly. At least one firm pays an investigator $350 a month. The highest salaries were not necessarily paid by the largest law offices, although the big firms did set their top secretarial salaries in the upper salary range.

Maintenance of law-office libraries is another large overhead item. One attorney reported an annual expense of only $75.00, but this was far from typical. Annual expenditures of $5,000 and $6,000 are not uncommon, and at least one firm spends $8,000 per year for books alone.

Problems relating to overhead and other aspects of law-office management are generally matters of individual concern, handled strictly according to the ideas of the individual firm. But some problems are of common interest and are solved more effectively following interfirm consultation. Managing partners of large firms in Boston and New York have formed law-office management groups to study typical questions in this field. The Boston organization, for example, has looked into the proposal of instituting periodic audits of firm books and fiduciary books and records, the audit made by independent certified public accountants. As a joint service, it also has explored the advisability of carrying lawyers' liability insurance and insurance protection against the loss of valuable documents belonging to clients. Discussions have also been held on the maintenance and disposition of old files, but no uniform policy has been adopted. According to the Gerhart report, lawyers preserve office files a minimum of three years before destroying them and keep them in their offices for at least a year. Files which are put in storage are kept a minimum of five years. Many firms and some lawyers, however, keep files in their offices almost forever.

WHAT ARE LAWYERS' WORKING HOURS?

Another important question asked by Gerhart related to the hours of work which are performed by attorneys and their employees. The shortest office hours recorded for law partners were from 9:00 A.M. to 4:00 P.M.; the longest, from 8:30 A.M. to 6:00 P.M.

Neither schedule, however, gives an accurate picture of the working day of the American lawyer. No records are available as to the number of briefs and legal memorandums which are prepared at home with the aid of the proverbial midnight oil, but every lawyer can testify that they are frequent. And no careful observer has ever taken a commuters' special during the rush hours without seeing some lawyer perusing legal newspapers, journals, and court decisions, keeping up with the law as it affects or may affect his clients. Figures on the office hours of nonlawyer employees are far better yardsticks of the extent of their services to the profession. The longest were from 8:00 A.M. to 5:30 P.M.; the shortest from 9:00 A.M. to 4:30 P.M., though presumably the short workday is stretched in emergencies, and the long one occasionally shortened "when the cat's away."

From all its quantitative statistical studies as well as its qualitative researches, the Survey found that lawyers generally believe the practice of law in partnerships to be preferable to individual practice. The lawyer is only as valuable as the service he renders, and that point is emphasized by the members of the bar preferring group practice. Those advocating the establishment of firms cite as advantages increased opportunities for mutual consultation and assistance, increased opportunities for specialization, greater flexibility, and more prompt and efficient service. They indicated their belief that attorneys also benefit from group practice in the form of larger and more certain income.

Individual practice has its own advantages, of course, and many lawyers feel that they can render better service alone, having full responsibility and immediate contact with every client. Some solo lawyers simply like the independence of individual work. Further, in the smaller communities, partnerships are often impractical.

One form of group practice is the sharing of office space with other lawyers, but the conduct of business is on an individual basis. Library costs, rent, stenographic expenses, etc., are shared under this arrangement, but no agreements as to partnerships or firms are involved. Reasons for preferring this mode of organization include independence and full responsibility, sole immediate contact with clients, better service, performance of his own work by each lawyer, suitability to small-town practice and freedom and selectivity.

HOW DO LAWYERS GET JOBS?

Save for occasional passing references, little has been said about employment opportunities for the newly admitted members of the bar or the problems of placement in the legal profession. More than half of the firms responding to the questionnaires on law-office management expressed the opinion that the profession is overcrowded, and 63 per cent flatly said "No" to the question, "Are there any openings for young lawyers in your office?" Only 20 per cent of the firms responded in the affirmative, and 14 per cent failed to give any answer. When youthful law graduates obtain employment, they find that starting salaries for lawyers recently admitted to the bar range from $20.00 to $75.00 a week. Law clerks not as yet admitted may receive as little as $5.00 weekly.

Assistance available to lawyers looking for employment is discussed in the Survey report by Louis A. Toepfer, assistant dean and director of admissions at Harvard Law School. Placement service is needed by two groups of lawyers: the large group of recent law-school graduates and a much smaller number seeking new positions after a number of years of practice. Almost all the work being done in the field today is directed toward helping the first group.

There is a great deal more to legal placement than the limited definition the term conveys. Placement means finding employment. But placement work in the legal profession takes on added meanings: the responsibility of advising and guiding young men bewildered by the transition from school to practice; the collection and distribution of information about fields of work, areas of opportunity, and salary scales; and the devising of personnel counseling methods which can be applied successfully within the unique relationship of the lawyer-employer and the lawyer-employee.

The majority of attorneys securing legal employment find positions through personal contacts and through such personal efforts as in-person canvassing of law firms and examination of communities potentially desirable as situations for the practice of law. The Survey questionnaires showed that a relatively small proportion of the bar is employed through the medium of placement services and that, of this group, the largest percentage consists of recent graduates assisted by the law schools.

No matter what the agency involved in placement—whether it is a school, a bar association, a public placement service, or a private employment firm—the machinery is about the same. Law schools have developed several methods. Twelve have established separate offices solely for placing their own graduates. Six use the placement facilities of the universities with which they are connected, and ten others use both the facilities of their universities and their own deans' offices. Eight schools have designated faculty members who are responsible for the placement work of the school, and five use both a special faculty member and their own deans' offices. Twenty-nine schools report that their placement work is a function of the dean's office.

In the thirty-six schools which undertook to estimate their 1949 placement expenses, the amounts varied from nothing to two instances of $12,000. The total spent by these schools was $80,600, an average of $2,239 per school.

In order to operate properly, a law-school placement service should perform five distinct functions: (1) maintain a complete library of current placement information; (2) organize local alumni placement committees in all areas where graduates regularly seek positions; (3) provide counseling on job-seeking procedures; (4) make surveys, through questionnaires and other means, of job possibilities; and (5) arrange interviews at the school for prospective employers.

Few law schools have come to the point where their placement offices embrace all five of these functions. The division of activities is as follows:

	No. of Law Schools
Five functions	13
Four functions	17
Three functions	16
Two functions	19
One function	32

The Survey found that the percentage of students substantially assisted in placement climbs fairly steadily as the number of functions increases. Schools carrying on none of the five report that they help on the average only 20 per cent of their students, while in schools using all five functions the proportion given substantial aid is 56 per cent.

Yet, measuring the results of placement work done by law schools is very difficult. No placement director can assess with any great degree of accuracy his influence in the success of his charges in finding employment. There is very little actual plucking of men from the classroom and inserting them into jobs. Most of the work consists of recommending a number of opportunities to each man and a number of men for each opportunity. Most of the actual effort remains with the person seeking placement.

With but isolated exceptions, the bar associations of the United States have not seriously concerned themselves with the placement problems of the profession. Many of them have recognized the existence of such problems, and a number have committees that work in the field, but very few have accomplished anything really constructive.

Whether the bar associations should be criticized for their failure to meet the problems of placement, it is difficult to determine. Many have made genuine efforts to work out useful programs, only to have the projects collapse from the apathy of their members. Several bar associations that sincerely tried to locate opportunities for position-seeking lawyers found their inquiries ignored. In Virginia, for example, the state bar mailed 3,300 cards asking (1) whether or not lawyers needed any help and (2) whether there was a need in the community for one or more lawyers. Only 50 per cent of the cards were returned. Eleven lawyers said that they would be interested in taking on a young associate. Thirty-five, including some duplications, replied that there appeared to be a need for one or more additional lawyers in their communities. The effort succeeded in turning up 46 leads in a field of 3,300 possibilities—an average of only 1.4 per cent.

Arizona reported that "our efforts have met with almost no results." Iowa complained about the "reluctance of those with possible openings to inform the Association headquarters." The officers of the Kentucky State Bar Association reported that they could give valuable aid in placement if the firms would only register their needs.

Not all developments have been so discouraging. In 1947 the Lawyers' Bureau of the Association of the Bar of the City of New York and the New York County Lawyers' Association established a placement bureau that has achieved distinct success. This bureau personally interviews each registrant, classifies his experience and interests, and refers him to those positions listed for which he might qualify. The bureau also tries to locate employment opportunities by communicating with law firms and business organizations, by mailing announcements and brochures to members of the bar, by placing notices in legal periodicals, and by answering advertisements. Since its establishment, more than 2,533 persons have registered with the Lawyers' Bureau, and it is estimated that an additional 4,000, exclusive of employers, have sought its advice. The bureau has arranged 2,722 employer interviews for its registrants and has submitted 3,718 résumés to employers.

Although the bureau, like other placement services, devotes its major efforts to counseling, it claims a placement ratio of 1 in every 8.9 registrants. Similar progress has been made by the Chicago Bar Association, which has served about 1,500 applicants and has placed 327 job-seeking members of the profession.

On the national scene, Dean Toepfer recommends that the American Bar Association take an interest in promoting the development of placement activity by state and local associations and by the law schools. An ABA office should be established, he urged, with the responsibility of providing the organized bar and the schools with information which would serve as a basis for placement counseling. This office would be concerned with the broad problems of placement across the country, serving as a clearinghouse for facts about where lawyers are needed and the relative prospects in given areas either for employment or for establishing a practice. It is not suggested by Dean Toepfer that the ABA run a placement office or that it should receive applications from either employer or prospective employee. Rather, it should be an information hub and a center for the study of placement methods, lawyers' needs, and similar subjects.

PROBLEMS OF RETIREMENT

Equally important to the American Bar Association, the organized bar, and the legal profession is the question of social security and retirement plans for lawyers. Self-employed attorneys, comprising the vast majority of the bar, are not eligible for social security benefits under today's laws; nor may self-employed lawyers participate in any retirement programs which they might set up for their employees under the provisions of the Internal Revenue Code. In addition, lawyers, like most other professionals, are excluded from existing state legislation providing compensation for disability caused by accident or sickness.

The Survey report by Harold O. Love, of the Michigan bar, advocates a twofold program: (1) amplifying and extending present social security legislation into a unified federal system in order to provide adequate minimum protection for all against socially created risks and (2) establishing legislation that would encourage an individual to set up for himself a tax-deductible retirement program providing for a standard of living comparable to that which he enjoyed during his productive years. Such a program also would enable his family to maintain that standard after his death.

Lawers are seldom thought of as needing the benefits of social security. There still remains the hangover of the old belief that the self-employed professional can take better care of himself than can the wage-earner; there still seems to be a common assumption that those who are self-employed have income from investments which are adequate for retirement needs. This is just not so. Most lawyers are no more able to save for the future than most nonprofessional employees—and they have the same needs to fulfil when their active earning days are over.

It is almost impossible today for younger lawyers to do what their predecessors at the bar could do a generation ago in the way of buying insurance and annuities. The younger men now are compelled to pay in increased taxes far more than the older men paid in premiums. Present rates of taxation make it difficult for anyone to achieve even modest security by accumulating reserves through private initiative. The self-employed lawyer thus finds himself unable to provide his own social security; yet he is excluded from coverage under the Social Security Act.

Love offered the following recommendations for expanded social security benefits: they should (1) provide coverage for all the people in the United States; (2) provide both protection against economic hazards involving the loss or interruption of earning power and income necessary to sustain life; (3) pay benefits for the entire period of need, not merely for a stated period of time; and (4) establish benefits sufficient to maintain a decent minimum standard of living.

But these proposals, described as "adequate minimum protection for everyone against socially created risks," are only the first step. There must, he asserted, also be legislation encouraging retirement programs. As the law now stands, the attorney is unable to set up any sort of pension plan in which money devoted to the plan can be deducted from his income tax. Corporations, on the other hand, establish retirement programs for their employees—including top-management officials—and are allowed to deduct the premiums from their taxes as a business expense.

The program advocated by Love would allow the individual lawyer to set up a fund guaranteeing him, at retirement (or his family, in case of his death), a standard of living equal to 75 per cent of that which he previously enjoyed. The contributions made to such a fund would be deductible from current income tax in the year in which they are made and would be invested in government bonds and life insurance policies. The recipient would be taxed when the benefits were made available. Love feels that this type of plan would "stimulate initiative and at the same time discourage indolence or further progress toward undesirable socialism."

New York State Attorney-General Nathaniel L. Goldstein has proposed a somewhat different plan. The lawyer's income, he points out, "is all earned and subject to the crushing weight of high surtaxes in the short period when his long years of effort come to fruition." He advocates that those who earn their incomes by personal practice of the law (and the other professions) be permitted to project a limited proportion of their earnings into the future, in order to escape the full impact of the surtax on peak earnings, and also to establish a fund for retirement, in the form of special, non-interest-bearing government bonds.

WOMEN AS MEMBERS OF THE BAR

Everything which has been said thus far about the lawyer in the United States has dealt primarily with the 199,052 male members of the bar. The nation's 5,059 Portias (2.48 per cent of the total) are in a special category—special in terms of numbers, opportunities, status in practice, and public relations within the profession. For, as Barbara Armstrong, the Survey's consultant in this field, pointed out, "when it comes to women who enter the law, the majority of large law offices still refuse (short of war) to interview them for jobs. . . . Women must work twice as hard as men for half the pay. And so far there have been relatively few women—although the number is steadily increasing—who have won positions of real distinction in practice, in legal service to the government or on the bench."

Of the 5,059 women at the bar in 1951, 3,003 were in cities with more than 200,000 population, and 2,056 were in the smaller communities. New York led in the state rankings with 958 female attorneys, nearly one-fifth of the national total. There were 426 women lawyers in California, 405 in Illinois, 311 in the District of Columbia, 278 in Massachusetts, and 245 in Texas. While complete breakdowns were not prepared in connection with the 1951 Martindale-Hubbell report, much additional data are contained in the special study made by Blaustein and Kaplan in 1948. The earlier statistics vary somewhat from those compiled in 1951, but the percentages are accurate for comparative purposes. The highest percentages of women lawyers, as compared with the male legal population, were found in the District of Columbia, Massachusetts, Vermont, Florida, Oklahoma, and Kansas. Comparatively few women lawyers are members of the bars of Rhode Island, Connecticut, West Virginia, Pennsylvania, Arkansas, and North Carolina.

Underlying these figures is woman's uphill struggle, through more than eighty years, for professional education, opportunity, and recognition in the law. It was not until 1869 in Iowa that the first woman lawyer was admitted to the bar, and even after that date many states denied the privilege of practice to members of the female sex.

The universities made it virtually impossible for women to secure an adequate legal education. Michigan admitted women students as early as 1870, and Yale and Cornell followed suit in 1886 and 1887, but they were the exceptions. The doors were barred at Columbia, for example, until 1929, and Harvard held out until 1950. Women still constitute a very small percentage of the law school's classes: at Cornell, Stanford, Southern California, and Michigan, between 3 and 4 per cent; at Yale and New York University, about 6 per cent; and at Columbia, 7 per cent. Law schools reporting to the Survey indicated that the aptitude and the general record of women students are at least as high as those of the men. Since women were first admitted at Cornell, three of their number have either led their classes or have been editors-in-chief of the *Cornell Law Quarterly*. At Columbia 24 per cent of the women have maintained "A" averages, a higher proportion than the men have been able to achieve.

Even more prolonged than winning the right to a legal education has been women's fight for admission to the bar associations. The American Bar Association did not open its membership to them until 1918, and not until 1937 did the Association of the Bar of the City of New York "stop making excuses (which hinged around powder rooms) and finally open its doors." The New York County Lawyers' Association, however, has admitted women members since its inception in 1908. Because of the denial of membership and because membership, even when granted, seldom brought with it the privilege of serving on committees and participating in the work of the organized profession, the women formed their own bar organizations. The National Association of Women Lawyers, which was formed in 1899, now has more than a thousand members, and numerous state and local bar groups have sprung up in the last twenty-five years. While these organizations have accomplished much, the fact remains, according to Mrs. Armstrong, that, "if women were given adequate opportunity and recognition by men's bar groups, the need for a separate women's bar with the inevitable duplication of committee work, community service, and recreational activity would in large measure be eliminated."

As far as the practice of the law is concerned, the dimness of the general employment picture is accompanied by the stultifying nature of the work the average woman performs in the law office. One study reported that 90 per cent of the lawyers wishing to employ a law clerk refused even to interview women, and such openings as there are often call for the additional skill of stenography. Most law schools have recommended that women seek employment in government positions requiring legal training, in probate and tax practice, in legal aid work, or in some professional capacity for either trust or insurance companies.

Absence of client contact marks the work of women at the bar, and women seldom become full members of their law firms. A number of large offices are quite willing to hire competent women on an equal footing with men for the first few years but then subject them to the ruthless pruning the firms do on "nonpartnership" material. Being unable to secure top positions, most women attorneys work diligently to achieve some lesser status, based on their technical proficiency, executive ability, or exhaustive knowledge of some particular field.

"Women have their best chance with the government," says Mrs. Armstrong, "where there is no client contact except at arm's length with worried citizens, where there is a tradition of civil service as opposed to the somewhat authoritarian structure in the law office, where real recognition is given for intellectual achievement and where there is not too much call, through the mass of the government pyramid, for imagination or daring. Not that women lack those qualities, but in normal practice they are rarely encouraged to show them."

So much for the statistics on the American lawyer; at least, so much for his numbers, distribution, status in practice, and economic situation. Future chapters are devoted to his professional activities, his services to the state and to the public, his education, his standards, and his activities as a member of the organized bar. But, before telling the story of what lawyers do, it is important to consider the lawyer and his public—what the layman thinks about the legal profession and the reaction of the bar to the problems of public opinion.

THE PUBLIC LOOKS AT THE LAWYER

When Alexis de Tocqueville visited the United States in 1835, he made a statement which has been quoted again and again in attempts to define the status of the American lawyer. "The profession of the law," he wrote in *Democracy in America,* "is the only aristocratic element which can be amalgamated without violence with the natural elements of democracy. . . . I cannot believe that a republic could subsist if the influence of lawyers in public business did not increase in proportion to the power of the people."

That is what De Tocqueville wrote; that is what most legal authorities believe; that is what is borne out by the findings of the Survey of the Legal Profession. The only trouble with the statement is that all too few people in the United States would agree.

Lawyers have never been popular in American society. Benjamin Franklin reduced his opinion on the subject to six simple words in *Poor Richard's Almanac:* "A good lawyer, a bad neighbor." Carl Sandburg expressed his views in poetry (in "The Lawyers Know Too Much"):

> Why is there always a secret singing
> When a lawyer cashes in?
> Why does the hearse horse snicker
> Hauling a lawyer away?

And so it goes. Whether in prose or poetry, over the radio or on television, in the movies or in just plain conversation, the lawyer is the convenient butt for the jokester, the target for the wit, and the villain prototype for the writer of scripts and scenarios. And there are even those who would agree with the Shakespearean character (in *II Henry IV*) who suggested, "The first thing we do let's kill all the lawyers." But why?

Probably the best answers to that "why" are found in the "Memorandum concerning Complaints against Lawyers," prepared for the Survey under the supervision of Director Smith.

It is a far from simple task to outline the specific criticisms which have been leveled against the legal profession. In part the complaints are not against the lawyers themselves but are directed against the administration of justice or even the law itself. Yet all the complaints are relevant. As Smith pointed out:

> The fact that a complaint is unfounded or can be proved untrue does not end the matter for our Survey. What people think is a fact itself. If they misjudge lawyers, that is due, in part at least, to the failure of the bar to make its work plain to the public. Because lawyers wield so much power in a democracy, it is essential for them to make their function plain to the people; they are stewards who must account for their actions.

Generally speaking, the Survey divided the subject of complaints into two categories: (1) complaints against the administration of justice and (2) complaints against the legal profession.

The primary criticism in the first category is that justice is complex and uncertain. Unfortunately, the charge is supported by ample evidence; and, unfortunately again, there is no simple solution. If a citizen is to know what he can and cannot do, the law must be certain. But organized society does not stand still. It is in constant movement, and the law must not lag too far behind. And a changing law, of course, is an uncertain law. This is a dilemma from which there is no escape.

But while the complexity and uncertainty of law are, to an extent, inevitable, there is no answer to the criticisms directed against "justice delayed" and the archaic court structures which exist in most jurisdictions. The bar has been and is working on these problems. Much of the "delay" in the courts is due to antiquated procedures, and such bodies as judicial councils have sought appropriate legislative reforms. The American Judicature Society and the various bar associations have accomplished much in the direction of achieving a modern, practical court structure. But mighty efforts will still be required to reorganize the present patchwork system—a system which grew out of the necessity of adapting ancient court structures to a rapidly growing nation.

Many complaints are also leveled against the legally technical methods used to settle disputes in the American courts and the rules of evidence which have been imposed to control the testimony presented before judge and jury. Businessmen became so outraged at the methods that, through their chambers of commerce, they set up arbitration procedures. The idea was to let a man tell his own story in his own words with no fuss, no objections, and with no lawyers to "distort" the truth. That did not work. Arbitration is a well-established procedure, and its use is growing. But the businessmen found that, if lawyers presented their cases in arbitration, the issue became clearer and less time was wasted. Today lawyers represent the opposing sides in many, if not most, arbitrations. In the field of evidence, such groups as the American Law Institute have done splendid work. These points are not meant to indicate that the present system of justice is perfect. Far from it. Improvements are not only possible but vital.

The administration of justice is also attacked as being too expensive. This complaint, in a sense, merges with the criticism of the legal profession for its alleged "high charges." Since the state provides the courthouse and pays the salaries of judges, jurors, sheriffs, bailiffs, etc., and since court fees are generally very small, the biggest expense in litigation is the attorney's fee. But are the fees too high?

Good legal work is not cheap, and no method to make it so has ever been discovered. The lawyer's education, which is his capital, is acquired at great expense. His clerical assistance must be of high caliber, because a mistake made in a lawyer's office can be costly.

Actually, the legal profession is the most competitive of all the professions, and a client who is dissatisfied with his attorney can easily find another. The lawyer cannot afford to charge exorbitant fees.

In some countries, including England, fees are regulated by statute. That plan has been tried in the United States and has failed. The prevailing philosophy in America has been to let client and lawyer agree on the charges—usually at the end of the case, when the results are known.

Notwithstanding the fact that deliberate overcharging is uncommon and that lawyers' fees are generally fair and reasonable, there still remain those who are unable to pay even minimum charges. And, if a person cannot afford an attorney, the denial of justice must be the result. This is a very real problem and one which must be, and is being, met by the legal profession. Solutions are found in the establishment of legal aid offices, lawyer-referral services, and other plans which are discussed in chapter iii.

The American bar has also been criticized in such characterizations as "lawyers are financially dishonest," "lawyers are liars," "lawyers are tools of big business," and "lawyers have too much power."

Financial dishonesty on the part of a lawyer is a rare occurrence. When it happens, it makes news. It is true that some readers of the sordid stories in the press conclude that lawyers are crooks. But, as stated by Elihu Root, "for every detractor, we find a thousand men and women who trust their lawyers implicitly in their most intimate and vital affairs, with the frankness and confidence of personal friendship, and who are justified in their trust."

Persons who voice the complaint that lawyers are liars have in mind, not the attorney in his office, but the attorney in court, especially in a murder trial. The suspicion is that the lawyer does not tell the truth because he is paid to lie. By inference, if one has enough money, he can hire the best lawyer to tell the best lies—and thereby be acquitted.

This is nonsense. Fidelity to one's client—a proud boast of the legal profession—has never included bribery, perjury, or the manufacturing of false testimony; such activities lead only to disbarment. However, Anglo-American law prefers to have the guilty escape rather than the innocent punished. And, under this conception, it is the defense lawyer's duty to say everything for his client that ethically can be said and to force the prosecution to go to the limit to prove its case. The general theory of American law is that the best chance to discover truth is in the conflict between the parties, each represented by counsel, and each lawyer doing his loyal best for his own side. This theory, though it is open to some question, seems to suit us best.

There is little to be said concerning the charge that lawyers are tools of big business. It is generally true that lawyers are conservative. Yet De Tocqueville contended that this was their supreme service to a democracy and that, without some such check, majority rule would soon destroy itself. It is also true that there is an overemphasis on business law in the profession. This situation, however, is tending to correct itself. Business will still have its staunch advocates, but equally staunch advocates now are in the service of labor and of government.

It is true that vast power has been lodged in the legal profession, but that certainly does not justify the complaint that lawyers have too much power. It is no exaggeration to say that a government of laws and not of men necessarily means government by lawyers to a very considerable extent. What is unfortunate, in this situation, is not the grant of power to the bar but the failure of the profession to make plain to the people the reasons for the grant and its meanings.

Over and above all these criticisms of the administration of justice and of the profession itself is a fundamental complaint. Mr. Smith puts it this way:

> The end of law is justice, and each man feels that he knows what is justice as well as any other man. He would like to be able to go into court and tell his story to the judge in his own words.

Men realize that they must have doctors for their health, engineers to build bridges, priests and ministers for their spiritual guidance.

But why should they have to pay someone to tell them what the justice of their cause is? That is bad enough, but what is infuriating is to be told in technical jargon they can hardly understand.

There is, of course, a ready answer to this fundamental complaint. The layman's trouble begins when he has a dispute with another layman whose idea of justice is exactly opposite. The law forces them to resolve their quarrel in court instead of by assault and battery. History has proved that to let a judge decide according to his own notions leads to arbitrary and capricious judgments. Hence the judge is required to do justice according to law. Hence lawyers are needed.

Lawyers would only be unnecessary if courts were unnecessary, and courts would only be unnecessary if law was unnecessary. And in the America of the mid-twentieth century there are few who would contend that law is unnecessary.

PUBLIC RELATIONS OF THE BAR

The task and accomplishments of the legal profession in creating a better understanding of itself by the American people are discussed in detail in the Survey's report on public relations, prepared by George Maurice Morris, of the District of Columbia bar.

Morris takes the position that "the lawyer has always had, and will always continue to have, an uphill struggle to win universal acclaim," and he adds another reason for complaints against lawyers. The lawyer, for the most part, lives by controversy. It is his job to advance one side—and one side only—of a dispute. Usually the people on the other side—particularly if it be the losing side—emerge with no great affection for the opposing counsel. The result is that persons are sometimes heard to swear by their own lawyers and to refer to all others as "shysters." Quips Morris: "The lawyer may know how to 'influence people,' but in the game of 'winning friends' the cards are somewhat stacked against him."

Yet there is much that can be done—and more and more lawyers, observing the efforts of the medical profession, the dentists, the bankers, and others to gain greater public understanding and approval, have advocated that the bar should also get into the business of "educating the public."

There is an important base upon which to build a public relations program for the legal profession—the organized bar. There has been increasing regard for the services and accomplishments of the various legal associations in recent years, and, while the lawyer as an individual may be suspect, the purposes and actions of the organized bar are respected.

Publicity being so obviously a major means by which information is spread, and something which money can buy, the lawyers who call for action in this field almost automatically think in terms of the mass media of communication. This results in buying advertising space in newspapers and periodicals, the purchase of radio and television time, and the distribution of printed pamphlets. Most of these activities have been directed to convincing the reader or the listener of the economic value of the lawyer's services to him. The public is told about some of the specific things which a lawyer does; instances where the timely employment of a lawyer would have avoided trouble and loss are recited, etc. However, because of lack of funds and the virtual impossibility of measuring results, this type of effort has generally been sporadic.

Many members of the profession have been singularly unenthusiastic about these programs. Their reluctance in permitting lawyers to advertise as a group when they may not do so as individuals has been largely overcome by the restraint and good taste of the advertising copy actually used. But they still have reservations. Their attitude seems to be that, in the long run, people will be valued at their true worth and that the true worth will be longer remembered if it is not self-proclaimed.

Rather than an "action" campaign to argue the virtues of the American lawyer, the Survey report urges caution. To begin with, it must be determined in whose interest a public relations program is to be operated. Should the program be dedicated primarily to gaining public acceptance of the organization which finances it, the individual members of that organization, all the members of the profession in the area served by that organization, or lawyers as a class?

And who are these people whose attitude toward the profession, or the lawyer, is to be improved? Is the program to be directed at potential clients, "persons of influence," legislators, journalists—or all comers?

Once these questions are answered—and once the answers are co-ordinated with the specific complaints against lawyers—a public relations campaign can begin. But, even in these days of super-selling, the best way to get a reputation for being honest, able, and public-minded is to demonstrate by deeds that one actually *is* honest, able, and public-minded. "Advertise your merits, if you like," says Morris, "but make sure that you hold to the first principle of advertising: 'See to it that the goods live up to the copy.' "

The "goods" have been and are being delivered by the organized bar. Higher standards of admission (see chap. vii) and stricter codes of ethics (see chap. viii) have been imposed and enforced. Work has been done in improving the administration of the courts, and the profession has performed yeoman service in the campaigns for the election or appointment of qualified judges (see chap. v). Further, the bar has sought to extend the availability of legal services to the poor and to those of moderate means by establishing legal aid offices, lawyer-referral services, etc. (see chap. iii).

As lawyers' services become available to all, regardless of economic circumstances, and as all people learn that those services are available, a foundation will be laid on which good will and esteem may be built. This is the best kind of public relations.

It is not enough, however, just to do a good job; the doing must be made known. And here the organized profession faces the ever present problem of lack of funds. The implementation of a public relations program, even with all the volunteer time a bar association membership can make available, costs money. It has been a common phenomenon in the organized bar to find a membership agreed, to the point of enthusiasm, on a public relations campaign. But a campaign involves costs—a competent and therefore expensive director or manager, clerical assistance and equipment, printing and mailing expenses, public relations counsel, and the purchase of advertising space or time. When these costs get piled on top of each other, spirits cool. Here are some of the alternative results which often follow: (1) the whole project gets shelved "for the time being"; (2) the membership votes to "give it a whirl" and, when the whirl is over, being unable to measure results in tangible terms, abandons the effort; or (3) the organization induces someone with a spirit of dedication, patience, and tenacity to take on the job of being "director" of the association's program. He must be prepared—underpaid, understaffed, and underfinanced—to do the best he can.

Recent years have seen much improvement in the scene. The bar has come to realize the need for qualified and well-paid professional public relations assistance, and numerous associations have added public relations counsel to their staffs. The American Bar Association has taken active leadership in the field, and its Public Relations Committee, under the chairmanship of Thomas L. Sidlo, of the Ohio bar, has been guiding the work of local bar groups. The ABA published its own volume last year on *Public Relations for Bar Associations* and now issues a *Public Relations Bulletin* five times a year. Both the book and the *Bulletin* are designed to assist the persons engaged in these activties in their work with the press, radio, and television, in establishing speakers' bureaus, in preparing and distributing pamphlets and other printed material, in conducting institutional advertising, and even in making motion pictures portraying the role of the lawyer in American society.

The job ahead, says Director Smith, is "to explain the relationship between lawyers and the law" and "to describe [the lawyer's] role in civilized society and especially in a democracy in words that would bring understanding."

CHAPTER II

Professional Services by Lawyers

WHAT DO LAWYERS DO?

Lawyer efforts run the alphabetical gamut from *argument* to *zeal,* dealing with matters ranging from *abandonment* to *zoning.* A complete list of the activities and services offered by the genus *Attorney* is impossible; in fact, it might even be easier to itemize the things lawyers do not do. Many lawyer functions are discussed elsewhere in this volume in sections devoted to public service, judicial service, and the contributions of the profession in such fields as legal aid and lawyer referral plans. But these categories still are only partial.

Nor is the answer to be found by analyzing the day's doings of the traditional lawyer stereotype. The attorney and counselor-at-law does go to court and does argue his client's cause before judge and jury—but this activity constitutes an almost infinitesimal portion of his day's work load. And it is not enough to describe the lawyer's role by citing the conclusion of the astute nine-year-old who, after being told about the activities of her practitioner father, stated simply that "lawyers help people."

Statistically speaking, of the 224,347 lawyers surveyed in the Martindale-Hubbell reports, 176,995 (78.89 per cent of the total) are engaged in private practice. After subtracting the number of attorneys now inactive or retired, the remaining 40,378 entries refer to members of the bar who hold judicial office or serve the profession in local, state, or federal government, private industry, or educational institutions. But statistics merely provide a convenient means of categorizing the profession, and the basic question still remains unanswered.

Essentially, the five functions of the lawyer are to be a wise counselor, to be a wise advocate, to work toward the improvement of his profession, to answer the call to public office if it should come, and, even if the call should not come, to lead public opinion. During any specific time in the practitioner's working day he is involved with at least one of these functions. He always has been.

In the growth of the law in the last half-century, however, the lawyer has met increased opportunities to counsel and to lead public opinion. In the last fifty years many corporations have become national in scope and character; government, at all levels, has found itself engaged in many new areas of regulation and supervision; and new laws have given rise to new rights and novel principles. The lawyer's role can no longer be confined to the specific controversies of John Doe and Richard Roe. His duties and obligations encompass virtually the entire range of human activity.

Briefly summarizing and outlining the lawyer's job, Chief Justice Arthur T. Vanderbilt of the New Jersey Supreme Court had this to say (in his *Report on Prelegal Education*):

> Lawyers carry on a wide variety of professional activities. They go to court, they appear before administrative tribunals and legislative bodies, but they also give advice in their offices to clients on every phase of the law and business and prepare documents of every conceivable kind for them. Lawyers may be general practitioners or they may be specialists and the number of specialties is almost unlimited. They may practice alone or aided by younger associates or they may be members of firms, large or small. Some become judges, legislators, mayors or governors. Others become district attorneys or public defenders, law enforcement officers or probation officers, law clerks or secretaries in the judicial branch of the government. Still others find employment in the executive department of the government, in the administrative agencies, or in local government either at the policy-making level or in various civil service positions. Some become law professors or engage in legal writing and editing or act as law librarians. Many join the legal staffs of private or quasi-public corporations and some of them ultimately become the officers or chief executives of such corporations. New outlets for professional activity are constantly being developed.

The expanded role of the legal profession is strikingly pointed out in the Survey report written by Zechariah Chafee, Jr., of the Harvard Law School, outlining the changes in the legal structure which he has witnessed in the forty years since he first entered law school. The four changes which he feels are most significant are (1) the enactment of workmen's compensation laws in all forty-eight states; (2) the advent of federal income and estate taxation; (3) the growth of administrative boards with wide discretionary powers; and (4) a changing attitude toward labor rights and regulations. Each of these developments has required the lawyer to add to his green bag of necessary knowledge and techniques.

Additional lawyer responsibilities have followed on the heels of each attempt to solve the problems which have faced American society.

Experiences of the depression brought forth a flood of statutes seeking to level out so-called financial inequities and standardize business operations. These laws created such administrative bodies as the Federal Security Agency and the Securities and Exchange Commission. Better transportation and increased consumer buying power made nation-wide industry possible, thereby increasing the occasions of intraindustry conflict and giving rise to such agencies as the Federal Trade Commission and private advisory committees and councils. The necessities of war spawned a new range of problems, including rationing, price control, and rent regulation. And the present requirements of national defense raise difficult questions in international law, negotiation of contracts, and arbitration of disputes.

In each of these developments the lawyer has had and continues to have an important role. New specialties have been created. And even the general practitioner, traditionally dealing with wills, real estate, and an occasional negligence case, now must meet and work with a constantly accumulating volume of new statutes and adjust to new patterns of relations.

Detailed data on the labor lawyer, the lawyer in government, the corporation counsel, and the workmen's compensation claims advocate will be treated later in this chapter. But before that it is necessary to consider some of the special conflicts which arise in performing the lawyer's job and some of the difficulties which a lawyer faces in achieving acceptance as an adviser.

THE LAWYER SERVING THE PUBLIC

Writing in *The Church Militant,* Director Smith noted some of the basic problems which the lawyer meets in performing his professional services. First, the lawyer faces a conflict between, on the one hand, supporting and maintaining the stability of the law and, on the other, advocating the need for legislative reforms to meet changing requirements of society.

Next, the lawyer faces and must resolve the conflicting loyalties he owes to his three masters—the client, the court, and society. In a very real sense the attorney is confronted with ethical problems greater than those of any other profession. The minister owes his obligation only to God, and the physician only to his patient (with some statutory exceptions). But the lawyer must decide whether the steps he should take, in serving a particular client, will also serve the best interests of the judicial branch of government and of society as a whole.

The third problem which confronts a lawyer is whether he should defend a client whom he knows or believes to be guilty. Here the lawyer, following the highest traditions of his profession, must fulfil his oath never to reject, "from any consideration personal to myself, the cause of the defenseless or oppressed." Yet, despite the necessity of adhering to this principle, it is not an easy task for the lawyer to serve a client whom he believes to be in the wrong.

Finally, the lawyer must decide how to provide assistance to families which cannot afford to pay regular fees for legal services and how much of his own time he can and will give to that end.

While the lawyer wrestles with these moral and professional problems, he must also continue to carry on the workaday tasks of his calling at the behest of that part of the public which is his clientele. Yet the greater portion of the public is not only unconcerned with the lawyer's problems; it scarcely sees fit to consult legal counsel about its own legal problems. Through omission stemming from ignorance—or through unwillingness stemming from hostility —a large share of the lawyer's potential public is not his public at all.

The need of the average American family for legal services is treated in a Survey report by Earl Lomon Koos. Replies to his questionnaire were received from 2,027 middle-class families in six representatives cities (Akron, Atlanta, Nashville, Oakland, Rochester, and Seattle), and 2,050 interviews were conducted with working-class families in the same communities.

While the number of middle-class families reporting the existence of a legal problem was 48.9 per cent, the percentage of working-class families facing such a problem was only 35.6. This does not mean that working-class families necessarily have fewer legal problems, explains Koos, since sociological studies have indicated that the middle class has a lower threshold regarding problems than the other group. The more significant fact is that 60.4 per cent of middle-class families with problems consulted a lawyer and that only 44.2 per cent of working-class families did so.

In each group some families declared that there were certain problems they would not take to an attorney under any circumstances. Those in the working class would not consult attorneys on problems involving insurance, personal debts, recovery of personal property, and complaints against another attorney. Middle-class families on the other hand, would forego a lawyer's services when the problems involved illegitimate children, adoption, separation, insanity, defamation, and the settling of estates. Apparently, working-class families attempt to deal with their financial problems on their own, while middle-class families prefer to handle personal matters by themselves.

The reasons given by both groups for not consulting a lawyer about these and other problems indicate once again the need for more and better public relations for the bar. As might have been expected, both economic groups gave financial considerations as a major reason for not consulting attorneys. This reason accounted for almost half of the working-class responses. Other reasons given were related: unwillingness to take "charity," unsatisfactory previous experience with a lawyer, and the belief that attorneys were too costly. Some respondents said that they did not know any attorneys to whom they might go. Others did not know that a lawyer could help them with their problems. A sizable number of those interviewed stated that they had received legal advice from nonprofessional acquaintances.

Koos believes that the failure of laymen to use legal assistance arises from a failure of communication—the lawyer's function is misunderstood or misconstrued. A total of 71.2 per cent of the middle-class families and 81.9 per cent of the working-class families saw the lawyer only as a person defending persons accused of violating the law. Other answers from both groups described the lawyer's role as keeping people out of trouble or helping clients find legal loopholes which would keep them within the law. None seemed to be aware of a need for the lawyer as a counselor in daily affairs. The most important conclusion to be drawn from this aspect of the study is that there exists an immediate need to educate the public as to the true function of the lawyer.

Existing service agencies of the legal profession also have to make their presence and usefulness known. In Rochester, the only one of the six cities surveyed in which the legal aid society has been working long enough to have become well known in the community, 30 per cent of the respondents had no idea that the agency existed. Another 23 per cent had a general idea that its services were available but did not know the name of the agency. Only 28 per cent knew of the existence of the agency, and these only in a general way.

THE LAWYER SERVING BUSINESS

In the newly opened and newly expanded fields which have developed in recent years, the Survey found the function of the lawyer to be more properly understood. This is especially true in regard to those attorneys who are serving industry, particularly those employed as corporation counsel. Two articles dealing with this modern phenomenon were prepared for the Survey by Charles S. Maddock, of the Boston bar.

His reports show that the number of lawyers who are serving a single corporation's interests is steadily growing. This can be attributed in part to the complexity of governmental regulations which make day-to-day counseling necessary. It is also the result of an increased realization of the benefits to be gained by having a counselor who is thoroughly familiar with the employing organization and its problems and who is readily available to serve directors, officers, and supervisory employees with their personal legal problems.

The Maddock study, made in 1949, covered 2,048 private organizations. It revealed that 5,428 attorneys were employed as house counsel. Of this number, 1,996 were employed by 231 industrial corporations having three or more attorneys in their law departments (Table 9). A total of 301 corporations employed two attorneys, and 769 employed one. The balance of the 5,428 lawyers employed directly by industry were divided as follows: insurance companies, 895; banks, 547; title companies, 315; colleges and universities, 239; and trade and other associations, 65.

Classified as a service organization of the corporation, and in this respect comparable to the personnel, traffic, and research de-

TABLE 9*

CORPORATION LAWYERS IN A GROUP OF REPRESENTATIVE INDUSTRIES

Industry	Number of Lawyers in Law Department					Total Companies	Total Lawyers
	3 or 4	5–9	10–24	25–50	Over 50		
Gas and oil	19	12	12	2	5	50	649
Railroads	13	15	11	3	......	42	409
Food, drugs, etc.	15	4	4	......	......	23	148
Public utilities (including telephone)	10	6	2	1	......	19	141
Chemicals	7	6	1	......	......	14	74
Heavy equipment	3	4	2	......	......	9	59
Consumers' goods manufacturing	4	3	1	......	......	8	44
Retail stores	1	4	2	......	......	7	54
Entertainment	2	3	1	1	......	7	74
Steel and aluminum	2	4	......	......	......	6	32
Electrical equipment	1	......	3	......	1	5	103
Automobile equipment	3	1	......	......	......	4	14
Rubber	1	......	3	......	......	4	51
Glass	1	2	......	......	......	3	13
Paper	2	1	......	......	......	3	12
Aircraft manufacturing	2	1	......	......	......	3	12
Publishing	2	1	......	......	......	3	12
Textiles	3	......	......	......	......	3	9
Tobacco	1	1	......	......	......	2	8
Air transportation	1	1	......	......	......	2	8
Automobile manufacturing	......	......	2	......	......	2	22
Unclassified	8	4	......	......	......	12	48
Total	......	......	......	......	......	231	1,996

* Source: Charles S. Maddock, "The Corporation Law Department," *Harvard Business Review*, XXX (1952), 119.

partments, the law department typically has at its head a man who, if not himself a corporation officer, reports directly to the president or a vice-president. He is usually held available for consultation by the board of directors and the officers regarding overall policies and plans of the company. Frequently the house counsel is a member of the board's important policy committees. Less frequently, he is himself a director.

Depending upon the nature of the business, the legal department may be subdivided into specialties, as, for example, patents and trade-marks, claims and litigation, etc. Peculiar operating conditions may result in a departmental organization in which one lawyer is assigned to a particular operating or service department. In large-scale operations spread across the country the legal department may be broken down into smaller units in key cities, with over-all direction from the central office.

Among the advantages of employing house counsel can be counted the immediate availability of the services of a lawyer who has, better than any outside attorney, a complete knowledge of the company's legal problems and their background. Concomitantly, this practice provides an opportunity for "preventive law"—the guidance of corporate activities, before decisions are made, into channels which will avoid undue legal risks.

There are likewise many disadvantages in the employment of house counsel, most of which are the result of the fact that the lawyer *is* an employee of the corporation. This status makes it more difficult for a lawyer to give advice to his superiors than it would be if he were guiding the same corporate officers in an independent capacity. Further, as an employee, it is frequently inconvenient or difficult to seek advice from outside specialists. In addition, his closeness to detail and his intimacy with the employer may blind the lawyer to the ultimate implications of local decisions. It may give rise to a temptation to consider problems in their business aspects rather than from their legal ramifications. Another disadvantage lies in the volume of work which may be forced upon the lawyer by individual members of the corporation, limiting the time he has available for analyses of legal trends and reflection upon their effects on current and planned programs.

The lawyer in a corporation legal department continually faces a great diversity of questions. The functions of the head of the department are similar to those of the senior partner in a private practice. This similarity extends to the organization and duties of the lower echelons, depending on the size of the department. Notwithstanding the similarity in organization, the functions of house counsel vary widely from industry to industry and from firm to firm. The requirements of the industries themselves, and the fact that some corporations limit their house counsel to general affairs, result in a wide range of services. But a number of these are common to all corporate lawyers.

In respect to planning and policy, counsel must advise on the legal aspects of the over-all company program, including expansion into new fields of operation, acquisition of established businesses, creation and operation of subsidiaries, relationships with existing subsidiaries, and problems of reorganization and consolidation. While initial sponsorship of such planning usually comes from the board of directors, evaluations as to the risks and opportunities involved in the proposals are sought from the legal department before final decisions are made. Obviously, evaluations as to planning are also received from the sales, production, research, and financial departments. But the use of the legal department at the outset probably eliminates a good number of unworkable, unenforceable, or disadvantageous suggestions without overburdening the other departments.

Planning, of course, is only one aspect of the work of the legal department. Among the financial problems house counsel are asked to deal with are those relating to the issuance of stocks and bonds plus the effect of changes in regulatory laws. A thorough knowledge of the impact of federal, state, local, and foreign taxation is invaluable in shaping the form which proposed operations will take. There are tax benefits, too, in advice as to timing expenditures and dividends, handling inventories, and dealing with other production factors. And the legal department must also work with the financial department in determining what advantages and disadvantages are involved in various methods of securing loans.

Some corporations combine the office of secretary with that of the chief of the legal department, thus permitting house counsel to handle such administrative details as stockholders' and special meetings; dividend announcements and payments; preparation of minutes, resolutions, and amendments; compliance with state filing and notice requirements; and the maintenance of other records. Where the two positions are not consolidated, the secretary usually seeks advice from the legal department on such matters. Corporate counsel are also called upon to advise on interpretation of charter and by-law provisions and similar matters.

Customary and specialized problems arising in the production and sale of the corporation's wares commonly receive the attention of the legal department. It advises on securing and protecting patents, trade-marks, copyrights, and trade secrets; interpreting the company's rights to such properties; negotiating contracts concerning their use; and avoiding conflicts with the rights of other companies. Where the volume of such work is small, however, some companies will choose to use the services of outside counsel for economy and efficiency. Other companies will retain or employ patent counsel regularly, even though they have no legal department at all.

House counsel will also handle contracts for the purchase of raw materials and facilities—drawing, interpreting, and approving them—and contracts for the sale of the finished product. In addition, these lawyers will analyze questions involving the possible or actual legal liabilities, of the corporation, in connection with its production operations and the products it makes.

Export and import laws, where pertinent, receive prompt attention from the legal department, especially where it is necessary to devise plans to permit smooth operation which is not only legal but profitable. Regulatory statutes—such as the Sherman and the Clayton ("antitrust") acts, the federal Robinson-Patman (Fair Trade) Act, state fair-trade and securities laws, and the pure food and drug acts found in many jurisdictions—also take up a good portion of the typical corporate law department's time, primarily in suggesting controls that will prevent violations. Where state and local laws restrict operations of the production department by imposing zoning restrictions, pollution controls, and such other legislation as smoke prevention, noise curtailment, and traffic regulation, the corporate lawyer may be called upon by his employer not only to guide company policy to avoid pitfalls but also to draft and foster desirable legislation, drawing on his knowledge of plant processes and the needs of the industry.

Another aspect of government relations which concerns the legal department with some regularity involves the interpretation of administrative regulations and appearances before administrative agencies. These appearances are usually in connection with current litigation but are sometimes for the purpose of advocating amendments to administrative rulings, a service to which the house counsel brings his intimate knowledge of business requirements.

The legal department will also handle such traditional tasks as the preparation and conduct of litigation, the investigation of claims, wills and estates of company personnel, and real estate. This practice includes negotiation for the acquisition of property, title searches, drafting of deeds and contracts of sale, closings, and the preparation and management of leasing operations.

Higher starting salaries than those offered by most law firms, plus relative job security and fringe benefits, are attracting more and more recent law graduates to the corporation law department. In turn, the corporations have gradually reversed their policy of seeking employees with several years of experience in private practice. The operating efficiency of a corporate law department seems to be enhanced by having counsel experienced in the operations and objectives of the employer. Some corporations have even instituted training programs for their young attorneys, similar to those established in the administrative and sales departments.

In addition to the financial benefits to be gained, the newly admitted attorney generally can obtain as good postgraduate legal training, serving a corporation, as he might gain in the average large law firm. And the company department may offer even greater opportunities than the firm for direct personal contact with clients. Whether a recent graduate or an experienced practitioner, the average lawyer in a corporation law department tends to remain with the company and does achieve a position of responsibility at as early an age as the attorney in private practice.

THE LAWYER SERVING LABOR

A detailed picture has been drawn of the labor lawyer in the Survey report by Robert M. Segal, of the Boston bar, on professional services to organized labor. The conclusion:

1. He is about forty-three years old, in a partnership, and has been practicing law about seventeen and a half years but has only been in the labor-law field about thirteen years.

2. He has probably had government training, although not necessarily in the labor field.

3. He has a college degree with a major in the social sciences and a law-school degree but no course in labor law.

4. Although he belongs to the local and state bar associations, he probably does not belong to the American Bar Association.

5. As for his income, he is probably on a retainer and nets about $12,500, which is higher than the average income for all lawyers in the United States. His top range is limited, but his lowest range is above the lowest range of all lawyers' incomes.

6. He probably feels that the stigma attached to being a labor-union attorney is decreasing but has not disappeared completely. Although he is accepted by the unions, which resent lawyers generally, he finds that unions still consider labor lawyers as "necessary evils" for emergencies only. In addition, he has lost general practice because he is a "labor lawyer." He finds that generally he can represent both AF of L and CIO unions but cannot represent employers as well as unions in labor matters.

7. Though some public officials in rural communities have an unfavorable attitude toward him, the labor lawyer feels that the courts today treat him fairly.

8. His work consists of: (*a*) regular appearances before administrative agencies; (*b*) court litigations; (*c*) approval and negotiation of collective-bargaining agreements; (*d*) arbitration work; (*e*) drafting legislation and speeches; and (*f*) public relations work for the union. For the considerable free or extra work which he is called upon to do, the labor lawyer is compensated by the satisfaction he derives from work which usually is in sympathy with his ideals.

With the exception of the southwestern states, labor attorneys are distributed geographically throughout the country on about the same percentage lines as the general lawyer population, with the heaviest concentrations in the highly industrialized Middle East, Central and Far West.

It is estimated that there are five hundred labor lawyers in the country, of whom about fifty are house counsel for labor organizations. Of the 213 attorneys responding to a Survey questionnaire, less than 13 per cent devote their entire professional services to labor unions. Approximately two-thirds of the lawyers spend the major portion of their time in labor work, and the remaining 22 per cent deal with union and labor problems to the extent of a quarter of their practice.

While most labor counsel find they must work exclusively for either the AF of L or the CIO, a relatively small percentage still manages to represent units of both organizations or of both organizations plus independent unions. In effect, there is a specialization within the specialty of labor law. Few attorneys can overcome the emotional, personalized aspects of labor practice to represent more than one union; fewer still can escape being labeled either an AF of L man or a CIO man.

Contrasted with corporate lawyers, labor lawyers have little opportunity to rise to executive positions in their clients' organizations or to receive the pension and bonus benefits that many corporations provide. And there are, Segal found, other deterrents to labor practice:

> Five out of every six labor lawyers report that they have lost general law business because of their relationship with labor unions. They report that businesses shy clear of them because of their work for unions or because of their label as "labor-union attorneys." In addition, because they are regarded as labor-union specialists, these attorneys often do not receive general legal work from members of the bar, from the general public, or even from the individual union members.
>
> Most labor lawyers claim that litigation work for labor organizations is the most lucrative phase of their labor-law practice. Workmen's compensation, administrative board work, and arbitration cases are also profitable fields of labor practice.
>
> On the other hand, consultative work for labor organizations is the least lucrative phase. This type of work consists of advice to the labor union, the officers of the union, and sometimes to the individual members of the organization. Unemployment compensation cases are also considered unprofitable. A large number of labor-union attorneys also report that contract negotiations are not very profitable, for the unions are not prepared to pay the attorney for the long hours and time spent in negotiating collective-bargaining agreements.

Individuals considering entry into this field must, for the present at least, also face prejudice on the part of employers, conservative members of the bar, the press, and the public. Even the rank-and-file union member shares in the dislike of the labor lawyer. This resentment finds one expression in collective-bargaining contracts which provide expressly that lawyers shall not sit for either side in negotiations or grievance-committee sessions.

Labor lawyers, however, do derive many advantages from their choice:

> Most labor lawyers report that the stigma is gradually disappearing. In fact, with the increasing importance of labor unions in politics, some labor lawyers are finding that the successful labor movement can offer

substantial support to individual political ambitions; many congressmen, senators, and governors were at one time counsel to unions, and many influential lawyers will take an occasional case for a union because of politics. In addition, one out of every four labor lawyers reports that some honors have been bestowed upon him as a result of his labor-union work; these honors include honorary membership in labor organizations, election to law-school alumni and bar-association councils, appointments to civic, social, and professional groups and committees, labor-management boards, and some political appointments.

As a specialist, the labor lawyer is able to perform valuable services for his client. Just as counsel in a corporation law department has the advantage of knowing the business logic of his employer's course of action, so the labor lawyer who regularly represents a single union has the advantage of familiarity with his client's needs and problems. There the similarity ends. Not only does the labor lawyer have a different orientation toward the mutual problems of industry and union but he spends a far greater proportion of his time on those problems, since, obviously, the union's concern with the firm is almost total, whereas, to the firm, employees constitute only one of its relationships.

Hearings before administrative agencies regularly take more time of more labor lawyers than any other form of legal work. Half the labor lawyers also spend a good deal of time in courtroom litigation. Although only one lawyer out of six is called upon for approval of collective-bargaining agreements, this work forms an important part of the practice of those lawyers so sought. Negotiation of the agreements is more common; one out of every five labor practitioners is regularly engaged in this service, and 75 per cent of all union counsel assists, frequently or occasionally, in labor-management discussions.

Grievance work prior to arbitration is normally performed by 20 per cent of the respondents. Arbitration itself occupies an important place for 30 per cent of labor lawyers and is undertaken occasionally by another 43 per cent. Internal affairs and management—the interpretation and revision of constitutions and by-laws, the conduct of meetings, etc.—continue to gain in importance, systematically engaging 15 per cent of labor lawyers and normally coming to the attention of half the group.

Impressive percentages of labor lawyers are involved in legislative activities—60 per cent being called upon to draft new laws (generally as counsel to state labor bodies) and more than half to argue before state and federal legislative bodies on their clients' behalf. It is in the legislative field, in strike strategy, and in contract negotiation that the labor lawyer usually is required to give continuing guidance; problems outside these three major areas receive attention only as they arise.

Notwithstanding the abilities that labor lawyers bring to bear in analyzing and advising on union questions, only four out of ten unions regularly heed the advice of counsel on legislation, strategy, and the settlement of contracts. In matters of discipline the percentage is even smaller, with unions completely ignoring lawyer guidance in 29 per cent of the cases and following the advice of their attorneys only irregularly in the remaining instances.

Even in the relatively short history of the labor movement there have been many changes in the nature of legal work to be performed on behalf of unions. Contract and grievance negotiations, once the source of bitter conflict, are now usually carried on in an atmosphere of mutual co-operation; attempts to insist upon procedural technicalities are resented by labor and management attorneys alike.

The nature of litigation brought into the courtroom has also changed. Once the principal sources of labor-law work were found in damage suits, criminal cases, and injunctive proceedings; now counsel are more frequently engaged in disputes over the enforcement of contracts and arbitration awards, problems relating to administrative decisions, and various internal union affairs. Where litigation before administrative agencies is involved, however, many unions prefer to handle their own negotiation and grievance problems, dispensing with counsel and relying upon the government agency or the arbitrator to discover the facts and see that justice is done.

Since unions recognize the necessity of favorable public relations, a substantial part of labor-lawyer activities includes addressing outside groups on labor topics, drafting speeches for union officials, writing articles for union publications, writing on labor matters for the general reading public, and appearing before legislative and administrative committees.

Because of the rapidly shifting internal political situation in many unions, most labor lawyers find it inadvisable to do legal work for individual members. The stereotype designation of "labor" lawyer is another factor preventing service to the rank and file, since few members consider their organization's counsel competent to deal with their personal legal problems.

WORKMEN'S COMPENSATION AS A LEGAL SPECIALTY

One type of legal problem involving large numbers of employees, to which labor lawyers might be expected to bring both understanding and experience, gives rise instead to another lawyer specialist. This is the field of workmen's compensation. As a subject of legislation it has burgeoned in twentieth-century American law. The reason for its growth—and the opportunities for assistance presented to practitioners in this field—is amply dramatized in the opening remarks of Joseph Bear in another Survey report. Drawing from Bureau of Labor Statistics figures, he indicates:

> A worker dies every twenty-nine minutes.
>
> Every five minutes one worker is totally disabled in industry; 100,000 are so severely injured every year that they can never work again.
>
> Almost every fifteen seconds some worker receives a temporarily disabling injury.
>
> In one year, these injuries resulted in the loss of 280,000,000 man-days—the equivalent of over 1,000,000 men kept out of work continuously for more than a year—and the relative proportion of fatalities and permanent disabilities is increasing.
>
> There were 19,000 amputations among servicemen during World War II, but more than 120,000 major amputations during the same period in our civilian population. Approximately 1,500 servicemen were blinded during the last war, but 60,000 civilians lost their sight during this period.
>
> The price we pay in money is at least $2,600,000,000 a year: about $7,250,000 each day for wage loss, expenses for medical care, overhead costs of workmen's compensation, damages to equipment and materials, production slow-downs, and time lost by fellow-workers.
>
> And the situation is getting worse.

Compensation laws have spread to all forty-eight states and the territories, and federal laws in this field cover longshoremen and harbor workers, private employees in the District of Columbia, and employees of the United States government. These statutes are based upon a relatively new concept in the law—liability without fault. The purpose is to make the industry in which injuries occur bear the major part of the accident burden that its workers may suffer.

By making the measure of damages for injuries sustained both fixed and certain, and by eliminating jury-trial procedures, the framers of the statutes sought to write out litigation and lawyers. However, despite the fact that all claims were supposed to be processed promptly by administrative tribunals, it was found that the system could not work without the services of the legal profession.

Most of the statutes contained provisions that an employee could be reimbursed if he suffered "a personal injury by accident arising out of and in the course of his employment." Because these words embodied a novel concept in the law, judicial interpretation became a necessity. Pressure by various groups brought countless amendments. And these turned an already complicated law into a labyrinth which only those trained in statutory interpretation could hope to penetrate successfully. Instead of establishing a lawyer-free law, the report indicates that "boards or commissions generally have come to frown upon an employee's appearing without counsel, or a layman's attempting to practice before them."

It is not every lawyer who is qualified to represent the injured workingman. Specialized training is necessary. To begin with, compensation work requires a comprehensive and intelligent acquaintance with all branches of medicine, since the lawyer must decide whether the injury at the basis of a claim has an industrial or a nonindustrial origin. Under fast-moving compensation procedures, the lawyer cannot always rely on his medical witnesses for guidance. Adjournments due to their absences cause unnecessary hardship to the client and may bring some loss of the attorney's prestige in the eyes of the administrative tribunal. And, because procedures are so rapid, the attorney must be well versed in the law which he is handling—there is no time to return to his library to search out a point. Finally, the lawyer must be an authority in his field, since he comes before commissioners and referees who are unusually expert as a result of devoting all their time to compensation matters.

Despite the need for compensation specialists and the growing opportunities in the field, most lawyers cannot afford to practice exclusively on the side of the injured worker. The average fee, according to the questionnaires, was 20 per cent of the amount awarded if the case was won or settled; there was no fee paid if the case was lost. Since these fees are set by the compensation tribunal, they are usually less than the fees charged by negligence lawyers working for their clients on a contingency basis. Further, the modest amounts which the injured workingman receives make it difficult, if not impossible, to raise fee schedules. Thus, compensation work on behalf of the plaintiff-workman cannot be profitable unless the lawyer is able to handle a great volume of claims.

Specialists in this area and lawyers working in the allied fields of admiralty, railroad, and personal injury cases formed their own association in 1946, the National Association of Compensation Claimants' Attorneys. This organization provides a valuable medium for the exchange of ideas and for further self-education. Its membership seeks to obtain legislation favorable to compensation claimants and to foster the teaching of compensation law in the law schools. They also seek to improve their own financial status, realizing that competent young lawyers are deterred from entering the specialty on the side of the workingman because of the inadequacy of fees.

LAWYERS SERVING GOVERNMENT

Compensation for legal services is likewise a familiar problem for lawyers in government. Wage scales at federal, state, and local levels are generally so low that most lawyers consider government service only as a training ground or as a stepping stone to better positions in private practice. The relatively low ceiling on government salaries tends to preclude the employment of lawyers with several years' private experience. By far the greatest number of men entering the public service are recent law graduates who, at this stage of their careers, are able to receive salaries from government comparable to those offered by the law firms. These men also find educational advantages in governmental work, having greater opportunities to see a case through to the end than in a private office.

Unless a case involving a municipality invokes a popular local issue, the work of the city, county, or township attorney receives far less public attention than is warranted by the importance of his service to the community. Charles S. Rhyne's report on lawyers in local government, including a study of the city attorney's work for the largest city in the world, shows the variety of matters that can come to the desk of a lawyer in local government:

> The Law Department of the City of New York is the largest municipal law office in the world, employing over 600 persons including lawyers, accountants, examiners and clerical personnel. It is headed by the Corporation Counsel who acts as attorney and legal adviser for all departments, bureaus, boards, commissions and agencies which comprise the City government. The Department deals with a wide variety of legal questions as illustrated by its 15 divisions which include: Admiralty, Contracts, Franchises, General Litigation, Real Estate and Condemnation, Tax, Torts and Workmen's Compensation.
>
> . . . .
>
> During 1950 more than 16,600 actions and proceedings were instituted or defended by the Department. In addition, during that year, 16,000 prosecutions were instituted by the department for violation of the Administrative Code, the Multiple Dwelling Law and numerous other rules and regulations pertaining to the safety, sanitary maintenance and fire protection standards of buildings.
>
> The Department conducted 112 condemnation proceedings in 1950 for housing, school sites, parks, streets and other public purposes. These proceedings resulted in awards totaling $32,455,786. There were 3,200 negligence actions against the City and its agencies, resulting in settlements and judgments which total $3,792,700. During the same period over 12,000 proceedings to review real estate assessment were settled, tried or otherwise disposed of, with reductions granted totalling $11,000,000. . . .
>
> The work of the Corporation Counsel includes every type of litigation except criminal law. Among the great variety of matters handled are the rates, franchises and taxes of public utility corporations, excise taxes, released time program of the schools, zoning, litigative matters arising out of construction of water supply systems, actions arising out of disciplinary action against school teachers refusing to answer questions concerning membership in the Communist party, and opinions on interpretation of law for every function of the city government.

Salaries for the full-time heads of municipal law departments range from the $3,850 received by the city attorney of York, Pennsylvania (population 56,712) to the $17,500 of the corporation counsel of New York City (population 7,454,995). Size of staff ranges from no assistants at all—again in York—to 125 assistants—again in New York. These include a chief assistant, 61 assistant corporation counsel, 44 deputy assistant corporation counsel, 10 associate assistant corporation counsel, and 10 junior assistant corporation counsel.

More than two thousand municipalities, all with populations in excess of 5,000, have made provisions either for regular legal departments or for the part-time employment of an attorney. Because of financial limitations, smaller communities employ counsel to handle legal problems only as they arise. In more than 80 per cent of the cities with populations of more than 5,000, the city attorney and his assistants hold appointive offices.

The nation's largest employer of lawyers—the federal government —also appoints its attorneys. And therein lies one of the major disadvantages of government legal service as a career. Failure to place legal work within the civil service structure may be politically desirable, but it becomes a serious drawback to those who want the permanency and security which government service usually brings. Other disadvantages to employment in the federal government are the limitation on top-range salaries and a recently developed negative public attitude toward federal employees.

The Survey report by Peyton Ford, Clive W. Palmer, and David Reich, however, points out that there are also many advantages in government service. Distributed among fifty-four different agencies of the executive department, 7,919 lawyers were finding (in 1952) ample opportunity within their own specialties to "take part in history" (Table 10).

The Department of Labor, the National Labor Relations Board, and similar agencies provide many positions of interest to lawyers desiring to work in employee relations. Similarly the Internal Revenue Service and allied boards attract attorneys making a specialty of taxation. And within each specialty the lawyer may well have a variety of functions to perform.

Every agency has lawyers who engage in litigation, either in court or before administrative bodies; who draft and take part in enforcing regulations; who prepare licenses, contracts, and schedules, insuring compliance with statutes; and who investigate violations. Government lawyers also are called upon to advise industries and individuals on the applicability of statutes and regulations to proposed ventures. Finally, within each agency itself, the lawyer serves as adviser to nonlegal personnel.

As an example of the scope of legal duties in a typical government agency, the Survey report outlined lawyer work in the Civil Aeronautics Board. The primary task of the CAB lawyer is to interpret the Civil Aeronautics Act of 1938—and related statutes—and advise the board on the legal aspects of proposed actions. He also represents the staff in formal proceedings before the board, performing all the tasks customary in lawyer litigation before the

TABLE 10*

ATTORNEYS EMPLOYED IN FIFTY-FOUR FEDERAL EXECUTIVE AGENCIES AND DEPARTMENTS

Agency or Department	No. of Attorneys	Agency or Department	No. of Attorneys
Bureau of the Budget	3	Federal Power Commission	49
Philippine Alien Property Administration	2	Federal Security Agency	98
Department of State	44	Federal Trade Commission	278
International Boundary and Water Commission	3	General Accounting Office	589
Treasury Department	550	General Services Administration	66
Department of Defense	29	Housing and Home Finance Agency	40
Department of the Army	600	Home Loan Bank Board	8
Department of the Navy	175	Public Housing Administration	106
Central Intelligence Agency	10	Federal Housing Administration	21
Department of the Air Force	125	Federal National Mortgage Association	17
Air Coordinating Committee	2	Indian Claims Commission	5
Immigration and Naturalization Service	214	Interstate Commerce Commission	253
Post Office Department	28	Maritime Administration	45
Department of Justice	1,651	National Capital Housing Authority	2
Department of the Interior	293	National Capital Park and Planning Commission	1
Department of Agriculture	232	National Gallery of Art	3
Department of Commerce	284	National Labor Relations Board	301
Department of Labor	194	Office of the Housing Expediter	162
Atomic Energy Commission	103	Railroad Retirement Board	24
Federal Reserve System	14	Reconstruction Finance Corporation	40
Civil Aeronautics Board	78	Securities and Exchange Commission	180
Civil Service Commission	16	Selective Service System	5
Displaced Persons Commission	33	Tax Court of the United States	32
Economic Cooperation Administration	13	Tennessee Valley Authority	46
Export-Import Bank of Washington	8	Veterans Administration	728
Federal Communications Commission	64	War Claims Commission	40
Federal Deposit Insurance Corporation	11		
Federal Mediation and Conciliation Service	1	Total	7,919

* Source: Ford, Palmer, and Reich, *The Government Lawyer* (New York, 1952).

courts. In addition, he serves in the quasi-judicial function of drafting the opinions issued by the board.

Other duties include the investigation of alleged violations; service as a hearing examiner; the interpretation of treaties, conventions, and agreements; interpretation of proposed legislation; and representation of the Civil Aeronautics Board in court proceedings. CAB counsel must also prepare orders and legal documents relating to operations of domestic and foreign air carriers, the regulation of airline consolidations, mergers and interlocking relationships, and the control of rate schedules.

In a true sense the government lawyer may be the most important member of the agency he serves. As Director Smith has observed, "What appears to happen is that if, in a given bureau in a department, there are a lawyer, an economist, a physician, a sociologist, a statistician, and an agronomist, the lawyer tends to become the nucleus of the group. He has to write the regulations and the reports, and both are instruments of power. The group is apt to meet in his office for conferences, and that fact is a psychological advantage."

Lawyers in federal service also have excellent opportunities for promotion to high executive positions. Several agencies, in fact, make it a practice to advance counsel to higher wage-scale positions after the completion of a specified period of service; for example, the Department of Agriculture. Those who ultimately decide against government service as a career still find that the experience gained is of great value either in private law practice or in business —especially if they have been engaged in highly specialized work dealing with problems of immediate importance to large commercial interests.

Few entrants into government legal work remain long enough to obtain the many advantages of advancement and training. There is no central recruiting system, and, since application must be made directly to a particular agency, some find out too late that they have chosen the wrong agency for their talents and interests.

Morale, of course, also is effected adversely by the lack of job security resulting from changes in political administrations, vagaries of budgeting, and the non-civil service status of the government lawyer. Elimination of these faults and an increase in the pay scale have been advocated by the Survey to insure the highest caliber of legal talent for public service.

The recent law graduate may forego some benefits by choosing government service in preference to private practice. Still, for acquiring experience, for treating problems which involve a great complex of considerations, and for rendering service to the public, legal work in government provides variety, interest, and immediacy.

More than that, government work has an inherent satisfaction—the lawyer in government is the lawyer for the people of the United States. His client is the government of the United States; it enables the conscientious attorney to serve without regard to the idiosyncrasies and peculiarities of the average client that is encountered in private practice. The lawyer in government does not see his client except in so far as his client is represented by the particular officer who heads the agency in which he is functioning. The government lawyer has the opportunity to assist in the development of the law from the viewpoint of the over-all public interest as against the normally purely private interest of outside practitioners.

The attraction of government is such that many a man with a highly successful practice has sought government service. Several such men, while initially undertaking the assignment for the opportunity it affords for publicity and fame, have remained on year after year in the government. They have discovered that there is an intangible reward in representing the people of the United States. They have found truth in the statement of Montaigne: "I am of the opinion that the most honorable calling is to serve the Public and to be useful to the many."

CHAPTER III

Availability of Legal Services

Joe Maffini, who makes $69.25 a week working for the Chicago street railway, decided he needed a lawyer. Mr. Caprecio, his landlord, had said to him: "Joe, you and your family got to get out. You make too much noise. Besides, you got two more kids than when you came in."

Joe knew no lawyer, and he was afraid to walk into a strange office. He went instead to the office of the Chicago Bar Association and asked for the reference attorney. He waited twenty minutes while three persons ahead of him had their turns.

"What's your problem?" asked Charles G. Lind, the reference attorney. Joe told him.

"Ever had a lawyer before?" Mr. Lind queried.

"No," said Joe.

Mr. Lind consulted a card file and then dialed a number. "Let me speak to Mr. Spather. This is Mr. Lind, the reference attorney for the Bar Association. After a short wait, he said, "Hello, Tom, how are you? Got a Mr. Maffini here. His landlord wants to throw him and his family out. Claims nuisance and violation of lease because two children born since they moved in. Will you handle it? Okay. Right now? Just a minute." He turned to Joe. "Can you go over right now?"

"Sure," said Joe. "Sure."

"Okay by him, Tom. Goodbye."

Lind wrote out Spather's name and address and the time of appointment on a form, which he gave to Joe.

"You understand that he will charge you $3.00 for the conference if it take less than thirty minutes, or $5.00 an hour, and that you and he will make your own arrangements as to other fees?"

"Sure," said Joe.

"And you understand that, when we refer you to Mr. Spather, the Bar Association is not saying that he'll win your case or even that he won't make any mistakes. We have investigated all the lawyers on our list, but we don't guarantee any of them. We do say that we believe they are competent and honest, and we help you get together."

"Okay," said Joe, standing up after he had signed a form incorporating these matters. "And thanks a lot."

With variations in personnel and circumstances, this scene is re-enacted daily in the offices of the Chicago Bar Association. It represents one form of legal aid; specifically, it is an example of the lawyer-referral plan, which will be dealt with later in this chapter.

PRINCIPLES OF LEGAL AID

The term "legal aid" as used here means providing lawyers for persons who are unable to pay fees for legal services. The object of legal aid is to make it impossible for any man, woman, or child in the United States to be denied equal protection and benefits of the law simply because he or she is unable to afford a lawyer. This goal has not yet been achieved, but important progress toward it has been made.

Legal aid is an essential part of the administration of justice in a democracy. Primary responsibility for its establishment and maintenance rests with the legal profession. It is especially important today because it touches our legal institutions in precisely those areas where they are vulnerable to attack and are being attacked.

It is a fundamental tenet of Marxian communism that the law, under our form of government, is a class weapon used by the rich to oppress the poor through the simple device of making justice too expensive. According to this view, lawyers are simply the hirelings of the propertied classes. The danger of this attack lies in the fact that it stirs a response in all who feel they have been denied their rights, for nothing rankles more in the human heart than a brooding sense of injustice. Illness we can endure, but injustice makes us want to pull things down.

To say that millions of persons in the United States are unable to pay for a lawyer is to tell the truth. But that fact alone does not prove that the Marxist indictment of our legal system is justified. For it can also be shown that legal aid offices in this country have given assistance to more than eight million persons and are serving more than three hundred thousand clients each year. These totals are relatively small, but they are showing steady growth.

Legal aid is not a new concept in America. The first important study of it was made by Smith in his *Justice and the Poor,* published in 1919. Smith, together with John S. Bradway, made another study in 1936, and in 1951 the subject was again thoroughly investigated by Emery A. Brownell, who published his findings for the Survey of the Legal Profession under the title "Legal Aid in the United States."

Legal aid is defined as the organized effort of the bar and the community to provide the services of lawyers free, or for a token charge, to persons who cannot afford to pay an attorney's fee and whose cases are unremunerative on a contingent-fee basis (that is, where the expected financial gain to the client if he wins his case will not be enough to pay his lawyer adequately). The term does not apply to the practice of lawyers simply giving free service (which they do to a greater extent than most people realize), because such practice does not provide the four basic elements which have been found essential for adequate legal aid service. These elements are: (1) a definite, convenient, and well-publicized place where the service may be applied for; (2) definite office hours; (3) a definite person in whom confidence may be reposed and who can give executive direction; and (4) a supervisory policy-making group to assure sound administration in the interests of the clientele, the community, and the bar.

In *Justice and the Poor* Smith found the major weaknesses of legal aid in this country to be (1) lack of funds; (2) constant change of personnel in legal aid centers; (3) lack of centralized responsibility or authority; (4) "desperate need of intelligent propaganda and missionary work"; (5) need for co-ordination of legal aid work in the fields of criminal and civil law; and (6) lack of means for putting the accumulated experience of legal aid organizations to use in various movements for improving the administration of justice.

Despite these handicaps, at the time of Smith's 1919 study legal aid programs were definitely established in thirty-four of the seventy-one United States cities then having a population over 100,000.

Beginnings had been made in ten others, while in the remaining twenty-seven cities of 100,000 or over there was no legal aid service available. In 48 per cent of the cities where legal aid was available, it was found to be satisfactory, and in the other 52 per cent it was unsatisfactory.

By 1950, legal aid offices for civil cases existed for eighty-four of the cities over 100,000 population, more than twice as many as were being serviced in 1917. But the growth of population has kept pace, with the result that in 1950 there were fifty large *unserved* cities, as against only thirty-four in 1917. On the matter of coverage, progress has also been slow. In 1917 legal aid facilities were able to meet 51 per cent of the need. Thirty years later only 55 per cent of the need was being met.

On the criminal law side, fewer than half the counties in the United States provide paid counsel for indigent persons accused of major criminal offenses. In most of these the fees paid are inadequate and take no account of the expenses and time involved in investigation. In 38 per cent of the counties no help whatever is provided, except privately through the charity of individual lawyers. Defender offices (public or private), considered essential in larger cities, have increased from five in 1917 to twenty-eight in 1949, a record of progress as limited as that of facilities for civil cases.

A minimum legal aid program includes these specifics:

1. In every metropolitan center of 100,000 or more population—and in smaller ones which are distinctly urban in character—a legal aid office should be open at least thirty hours a week at specific times and with at least one full-time attorney available.

2. In every other city or county of more than 50,000 population there should be an office open at least twelve hours a week.

3. In every other county a lawyers' committee, or other agency, should exist to take care of legal aid matters throughout the county.

4. Every state should have a state bar association committee to supply over-all support and supervision of legal aid.

5. In all larger cities there should be an organized defender system for criminal cases.

6. In all counties not served by a defender office, adequately compensated assigned counsel should be provided.

7. Effective minimum standards, policies, and personnel practices

should be formulated to govern the work in both the criminal and the civil fields, the object being (*a*) to assure a quality of service equal to that of other law offices in the community, (*b*) a complete meeting of the actual need, and (*c*) a sound integration with private law practice and other basic community services.

Leadership is a major factor in developing an adequate network of legal aid service. Leadership must come from the legal profession primarily, but it must also come from the community at large. Until recently, the movement has lacked sufficient strong leadership, but there are hopeful signs that this handicap is being overcome.

"It can truthfully be said," wrote Reginald Heber Smith, "that our legal aid facilities must be doubled, that it must be done speedily, and that the legal profession needs bestir itself. American lawyers and bar associations cannot escape a measure of criticism, and they have been criticized by many of their own leaders. But a substantial measure of praise is also in order because it is equally true to say that, by virtue of the leadership and support of lawyers, more legal aid is provided in the United States than in any other country in the world."

LEGAL AID TODAY (CIVIL LAW)

By 1950 there were a hundred and twenty-four cities of 100,000 population or more. Of these, fifty-six had legal aid offices with paid staffs. Volunteer staffs served legal aid offices in seventeen more, making the total seventy-three. Compared with the situation nearly thirty-five years earlier, the "satisfactory" ratings had climbed to 59 per cent, an increase of about 10 per cent. In addition, legal aid services were found in nineteen smaller cities of less than 100,000 population. All this improvement, it was found, had taken place since World War II.

There were eight states in 1950 in which there was not a single committee of either state or local bar associations devoted to legal aid. These states were Alabama, Mississippi, Montana, New Mexico, North Dakota, South Dakota, West Virginia, and Wyoming. The need for legal aid was found to be substantial and critical in Alabama, Mississippi, and West Virginia, with three thousand needy cases reported every year in Birmingham alone.

One fact that needs to be kept in mind is that none of the factors which create the need for legal aid remains static. Two world wars, astonishing technological developments, and an accelerated expansion of mass production in industry—based on an ever rising standard of living for a steadily increasing number of people—have wrought many changes in family life. There have been marked changes in buying habits, in housing, and in ways of making a living. These changes have multiplied the problems of people everywhere by complicating their relationships—between employer and employee, buyer and seller, landlord and tenant, husband and wife, parent and child.

All phases of this dynamic evolution have required proportionately increased regulation by law. An overwhelming number of laws now affect more and more people and in more and more areas of their lives. Disagreeable as it may be to some, this trend is unavoidable in a society which believes in the preservation of order—and of freedom and opportunity—by law rather than by force. But laws create legal obligations, as well as legal rights, for the poorest as well as for the richest citizen. Obviously, then, as laws increase in number and complexity, the need for lawyers' services for all economic groups is greatly intensified.

How much progress has been made? Brownell found it to be "the unhappy truth" that practically no progress in the development of legal aid had been made from 1916 to 1947. Growth in the last thirty-five years has occurred almost entirely since the war. "Like the Red Queen of *Alice in Wonderland,*" said Brownell, "the legal aid forces have been obliged to run as fast as they could to stay where they were."

WHAT LEGAL SERVICES ARE NEEDED

To understand better the true significance of legal aid—to the public and the profession—it is necessary to examine the nature of people's need for legal services. Scientifically conducted studies and the experience of legal aid offices throughout the country show that the main types of problems are "economic," "family," and "property," with the variation in frequency depending largely upon the economic status of the clientele. It is particularly significant, however, that approximately three-fourths of the problems coming to legal aid offices require consultation service only or referral to some other legal or social service. Only 5–10 per cent involve litigation.

It is clear therefore that the greater part of the lawyer's professional service is out of court and is devoted to tasks of counseling, mediation, drafting of papers, and other office work. This points up the need for consultative services which sociologists have found to be increasingly urgent in our complex and perpetually baffling society. The well-being of all citizens is promoted by receiving timely advice from lawyers on the many and frequent questions of law affecting their lives, their property, and their opportunities.

Some typical cases from legal aid files will show more precisely the kind of problems in which the average person feels the need for expert help in the field of law. The few given here are documented as of the time of the first interview, with only a suggestion as to the probable course of action.

Mrs. P. reports that her husband failed to send the support that was provided for in a separation agreement prepared several years ago. She would like him to return to her, but he refuses. He has been regular in his payments heretofore, and we shall probably be able to get payments resumed by having an interview with the husband.

A young married veteran seeks advice as to how he should protect his interests in a small partnership venture which has been proposed in which he would have a subordinate but perhaps satisfactory position. He has no job at present, and this seems like an opportunity, but he will have to borrow on his insurance, his only resource, to go into the deal.

Mr. R. needs an attorney. He is being sued for rent but has receipts showing that he does not owe what is claimed. It appears he is able to employ an attorney but was under the mistaken impression that it would cost more than the rent claimed. He has never before consulted an attorney.

A middle-aged maiden lady is worried about her interest in a cemetery lot left to her by her stepmother. The husband of a deceased sister who also had an interest in the lot had indicated his intention of appropriating the entire lot.

Mr. Y., born in Syria but applying for citizenship, is in the carting business in a very small way. He earns from $25 to $30 a week. A wife and baby are dependent upon him. Due to poor business, he became in arrears on the instalment contract under which he was buying his truck. He had scraped together enough to make up the deficiency, but the finance company which held the contract was insisting upon extra charges which he could not meet. If he loses the truck, he and his family will need welfare.

At the request of the Family Service, Mr. and Mrs. S. have called for a conference to talk over their legal rights and obligations. It develops that an interfering mother-in-law and the difficulty of existing upon the relief budget are the major causes of marital friction. The parties are now separated, and, while immediate reconciliation is impossible, many of the friction points have been smoothed out, and it appears likely that, with the help of Family Service, we can bring about a re-establishment of this home.

These are not weighty matters of corporation and business law, or lucrative problems of trust and estates, or the subjects of hotly contested litigation which in the popular mind constitute most of a lawyer's practice. They are the everyday problems of plain people but as important to the total well-being of the community as are the cases which attract public attention and involve large interests. They require service of a less dramatic nature, and they are less time-consuming, but they require expert knowledge, a sympathetic understanding of people, and professional skill.

The average citizen should be conditioned to be as aware of the legal pitfalls that may confront him as he is of his physical health. More and more it is becoming routine for people to consult their doctors, as their dentists, at regular intervals for a physical check-up. A generation ago this type of "preventive medicine" was rare. Public health education, stimulated and directed by both laymen and doctors, with private and public funds, has brought about a more intelligent and efficient use of medical services than was true in the old days when the doctor was not called until the patient was very sick. Today's preventive approach has benefited both the public and the medical profession.

The same approach could well be applied to the legal profession to bring about more "preventive law practice." But the success of such a trend will depend largely upon the lawyers themselves; the public will not demand it, any more than the public demanded preventive medicine. Popular ignorance in the matter of lawyers' fees is probably the greatest single deterrent to its spread. Here is the most harmful mystery concerning lawyers' services. In no community is there a commonly known consultation fee. Not even the simplest of the ordinary services bears a known price tag.

In a recent Survey study ("The Family and the Law," by Earl Lomon Koos) it was found that four out of five families studied in six cities had legal problems. Of those who had never consulted a lawyer, 60 per cent were under the impression that a lawyer's advice would probably cost between $25.00 and $75.00. Despite the fact that many lawyers charge nothing for consultation, no family was found that appeared to realize this.

Koos also found evidence of widespread misconception of a lawyer's function. More than 70 per cent of the middle-income group studied, and more than 80 per cent of the lower-income group, believed that the lawyer's principal job is "defending people who are presumed to have violated the law."

The law is popularly regarded as a negative and restraining force, something darkly mysterious and forbidding. Most people do not see it as a constructive device for regulating human relations in a way designed to give maximum opportunity and freedom to the greatest number. When the law is thought of as something to be feared and shunned, quite obviously the lawyer's chief purpose is thought to be that of protecting the citizen against it.

Much basic educational work must be done if all these popular misconceptions are to be dispelled. Legal aid organizations are an essential element in such a program. Not only are they indispensable instruments of everyday justice but they are also effective laboratories in which the legal profession can discover how to improve its usefulness to society. They also constitute a vehicle for public relations solidly based on service in behalf of constitutional rights.

ELIGIBILITY FOR LEGAL AID

To determine a set of rules or standards of eligibility for legal aid is one of the more vexing problems in the whole question.

"We believe that every man accused of serious crime is absolutely entitled to counsel and that, if he is too poor to employ one, society must furnish him one," said the Committee on Legal Aid Work of the American Bar Association in 1937. This principle is, however, still in the process of becoming effective. As courts and legislatures have sought to extend this protection to more and more citizens, the need for organized legal aid in criminal law becomes more apparent.

The federal Constitution and many state constitutions grant to the accused the right to be represented by counsel in a criminal trial. But, in the absence of such a right under the English common law, these constitutional provisions have been construed until recently as merely guaranteeing the *opportunity* to be represented by counsel if the accused is able to secure an attorney through his own effort and resources. Both federal and state governments provide for assignment of counsel in capital offenses, and the Federal Rules of Criminal Procedure now provide for it in federal cases, but the states have been far from uniform (except in capital cases) in progressing to this concept of justice. In only about one-third of them is assignment mandatory in felony cases other than capital offenses.

It is necessary to emphasize the general policy, scrupulously observed in all legal aid organizations, that legal aid is not competitive with the private practice of law. A general rule of eligibility is found in nearly all such organizations, public and private, which limits service to persons "who, from poverty, are unable to procure it elsewhere." The principle of this rule is clear enough; the problem lies in drawing up a set of conditions which clearly, fairly, and accurately determine what constitutes need. Obviously it is impossible to frame a standard of eligibility that could be applied uniformly in all parts of the country at any one time. Local conditions vary too much.

The matter of who determines eligibility is important. Neither the bar nor the public is served if the question of standards is left exclusively in the hands either of lawyers or of laymen. Experience has shown that a governing body representative of both the public and the bar is most satisfactory. Generally, it has been found wise also to leave a certain amount of discretion as to border-line cases in the hands of the lawyer in charge of the legal aid office.

A number of factors go into the determining of eligibility for legal aid service. Family income is considered as a starting point in most offices. Other factors include bank accounts or convertible assets, ownership of home, ownership of automobile, unemployment, debts, and number of dependents. The precise point at which each or all of these factors become critical will of course vary a good deal from one locality to another and perhaps even from one year to the next.

Policy statements on eligibility differ a good deal in legal aid centers. A number of them restrict services to applicants "whose net income together with any other resources is not more than the amount necessary to purchase the minimum necessities of life, based upon accepted relief standards." Another way of putting the test appears in the manual of the Harvard Legal Aid Bureau: "Would the payment of a fee to an attorney seriously impair the client's ability to furnish himself and his family with the bare essentials necessary to keep them decently fed, clothed, sheltered and living together as a family?"

The manual of the Legal Aid Society of New York poses this query as the test: "Could a competent private attorney be found to take the case for whatever fee, direct or contingent, the case might yield?"

Somewhat more liberal perhaps is the statement of the principle by the Boston Legal Aid Society: "The question to be decided is whether or not by taking the case we are aiding in securing substantial justice which would not be secured by using the average private lawyer if paid a proper fee."

It will be noted that in all these statements certain qualifying terms invariably appear, terms which are difficult to define precisely. What constitutes "decent" feeding, clothing, etc.? What are the measures of "competency" in a lawyer, and what is an "average" lawyer? The ultimate necessity of a measure of discretion would appear to be unavoidable.

In connection with the nature of cases accepted by legal aid offices, the trend is toward the removal of all restrictions. Some organizations continue to list certain types of cases as unacceptable. Brownell suggests that the real reason often lies not in the nature of the case itself but in the fact that such cases are productive of a reasonably compensatory fee. "It is regrettable, however," he says, "that due to lack of support, adverse public opinion, or the opposition of the local bar, some legal aid organizations are obliged to reject certain types of cases even if it is conceded that the applicant is unable to employ a lawyer. An applicant can hardly feel equal before the law if his case is legally meritorious but is rejected solely because of its nature."

Types of cases which are often rejected by legal aid offices include divorce and annulment of marriage, bankruptcy, workmen's compensation, personal injury and tort cases, court cases, and adoptions.

LEGAL AID ORGANIZATIONS—CIVIL

There are several different organizational plans for legal aid. Of the ninety legal aid offices operating in the United States in 1950 (not including volunteer facilities), thirty-seven of them were organized in the form of legal aid societies, thirteen were departments of social agencies, twenty were bar-association offices, eleven were public bureaus, and nine were law-school clinics. Each of these types will be described briefly.

Societies.—The legal aid society, the most common form of organization, is characterized chiefly by having organic independence and its own governing body. All cities in the United States over 1,000,000 population, except Chicago, have legal aid societies. Most of these have salaried lawyers on their staff. The Legal Aid Society of New York, established in 1876 and the oldest in the country, set a pattern for development in other cities, especially in the East, with its efficiency and prestige. Independent existence is perhaps the strongest asset of the society form of organization. Being "on its own" gives it better status among other community agencies and yet assures its standing as a law office in the eyes of lawyers.

Departments of social agencies.—This form has been notably successful in Chicago, the second city in the country to establish organized legal aid service. Over-all management lies in the board of the parent-organization, but it is standard practice to delegate actual policy and operations to a committee which represents the bar as well as the agency board. As a means of getting legal aid started in a community where funds for the purpose are limited, or for demonstrating need and usefulness, the agency-sponsored type has been invaluable.

Public bureaus.—The public bureau legal aid office is similar to the social agency department type, the distinction being that the public bureau is supported entirely by public funds. An advantage is that this form seems to carry less suggestion of charity and takes on more the character and prestige of a public service. It is generally better known than the privately supported office. Despite these advantages, the history of the public bureau type of legal aid office has not been encouraging. In several cities support has been grossly inadequate and reluctantly provided, with the result that high-quality personnel is not attracted and the service becomes shallow and perfunctory.

Bar-association offices.—The type of legal aid office that operates as part of a bar association has increased quite rapidly in recent years. This indicates a growing awareness in associations of the need for organized service. The bar-association office with a paid staff is more successful in meeting the needs of the community than is one operated on a volunteer basis.

Law-school clinics.—Legal aid clinics operated by law schools are of two types: (1) those actually conducted by or affiliated with a law school and providing direct service to clients and (2) those which are operated co-operatively by a law school and an established legal aid office. The values of the clinic as a teaching device have been demonstrated clearly and convincingly over the last thirty years. Since this type of legal aid organization obviously bears responsibility to the law student, on the one hand, and to the public, on the other, the result is an altogether different type of organization than the more conventional forms of legal aid setups. The oldest clinic is the Harvard Legal Aid Bureau, established in 1913. In it great care is taken to give the utmost freedom from academic control and to safeguard the client from the inexperience of the students who conduct the work.

Volunteer legal aid services.—In smaller communities, where the need for legal aid exists but where funds and facilities for providing it are scanty or altogether lacking, attempts to meet the need on a volunteer basis are often found. The simplest plan is for the local bar association to have a standing committee on legal aid, to announce the fact publicly, and to see that all health and welfare and other public officials know about it. Such publicity bears frequent repetition. No matter how well such a plan is carried out, it cannot work as satisfactorily as a regularly established office.

Experience and documented studies show that both a definite office and a salaried lawyer are essential for adequate service. Busy lawyers cannot give the necessary time to the kind of troubled and confused clients who come to legal aid offices. Other lawyers, for their own economic reasons, must look first to their paying clients. Finally, in many of its aspects legal aid is a specialized kind of legal work, requiring specialized knowledge and experience.

The effectiveness of any legal aid organization, regardless of the form, depends upon the extent to which it observes these essential principles:

1. The service should be equal in quality to that of the private law offices in the community.

2. The scope of the service and the policies of eligibility should be clearly defined in order that there may be no competition with private practice and in order that those entitled to use it may feel welcome.

3. There should be a definite, well-publicized place for the reception of applicants which is accessible to the persons who need the service and convenient to courts and social service agencies.

4. It is necessary to have definite and regular office hours to fit the convenience of working people who cannot afford time away from jobs.

5. A definite person should be in charge. This is the most difficult requirement for a volunteer plan to achieve. It is customary for clients to repose confidence in individuals rather than in organizations or offices. Moreover, working organizations need continuous administrative direction—someone to interview applicants, apply policies, keep records, and make reports. But in the case of volunteer-staffed organizations, if the reception of clients is conducted understandingly and referrals to the volunteer services do not involve needless trips and repetitious recitals of their problems, it may have good prospects for success.

6. A supervisory group is essential—one which assures sound legal policies and is representative of the community. The right kind of governing body helps to inspire the confidence of clients, relates the work to other community services, and advances the best interests of the legal profession.

LEGAL AID ORGANIZATIONS—CRIMINAL

Three general systems exist in this country by which counsel is provided to indigent and unrepresented persons accused of crime. These are (1) unpaid counsel, assigned by the courts, serving in response to public and professional duty; (2) assigned paid counsel, with compensation fixed by statute or by the court; and (3) defender offices, publicly or privately financed, involving counsel whose primary task it is to meet this need on a continuing basis.

On the basis of population for the country as a whole, some system of paid assigned counsel prevails for 64.5 per cent of the people, public and private defender systems serve 13.7 per cent, and for 21.8 per cent of the people there is either unpaid assigned counsel or no legal aid service at all for criminal cases.

Assigned unpaid counsel.—This practice is traditional and widespread. In eight states (Alabama, Florida, Maine, Massachusetts, Mississippi, Pennsylvania, South Carolina, and Texas) counsel is assigned only in capital offenses (those punishable by death). In the other forty states assignment of counsel is mandatory in only eighteen and discretionary with the court or only at the request of the defendant in the remainder. All too often the accused may waive his right to counsel.

Assigned paid counsel.—Where counsel is assigned in other than capital cases, compensation for the attorney is provided for in twenty-one states. In five of them the fee is left to the discretion of the court with no limit set. In six others the statute provides for an allowance for each case regardless of time spent, with the court awarding the fee within various limits. The fee is discretionary but has a fixed maximum in six states, and in the remaining four a maximum per day is fixed by law. Two states, Connecticut and Rhode Island, have complete coverage by public defender offices.

Only twenty-three states provide any compensation for other than capital cases, and in a majority of these the maximum fees are grossly unremunerative. Among the states that pay nothing except in capital offenses are some of the more populous where there is a relatively high volume of criminal prosecutions.

Defender organizations.—The impracticability and other serious drawbacks of the assigned-counsel system have led to the establishment of organized facilities for legal aid in criminal cases. These are of two kinds: public defenders and voluntary defenders. The essential difference between the two is that public defender offices are supported by taxes and that the others are financed largely by private contributions and Community Chest funds. In the case of public defenders, great importance rests with the method by which they reach office—whether by appointment (by judges, city council, or county commissioners) or by general elections, or otherwise. Generally speaking, that system is best which gives the defender a maximum of independence to serve the best interests of his clients and reasonable assurance that he will continue in office so long as he does his job well.

The assigned-counsel system is considered unsatisfactory by many authorities.

The conditions which prevailed when it grew up have changed drastically. This was clear to Smith as early as 1917, when he said, "The truth about the assignment system in criminal cases is that as a whole it has proved a dismal failure, and that at times it has been worse than a failure." George N. Wickersham in his report as chairman of the National Commission on Law Observance and Enforcement (1931) declared, "As things go in the average city, the system of assigned counsel is not efficient and it is not economical." Supreme Court Justice Wiley Rutledge has called it "a barbarous system." Judge J. Edward Lumbard, Jr., of the New York Supreme Court has asked: "Were the system the same on the other side of the fence, would it be logical for us to expect efficient prosecution of criminals by a district attorney who is neither paid nor reimbursed for his expenses? The question is, of course, ludicrous, but if we are to uphold our constitutional guarantee that every man is equal before the law, it is one which must be solemnly considered."

Except possibly in a few rural areas, the assigned-counsel system has "failed miserably," Brownell concluded, to afford the equal protection under law which it pretends to give and which the Constitution of the United States contemplates. It has failed for these reasons:

First, many large and populous sections of the country do not provide this protection at all.

Second, other sections, also populous, although assigning counsel in at least some of the more serious offenses, fail to compensate the attorney either for his labor or for his expenses of preparation for trial.

Third, in only a few sections is the compensation to the attorney worth his time.

Fourth, in most states counsel is not assigned early enough in the proceedings.

Fifth, too frequently, young, inexperienced, or unqualified lawyers are assigned to match skilful, full-time prosecuting specialists.

Sixth, the number of available qualified attorneys in private practice in the larger metropolitan areas is insufficient to undertake the quality of representation needed.

Seventh, the protection is too easily waived.

"This country cannot afford to go on permitting thousands of its poorer citizens each year to face criminal prosecution without the minimum protection of representation by competent legal counsel," Brownell declares. "The long and wistful attempt to meet so large a need by the volunteer assistance of individual lawyers is a complete and abject failure."

Similarly, arguments for and against public defenders have been expressed freely and feelingly for many years. The advantages of defender offices may be summed up as follows:

1. The quality of legal assistance for defendants without means is improved because of better facilities for investigation of both the facts and the law and by the opportunity for specialization.

2. Adequate and competent assistance can be extended to all defendants who are unable to employ their own counsel, whereas under existing conditions many are obliged to do without legal aid of any kind.

3. In the more populous areas the plan is more efficient and economical than the assignment of counsel on a fee basis, especially if the fees are as substantial as they ought to be to assure competent service.

4. A distinct saving of time results in always being prepared and avoiding unnecessary procedural delays. Continuances must often

be asked by assigned counsel, since they have other work to attend to. The less time spent awaiting disposition of a criminal case, the better. This is especially true in the cases of innocent persons and youthful defendants.

5. Unnecessary trials are avoided, and the duration of trials is shortened. This results from the opportunity of making more complete investigations. The Los Angeles public defender claims, for example, that this procedure alone saves the county more than the cost of the office.

6. The general tone of the criminal court is raised. Fewer unscrupulous and perjured defenses are attempted, and the obnoxious type of "jail lawyer" is eliminated from practice.

There are arguments against the defender system too. Some of them are conflicting, such as the view that public defenders become overly hardened to the point of indifference and the opposite claim that they become "too sentimental with criminals." Another objection, that the defender system denies the defendant the right to choose who shall represent him, applies with equal force to the assigned-counsel system as it operates in most states. The most common argument againt the public defender system, however, rests on the charge that politics and graft can adversely affect operations. This objection does not apply in the case of privately supported defenders. As to the publicly supported office, there is no inherent reason why a public defender should not be as conscientious and trustworthy as the judge who sits on the bench.

SERVICES NOW AVAILABLE

Records of legal aid work in the United States show a steady growth since 1876, when the first organized service began. Taking the figures for all legal aid organizations reporting, and including both criminal and civil cases, the picture, by decades, is shown in Table 11.

Costs have increased but not proportionately. Prior to 1918 few criminal cases, more costly to handle, were accepted. Considering the reduced value of the dollar, the average unit cost of $4.40 per case in 1948 (the last year for which figures are available) is astonishingly low.

The figures shown in the last column of Table 11 are incomplete, because most offices record only the actual funds which pass through their books. In any case, the amount of money collected for clients is but a small measure of the economic importance of legal aid offices to their communities and an even less adequate measure of their social importance.

A study of the type of service rendered by legal aid offices, measured by the amount of staff time given to each kind, shows that 34 per cent of time is devoted to interviewing clients and witnesses, 15 per cent to court work, 11 per cent to dictation, 10 per cent to law study, 8 per cent to conferences other than with clients

TABLE 11

NUMBER OF CASES OF LEGAL AID, COST OF OPERATION, AND AMOUNTS COLLECTED, BY DECADES, 1876–1946

Year	No. of Cases	Cost of Operation	Amounts Collected for Clients
1876	212	$ 1,060	$ 1,000
1886	3,462	3,820	19,357
1896	15,017	13,450	76,695
1906	37,603	53,347	99,049
1916	117,201	181,408	340,199
1926	152,214	369,264	645,991
1936	260,400	577,220	526,903
1946	301,628	1,033,812	751,706

or witnesses, 7 per cent to investigation of facts, and 7 per cent to all other types of work, mainly administrative.

A majority of the problems—58 per cent on the average—are taken care of by a single consultation between client and attorney. An average of 5 per cent of all cases require court work, but—as is true with most averages—this figure is misleading. A high proportion of court cases would not necessarily mean that a legal aid office was doing more effective work. It could well mean the contrary if the office is not well known, has limited contacts, and is discovered by persons whose need for a lawyer has reached a critical stage. It is always an aim to avoid litigation whenever possible, and legal aid offices are notably successful in this.

Statistics do not reveal several types of special service rendered by legal aid offices. A dramatic example of such work was that done by the Louisville Legal Aid Society in securing the abolition of a costly, archaic, and unjust system of magisterial courts. Legal aid societies in various cities have initiated successful movements to correct abuses of instalment selling, wage assignments, and small loans. In many places their leadership has helped establish small-claims and domestic-relations courts.

Difficult as it is to show by statistics the true nature and extent of legal aid work in civil cases, it is even less feasible to do so with criminal law work. Because of wide procedural differences in the forty-nine separate jurisdictions, it has not been possible to develop a uniform system of statistical reports comparable to that used for civil cases.

Some notion of the type of service given by legal aid in criminal cases can be gained from a consideration of the steps involved in preparing an adequate defense. The Philadelphia Voluntary Defender Association lists the following items, most of which are required whether a plea of guilty or not guilty is entered: (1) a thorough interview with the defendant; (2) clearance with the Social Service Exchange and contacts with social agencies to which the defendant may be known; (3) preparing an abstract of the formal charges against the defendant; (4) securing a transcript of the police report on the crime; (5) transcribing the testimony from the magistrate's record of the preliminary hearing; (6) obtaining the defendant's work record and other pertinent social history; (7) securing previous police records on the defendant, if any; and (8) interviewing and subpoenaing witnesses.

WHO RENDERS THE SERVICE?

Legal aid is no exception to the truism that the vitality of an organization and the quality of its service depend directly upon its personnel. Excellence of staff cannot overcome a structurally poor organization, but a poor staff cannot make even the best-planned office a good one. Several general observations as to the nature and purpose of legal aid are pertinent to any consideration of staff.

First, legal aid clients, by and large, are persons less favorably endowed and more harshly treated by life than the majority of private clients. Accordingly, special skills in dealing with them are called for. Often their confidence is not easily won.

Second, in a real sense and to many citizens, legal aid offices are representative of the bar. The work is done by lawyers, and inevitably they will strive to interpret to their clients the general fairness of the law and the function and integrity of lawyers. To the degree that they succeed, public faith in our institutions of justice is restored and strengthened among men and women who may well, in the main, be ignorant of the law or cynical toward it, or both.

Third, in the larger cities the legal aid office must take on many

TABLE 12

SALARIES OF PAID EXECUTIVES IN LEGAL AID OFFICES, 1947

No. of Cases Annually	Annual Salary on Full-Time Basis			No. of Years with Agency (Average)
	Range	Average	Median	
Less than 1,000	$1,200–$ 8,400	$4,393	$4,500	8
1,000–3,000	2,400– 8,400	4,504	4,540	8
3,000–6,000	3,733– 9,000	5,517	5,070	20
More than 6,000	4,720– 10,250	7,253	6,000	14

of the characteristics of a large law firm, particularly in the training of personnel and distribution of work. Whether large or small, the legal aid office must maintain certain vital community relationships. These factors point up the importance of staffing the office with attorneys who can make positive contributions to the broad goals.

Fortunately, legal aid work has attracted many executives of high caliber in its history but all too often at an unfair and heavy personal sacrifice on the part of the individual. The figures in Table 12 for salaries of paid executives in legal aid offices reveal the relatively unremunerative nature of this field. These salaries do not compare favorably with the earnings of lawyers in private practice. In 1947 the median net income of salaried lawyers in the United States was $6,225 annually. The mean net annual income of nonsalaried lawyers was $7,432.

Despite the low salaries, the average tenure is fairly long. Scores of capable young lawyers have been drawn into legal aid, seeking both experience and an opportunity for humanitarian service. In the flush of professional idealism and with a compelling awareness of the need, many have been inspired to forego more remunerative openings and continue in the work. The longer they remain, the slimmer grow the opportunities for change and the more wedded they become to the intangible satisfactions of legal aid service. It is not a healthy situation. If the legal aid executive is a good one, he deserves better compensation. If he is a poor one, he should not be kept on solely because he can be hired cheaply.

In about one-fourth of the legal aid offices where the executive is engaged on a full-time basis, he is permitted to accept an incidental amount of private work for friends and relatives. From the individual attorney's standpoint, the part-time executive arrangement is substantially better. The organization may suffer, however, particularly if it is a larger office. It is difficult to divide loyalties between the responsibilities of the legal aid office and the fluctuating demands of a private practice. Inevitably there are times when one or the other must suffer.

Salaries for assistant staff attorneys in legal aid offices are, with few exceptions, lower than those paid to lawyers in other comparable legal positions. In about half the offices the assistant attorneys are not wholly dependent upon their legal aid income. Usually the part-time lawyers have stipulated hours for service at the legal aid office and return to their private offices for all personal legal work.

It is surprising to find members of the bar in a number of cities being responsible for depressing the level of salaries paid to legal aid attorneys. Partly out of a desire to make economical use of available funds and partly through lack of understanding of the specialized nature of legal aid work, lawyers on directorships and Community Chest budget committees too often take the position that any young lawyer is capable of handling the job and that the salary need be no more than enough to attract an attorney who is free at the time. Where legal aid has been conducted as part of the program of a social agency, there has been the greatest difficulty in getting lawyers' salaries raised to the level of social workers', despite the fact that their training and experience is at least equal.

Salaries in legal aid work on the criminal side are substantially higher than those paid on the civil side. Not only is the specialized nature of the practice more generally recognized but the higher incidence of court work requires the employment of attorneys who have better than average skill in the trial of cases. Defenders in charge of offices were paid, in 1947, an average annual salary of approximately $6,600.

Qualifications for positions on legal aid staffs have been precisely defined in only a few places. In general, the aim has been to secure lawyers who possess (1) a legal knowledge and ability at least equal to that of the average practitioner in the community; (2) a sincere interest in the objectives of the service; and (3) the judgment and tact necessary to apply office policies to given situations without friction with the applicant, the bar, the social agencies, or the public.

WHO BEARS THE COST?

Lawyers cannot alone bear the cost of adequate legal aid service any more than the doctors can carry the costs of necessary free medical services in the field of health. Where lawyers have tried, they have failed to raise enough money, despite the fact that legal aid work, when understood, makes a strong appeal to the bar.

Throughout the nation, the greatest single source of legal aid financial support is the Community Chest system. The following breakdown shows the sources of support on a percentage basis:

	Per Cent
Community chests	60.0
Other contributed funds	14.0
Tax funds	9.5
Bar associations and lawyers	8.5
Clients	6.0
Capital income	2.0

With legal aid accepted as a participating agency of the Community Chest, the bar can be counted on to do its full share. Indeed, because of the bar's special concern for legal aid, it has an added reason for responding with both money and effort to a Community Chest drive.

It is encouraging to note that the increased taxation of recent years has not curtailed the steady growth of philanthropy. On the contrary, according to a recent study, the widespread plan of federated fund-raising through community chests has substantially increased both the number of givers and the total amounts contributed to social welfare. This growth is impressive—from 240 chests raising $58,003,965 in 1925 to 1,318 campaigns raising $192,-933,988 in 1950.

Widespread participation in community chests has been of great benefit to the legal aid movement and is primarily responsible for maintaining the service as a predominantly private enterprise. The preventive aspects of legal aid are strongly appreciated by those who manage federated fund-raising agencies. Other participating agencies in the social welfare field find legal aid service an indispensable resource. When tied in with the community's principal effort for meeting social needs, legal aid finds itself in a most congenial climate for steady growth and widespread acceptance.

Legal aid has lacked, and still lacks, the popular appeal which most health and welfare agencies possess. It is likely that the dramatic possibilities of the work have not been fully exploited, but the fact remains that legal aid does not have the emotional pull of an appeal for help for underprivileged children, for instance.

Legal aid lawyers, like most lawyers, are not publicity-minded. In addition, there are some inherent limitations which stand in the way of making the service widely appealing as a charity. For one thing, the general public is not aware of its own need of legal services. Physical distress, be it hunger or sickness, is self-evident. So, to a lesser extent perhaps, are emotional ills. But to appreciate why the poor are denied justice and to see the need for organized legal aid service require a knowledge and understanding of our legal institutions which few laymen possess. While it may be relatively easy to win the backing of leading business figures, clergymen, social workers, and other civic leaders, it is quite another matter to convince the man on the street, unless he happens to be in need of help himself. Fortunately, it is the group which appreciates the importance of legal aid that constitutes the backbone and leadership of the community chests.

There is no doubt another reason for the lack of widespread popular appeal of legal aid. Its major function of making the law equally available to citizens seems so logically a part of the routine administration of justice that it is difficult for many people to conceive of this as a responsibility of private philanthropy. Since equality before the law is a cornerstone of democratic government and since legal aid is necessary to achieve that equality, it seems plausible that legal aid should be a public function, much as the providing of judges—which itself was once a private function. If the state enacts the laws, engages the judges, clerks, sheriffs, district attorneys, jurors, and provides all the physical equipment for administering the law, there is a tendency to ask why it does not furnish the one remaining essential ingredient—the service of a lawyer?

To the person able to hire an attorney, the answer is simple. He wants a lawyer of his own selection, a lawyer who has no interests or loyalties adverse to his own, and who will not hesitate to challenge the state—if need be—to protect his client's right. To the person who is not able to pay a lawyer's fee, the answer is not so simple. It is not practicable, in the cities at least, for him to have counsel of his own choosing, but, since the lawyer provided for him must be paid by someone, does it make a difference whether it be the state or a private philanthropy?

The answer is to be found in the experience of the public and private legal aid offices, and it seems to be that the source of the lawyer's fee—in and of itself—has little effect upon either the competency or the zealousness of his service. An independent bar, like an independent judiciary, is indispensable to liberty and equal opportunity. But just as judges are uninfluenced by the fact that they are in the pay of the state, so legal aid attorneys—to the extent that they have like status and freedom from political control—are committed to fulfil their professional obligations.

The effectiveness of the service is directly related to the degree of professional independence which is permitted. This is a controlling factor, whether the service is publicly or privately financed. Those public bureaus which are financially starved, or which are used to reward the politically faithful, render a wholly inadequate service. Likewise, the privately supported bodies which have insufficient funds or which have governing bodies that are narrow or indifferent fail to meet the need too.

The Survey Council of the American Bar Association has stated the issue of legal aid in terms of these two basic propositions:

Proposition 1: That an independent bar is just as essential to the preservation of freedom as is an independent judiciary or the bills of rights in our federal Constitution and state constitutions. This proposition is far more important than the American people in general yet realize.

Proposition 2: That there is an ever present danger that a grant of governmental money will be followed by governmental control. In other words, if the government becomes the lawyer's paymaster, it may soon become his master as well.

One reason why the average American does not appreciate the importance of an independent bar is that he still thinks of litigation in the courts as consisting mainly of suits between private parties. He thinks of lawsuits arising out of automobile accidents, domestic troubles, and disputes over contracts and property.

But that is only part of the picture. Government (federal, state, and local) is looming larger and larger in the role of a party to litigation. In all criminal cases, of course, the state is a party because it is the prosecutor. In all tax cases government is a party, either defendant or plaintiff. Government commissions, bureaus, and agencies of all kinds have multiplied profusely in recent years, and they all enforce their rules and decisions by going into court as the complainant party.

Whenever the government in any form is a party to litigation, its lawyer is paid out of the public treasury. This is where the question touches the issue of legal aid. If lawyers for all the poor are to be paid out of public funds, would the next step be to provide persons of moderate means with lawyers paid wholly or in part out of public treasury? How far could we go in this direction and not destroy the independence of the bar? Thus at the bottom of the legal aid problem lies this question: If legal aid attorneys receive their fees from public funds, will that be the first step, the entering wedge, into "socialization" of the legal profession? There appears to be no ready answer to that question.

In 1950 the House of Delegates of the American Bar Association resolved as follows:

1. It is the primary responsibility of the legal profession, as part of its high tradition of service to the public, as an expression of its devotion to the ideal of equal justice for all, and in order to forestall the threat to individual freedom implicit in growing efforts to socialize the legal profession, to assume through its bar associations and in conjunction with other social and welfare agencies, the leadership in establishing and maintaining adequate organized legal aid facilities in all parts of the country.

2. Legal aid facilities should be established and maintained so far as possible as a privately supported community service and, in any event, without governmental control or influence over their operations.

The practical issue, therefore, becomes whether the bar will bring about the very evil it fears by failing to proceed with genuine diligence in building up legal aid wherever needed and to the extent needed. Judgment will be rendered, not by the lawyers themselves, but by the American people.

THE NATIONAL LEGAL AID ASSOCIATION

Legal aid work in the United States had been carried on for thirty-five years before a central unifying power was created. This was the National Alliance of Legal Aid Societies, established in 1912. Reorganization as the National Association of Legal Aid Organizations took place in 1923, and in 1949 the present National Legal Aid Association was formed. Each reorganization strengthened the association and broadened its representation among laymen as well as lawyers.

As now constituted, the National Legal Aid Association is in a position to provide effective national leadership to the legal aid movement. Given adequate financing, the way is prepared to undertake full-scale, nation-wide promotion.

One of the important functions of the National Legal Aid Association is the formulation of standards of operation. It has also been its policy to supplement this with various "recommended practices," some of which may ultimately become standards. A summary of standards and recommended practices follows:

STANDARDS

Every legal aid association should:

1. Have a responsible and informed governing body, preferably a board of directors, which shall fairly represent the legal, social, and civic interests of the community and which shall meet at least quarterly.

2. Unless its case load is less than four hundred cases a year, have at least one or more full-time attorneys.
3. Provide sufficient space in the office for privacy of interviews between attorney and client.
4. Maintain active and friendly relations with other social agencies and with the organized bar.
5. Provide, either by qualified staff personnel or through co-operating social agencies, for social investigation of domestic-relations cases where there are social factors which require consideration.
6. Make use of the social service exchange when and where its work will benefit thereby and register its own cases therein when it is of distinct community advantage to do so and where it will not violate the confidential relationship of attorney and client.
7. Act in advisory capacity to social workers relative to the legal aspects of problems faced by their clients whenever requested to do so.
8. Keep such financial and case statistics as will accurately reflect the nature, volume, cost, and effectiveness of its service and publish them annually.
9. Maintain an active membership in the National Legal Aid Association, accepting proportionate responsibility for the support of its program and co-operating with it for the improvement and extension of legal aid service by committee service, the furnishing of data, and otherwise.
10. In accordance with rules adopted by the National Legal Aid Association, accept for prompt service or referral all cases which are sent to it by other legal aid organizations.
11. Make adequate provision, preferably through a reference list maintained by the organized bar, for securing private counsel for applicants in cases which it cannot handle.
12. Be alert to the needs of applicants for social or health services and make use of the community's resources for such problems.
13. So far as possible, provide for the advancement of legal expenses in cases where the client's lack of funds for such costs would result in a denial of equal justice.
14. Undertake appeals to right palpable miscarriages of justice or, when costs are available, to establish useful principles.
15. Accept a divorce case, first, where social need exists; second, where there is a good prima facie case; and, third, where the client cannot afford to employ counsel.
16. Further desirable legislation in its own community or in the state legislature when in aid of its purposes.
17. Welcome intelligent surveys of its service and operation.
18. Prohibit the acceptance by any of its staff attorneys for private work, directly or indirectly, the case of any person applying for legal aid.
19. Establish contacts with the sources of legal aid cases where essential to adequate service in special types of cases, such as workmen's compensation cases, seamen's cases, veterans' cases, etc.

RECOMMENDED PRACTICES

Every legal aid organization should, as far as conditions permit:

1. Provide for legal aid in criminal cases where there is no statute providing for the assignment of counsel or for a public defender or where the circumstances are such that the defendant cannot obtain proper representation in any other way.
2. Have an attorney whose business it is to investigate and handle workmen's compensation cases where they are not acceptable to the bar and representation is needed.
3. Make every effort to establish a small-claims court in the community.
4. Make every effort to establish a domestic-relations court in the community.
5. Whenever a client presents evidence of improper practice on the part of an attorney, undertake to present the matter to proper authorities for disciplinary action.
6. Co-operate with other agencies, when necessary and proper, in the securing of such new legal machinery for social betterment as the community requires.
7. Accept bankruptcy cases only in instances where everything possible has been done to make an adjustment with creditors and where it is obvious that a client will never be able to pay his debts and will be harassed by creditors for a long period.
8. Except for good cause in individual instances, accept personal injury cases in which the client is unable to pay any fee and in which the amount of recovery is not sufficient to induce a reputable attorney to accept the case on a contingent-fee basis.

LAWYER-REFERENCE PLANS

The lawyer-reference plan, in its various forms, is a method by which persons needing legal advice and help are directly and properly brought into contact with lawyers who are able and willing to serve them.

"The plan is simple, inexpensive, and efficient," writes Reginald Heber Smith. "It is in accord with all professional standards and ethical principles. It benefits everyone concerned. No longer an untried experiment, the lawyer-reference plan may prove to be an outstanding contribution by the organized bar to a more perfect attainment of our American concept of democracy."

The lawyer-reference plan is simply a device for helping clients find lawyers and lawyers find clients. It is defined more completely as an agency through which a member of the general public can be referred to a competent and reliable lawyer who for a fixed, moderate fee will be willing to give consultation on a legal problem and then render further legal service for a moderate fee if such additional service seems dsirable and necessary.

The lawyer-reference plan is not to be confused with organized legal aid service in any of its various forms. Legal aid exists to serve the indigent. It operates in an office of its own, established for that purpose, in which the service is actually rendered. Under a lawyer-reference plan the client pays a fee and sees the lawyer in the latter's private office.

The lawyer-reference plan is designed to fill the gap between organized legal aid, on the one hand (a service for persons without means to pay attorney's fees), and regular private law practice, on the other. Its aim is to help persons of moderate means find a good lawyer who will not charge them too much.

In cities where a lawyer-reference plan does not operate, professional ethics make it difficult for legal aid offices, bar-association headquarters, or private law offices to direct people who fall in this middle group. To refer them to the classified section of the telephone book—all that ethics will permit—is no answer to their problem.

Everywhere, and especially in big cities, there are thousands of men and women who do not personally know a single lawyer. Being of modest circumstances, they hesitate to pick one "out of the hat" for fear they will be charged a huge fee. They know so little of the legal profession that they do not even realize that it is standard practice for lawyers to adjust their fees to the needs and condition of their clients.

Only one rule is imperative for the operation of a lawyer-reference plan: it must be conducted by, or under the auspices of, a bar association. The organized bar must vouch for the plan, must be responsible for its integrity, and must make it known to the public.

Other appropriate rules are merely matters of common sense. They include these:

1. There must be a definite office, easily accessible to the public and open during the usual business hours.

2. In the office there must be at least one person who has a sympathetic liking for human beings, who has been trained to evaluate problems, who has technical proficiency, and whose impartiality is known to the bar.

3. There must be a bar-association supervising committee whose members the person responsible for referring clients can easily consult.

4. It is of the highest importance that it be stated, and reiterated, that all this is being carried on by the bar *collectively*.

The elements of a lawyer-reference plan include the following:

Referrer.—He may be called the "reference attorney," or the "executive director of the lawyer reference plan," or have no title at all. The important thing is that there be some one person who does the referring. A face-to-face interview is essential if the referrer is to make a sound judgment of the applicant and his case. Telephone and mail requests for reference should, therefore, be discouraged.

Place.—The referrer must have a definite place where he can be found by the public at regular hours. The location should be convenient to lawyers' offices, courts, and legal aid and social agency offices. Frequently the referrer is stationed in a bar-association office or legal aid center.

List of lawyers.—The referrer needs a list which is better than the classified pages of the telephone directory. The best method is to circulate a questionnaire among lawyers and to make up the list from those who respond. The questionnaire should be complete enough so that the lawyer can be accurately classified by the referrer, and it should show without doubt that the participating lawyer fully understands the plan.

Publicity.—The best-conceived lawyer-reference plan will get nowhere unless the public knows about it. Because of traditional concepts of ethics, publicity is a delicate subject with most lawyers and bar associations. The purpose and need of publicity for a lawyer reference plan, its propriety, and the techniques to be used therefore require careful appraisal.

Such plans are relatively new in the United States, the first one having been organized in Los Angeles in 1937. By 1950 the idea had spread to more than twenty major cities in the country, and today they are available in some one hundred communities. It is highly probably that, even in the cities where the plan is functioning, the average citizen has never heard of it or, if he has, does not understand what it can do for him. The lawyer-reference plan thus has made but a bare beginning, however promising of future development that start may be.

"In the lawyer-reference plan," wrote Reginald Heber Smith in his Foreword to the Survey report on the subject, "we are not dealing with a superficial matter. More is involved than simply putting deserving persons in touch with competent lawyers. What really is at stake is whether the organized bar is competent to meet the needs of a democratic society in the mid-twentieth century."

Through referral plans—and through the bar associations in many other ways—will come answers to the problem of providing that constitutional necessity, adequate legal service for every citizen.

Brownell writes:

> The need for organized legal aid service is so essential to a proper administration of justice and to the everyday welfare of vast masses of the population that the public will insist upon having it—even as the public has insisted in England, Sweden, and elsewhere—by one way or another. Unless the bar recognizes this certainty, the people in blind desperation may choose a system which, at best, may fail to fulfil their needs and, at worst, may be disastrous to their liberties.

Chief Justice William Howard Taft wrote in 1926:

> The real practical blessing of our Bill of Rights is in its provisions for fixed procedures securing a fair hearing by independent courts to each individual. . . . But if the individual in seeking to protect himself is without money to avail himself of such procedure, the Constitution and the procedure made inviolable by it do not work for the equal benefit of all. Something must be devised by which every one, however lowly and however poor, however unable by his means to employ a lawyer and to pay court costs, shall be furnished the opportunity to set fixed machinery of justice going.

Justice Taft's view has been shared by every succeeding chief justice and by every thoughtful leader in the legal profession. The individual does not exist to serve the state. The state exists to serve the individual. The object of law is to protect the dignity and worth of every human being, whatever his income.

If law is to fulfil its mission, the facilities of legal aid in the United States must be strengthened, for in legal aid is found the tested and the only means of assuring that every citizen stands equal before the law.

CHAPTER IV

Public Service by Lawyers

THE LAWYER IN THE LEGISLATURE

The prominence of lawyers in legislative affairs, both federal and state, is a matter of common knowledge to the lay public. This familiar political phenomenon was the subject of a study for the Survey by Harry W. Jones, Columbia Law School professor.

The powerful position of the legal profession with respect to membership in American legislative bodies, Jones observes, is a striking demonstration of De Tocqueville's thesis that "the government of democracy is favorable to the political power of lawyers."

To illustrate the customary lawyer dominance of lawmaking bodies, the United States Congress can be taken as an example. Studies of the occupational backgrounds of members of the Seventy-first to Seventy-fifth Congresses showed that the proportion of lawyers in the Senate during this period ranged from 61 to 75 per cent and in the House from 56 to 65 per cent. These percentages are probably representative of the makeup of Congress since then and for many years before.

As additional evidence, it has been noted that lawyers who were leaders in the Eighty-second Congress included the Speaker of the House, the Vice-President, the president pro tem of the Senate, House and Senate majority leaders, and twenty-four of thirty-four standing-committee chairmen.

In the forty-eight state legislatures the position of lawyers has always been strong, although the figures are not so striking as they are for Congress. Other occupational groups, especially farmers and merchants, are also powerfully represented. It is a fair estimate that the legal profession has provided about one-fourth of the total number of state legislators since 1900. This, of course, is a share overwhelmingly in excess of the proportion of lawyers in the total population and represents the largest single occupational group in the state legislatures.

Why are so many lawyers found in federal and state legislative assemblies? A few generalized answers seemed indisputable. First, lawyers are more strongly attracted to public service as legislative candidates than are other professionals generally. This is particularly true of young lawyers outside the metropolitan areas. The personal characteristics and inclinations that cause men to seek legal training are such as will also pull them into active political affairs. This affinity is indicated by the fact that in many state university law schools there are often members of the state legislature in the student body.

Second, candidacy for the state legislature is, in many parts of the country, a traditional form of professional advertising, and of course a perfectly legitimate one. Even the unsuccessful candidate brings his name to the attention of prospective clients. If he wins, the lawyer attains valuable standing in his community and has exceptional opportunities to meet persons of state-wide political and business influence. A veteran lawyer-legislator once summed it up by saying, "A seat in our state senate is worth $10,000 a year to a practicing lawyer, even if he is a man of absolute professional integrity."

Added to these two factors is the further consideration that attendance at a legislative session works no particular hardship on a lawyer's practice. On the other hand, it is usually difficult if not impossible for other men to devote even sixty days every two years to a task that takes them completely away from their business or profession. Farmers are frequently in the same position as lawyers in this respect, and indeed it is farmers who comprise what is usually the second largest occupational group in the state bodies.

The conditions described above apply more especially to state legislatures. What are the reasons for the large numbers of lawyers in the national Congress, where the percentage is at least twice as great?

One partial explanation certainly lies in the fact that membership in Congress is not a part-time avocation for sixty days every year or two but a full-time job requiring the legislator virtually to abandon his private business and professional activities. A lawyer can leave his practice for two years or six, or for an even longer time, with some assurance that he can return to his practice with professional skills unimpaired and with the prospect of newly attracted clients to replace those he might have lost during his years in Washington.

A physician could not leave his practice or a businessman his establishment with any such assurance. These advantages, plus the fact that political activity has unique business-getting value for the lawyer, combine to make lawyers more readily available as congressional candidates.

Thus, whether for the part-time demands of service in the statehouse or for full-time demands of one or more terms in Washington, the practice of law lends itself congenially to a blending of the two careers.

It would be unrealistically cynical, however, to account for the prevalence of lawyers in legislative positions entirely in terms of their greater availability as candidates. Beyond doubt, the most important single factor is the marked tendency Americans have always shown to choose lawyers for positions of high political responsibility. To couple this well-established public preference with some other public attitudes is to suggest, says Jones, this paradox: "The public is often severely critical of lawyers *as lawyers,* but it has a marked preference for them as public officials."

What are the effects on legislative functioning of the strong representation of lawyers in the lawmaking bodies? On the surface there is no noticeable difference between the lawyer-legislator and his nonlawyer colleague. About all that can be said is that the lawyer is more likely to concern himself with questions concerning the language of proposed bills or with the constitutionality of legislation. There is an observable tendency on the part of nonlawyer members to defer to the judgment of their lawyer colleagues on such "legal" questions.

In the state legislatures, particularly in states where bill-drafting services are not available, a lawyer-legislator usually does a substantial amount of actual drafting. The great usefulness of a competent lawyer in the typical state legislature is principally a matter of his ability to detect and correct "sleepers" and technical defects in bills drawn up outside the legislature. Almost every state legislature has a few lawyers in it who are looked upon as experts in this technical phase of lawmaking.

In matters of policy, as distinguished from statutory technique, it is a familiar assertion that the presence of a large number of lawyers tends to exert a "conservative" influence on the legislative body.

The "overrepresentation" of lawyers is a familiar theme in political science literature. It is certainly true that this alleged conservatism of lawyer-legislators operates with respect to proposals for drastic changes in areas of the law—such as procedure—where lawyers have something of a professional vested interest. But there is no evidence that lawyers in Congress and the state legislatures are, as a group, any more conservative than other members on general social and economic issues.

It is of course true that legal training and law practice develop certain traits of mind which most lawyers have in common. These prevailing professional attitudes would certainly include a preference for the case-by-case approach in attacking a problem, skepticism toward broad doctrinal generalizations, and a strong desire to seek out the precedents for any projected course of action. The presence of many legislators possessing these mental traits will of course affect the functioning of any lawmaking body. This, however, is hardly conservative in the sense of the familiar journalistic division of all men into "liberals" and "conservatives," according to their views on specific social and regulatory issues.

THE LAWYER AS LAWMAKER

Sound legislation is more than a matter of good intentions and enlightened political choices. Hard technical work has to be done before the best lawmaking idea can be made into a clear and enforceable statute. Every legislative body needs both legislative reference services and bill-drafting assistance.

Legislative reference bureaus, as such, are largely staffed by research librarians and specialists in social science discipline. Bill-drafting, however, is a lawyer's job. The attorneys now employed in the official drafting offices of Congress and state legislatures are in the most strategic position of all to influence the technical side of the legislative development of the law.

Bill-drafting is lawyer's work, not because lawyers have any special facility with words, but because mastery of existing law is called for at every stage in the performance of a drafting assignment. A statute drawn up without sufficient attention to laws already on the books, as well as to the state of relevant judge-made law, inevitably raises vexing problems of interpretation.

It must be remembered that legislatures are political bodies and that no amount of technical services will change their essentially political character. The finest draftsmanship in the world cannot bring about the adoption of wise legislative policies if the elected members of a representative body are mediocrities or worse. In fact, the professional draftsman regards himself strictly as a technician and not as a policy-maker in his own right. Nevertheless, competent legislative research and sound drafting can contribute notably to wise legislative decision.

Technical drafting services of high professional excellence have been furnished to the British Parliament since 1869 by the Parliamentary Counsel to the Treasury. In the United States the first bill-drafting offices seem to have developed as by-products of the state legislative reference bureau movement, which began with Wisconsin's bureau in 1901. By 1938 forty-two states had established similar legislative reference services. This historical tie between research and drafting explains the curious situation, still existing in several states, in which drafting duties requiring legal training are delegated to persons trained in library reference work.

At the national level the Office of Legislative Counsel of the Congress was created in 1918. The legislative reference service of the Library of Congress had been organized some four years earlier. The form of organization of the Office of Legislative Counsel was, in part, patterned on the British Office of Parliamentary Counsel. A small but busy organization, the Office of Legislative Counsel consisted of only twenty-one lawyers in 1951, ten on the House side and eleven on the Senate. These two small staffs carry a heavy load, each office being likely to do as many as two thousand separate jobs of research, consultation, and drafting in the life of a Congress. There is no rule of either House or Senate requiring consultation with the office, and assistance is given only on request.

State legislatures have urgent need for professional research and drafting assistance. Legislative power is exercised by part-time lawmakers who meet for a few weeks every year or every other year. Their compensation is normal, if not meager, almost everywhere. Most of them cannot afford to devote time to legislative work except during the brief and usually hectic period of the actual session. It costs little to make first-rate bill-drafting services available, and the investment, where it has been made, has paid rich dividends in improvement of the quality of the state legislative product.

Almost every state now has one or more agencies devoted wholly or in part to the legislative development of the law. These agencies vary so greatly from state to state, in function as well as in name, that it is impossible to put together anything like an orderly table of state legislative services.

In the forty states for which specific information is available, the basic job of providing technical bill-drafting service is handled in one of four ways:

1. In twenty states the drafting is part of the work of the legislative reference bureau or legislative reference library.

2. Nine states have separate bill-drafting staffs on something like the congressional pattern.

3. In seven states drafting work is performed by lawyers assigned from the staff of the attorney-general of the state.

4. In four states there is a statutory reviser, appointed either by the attorney-general or by the state supreme court, who is on call as a bill-drafter during legislative sessions.

The prevailing approach of treating bill-drafting as a phase of legislative reference work is open to serious question. Few persons trained for social science research have the legal background necessary for effective legislative drafting. There is no objection, however, to bringing legislative reference service and bill-drafting together in one agency, as in Virginia, provided (1) drafting is considered a separate function and given equal prominence with reference work; (2) the head of the combined agency is a lawyer or, if a nonlawyer, is capable of choosing good lawyer subordinates and delegating responsibility to them; and (3) bill-drafting is treated as a professional job for lawyers and not as an occasional venture for staff members without legal training.

For several reasons it is difficult to secure and retain lawyers of outstanding professional competence and resourcefulness for legislative drafting offices. Political considerations often control personnel selection, for one thing. Another factor is the rate of compensation, which in most states is entirely too low to attract able lawyers, California being a notable exception.

In the smaller states especially, reasonable year-round compensation for drafting services will not be provided unless legislative leaders can be convinced that there is important work to be done by the draftsmen between sessions. One has only to leaf through the awkwardly drawn and conflicting laws enacted at almost any state legislative session to see how profitably a full-time lawyer-draftsman could have been employed in the orderly advancement of important programs. Competent drafting service, available on a year-round basis and actually used by the legislators between sessions, could do much toward preventing the customary pre-adjournment log jam which makes a farce of all too many state legislative sessions in their closing days.

Bill-drafting and interim statute revision are frequently combined in the same office. This is done in Florida, Kansas, Kentucky, Minnesota, New Jersey, North Carolina, Wisconsin, and several other states. Reports indicate that the combined assignment is manageable and helpful.

It is hard to generalize about agencies as varied as legislative drafting services in the several states, but certain basic conclusions seem clear. The poor technical quality of most state legislation is itself strong evidence that few states enjoy adequate bill-drafting aid and that legislators do not take full advantage of the few first-rate services that do exist. No other step could do so much to improve the clarity, consistency, and predictability of American law as would the creation of a really excellent drafting service in each state.

The essential prescription for curing the technical ills of state legislation, Jones declares, is a series of state offices in which good lawyers have the opportunity to act as lawyers in giving professional advice and assistance at every stage of the complex process of clarifying legislative policy decisions and translating them into soundly drafted and effective laws.

THE LAWYER IN CITY HALL

The role which lawyers have played in local government in this country has not been glorious, declares Murray Seasongood, an eminent lawyer who has long led the fight for good government in Cincinnati and Hamilton County, Ohio, in reporting on this subject for the Survey of the Legal Profession.

Local government is, he maintains, the most important segment of governmental administration in our nation. Its financial requirements are huge; it is the branch of government which most directly and most frequently affects the ordinary citizen. Though commonly referred to as the "lowest" level of government, it is so in the sense that the foundation is the lowest part of a building—and the most important. As that branch of government closest to the citizen, local government is also the yardstick by which he judges government as a whole. Moreover, state and national leaders are often men who "cut their teeth" at the local political level; consequently, the tone of state and national politics is largely established by the spirit pervading the local political groups.

These observations should be rather obvious, but to the American lawyer, Seasongood holds, they are not. His record of participation in local political affairs seems to indicate a lack of understanding, callous indifference, or sometimes actual hostility. With few exceptions, lawyers have not busied themselves with the functioning of local government. Of those who have, only a fraction have done so unselfishly and as a civic duty. The great mass of lawyers supinely accept evil political conditions in their locality or, worse, abet them, Seasongood charges. The "political lawyer," the lobbyist, or the fixer is the all too common conception of the lawyer in local politics. Fiction, screen, and radio and television reflect this stereotype.

For the "existing lamentable situation in local government" which he deplores, Seasongood ascribes several causes, including "a shaky sense of public morality that pervades much of the thinking on local public questions." The greatest cause, however, is ignorance of the aspirations and importance of local government, he says. This lack of knowledge, in turn, is the result of "faulty or no teaching" about local government in schools, youth organizations, colleges, and law schools.

Singling out the law schools for sharpest attack, Seasongood points out that, while some of them give courses in legal ethics, not one gives courses in public legal duties. In perhaps half of the law schools there is no course on the law of municipal corporations, and in only a very few schools is such a course required. "The law schools still seem to think their primary function is to teach law students to become successful practitioners serving industry and individuals," he states. "This though the need for competent legal advisers in city and county law departments is great."

Seasongood calls upon the legal profession to work for a re-emphasis in education, from the earliest period, that will bring about a new and higher morality in the conduct of local affairs. The practice of law can be improved only through a realization of the connection between good legal administration and sound local government, he says. "Good local government and the standing of the legal profession are intertwined. Together they will either advance in esteem, or much of the practice of law will flounder in the slough of disaffection."

The most common form of direct service of lawyers in local government is their work as "municipal law officers." This term covers all attorneys for local government, regardless of title. They may be called, in various places, city attorney, city solicitor, director of law, county attorney, city counselor, or corporation counsel.

Municipal law officers are specialists in advising municipalities of their legal rights and duties as established by state laws and city charters and as elaborated by city ordinances and other regulations. Since municipalities are creatures of the state, with all their powers expressly delegated to them by the state, practically every municipal action requires study of the city's legal authority. Cities then must have competent legal advice in order that they may carry out their vital public services. The lawyers who give them this advice occupy a very important place in public life today.

There are more than two thousand municipalities in the country with a population in excess of 5,000. In each of these provision has been made either for the creation of a legal department or for the employment of an attorney to handle city legal matters. In the latter case the attorney is often employed on a part-time basis. Many smaller communities (below 5,000) do not have even a part-time city attorney and must content themselves with employing special counsel when the need arises.

The role of municipal law officers is relatively unheralded and is largely unknown to the general public. The practice of municipal law has been characterized—probably with some justification—as prosaic and routine. Consequently, it is not widely noticed except when some especially "hot" local issue comes up. Yet the vitality and efficiency of the entire city administration frequently depend upon the advice of these lawyers.

In 1889 Lord Bryce, who said of local government that it is "the best school of democracy and the best guarantee of its success," could also say, "The government of cities is the one conspicuous failure of the American democracy." To the extent that the great English critic's harsh judgment may no longer be valid—and there is wide agreement that much progress has been made in the last fifty years—the municipal law officer may claim a share in the credit for improvement, so closely is his work woven into the whole fabric of local government. And, to the extent that Bryce's charge still stands unrefuted, the municipal law officer must shoulder his share of the blame.

For the law student who may wish to pursue a career in municipal law, there are courses in that field in roughly half of the law schools. Less than a third of the states, however, include the subject in the state bar examinations. This indicates that the field is not broadly recognized. By contrast, questions on the law of private corporations appear on the examinations in forty-six of the states.

In 89 per cent of the cities over 5,000 the municipal law officer is appointed by the mayor, the city manager, or the council. In the others he is elected. Tenure of office is usually prescribed in the organic law of the municipality, but it is not unusual for tenure to be at the pleasure of the appointing authority. In the larger cities there are legal assistants to the city attorney (or whatever his title), and in some cases they are under civil service, although this is the exception rather than the rule.

The duties of the municipal law officer are many. He must represent the city in its litigation; provide legal advice to municipal officials; draft ordinances, resolutions, contracts, leases, and other documents; approve bonds and obligations; and discharge all other duties of a legal nature imposed upon a municipality.

Considering their qualifications and their responsibilities, municipal law officers are generally underpaid. Only in the very largest cities do the salaries even begin to approach the level for comparable work in private practice. The highest salary (as of 1950) is paid in New York City, which has the largest municipal law office in the world. The head of the city's huge law department is paid $17,500 a year. In only twelve other cities is the chief municipal law officer's salary above $10,000. These are Los Angeles, Port of Oakland, San Francisco, Washington, D.C., Miami Beach, Chicago, Baltimore, Boston, Detroit, Newark, Dallas, and Houston.

Typical salary scales in other large cities are: Denver, $5,000; Hartford, $7,500; Indianapolis, $6,000; Louisville, $5,000; New Orleans, $7,680; Minneapolis, $7,920; St. Louis, $8,532–$9,300; Omaha, $7,980; Cleveland, $9,186; Portland, $4,800–$5,700; Pittsburgh, $8,000; Seattle, $7,500; and Milwaukee, $9,600. In Kansas City the salary ranges from $8,860 to $11,860. Many medium-sized cities pay less than $6,000 a year for full-time attorneys. (All figures are for 1950.)

Considering the highly valuable and essential services rendered to the public by municipal law officers, this low compensation becomes doubly deplorable, for sound legal advice and counsel are as important to municipalities as they are to any private business. The importance of the services of municipal legal officers was stated succinctly by Charles S. Rhyne in a Survey report in these words: "Without their lawyers, local governments simply could not operate."

LEGAL ASSISTANCE TO SERVICEMEN

In World War II and again throughout the Korean trouble, thousands of lawyers served the government in a multitude of ways—both in uniform and as civilians. Many of those in uniform were in the Judge Advocate General departments of the Army and Navy and, later, the Air Force. Others were prominent in Intelligence activities and in General Staff work. It was lawyers who, to a large extent, handled the contracting for weapons and equipment. But, in or out of service, one of the most important public responsibilities taken by lawyers was that of legal assistance to members of the armed forces.

The record of the legal profession's activities in this field is covered in "Legal Assistance for Servicemen," a Survey report by Milton J. Blake, from which the following material is drawn.

"Legal assistance" is used here as a broad term to cover that form of legal service whereby persons in the armed forces and their dependents may obtain "competent, reliable, and sympathetic legal counsel who will give due consideration to their ability to pay reasonable fees for needed service." The term includes and is broader than "legal aid." It also includes the services that are rendered without charge by "legal assistance officers" as part of their official duties. Generally, the term includes legal services in all branches of the law, except those involving criminal matters (courts-martial) and official, administrative matters of the armed forces.

Historically, legal assistance had been rendered unofficially to servicemen by judge advocates and legal officers whenever they could. As there were comparatively few such officers and as they were much occupied with official duties, the amount of legal assistance they could provide was very limited. Likewise, the organized bar had taken little, if any, action in this field, except for some local unorganized efforts during World War I.

Hence, it may be said that legal assistance for servicemen before 1940 was so sketchy, unorganized, and unknown as to be practically nonexistent. After 1940 development was rapid, both in the organized bar and within the service branches themselves.

Following the proclamation of the limited national emergency (September 8, 1939) and passage of the Selective Training and Service Act (September 16, 1940), many persons were brought into the service from civilian life—many of whom had little advance notice or opportunity to arrange their personal affairs. To provide a measure of protection for such persons, the Soldiers' and Sailors' Civil Relief Act was approved on October 17, 1940. Although this act provided legal remedies and relief, it did not work automatically; legal advice and assistance were necessary to obtain its benefits.

Bar associations in many localities began to establish committees of volunteer lawyers to assist service personnel with their problems. Legal aid organizations also recognized the situation as a newly arisen need for their services. The first nation-wide organization to handle legal problems for servicemen was the American Bar Association, the work being directed by the organization's Committee on National Defense, later renamed the Committee on War Work.

In the fall of 1941 the office of the Judge Advocate General of the Army began a study of the problem of how professional legal counsel for soldiers could be provided. Under the Service Extension Act of August 18, the period of service had been lengthened from one year to two and a half years, thus creating a new situation with regard to the adjustment of personal legal affairs.

With the coming of actual war, the volume of legal problems for servicemen and their dependents grew enormously. Many of these problems were novel in legal jurisprudence and required the development of laws and procedures to obtain adequate and just settlement. All this served to emphasize the need for making adequate legal service available.

In the Army's study it was found that three basic factors were involved in the problem: (1) the providing of counsel within the Army; (2) the providing of civilian counsel where necessary; and (3) the providing of a method of contact between the serviceman and the lawyer in the service and the civilian lawyer, in order that the latter two could help the first.

The need for providing counsel within the Army grew out of the fact that the Judge Advocate General's department had not been growing in proportion to the Army as a whole. Consequently, members of that department were increasingly preoccupied with their primary duties as legal advisers to commanding officers, leaving them less and less time for personnel needing legal help. The need was met by the use in legal assistance work of those lawyers who were coming into the Army in increasing numbers in branches other than the Judge Advocate General's department.

Provision of civil counsel became necessary for two reasons. First, War Department directives prohibited the appearance of military personnel before civil courts as counsel for civilian clients. Second, the proper handling of a serviceman's legal problem often required representation in court or otherwise at places far removed from the Army camps. It was clear that the Army would be unable to provide the needed legal service wholly within itself, as in the case of medical service. The solution of this part of the problem was through the use of volunteer civilian lawyers working through the bar organization.

The third factor—that of establishing a means of contact between the serviceman and the military and the civilian lawyers—called for the development of an over-all system which would correlate legal assistance activities not only throughout the military establishment but also with the civilian bar on a nation-wide basis.

Based on the Army study, and after conferences of the War Department and the American Bar Association, in 1943, there was established, for the first time in the history of the armed forces, an official, uniform, and comprehensive system for making legal advice and assistance available to military personnel and their dependents in regard to their personal legal affairs. From the beginning of its development and throughout its operation, the Army Legal Assistance Plan was a joint effort of the Army and the bar.

Upon adoption of the Army plan in March, 1943, and after a series of exploratory meetings, collaboration between the American Bar Association's Committee on War Work and the Judge Advocate General of the Navy moved rapidly toward fruition. Adoption of a plan similar to the Army's was announced in June, 1943. Responsibility for legal assistance in the Navy was placed directly under the Judge Advocate General, as in the Army, instead of under the Bureau of Naval Personnel. It is noteworthy that the legal assistance systems in the Army and Navy were so similar and consistent that the matter posed no problem in the "unification" of the armed services which came after the war.

With the formation of a separate Air Force after World War II, that branch of the service established its own legal assistance program, which is substantially the same as those in the other two branches.

The essence of the Army and Navy legal assistance plans can be expressed in terms of two goals: (1) to assure service personnel of legal advice and assistance from lawyers in the service, designated as legal assistance officers and assigned to duty as such by their commanding officers, and (2), in cases where needed legal service involves court appearances or otherwise requires the services of civilian lawyers, to provide a method of reference of such cases by legal assistance officers to committees on war work of the various bar associations or to established legal aid organizations in the larger cities.

Under the plan legal assistance is available, in each service, to personnel (and their dependents) of the other services and also to other persons serving with the armed forces. Thus, a soldier can obtain help at a Navy legal assistance office and vice versa. Further, a Red Cross worker, for example, can get such service from either the Army or the Navy.

Legal assistance officers are accorded two special privileges not usually granted members of the armed services: (1) There may be direct (rather than "through channels") correspondence between the Judge Advocate General of either service and the legal assistance offices, which may also correspond directly with each other and with civilian lawyers. (2) Matters about which legal assistance officers are consulted are confidential and privileged. Their disclosure may not be ordered by superior authority.

These provisions are fundamental to the plan. They are exceptions to normal military and naval routine, and the granting of these exceptions is greatly to the credit of the armed forces and the wisdom and understanding of the officials concerned.

Although not directly involved, the question of "socialized law" was considered in the development of the plan. Those involved in the planning were on constant guard against steps in that direction. Proof that the legal assistance plan did not become a form of "socialized law" is the fact that it contains no provision for compensation of civilian lawyers out of public funds. Hence, in the "external" phase, it was and is simply a method of referral of servicemen's cases to civilian lawyers without any governmental subsidy or control.

On the contrary, it might be said that the support of the plan by the civilian bar was itself a step to head off any such development. At the start of the operation there was some misunderstanding, as in the case of the commandant of a naval district who was advised by a civilian lawyer to have no part of the plan because it was "socializing" the law. In every known case, however, a complete understanding of the plan dispelled all such objections.

LEGAL ASSISTANCE IN THE SERVICES—IN OPERATION

Actual operation of the plan got under way in 1943 with close and harmonious collaboration between the two service branches and the organized bar. The similarity of the two (after the war, three) plans was helpful for smooth operation.

In effect, there was created a huge legal network which linked Army and Navy posts, installations, and activities all over the world with one another and with civilian lawyers in every part of the United States. A civilian lawyer participating in the plan might have referred to him on the same day a case from a legal assistance officer in England, another from China, a third from a different state, and still another from a different county in the same state. Army memorandums and Navy letters on procedures were circulated throughout the operation of the plan, aiding in achieving effective, efficient, and uniform service.

During the first six months of the plan's operation approximately six hundred legal assistance offices were established in the Army (including the Army Air Forces), and by the end of the first year about eight hundred and fifty offices were at work. A year later the

TABLE 13

AVERAGE NUMBER OF OFFICES AND ESTIMATED NUMBER OF CASES HANDLED BY ARMY LEGAL ASSISTANCE

Year	Average No. Offices in Operation	Estimated No. Cases Handled
March–December, 1943	600	1,200,000
1944	1,000	2,800,000
1945	1,450	4,000,000
Total	....	8,000,000

total was over twelve hundred, with most of the expansion coming in overseas installations. On V-J Day (September 2, 1945) the peak of more than sixteen hundred offices was reached.

In the Navy there were 465 legal assistance offices in operation by the end of 1943. A year later this had increased to 716, and at the peak (October 1, 1945) there were 1,023 offices.

The estimates of the work done by the Army legal assistance offices are given in Table 13. Of the total volume, approximately 20 per cent related to taxation (mostly income tax), 21 per cent to powers of attorney, 19 per cent to wills, 8.5 per cent to domestic relations, and 25.5 per cent to all other legal problems.

In the Navy the types of cases fell into about the same percentages, and the total number was relatively comparable.

Domestic-relations cases and "all other" problems comprised the bulk of the cases referred to civilian lawyers for final disposition; hence the relative percentages of types of cases handled by the civilian bar differed materially from those handled by the legal assistance officers. Divorce and separation problems constituted most of the domestic-relations cases. They continually grew in number as the war progressed and as the strain on normal marital relations was increased by long enforced absences and abnormal domestic conditions. The operation of the legal assistance plan undoubtedly helped keep this explosive problem from getting out of hand and thus benefited morale, both in the armed forces and at home.

The number of cases handled by the civilian bar in co-operation with the legal assistance plan cannot be estimated with any high degree of accuracy. It is believed that between March, 1943, and December, 1945, approximately two million cases were handled for servicemen by civilian lawyers, either directly or on reference from legal assistance officers. It is also estimated that at least twenty-seven thousand lawyers actively participated in the plan, and it is probable that there was at least one participating attorney in every county in the United States.

Reports from the military services and other sources indicate that, almost without exception, excellent co-operation was received from the civilian bar. Very few complaints were made, and those, on investigation, were found in nearly every case to be groundless or based on misunderstanding. The over-all record speaks eloquently in praise of the bar as a whole, considering the volume and nature of the work and the number of persons involved. This result was largely attributed, it is felt, to the care that was exercised by the several bar organizations in selecting the personnel of the war work committees. The membership rolls contained the names of many judges and public officials and other recognized leaders in the bar.

Much of the civilian lawyers' time was given without charge to servicemen and their dependents. In some types of cases and under some circumstances, modest fees were charged. It was understood by all concerned that an out-and-out policy of 100 per cent free service would be neither wise nor proper. Many kinds of legal matters involve extensive service requiring much of a lawyer's time and often resulting in substantial monetary benefits to the person served. Accordingly, it was provided in the legal assistance plan that "in any proper case the legal assistance office may refer the serviceman to civilian counsel for retention . . . upon the usual civilian basis." It was impossible to set out a formula as to what constituted a "proper case," so the matter was left to the individual bar organizations to determine.

In practice, little difficulty was encountered with respect to fees charged by civilian lawyers to whom legal assistance officers referred cases. It was uniformly reported that the fees charged were low—usually the minimum standard or less. Generally servicemen wished to pay for their legal counsel to the best of their abilities in preference to being "charity patients."

With the end of the war the problem arose of whether the legal assistance plan should be demobilized or continued as a peacetime policy. Immediately following V-E Day the American Bar Association, through its board of governors, recommended to state and local committees that their services be vigorously continued and be extended to any veteran for at least six months following separation from the service.

Further study of the question brought civilian and armed forces representatives to the conclusion that the legal assistance plan should be continued as a permanent activity in the armed forces. Because prompt action was taken, there was no serious break or lapse in the system, and the plan continued in operation during the period 1946–50 with only some necessary readjustments.

An interesting and significant by-product of the legal assistance plan was the impetus it gave to the organized bar's acceptance of the principle of low-cost legal service. On October 20, 1946, the House of Delegates of the American Bar Association adopted a resolution with reference to legal assistance for the armed forces *and* low-cost legal service for the general public. That part of the resolution dealing with the latter is quoted as follows:

> WHEREAS, the American Bar Association believes that it is a fundamental duty of the Bar to see to it that all persons requiring legal advice be able to obtain it, irrespective of their economic status, and has recently approved and made an appropriation to increase the extent and efficiency of legal aid service in various parts of the country;

Resolved, That the Association approves and sponsors the setting up by state and local Bar associations of lawyers' referral plans and low-cost legal service methods for the purpose of dealing with cases of persons who otherwise might not have the benefit of legal advice.

The wartime legal assistance plan gave the bar its first experience with "mass legal service." The millions of persons who had been served under it represented a fair cross-section of the American people; thus the plan provided a means of measuring the civilian problem of providing legal service to persons of moderate means. Here was a method which could be extended voluntarily by the legal profession to the whole of the people, without the interposition of governmental control or subsidy—the answer, or at least a possible answer, to "socialized law."

In the civilian phase of the plan it was found that from 10 to 20 per cent of those served could afford no fees whatsoever. Another 10–20 per cent could well afford lawyers' fees at the going rate. The remaining 60–80 per cent could pay something and generally wished to pay a reasonable fee or as much as they could. This experience underscored the problem of making adequate legal service available to this largest segment of the population. It was to help meet this problem that the resolution quoted above was adopted.

Thus the operation of the legal assistance plan in the armed forces had additional beneficial effects on another activity of the American Bar Association, of ultimate benefit to the plan itself. Where lawyer-reference services had already been established, the facilities of such offices lent themselves readily to use in the legal assistance plan. As that plan continues to operate, this development seems likely to become more and more mutually beneficial to these two separate yet interrelated activities of the bar. The significance of this cannot yet be fully assessed.

The outbreak of the Korean war in June, 1950, further justified the policy of maintaining the legal assistance plan in the armed forces. There was no two years' delay, as in World War II, in getting a plan into operation. Prompt action was taken by both the bar and the armed forces to meet the increased need for legal services.

What lies in the future for legal assistance cannot be forecast, the question depending, as it does so largely, on developments in the international situation. It appears clear, however, that the United

States armed forces will be large for some years to come. Consequently, there will be a need to maintain the legal assistance program at a commensurate level.

THE LAWYER AS A FIGHTING MAN

Apart from the lawyers in uniform whose duties were largely of a professional legal nature, there were others whose wartime service was unrelated to their professional training and experience. An interesting commentary on what might be called "the lawyer as a fighting man" is found in "Lawyers as Operations Analysts in the Army Air Forces in World War II," a Survey report by W. Barton Leach.

In an introductory note to Professor Leach's report, Reginald Heber Smith, director of the Survey, says:

> Many of [those who planned the Survey] believed that our best law schools . . . give the finest *intellectual discipline* to be had anywhere in the country, and perhaps in the world. Furthermore, we felt that this discipline was, in no small part, the result of the case method or problem method of instruction.
>
> An excellent way to test our belief was to ascertain what lawyers did in World War II, not as lawyers dealing with legal problems and not as soldiers, but as a group who were called upon to solve entirely new problems of all kinds for our armed forces. We wanted to find out how well they were able to stand up under such a severe testing when the stakes involved, not the fate of a client in court, but of a civilization engaged in a world-wide struggle for existence.

Leach, who played a key role in setting up the Operational Research Section of the Army Air Forces, reports that "lawyers proved capable of doing the most exacting tasks of investigation and analysis." They made recommendations of "significant improvements" in the strategy and tactics of all kinds of air operations.

As a specific example, Leach tells of a lawyer who served as head of the Bombing Accuracy Subsection of the Eighth Air Force. His two colleagues in this highly technical and important project were trained scientists—a mathematician and a biologist. One of these scientists said, in surprise, of the lawyer, "Why, he's as good a scientist as I know." By this he meant that the lawyer was a man who could recognize the difference between a fact and an assumption, who could search out the relevant and discard the irrelevant, and who could proceed through various phases of intermediate conclusions to a final recommendation of corrective action. This particular job, incidentally, was credited with playing a significant part in increasing fourfold the percentage of bombs dropped which actually reached the target area.

Lawyers proved particularly useful as heads of operations analysis sections, exercising in this new area the familiar technique of making complex subjects understandable to a nontechnical audience. The procedures that are so successful in presenting a medical case to a jury or a patent case to a judge proved equally effective in presenting conclusions on mathematical and scientific data to combat crews and their commanders.

"The general pattern of the overseas sections was one of success, occasionally dramatic success," says Leach. "The men who were engaged in this work were under all the difficulties of military personnel without the kudos and perquisites of military rank. (In this particular type of duty the specialists served as civilians.) Their enterprise was so highly classified that they could tell practically nothing to their families or friends. Two of them lost their lives."

When the enterprise was disbanded shortly after V-J Day, General Spaatz paid high tribute to the analysts. "They stayed on the job, mastering the hard realities of combat operations and acquiring the confidence of the officers at whose side they worked," he wrote.

High praise for lawyers' services in another branch of the service, the Navy, was forthcoming in a Survey report prepared by Admiral Denfeld, head of the Bureau of Personnel during World War II. More than eleven thousand lawyers served in uniform with the Navy, he reported. The vast majority of these did not perform legal duties but were fighting members of the Navy's team.

In addition to the uniformed lawyers who served as legal assistance officers, the Navy "needed and obtained the services of many distinguished lawyers who came to us in their civilian capacities," said the Admiral. During the war the Navy found it necessary to operate "one of the largest law firms ever to engage in the practice of law." In addition to operating the greatest naval military machine in history, the Navy was conducting a gigantic business enterprise. Its buying and construction program involved approximately a hundred billion dollars, and it operated a three-billion-dollar Navy-owned industrial plant.

To handle the Navy's huge commercial law needs a group of 125 lawyers worked as a civilian law firm rather than as a government bureau. "This group of lawyers successfully cut through barriers of red tape and solved with celerity the thousand and one unprecedented legal problems created by the Navy's wartime needs," declared Admiral Denfeld.

Speaking for the Army, the late Robert P. Patterson wrote shortly before his death:

> In the War Department the entire membership on the secretary level was made up of lawyers. That included Secretary Stimson, Under Secretary Patterson, Assistant Secretary McCloy, Assistant Secretary for Air Lovett, Special Assistant Bundy and Special Assistant Amberg.
>
> The work done by lawyers in the Army was of the greatest significance and was by no means confined to the Judge Advocate General department. To a large extent lawyers were handling the contracts for weapons and equipment. They were also prominent in Army Intelligence activities and in General Staff work. Over and above these, there were of course thousands of lawyers serving in the line, doing combat duty.

In sum, a comprehensive and objective examination of the record indicates beyond all doubt that in World War II and since, in uniform and as civilians, as lawyers doing work for which they were trained, as specialists in nonlegal work, and as fighting men, the members of the legal profession served their country well.

THE LAWYER AND CIVIL SERVICE

"History does not furnish a better example of the leadership and self-sacrifice of leaders of the bar than the story of the reform in civil service in the United States," says H. Eliot Kaplan in reporting on this movement for the Survey of the Legal Profession.

Among the early crusaders for civil service reform, noted legal figures were in the van, as well as illustrious and dedicated laymen. Organizationally speaking, most of the credit belongs to the National Civil Service League, which was formed in 1881. Another leading group has been the New York Civil Service Reform Association, also organized in the eighties. More than 90 per cent of its membership has been and still is composed of lawyers.

The New York association, a relatively small group, was responsible for the adoption of the original civil service law in New York in 1883. It was introduced by Assemblyman Theodore Roosevelt.

Other early leaders included Elihu Root and Joseph H. Choate. Through its Voluntary Law Committee this Association has sponsored and instituted over one hundred proceedings in the courts seeking enforcement or practical interpretation of the civil service laws. In all but ten cases it has been successful in sustaining its position. It has been conservatively estimated that the savings to taxpayers, directly and clearly attributable to these cases, has been over $10,000,000 a year. Yet it cost the taxpayers nothing to bring about these results, as all proceedings were carried on by the committee without cost for lawyers' fees.

One proceeding prevented a $250,000 pension grab by a former mayor. Another swept off the payroll hundreds of "rat catchers" in the New York City Health Department. A third put an end to the employment of hundreds of lifeguards who, it was discovered, could not swim a stroke!

Most of the New York group's proceedings involved the clarification and establishment of major principles of the merit system. One case established the principle that no person may have a legal appointment to a position under civil service rules until the civil service commission has first passed on his qualifications. Another brought clarity out of confusion in the matter of civil service preference to war veterans.

Many other examples in many other states could be shown to illustrate the effectiveness of civil service reform and the leadership of lawyers in pressing for those reforms.

With a public payroll now aggregating over sixteen billions of dollars to provide for a vast legion of six million public employees, the challenge to the bar to carry on in the struggle for civic righteousness and administrative competence is one it must not fail to meet. "The bar is obligated to continue this effective leadership," says Kaplan.

THE DILEMMA OF DIVORCE

With cheerful candor, Judge Paul W. Alexander admits that it would probably surprise most lawyers, and certainly an overwhelming majority of the public, "if it were to develop that the legal profession has ever done anything in the field of divorce that might, by some strained construction, be regarded as a service to the public."

To some people, he says, the lawyer is the villain in the piece "who in the first instance advised Jane that divorce was the remedy for her ills; who told her just what she must produce in the way of evidence, and how and where to get it; who conspired with her and her husband to pull the wool over the judge's eyes so that he could see plenty of evil in the defendant and naught but good in the plaintiff. The lawyer is the knave who pocketed the exorbitant fee for failing to procure enough property and alimony for the wife or support for the children—and who, at the same time, outrageously robbed the husband, practically driving him into bankruptcy and putting him in a financial strait jacket for the rest of his life!"

This attitude has a prevalence that would be hard to measure. In part it stems from what a psychologist would call a "simple projection": Jane is dissatisfied with her marriage; she demands a divorce to remedy her unhappiness. When the remedy turns out to be less than perfect, she turns against the lawyer.

In his report on divorce for the Survey of the Legal Profession, Judge Alexander states that there are two facts about divorce which seem to have escaped the legal profession as a whole and the public too:

Fact One—Divorce has rather suddenly become big business, and this business is by no means confined to Reno and the other so-called "divorce mills." They handle less than 3 per cent of all divorce cases in the United States.

Fact Two—The problems presented by divorce are largely social rather than legal.

With regard to the first fact, in a great many cities the number of divorce cases filed annually exceeds the number of all other civil actions combined. If divorce is such a big business—and since it always takes one and often two or more lawyers for every divorce —how is it that the legal profession itself is not more familiar with the facts on divorce?

For one thing, many lawyers do not take divorce cases. In most cities the divorce business is almost monopolized by lawyers who seem to specialize in it. They constitute what is sometimes referred to as the "divorce bar." Thus, divorce as an aspect of the practice of law may well be of little or no direct professional concern to the great majority of lawyers.

As to the second fact—that divorce is more a social than a legal problem—it is common knowledge among leaders of the bar that the average lawyer will try his best to reunite estranged couples and to prevent divorce before agreeing to institute legal proceedings. Depending on their religious and moral indoctrination, people may feel that all divorce is evil and that any lawyer or judge involved does a disservice to the parties and to the public as well. Or they may believe that divorce is a necessary remedy for impossible marital situations and that the lawyer who aids in cleaning up the debris of a ruined marriage serves both his client and the public. Regardless of the differing views, nearly everyone agrees, says Alexander, that, "since the family is the unit upon which our society is founded, the lawyer who succeeds in salvaging one foundering marriage and re-launching it on an even keel makes a contribution to the preservation of family life and not only serves the individuals but commits an act of public service."

The number of cases where lawyers have thus acted can never be known. Instances of it come to light every day in the larger divorce courts. Even members of the "divorce bar" make gestures in this direction with surprising frequency. (Alexander tells of the octogenarian lawyer in West Virginia who boasted that he had not had to file a divorce case in the sixty years since he discovered the secret of persuading the wife to bake her husband his favorite pie or inducing the husband to surprise his wife with a bouquet of roses.)

For this little-known and undocumented type of public service the bar receives little credit. The remarkable thing is that so many lawyers try hard to mend broken families while realizing that their only reward, if any, will be in heaven. Not only is the lawyer in such a case almost sure to beat himself out of a fee; he is apt to alienate a friend and lose a client. Divorce-seekers seldom consult their lawyer—they tell him. They go to lawyers to get riddance, not reconciliation, and, when they do not get what they want, they may be pretty unpleasant about it. Moreover, efforts to dissuade can be very time-consuming and often downright harrowing.

Most unfortunate of all, the lawyer undertaking the preventive role is largely out of his element. True, legal "preventive medicine" is widely taught and practiced. But, in applying it to divorce, the lawyer is confronted with a social problem. By training and experience he is a counselor-at-*law*, not a marriage counselor. The law has traditionally shown a reluctance to stray off its reservation, which again points up the handicaps of the lawyer when confronted with a marriage failure.

Judge Alexander observes:

> A family may be likened to a watch, with its mainspring, its fine hairspring, and delicate balance wheels. . . . When a watch gets out of adjustment, we don't smash it and bury it; we take it to a watchmaker. He has fine tools and he has know-how. He is equipped to do a repair job. When a marriage gets out of adjustment, it is customary for the spouses to smash it and take it to the law for burial. But the law, unfortunately, until quite modern times has had neither the inclination nor the fine tools nor the know-how to do a repair job. . . .
>
> Heretofore, it's been something like taking our watch to a watchmaker who had only one tool, a meat cleaver. The law has had only the equivalent of a meat cleaver. And, when the hapless family has come before it, the law mechanically has obeyed the injunction of the Queen of Hearts—"Off with its head!" Of course some watches are broken beyond repair, and some families are broken beyond repair. But nobody knows and nobody ever will know how many of the marriages that have been decapitated by the law were still viable.

Alexander urges forbearance in blaming our system of legal education for this state of affairs. Who ever heard, he asks, of a student going to law school with either the hope or the expectation of becoming a specialist in domestic relations—a divorce lawyer—or, still less, a marriage counselor?

Evidence of the lawyers' recognition of the social problems involved in divorce and of their eagerness to make their profession more responsive to this great modern problem is found in the establishment of the Interprofessional Commission on Marriage and Divorce Law in 1950. This body is a direct outgrowth of the National Conference on Family Life held in Washington in 1948. One of the conference's ten sections was the legal section, and, although greatly outnumbered by sociologists, social workers, and specialists in other fields, the lawyers carried the ball with their definite proposals for concrete action. According to one newspaper writer, they stole the show with their exciting and challenging report.

This report of the legal section at the National Conference on

Family Life scathingly denounced the evils of present divorce laws and offered challenging suggestions for their basic reform and for the establishment of family courts to implement them. Along with the several proposals for changes in faulty divorce-law procedure were suggestions for the improvement of marriage laws, such as putting the brakes on hasty and ill-advised marriages.

The resultant commission is now conducting research necessary to the drafting of a model act or series of acts designed to achieve its objective, which is stated as follows:

> The ultimate purpose of this organization shall be to bring about improvement in the laws of the several states relating to marriage and divorce and allied phases of family life, to the end that the law, in both philosophy and procedure, may tend to conserve, not disserve, family life; that it may be constructive, not destructive, as to marriage; that it may be helpful, not harmful, to the individual partners and their children; that it may be preventive rather than punitive as to marriage and family failure.

It is too early to predict the degree of success which the Interprofessional Commission on Marriage and Divorce Law will achieve, Judge Alexander concludes. But one thing stands out clearly, he declares: namely, that, although divorce may be both unpleasant and unprofitable, and although neither legal tradition nor legal education equips the lawyer with a peculiarly social conscience or with special interest in the preservation of family life, the legal profession has demonstrated that it does have a social conscience. It has demonstrated its eagerness to improve the law as a social instrumentality. It has demonstrated its concern with the protection of family life by assuming leadership in invoking the co-operation of any and all other professions that may have something to contribute toward this goal "whose compelling importance is concurred in by *all* professions, *all* faiths, and *all* classes!"

THE LAWYER SERVING IN ARBITRATION

Arbitration of disputes, according to an early writer on the subject, probably had its rise in the very infancy of society. "Whenever any parties had a dispute respecting the rights to a valuable subject which . . . it was inconvenient to settle by mere appeal to force and violence, but which nevertheless required to be brought to a settlement, nothing seems more likely than that they should bethink themselves of the expedient of referring the question to some mutual friend or neutral third party as an umpire between them and agreeing to abide by his decision." Thus wrote John Montgomerie Bell in 1877, as quoted by Frances Kellor in a report on arbitration for the Survey of the Legal Profession.

American arbitration has its roots in the mercantile and legal systems of arbitration in England. They have been inherited, one by way of the mercantile and trade organizations and practices, carrying forward the voluntary free-will tradition; the other by way of court decisions establishing the common law, and later the statutory laws of the various states in this country.

The two procedures—mercantile and legal—have advanced side by side and have been neatly dovetailed, so that, where one system fails, the other is found to apply. In the history of the two types of arbitration there is a great difference in that the one has largely been recorded and the other has not. When an issue arising out of arbitration is taken to court, it is examined and recorded; when an issue is taken to a trade tribunal, it is frequently disposed of without recording.

The general effect of this dual inheritance of arbitration has not been wholly beneficial, for it repeated in America the experience of England and caused tension between the bar and business. The inheritance brought to the United States the differences, the antagonisms, and the anachronisms which had persisted in England over the centuries. Among them was the long-standing opposition of bench and bar to any granting of legal right to submit future disputes to arbitration.

Under the Federal Arbitration Law (1925) and in those states where arbitration clauses are legally valid and enforceable, the growth of legal arbitration has been phenomenal, and its practice by the legal profession flourishes. Delay in the granting of this right, however, encouraged the use of voluntary good-will arbitration through business organizations. A survey made in 1945 showed that fairly uniform modern arbitration laws had been adopted in fifteen states and by Congress as a federal act applicable for interstate and foreign commerce. Generally speaking, though, the legal right lagged far behind the exercise of the natural or free-will right, with lawyers engaged in advancing arbitration within the judicial system and businessmen in its advancement within the business system. The two did not fully unite their efforts until 1920, when reformation of American arbitration law began.

Arbitration did not become a matter of popular concern until it became a vital factor in labor relations. Then it became a dramatic factor in the lives of millions. It entered the shops, factories, and offices, the homes and the schools; it haunted communication lines and transportation systems; and it was found wherever labor and management were in disagreement.

Through the impetus given arbitration by its introduction in collective-bargaining agreements, it has advanced immeasurably as a way of thought and life in America. Added to this, events following two world wars made a great contribution. The National Recovery Administration and then the National War Labor Board were governmental agencies which favored arbitration. What commercial arbitration failed to dramatize, industrial arbitration brought vividly to the attention of the American people. It was also the open door through which lawyers found a new practice of arbitration, for the "labor lawyer," specializing in labor relations and arbitration, materialized out of industrial arbitration.

Records of the American Bar Association show that for the year ending in 1926 only 36 per cent of the parties to arbitration (in those cases which reached the hearing stage) were represented by lawyers. By 1947 lawyer participation had increased to 91.6 per cent of the cases.

The Kellor study reveals that the lawyer's early stake in arbitration lay in the occasional case that found its way to court, in legislative assemblies where he served on committees that considered arbitration laws, and in judicial councils or bar groups where legal questions involving arbitration were threshed out. His interest lay in appeals from court to court on procedural questions. It lay in opposition to arbitration as a possible competitor of litigation.

The lawyer's future stake in arbitration lies in his participation in all movements that improve the standards and techniques of arbitration in the interests of human welfare, including instruction in the law schools and bar associations. It lies in his interest in the development of arbitration as a profession. It lies, finally, in his vision in helping to build arbitration as a science of ameliorative behavior as an offset to the science of force.

THE PROBLEM OF UNAUTHORIZED LEGAL PRACTICE

The fight against unauthorized practice of law is really the fight against unqualified practice. Authorization alone does not qualify a man to practice law, or any other profession or trade, for authorization is always granted only subject to the demonstration of competence and the pledge to abide by certain standards. It follows that the unauthorized practitioner is not likely to be competent and—in the case of the law—is plainly not subject to discipline for unethical conduct.

The prevention of unauthorized practice is part of the public service of the bar. Many lawyers seem to regard the effort as something necessary merely to prevent competition. This misguided attitude is often expressed in the charge that laymen are "taking the bread and butter" of the lawyers, as though that alone were the reason for prosecuting them. Strongly to the contrary, it is the public, not the lawyers, which is entitled to the protection. Were laymen permitted to practice law, this in itself would make futile any program seeking to maintain a high standard of education, training, and character for lawyers. Thus, public protection against unauthorized practice is not only a part of the entire bar program but a necessary corollary to much of it.

Laws exist in every state to provide this protection. But the fight against unauthorized practice involves more than punishing offenders. It also involves a better understanding by the public, and by laymen whose business or services may impinge upon the field of law, of what may with propriety be done and of what may not be done. Boundaries between the law and accounting, for example, are not made of stone or drawn with white lines, but there *are* boundaries—important ones.

The members of the bar who have devoted themselves to the elimination of unauthorized practice have usually had their motives misinterpreted by the public as an attempt to protect their "business." More lamentable is the fact, as indicated above, that some members of the bar itself misunderstand the movement. One of the reasons for the latter's misunderstanding is that until recently there was no adequate and comprehensive source of information on the subject. This need has been filled by a thoroughgoing study of the unauthorized practice of law by Edwin M. Otterbourg as a contribution to the Survey of the Legal Profession.

A lawyer is responsible to his client and, if need be, can be held accountable to that responsibility. When a layman engages in unauthorized practice of law, what happens to the person advised is not the layman's responsibility. From this it is clear that unauthorized practice of law is a public danger. A few examples will illustrate the point.

A real estate broker conducted what a court afterward defined as a "bootleg law business." Relying on his assumed honesty, an old, illiterate, and feeble woman executed her will and a deed of real estate without consulting her attorney. After her death, extended litigation resulted in the denial of probate of the will.

A shrewd and unprincipled certified public accountant found a lucrative field in giving legal advice to aliens. Eventually he was sentenced to a federal prison, but how much harm and suffering he caused cannot be reckoned.

A man relied on the advice of an insurance agent in an important matter involving taxation questions, and after his death his estate suffered an adverse decision in a suit by the government.

Literally thousands of examples could be cited—not to suggest that accountants, real estate brokers, and insurance underwriters are unscrupulous, but to show that there are certain areas related to their work, and to the work of many other laymen, where competent professional legal advice is necessary in the public interest.

Legal ethics prohibit advertising and solicitation of professional services. Laymen are under no such restriction. Many legitimate modern business activities, because of their nature, sometimes overlap into the field of law. An uninformed public too often expects such concerns to give legal advice and to render legal services which the public has been led to believe are merely incidental adjuncts. This misconception on the part of the public has been brought about largely by advertising and solicitation by business concerns having something to sell which, as a sales inducement, either explicitly or implicitly offer to throw in legal advice and service as well.

The refrain, says Otterbourg, goes something like this: "Buy from us—hire us. Although we are not lawyers, you will receive valuable legal services and advice for nothing or practically nothing, just as good as the genuine article and even better. When it comes to buying a piece of real estate, making a will, creating a trust, setting up a complicated life insurance program, or handling a tax controversy with the government, you really don't need a lawyer at all. We, laymen though we be . . . have become 'experts' and 'specialists' and know the law even better than the lawyers."

Unquestionably, large segments of the public mistakenly believe that experienced laymen in certain specialized fields are both competent and qualified to give them advice as to the law in those fields. Until the legal profession finds a way to disabuse the public of that impression, a great deal of unauthorized practice by so-called "specialists" may continue.

A sequel to this erroneous impression on the part of the public is the pressure now felt in certain quarters for law schools to make it possible for students to become "specialists" in some field of the law by means of a short cut of some kind in legal study. No theory could be in greater error. The law is indeed a "seamless web," and competent legal advice in any branch of it necessarily involves a knowledge and application of the fundamental basic principles of substantive law.

World War II gave great impetus to the unauthorized practice of law. Many members of the legal profession were engaged in national service of one kind or another, and the war itself created many new laws, regulations, rules, and controls which tremendously increased the public's need for legal advice. If there is more unauthorized law practice today than there was fifty years ago, it is doubtless in proportion to the people's greater need for lawyers' services.

Shortly after the end of the war a program called the Postwar Plan for the Suppression of the Unauthorized Practice of Law was announced by the American Bar Association. The plan contains three major recommendations: (1) greater education of lawyers, particularly in the fields of taxation, labor law, and administrative tribunal practice, through modification of existing curriculums of the country's law schools and also postgraduate courses for lawyers; (2) a national publicity campaign to make the public aware of the advantages of consulting a lawyer on every legal problem;

and (3) further development and extension of the educational campaign through conferences with those laymen in businesses which involve a knowledge and application of law, so that these will not cross over into the field of actually practicing law.

The bar program, which includes legal aid and lawyer-reference plans as well as the fight against unauthorized practice, as analogous to the programs undertaken by the medical profession for the protection of the public. When a person has a pain he knows it, and he knows he may need a doctor. The medical profession has gone to great lengths, however, to educate that person not to consult a quack, use a patent medicine, or indulge in self-treatment. In the field of law, however, it is less likely that the person will know when he has a legal problem or, recognizing it, that he should see a lawyer.

As has been previously indicated, the public will not support the legal profession's campaign against unauthorized practice if it believes the primary motivation is selfishness on the part of lawyers seeking to protect their interests. For that reason it is essential that, when any action is taken by a bar association against unauthorized practice, not only should full publicity be given to the action but the publicity should stress that the basic aim of the action is to protect the public from harm. Whenever possible, examples of the damage that can result from unauthorized practice should be spread before the public.

While recognizing the need for greater publicity, Otterbourg cautions against any lowering of professional standards with respect to advertising. The existence of these very standards is in itself one of the strongest claims the profession has upon the respect of the public. Indeed, it is one of the strongest arguments against permitting unauthorized practice. Were employment of lawyers to depend upon who could blow the loudest trumpet or who had the largest advertising budget, the profession would soon lose all status as such.

The road to public support of the bar's effort to prevent unauthorized practice has been opened and marked in every one of the forty-eight states with statutes. Utopia can never be attained, but, by continuing and broadening its efforts, the organized bar, for the protection of the public, can surely reduce to a minimum this display of irresponsibility.

CHAPTER V

Judicial Services

Many New York papers indignantly carried in May, 1951, a story of a seventy-six-year-old woman who sued to recover damages for injuries resulting from falling into a sidewalk hole in November, 1949. She was in ill-health. Her case could not be reached for trial until late in 1954. Her sole income was an old age pension. The old woman's condition was such that there could be no assurance that she would be physically able to testify at the trial forty months hence. She applied for an early trial, only to meet opposition and denial.

In another case, begun in December, 1939, in an eastern state, the plaintiff was injured by a falling ceiling. For twenty-two months after the accident he was unable to work. During this period his only income was workman's compensation of $28.00 a week. The case was reached for trial eight years later on November 12, 1947, and he obtained a verdict. The court set the verdict aside, however, and dismissed the complaint. On appeal, the order was affirmed, but the high court reversed and ordered a new trial on the ground that there was sufficient evidence to justify the verdict. The case required the services of thirteen judges. It was finally settled on February 1, 1950, a decade after it was started.

In the same jurisdiction a case was begun in August, 1945, and ended in June, 1949, after three years and nine months. A brakeman was killed leaving the railroad yard at the end of his day's work. He left a twenty-nine-year-old widow and five small children. During these three years and nine months, while she waited for a decision, the widow was forced to live on borrowed money and eventually had to break up her home.

A family consisting of a couple and their two children lived upstairs in a tenement. One morning the father went to the street door to get a bottle of milk. On his way back he leaned on the stair rail; it broke, and the man fell and was killed. This happened in 1939. In January, 1940, the widow brought suit. The trial was reached in January, 1944—four years later. Plaintiff recovered a verdict of $20,000. It was set aside. Eighteen months later an intermediate appellate court sustained the trial judge in setting the verdict aside. The high court reversed and directed a new trial. This occurred eleven months later and resulted in a verdict, in October, 1946, of $30,000. The defendant appealed and lost, and, finally—after six years, nine months, and five days—the widow won her case. The services of fourteen judges (there would have been nineteen had not five of them heard the case twice on appeal), twenty-four jurymen, and five or more attorneys were used.

It is no secret that the cost of justice can be very high for those seeking it. Dockets are crowded; it may be many months or even years before a case is brought to trial. And, once the trial has been reached, final judgment may be delayed additional months by a series of motions and appeals, all calculated to wear down the opposing side. All this amounts to a substantial denial of justice.

This question—the cost of justice—was dealt with by Harry D. Nims in a Survey of the Legal Profession report in a manner which raised searching questions and proposed an answer.

The parallel between the medical and legal professions, often brought out in the various Survey reports, is again cited by Nims in this connection. The cost of medical care and of justice, he observes, is unsatisfactory to the public and to the respective professions involved as well. To some extent, the public has taken the legal situation into its own hands. Many controversies now are settled by arbitration. And only a small percentage of the cases begun in the courts ever reaches trial.

Nevertheless, the cost of litigation remains an important problem to millions of persons each year. Assuming two parties to a case, approximately 1,330,000 persons used the courts in one year in the states of New York and California alone.

HOW NOT TO SETTLE A LEGAL ARGUMENT

In the disposition of legal controversies there are two distinct and opposite methods of approach—the conference method and the adversary system.

The conference method seeks to find the points of agreement

between the two parties and to build upon them. In the adversary system the points of difference are accentuated, and conflict is heightened.

The adversary system, says Nims, is responsible for much of the cost of justice. Under it the litigant feels he has an inherent right to use the court pretty much as he pleases so long as he keeps within the rules. He may bring appeals he knows will not succeed but which he knows will impose substantial expense and delay on the adversary. He may make unnecessary motions; he may take extended depositions on matters not essential to a decision; he may employ other proceedings for the same purpose. While all this involved, tedious, and expensive process is going on there seems to be no means by which his adversary can protect himself from the hardship and cost which such tactics impose.

"The court's attitude [in the adversary system] seems to be a form of the 'all's fair in love and war,'" says Nims, "and the case is allowed to run its course, sometimes for years or until one party or the other, worn out and discouraged by the work and expense, quits or settles."

In this connection Nims cites a study of the use of motions which was made in New York in 1951. An examination was made of docket entries in civil cases begun in 1942 in the supreme court, New York County, in cases where more than a normal number of motions had been used. Thirty-one such cases were investigated. It was found that from ten to thirty-eight motions had been entered in these cases and that the time lapse from date of service of summons to date of judgment in the cases ranged from thirteen months to nine years.

One of the cases studied, for example, was action brought by a small corporation against former officers and directors for dereliction of duty and for an accounting. The case was begun April 7, 1942. From then until it was settled the case was in the courts five years and eight months. The services of thirty-one judges were used, six opinions were written, and there were two appeals. What this case cost the plaintiff only he knows, but it is safe to say that it was a sizable sum. The problems involved were largely questions of law. It was not a jury case. No backlogs of untried cases or calendar delay prevented this case from being reached for trial promptly, because most, if not all, of the time it was pending the nonjury calendar of the court was not more than six months in arrears.

It can hardly be doubted, Nims declares, that if, soon after answer had been filed, these cases had been considered by counsel for both parties with a judge and the questions involved in the motion had been discussed, most of them could have been disposed of then and there. As it was, in one of them nearly three years elapsed before even the issues at stake were defined.

Also contributing to the cost of justice are orders for new trials. Such orders may be based on error in the trial or in prior appeals. They may require a repetition of the whole litigation, which may delay settlement for years and add materially to the expense. Involved in this problem are the efforts of counsel to create and promote error in the hope that it will bring a new trial or one or more appeals. This is to use the courts not as an agency to reach the truth but to drag out litigation, increase the cost, and so perhaps induce the opponent to compromise.

A real estate case in France is said to have lasted two hundred and seventy years. "We have done far better than that," says Nims, "but in some localities, as a matter of routine, it takes as long—and sometimes more than twice as long—to get a case through the courts . . . as it takes a boy or girl to go through college; and, if a new trial be granted, the time involved may be still greater."

Actual contact with litigation seems to have a peculiar psychological effect on some people with respect to delay. Most of us are ready to criticize court delay, but let the critic be sued, and often he welcomes and urges his lawyer to use all the devices that will produce delay, and there are many. While the case is pending, his opponent's witnesses may die or move away or their memory of the facts involved may grow dim, all to his advantage. Records may be lost, and presently, as the months slip by and his opponent is forced to meet the expense of motions, depositions, examinations before trial, and other procedural devices, his zest for the conflict may lessen, and favorable compromise becomes easier. Many a defendant therefore welcomes and approves and is willing to pay for the use of all the delay-producing measures that counsel can suggest.

Delay tactics have great attraction for the plaintiff with a sham case and for the defendant with a weak case or no case at all. Sham cases would be few indeed if litigants knew that shortly after their case is begun they must face a judge and explain their contentions.

Another technical source of unnecessary expense to litigants is found in the cost of printing the record of an appeal. The practice has increased substantially in recent years and has become a serious problem for the litigant of small means. Chief Judge John J. Parker of the United States Court of Appeals for the Fourth Circuit is commended by Nims for the view that an appeal should not be considered a new proceeding but merely a continuation of that begun in the trial court. "As every lawyer of experience knows," wrote Judge Parker, "there is no sense in printing the entire record. Nobody reads it or ought to read it."

The time consumed in the process of fixing the amount of damages is another factor in increasing the cost of justice. A recent equity case was in the courts for twelve years and three months, and it cost the plaintiff about $71,000 to recover $117,500. Here the plaintiff won his case, but it took him nine of the twelve years to find out *how much* the defendant owed him! The additional three years were spent in appealing the case.

It is not at all uncommon for accounting proceedings to last ten years or more. Nearly thirty years ago a leader of the bar wrote, "There is a complete failure of justice in almost every case in which supposed profits were recovered or recoverable." Patent cases sometimes last as much as fifteen years, and the settlement of estates may drag on for years; both may involve accounting proceedings. The procedure now commonly used in such cases is unnecessarily complicated and technical, in Nims's view. It involves far too great an expenditure of time and money. It lends itself readily to abuse in that it can be employed to wear down opponents with limited resources, and it can be used in such a way as to amount practically to a denial of justice.

The price in terms of human hardship is another aspect of the cost of justice. The facts of this phase are hidden away in the life-stories of those who have turned to the courts for justice. Few, if any, American writers have been inspired to tell the public of the social consequences of contact with the courts, as Dickens did for the English public in *Bleak House* and Samuel Warren in *Ten Thousand a Year.* These stories reached the hearts of the English people and aroused their determination to obtain justice that gave more consideration to human values. They also aroused the bitter opposition of lawyers and judges. In the end this opposition failed, though it did postpone the measures which gave England the justice of which her present-day judges and lawyers are so justly proud.

In this matter of the cost of justice there arises a basic question: What is the *real purpose* of the courts? Should they confine most of their efforts to trial in the courtroom, or should they give all possible help to litigants in all cases on their dockets—whether those cases are on trial or may not be tried for months or years to come?

Usually at least one of the parties is seeking the aid of court, not so much to try his case as to dispose of it quickly and with the least possible expense, preferably without a trial. If the courts have the obligation to aid those with that goal, they cannot meet that obligation by concentrating their effort on trials and paying little or no attention to a case until it reaches the trial room, often many months after it was begun.

HOW TO REACH LEGAL AGREEMENT

The conference method, as opposed to the adversary system, provides a method by which the courts can aid those litigants whose primary concern is for settlement, as promptly and inexpensively as possible. The method is described and provided for in Rule 16 of the Rules of the United States District Courts, which says, "In any action the Court may at its discretion direct the attorneys for the parties to appear before it for a conference to consider (1) the simplification of the issues."

Judge George T. McDermott of the United States Court of Appeals for the Tenth Circuit in 1934 told how he discovered and used the conference method:

> Quite by accident . . . I stumbled onto a method of getting at the nub of a litigation at the beginning instead of at the end. . . . I see no reason why a rule requiring a few minutes' face-to-face conference between the parties, their counsel, and a trial judge, within a few days after a case is filed, shouldn't extend the practice to all cases in this country. . . .
>
> I first came onto the idea in some strike lawsuits brought to cloud the title to producing oil leases. . . . Plaintiff's counsel never dreamed of

winning; he did know the lessee couldn't drill without getting pay for his oil; so he figured, too many times correctly, the lessee would pay a substantial sum to release the pipe line runs. Kansas lawyers struck upon the idea of filing an answer the day after the summons was served, and at the same time they served notice . . . of a motion for immediate trial, setting out the irreparable damage flowing from the delay. That brought the parties face to face with the trial judge immediately.

. . . When plaintiff's counsel appeared on the motion . . . he was put to the rack of the questions, "Just what is your claim?" and "Why not try it next week?" These queries ended his effort to use the process of the court for extortion.

. . . You'd be surprised how many dilatory motions . . . can be disposed of by such a conference. . . . A lawyer with a trumped-up case, unless it is a case founded on perjury, doesn't want to stand up and tell it to the judge. A defense lawyer with no weapon but delay has a bad half-hour in such a conference. And in bona fide controversies, it shortens immeasurably the time for its solution to get at the crux of the case ten days after it is filed, instead of in the court of appeals two years later.

Data now available show that 60–90 per cent of the cases pending in our courts are never tried. This means that most of them do not require a formal trial and that most people go to court not to try their cases but to end their disputes in other ways.

Reducing the cost of justice is no easy problem. The average citizen takes no interest in the courts until he becomes personally involved. Hence, the cost of justice is not likely to be reduced by the efforts of laymen.

Most corporations use the courts at one time or another, and some use them almost continuously. Corporations usually have ample resources and the knowledge to attack this problem, but they take little or no interest in it. If they are sued, delay is often an asset to them. They are satisfied with the status quo. This seems to be especially true of the insurance companies, which defend most tort cases. They have the resources to bring about improvements if they desired it, but there is yet to appear any evidence of serious effort by an insurance company to simplify or improve court procedure or to reduce its cost.

"We lawyers seem to possess a strange blindness to the expense and hardship of litigation," writes Nims. "We readily admit they are sometimes serious, but we say that we are merely using the methods which all our associates use and that we work under traditional rules and conditions applying to all of us which we cannot change. 'Too bad for the litigant,' we say, 'but it can't be helped.' "

Tradition encourages lawyers not to end disputes in the simplest, least expensive way consistent with a proper decision but to stage a contest, using every possible device and strategy which the rules afford. The fault does not lie entirely with the lawyers. Much of it lies with the system itself and the rules which all must use.

Nims concludes emphatically, however, that the cost of justice *can* be reduced. Our courts have an "inherent power," he points out, quoting Brandeis, "to provide themselves with appropriate instruments required for the performance of their duties." Yet for some reason very few of them have employed this power to lessen the cost and hardship of litigation by supervising the use which is made of their facilities. Until recently it could be argued that no practical means was recognized whereby this could be done. It has now been well demonstrated, according to Nims, that such regulation and supervision can be done by the conference method.

In conferences between the judge and the lawyers (and the parties to the suit themselves if they so desire) it is possible to discuss practically every phase of the case, including preparation for trial. It has been found that, in such conferences, the preparation for trial and the trial itself are simplified and shortened to an amazing degree. What is equally important, the work of the judge, both before and during the trial, is materially reduced.

For example, in the court year 1950–51 the Third Judicial Circuit Court of Michigan assigned twelve judges to trial work. They disposed of 769 law cases and 610 chancery cases by trials. During the same year one judge assigned to jury cases disposed of 1,284 cases by conference procedure. Another judge assigned to chancery disposed of 3,934 cases by this method. The chief judge stated that these figures represent about the average for the preceding five years. This court is now holding conferences in all cases soon after issue is joined.

The supreme court of New York—not an appellate court—in 1949 assigned two of its judges in New York County to call pending tort jury cases into conference, with the single purpose of eliminating those that could be settled. These conferences were held in chambers. In the six months ending June 30, 1950, a total of 8,690 cases were ended in this way.

The conference procedure has been criticized as denying litigants the benefits of a formal trial and as forcing settlements. If those who entertain such beliefs, says Nims, were to sit in with one of the judges conducting these conferences, there is every reason to believe their doubts would disappear.

> May it not be possible that in the development of this conference procedure a new function and opportunity for our judges will emerge? Perhaps no longer will they serve largely as umpires presiding over legal battles. Perhaps more and more they will use their prestige, their influence, their authority, their wisdom, and their humanity to heal the differences that separate those who come to court seeking aid.
>
> Especially is this possible with respect to thousands of cases which trained lawyers and judges know involve far too little to warrant the use of the ponderous, expensive facilities of a jury trial. . . . Many cases can be ended soon after they are started, always preserving the right to trial for all who wish one.
>
> Such procedure is not theoretical; its practical usefulness has been established in many cases and in various courts. By its use the cost of justice to many, in both human and financial terms, can be definitely reduced.

PROBLEMS OF JUDICIAL PROCEDURE

The most effective and at the same time the simplest system of procedure yet developed in our law is that set forth in the eighty-six Federal Rules of Civil Procedure and the sixty Federal Rules of Criminal Procedure, concerned with the progress of a case from inception to conclusion. These federal rules, as the latest and most advanced system known to the common law, furnish a sound standard for evaluating the procedure of the several states. It is no accident that the federal rules have now been substantially adopted in seven states and to a considerable extent in several others. Further acceptance seems highly probable.

Fundamentally, there are but a few questions—ten, to be exact—to be answered with regard to procedure in any case:

1. In what court suit may be brought—jurisdiction.
2. Who may sue whom—parties.
3. Where suit may be brought—venue and transfer of cases.
4. How to get the defendant or his property into court—process.
5. What relief is sought—remedies.
6. How to state the controversy—pleadings.

7. How to prepare for trial—pretrial procedures.
8. How to litigate the controversy—the trial.
9. How to correct trial errors—judicial review.
10. How to enforce a judgment—execution.

There are of course a considerable number of subordinate questions which cluster around these ten fundamental inquiries. One of the marks of a real lawyer is to know the question in a case when he meets it. This he can do only when his study has familiarized him with the variety of questions which arise in specific cases.

A leading authority on procedure, Chief Justice Arthur T. Vanderbilt of the New Jersey Supreme Court, has called procedure one of the three "chief instruments in the lawyer's kit." (The other two are skill in research as to both facts and law, and skill in legal reasoning.) With these three the lawyer is equipped to solve any problem in the law. But, Justice Vanderbilt notes in his authoritative textbook, *Cases and Materials on Modern Procedure and Judicial Administration,* not only have the essentials of procedure been neglected in the law schools but procedure has been looked down on by law students, by most law professors, and by many practitioners. He speaks of this as a "professional allergy to procedure." Even an office practitioner who never goes to court works, or at least should work, with the thought in mind that his labors may some day be put to the acid test of litigation. It will do a lawyer little good to know all the substantive law in the books if he does not know how it is actually applied in practice.

A desire to excel in giving his clients the highest kind of professional service is one sound reason for a lawyer's mastering procedure. But there are deeper reasons. No substantive rights—not even those guaranteed by federal and state constitutions—are really assured to one until he is assured of the most fundamental right of all: the right to a fair trial, in both civil and criminal cases. Even today after several centuries of development, a fair trial is not always assured in its entirety by our constitutions, statutes, rules of court, decisions, and practices. As every lawyer knows, and every law student should quickly learn, the right to a fair trial is still being developed in the courts. To be sure, more progress in this vital matter has been made in the last fifteen years than in the entire preceding century, but much remains to be secured.

Quite as fundamental as the right to a fair trial in the protection of all our substantive and procedural civil rights is the due enforcement of the criminal law. It will do one little good to obtain his just desserts in the civil courts if he is deprived of them through some unpunished breach of the criminal law. Many lawyers, and most laymen, take the enforcement of criminal law for granted, but this is scarcely warranted by the facts.

The essentials of civil and criminal procedure should be considered together, for they have much in common and are interrelated historically. The first aim of the law, both civil and criminal, has always been to preserve order. In both branches, procedure is basic.

Procedure under the federal rules, or indeed in any system, is largely concerned with answering the ten major questions listed previously and with solving four sets of major problems revolving around the manpower of the courts. These four great sets of problems are:

1. *Matters concerning the judiciary.*—How are the judges selected? What is the tenure of their office? Is their salary adequate today in comparison with what lawyers make? What standards govern their conduct? These problems of judicial selection, tenure, salaries, and ethics, go to the heart of any judicial system, the quality of that system depending so much as it does on the character and professional qualifications of the judges selected to man it.

2. *Matters concerning the jury.*—It will do a litigant little good to have his case tried by competent lawyers before the ablest judge on the bench if the jurors chosen to pass on the facts are not both honest and intelligent. In the enforcement of criminal law the selection of a proper grand jury is quite as important as the choice of a proper trial jury. The selection of jurors, therefore, is a vital matter in the due administration of justice.

3. *Matters concerning the bar.*—Cases in trial courts are not tried by judges and juries alone. Lawyers play an essential part not only in presenting the evidence to the court through witnesses and documents but also in arguing the facts to the jury and the law and the facts to the court. A judicial system in the long run can be no better than its bar and ultimately is based upon the professional responsibilities of the legal profession as a whole.

4. *Matters of judicial administration.*—To have judges, jurors, and lawyers work together effectively requires judicial administration. This involves the co-ordination of every branch of the judicial establishment; the collection of judicial statistics from the judges and court clerks and the compilation and periodical publication of these statistics; the assignment of the judges where they are most needed and to the kind of work for which they are best fitted; the drafting and promulgation of rules of court governing practice before both trial and appeals courts; and the setting-up of judicial conferences made up of the judges and representatives of the bar and the legislature to consider such amendments to the rules and practice as experience proves necessary. Strangely enough, Vanderbilt observes, in a country distinguished for managerial talent and executive technique, the art of judicial administration is still in its infancy.

Each of these ten fundamental questions and four sets of subjects having to do with procedure should be approached in the spirit of our modern rules of court—that a trial or an appeal is not a sporting event, in which the rival lawyers are the leading players, but an orderly search for the truth in aid of the administration of justice.

This in turn involves a firm grasp of the fundamental axiom that the courts exist not for the benefit of judges and lawyers ("though they often seem to think so," Vanderbilt interposes) but primarily for the litigants. It follows that the test of every rule of court should be not what is most convenient for the judges and lawyers but what is best for the litigants. This is not an easy idea for some judges and lawyers to grasp, but it is fundamental to any real progress in judicial administration.

Specifically, at each point the inquiry should be: "Does this step contribute as much as possible to a fair trial?" Viewing it in this light, the lawyer and the law student may be less inclined to think of procedure as subordinate to substantive law. They may recognize instead that procedure and judicial administration are integral elements of first importance even in an office lawyer's work and that all legal rights depend directly on the right to a fair trial under sound rules of procedure administered by honest, intelligent, and competent judges, jurors, and lawyers.

It is a strange phenomenon of the law, Justice Vanderbilt has observed in the Survey's report, "Minimum Standards of Judicial

Administration," that the legal profession is, on the whole, indifferent to the defects in our procedural law. While our substantive law, dealing with legal rights, has been developing from year to year—thanks to the unstinted efforts of judges, lawyers, legislators, administrative officials, and law professors—the procedural law, which deals with the means of enforcing those legal rights, has been relatively neglected.

Perhaps the situation is akin to the case of the shoemaker's barefoot children; lawyers are so preoccupied with the substantive problems of their clients that they have little time to devote to the great problems of ways and means in the law. Or perhaps lawyers in general are loath to change their own world of procedure, even in favor of something conceded to be better.

Whatever may be the reason for neglect, there is no escaping the uninspiring contrast between the streamlined efficiency of our modern world of commerce and industry and the cumbersome, inefficient, and anachronistic judicial machinery. In many states up-to-the-minute business organizations have to rely upon outmoded procedures, some of them medieval in origin, to enforce their legal rights.

Although at times procedural reform in this country may have seemed to move at the pace of a glacier, it may be well to recall that in England the agitation for improving the methods of the courts continued well over a century. For example, it required a series of campaigns from 1836 to 1907, the conviction of many an innocent man, and twenty-eight separate bills to obtain as fundamental a right as an effective appeal from a judgment of conviction in a criminal trial court. The struggle for procedural reform in England was won, moreover, in the main by laymen, though a few courageous and farseeing members of the bench and bar provided the required leadership.

The average lawyer's aversion to all problems of procedure stems largely from his law-school days. Until recently at least, courses in procedure have usually been the most unpopular in the curriculum. The law student generally learns enough procedural law to pass the bar examination and then centers his attention on substantive law, usually private substantive law, the "bread-and-butter" subjects. To this law-school aversion is added the fact that, once admitted to the bar, the lawyer has a "vested interest" in procedural law as he knows it. Any change in procedure will jeopardize his slight learning in the field. He resists the very thought of having to learn a new system of procedure, even if it is in fact a much better one, declares Vanderbilt.

STANDARDS OF JUDICIAL ADMINISTRATION

In any period of unrest and conflicting political, social, and economic ideas, the law and the courts are peculiarly subject to attacks by enemies both within and without the country. These attacks center not on the substantive body of the law but on its defects of procedure or personnel. In 1937 these considerations combined to induce a group of eminent judges, lawyers, and law professors in the Section of Judicial Administration of the American Bar Association to apply themselves to the task of recommending standards necessary to make law procedure workable and thus save our entire body of law from attack. This group was under the leadership of Chief Judge John J. Parker of the United States Court of Appeals for the Fourth Circuit. Their recommendations were embodied in seven reports dealing with judicial administration, pretrial practice, trial practice, trial by jury and jury selection, the law of evidence, appellate practice, and administrative agencies.

Basic to these reports was the conviction that the battle for improved judicial procedure had to be fought on a nation-wide front if it was to be won in time and that this could be done successfully only with the aid of the entire legal profession and of intelligent and public-spirited laymen.

In writing an Introduction to the reports, Justice Vanderbilt emphasized the fact that they dealt with the *minimum* standards that were needed in a *practical* way to make our court procedure work in the twentieth century.

> Note well the words "minimum" and "practical." The reports are entirely utilitarian in their objective. They were prepared with a realistic consciousness of the very genuine difficulties involved in inducing our judges and lawyers to change any of their working habits in the field of judicial procedure. Hence the recommendations of the seven committees are limited in number to those matters which are absolutely essential if the administration of justice in America is to be responsive to the needs of our times. They are confined to matters of *fundamental importance*. . . .
> . . . Some day . . . a more enlightened generation will look back on

these reports and wonder that it should have been necessary to write them, necessary to agitate for the recommendations set forth in them and necessary, perhaps, in some states to invoke the aid of enlightened and farseeing laymen to bring about their adoption.

There is nothing radical or experimental about any of the committees' recommendations. The key ideas are so simple as to be almost axiomatic. For example:

Practice and procedure in the courts should be regulated by rules of court; and to this end the courts should be given full rule-making power.

To have effective judicial machinery within the state, it is not sufficient that each judge shall discharge his functions efficiently in the trial of a case. Some judges or judges within the judicial system in the state must be charged with the responsibility of the efficiency of the system in the state as a whole.

Courts in the metropolitan areas should make provision for pretrial hearings, and other courts should give consideration to the procedure with a view of adopting it if justified by local conditions.

Jury service is the chief remaining governmental function in which lay citizens take a direct and active part, and trial by jury is the best means within our knowledge of keeping the administration of justice in tune with the community. It is highly important that everything be done which can be done to insure the most efficient methods of jury selection and trial procedure.

Jurors should be selected by commissioners appointed by the courts.

The common-law concept of the functions and the authority of the trial judge should be uniformly restored in the states which have departed therefrom.

Surely these ideas are not revolutionary, exclaims Vanderbilt. On the contrary, some of the recommendations involve a return to common-law concepts that were unwisely abandoned a century or so ago by various states; others represent the gradual advance in simple, common-sense methods of judicial administration.

These recommendations of the American Bar Association—the minimum, practical standards of judicial administration—present a definite challenge to all who understand the importance in our system of government of respect for the law. Respect for law is impossible without respect for the work and the working methods of the men, both judges and lawyers, who help administer the law. It is in the courts, and not at the hands of the chief executive or the legislature, that men and women feel the keen, cutting edge of the law; and they therefore judge the law by what they see and hear in the courts, and by the character and manners of judges and lawyers, quite as much as by the law itself.

"Viewed in this light," says Vanderbilt, "what seems at first blush to be a mere matter of judicial and procedural machinery suddenly is seen to be of prime importance. . . . What more important cause can there be to engage the support of any intelligent citizen, be he lawyer or layman?"

The recommendations put forth in the seven reports are here summarized briefly, together with the conclusions of the committee in each case.

Judicial selection, conduct, and tenure.—The committee's recommendation, adopted by the American Bar Association in 1937, as the plan offering "the most acceptable substitute available for the direct election of judges" calls for: (1) the filling of vacancies by appointment (by the executive or some other elective official or officials) from a list named by another agency, composed in part of high judicial officers and in part of other citizens, selected for the purpose, who hold no other public office; (2) if further check upon appointment be desired, such check may be supplied by the requirement of confirmation by the state senate or other legislative body; (3) the appointee after a period of service should be eligible for reappointment periodically thereafter, or periodically go before the people on his record, with no opposing candidate, the people voting upon the question "Shall Judge Blank be retained in office?"

The appointive system (and its alternative, the "Missouri Plan" advocated by the American Bar Association), to which all studies point as being best for the proper selection of the judiciary, is utilized in only nine jurisdictions. In three, all judges are so appointed; in three others, there are some exceptions; in two, only appellate judges are so selected; in one, only trial judges are so appointed.

The most-criticized method of selection is by popular vote. This usually involves the selection of candidates by party convention or party primaries. It is used in more than two-thirds of the states. While partisanship is not altogether absent in the selection of judges by methods other than popular election, other factors are influential.

Although no great volume of criticism of the judiciary is forthcoming in those states having popular election of judges, the dissatisfaction of the bar in these states is shown by the sentiment in about two-thirds of them for a change to the "Missouri Plan." In contrast, there is no sentiment favoring a change to popular election in those jurisdictions in which the judges are not so selected. And there is general approval of the courts. Such criticism as does exist in the states with popular election is aimed most heavily at the lack of learning or legal ability in the elected judges.

The problem of finanical security is important in obtaining fit persons for judicial office, and an attempt is being made to provide salaries commensurate with the importance of the office. Judicial salaries do not, however, in reality approach the amount of financial reward that can be secured by an outstanding lawyer in ordinary professional life. Therefore, provision for retirement in case of illness or because of age is essential if judicial positions are to attract the most suitable lawyers.

The present trend seems to be toward methods of selection, tenure, and recompense which will result in higher qualifications for judicial office.

Managing the business of the courts.—In July, 1938, the American Bar Association adopted the committee's recommendation (1) that provision should be made in each state for a unified judicial system, with power and responsibility in one of the judges to assign himself and the others to judicial service so as to relieve congestion of dockets and utilize available manpower to the best advantage; (2) that judicial councils should be strengthened with representation accorded the bar and the judiciary committees of the legislative department; and (3) that quarterly judicial statistics should be required.

These recommendations, says Vanderbilt, originated in the obvious necessity for improving the business methods of the courts in order to enhance their efficiency in performing their judicial functions. The first recommendation is the most important. It calls for the management of court business in a systematic manner, under the direction of one judge given adequate power and proper responsibility.

But, although the recommendations of the American Bar Association on the management of the business of the courts are fundamental to the successful operation of any judicial system, none of them has as yet met any general acceptance in the states—this despite the outstanding example set by the federal judicial system on all points here under consideration.

As to the first recommendation, there are eleven states which have substantially no elements of external control in their judicial systems. Another seventeen states have merely a minimum of such control. Sixteen other jurisdictions exercise a substantial degree of control over one or two of their sets of courts. Finally, there are only five jurisdictions wherein a substantial degree of control is exercised over nearly all the different sets of courts in the respective systems.

In four of the first group of eleven states the desirability of some measure of judicial unification has been indicated. In five of the second group there is evidence of dissatisfaction with the status of court administration. Since the states comprising these two groups are primarily rural, with few centers of concentrated population, it is probable that there is not such pressure on the courts as develops in metropolitan areas, and for that reason the need for court unification and improvement in management has not yet made itself felt.

Rule-making: The judicial regulation of procedure.—The committee recommended that practice and procedure in the courts be regulated by rules of court and that, to this end, the courts should be given full rule-making power. The recommendation was adopted by the American Bar Association in July, 1938.

No clear-cut picture of the regulation of procedure in the various states emerges from the committee's survey of existing practices. Common-law rules still underlie our thinking on procedure, particularly in the field of evidence and in those courts where there is little local rule-making. Statutes are utilized for rather complete code regulation in some states and for major piecemeal regulations in others.

A definite trend is apparent, however, toward the granting of full rule-making authority to the court of last resort. And, spurred by federal example, more courts are exercising their admitted rule-making power to a greater extent now than ever before. As evidence of this, the Federal Rules of Civil Procedure have been followed almost completely in Arizona, Colorado, Delaware, Maryland, New Jersey, and New Mexico, and to a lesser degree in Iowa, Missouri, and Texas. Certain details of the federal rules have been incorporated in the rules of North Dakota, Pennsylvania, South Dakota, and Washington.

The selection and service of juries.—The following recommendations were adopted by the American Bar Association in July, 1938: (1) that jurors should be selected by commissioners appointed by the courts; (2) that in the metropolitan centers some such system as that now in use in Cleveland, Ohio, should be adopted; (3) that the examination of prospective jurors should be in accordance with the procedure outlined in Rule 47 of the new Federal Rules of Civil Procedure: "The Court may permit parties or their attorneys to conduct the examination of the prospective jurors or may of itself conduct the examination. In the latter event, the Court shall permit the parties or their attorneys to supplement the examination by such further inquiry as it deems proper or shall itself submit to the prospective jurors such additional questions of the parties or their attorneys as it deems proper"; and (4) that, for prospective long trials, one or more jurors in addition to the regular panel should be selected and impaneled to sit as alternate jurors, in accordance with the practice authorized and regulated by Rule 47 of the new federal rules.

As background for these recommendations, Vanderbilt points out that trial by jury, despite the guaranties embodied in the federal and state constitutions and the lip service frequently accorded to it, has been the subject of much criticism over the years. Basic to the committee's recommendations was the conviction that the efficiency of jury trials must be increased if they are not to be discarded completely. The efficacy of jury trials depends as much upon the caliber of the jurors as on the character and training of the trial judges and the powers accorded them in the conduct of jury trials.

The caliber of jurors, in turn, depends upon the mode of selecting them. In selecting, the elimination of political influence is of paramount importance. This can never be accomplished when the jury commissioners are politically elected or appointed officials. Therefore, the recommendation for the appointment of jury commissioners by the courts is a fundamental one.

The need to acquaint the juror summoned for service with the general nature of his duties, the proper quartering and protection of the jury in all cases, and the instruction of the jury orally in language it can understand were also considered important by the committee which studied these problems in detail, although no specific recommendations were made on these points.

In the problems of jury selection the basic consideration is this: Having assumed the continuation of the present system, the next question is, "What *kind* of a jury do we want?" Should it be strictly a cross-section of the community, or should it be selected solely on the basis of ability to understand and decide cases? The problem is to find honest jurors with sufficient intelligence to understand the issues presented and yet be representative of the community.

The problems of the care and comfort of jurors while waiting assignment and the protection afforded them against improper influence during the course of a trial have not been given too much attention. In only five states are the accommodations for jurors "excellent" and "comfortable," according to the committee's survey. In only seven other states are they "adequate." In nine jurisdictions no quarters at all are furnished jurors waiting service. Conditions in the remaining states vary and for the most part do not seem to be adequate.

Jury protection also varies considerably from state to state. In twenty-nine states jurors are allowed to separate both during the day and at night, with a warning not to discuss the case. In thirteen states jurors are completely segregated during the entire trial of criminal or capital cases. Five jurisdictions guard the jurors during the day but allow them to separate and go to their homes at night.

Further study of these related problems would seem necessary as one step to the establishment of proper standards for the promotion and achievement of efficiency in jury trials generally.

Pretrial conferences.—Recommendations adopted by the American Bar Association, in July, 1938, form an interesting background for the discussion of the pretrial conference in the Nims report earlier in this chapter. The ABA recommended (1) that courts in metropolitan areas should make provision for pretrial hearings, and other courts should give consideration to this procedure with a view to adopting it if justified by local conditions; (2) that whether the pretrial hearing should follow closely the joinder of the issue or should be postponed until shortly before actual trial must be determined by the individual needs in each jurisdiction; (3) that the pretrial hearing should be had before a judge; and (4) that a pretrial hearing need not involve a disclosure of the details of proof which counsel prefers not to disclose.

The pretrial conference is an outstanding recent development for the improving of trial practice. It is important as a method of simplifying the issues, providing for the amendment of pleadings where necessary, obtaining admission as to the uncontroverted facts and undisputed documents, restricting within reasonable bounds the number of expert witnesses, and considering such other matters as may aid in the disposition of the action. Its incidental benefits include the settlement of many cases which should never go to trial, the achievement of a stabilized trial docket, and, most important of all, a court which is adequately informed in advance of the trial as to the issues on which it will be called to rule. This in turn has the desirable effect of decreasing errors of law and minimizing appeals.

The general nature of the pretrial conference is an informal discussion between court and counsel, preferably held in open court. Here the judge and the attorneys seek to state the issues in dispute. While the pretrial conference does not partake of the nature of an arbitration, and ordinarily the judge will not take the lead in trying to settle cases, an agreement is very often reached or at least initiated in such a conference.

Although the pretrial conference is a somewhat novel device, it has met with surprising acceptance. Originating in Wayne County, Michigan, in 1929, it is now provided for in the majority of jurisdictions. Because of its relative newness, the method's full effects on trial proceedings have not been completely assessed. However, its success in the federal courts has been such as to prompt the Judicial Conference of the United States report to state: "[The pretrial conference] has demonstrated beyond peradventure that pretrial procedures result not only in greater efficiency in the judicial processes, but in great economies in time and money for the courts, the litigants and the public."

Trial practice.—These recommendations regarding trial practice were presented by the committee and adopted by the American Bar Association in July, 1938:

1. The common-law concept of the function and authority of the trial judge should be uniformly restored in the states which have departed from it.

2. After the evidence has been closed and counsel have concluded

their arguments to the jury, the trial judge should instruct the jury orally as to the law of the case. He should have the power to advise them as to the facts by summarizing and analyzing the evidence and commenting upon its weight and credibility, always leaving the final decision on questions of fact to the jury.

3. The trial judge should at all times be the governor of the trial in the sense of actively, and firmly when necessary, requiring that the proceedings be conducted with dignity, decorum, and the avoidance of waste of time.

4. The provisions of the new federal Rules 26–37 relating to discovery (a proceeding for obtaining before trial, information relevant to the issues) should be adopted in all the states.

5. The trial court should be authorized in its discretion to submit specific issues to the jury to be considered in connection with a general verdict, in accordance with the practice prescribed by Rule 49 of the new federal rules.

6. The trial judge should have the power to grant a partial new trial where in his judgment the several issues in the original trial are clearly and fairly separable.

7. The practice of granting judgment *non obstante verdicto* should be uniformly adopted; this permits the court to enter a verdict contrary to that of the jury on the ground that the latter had no reasonable basis. This practice should be extended to authorize judgment on a motion, in accordance with the original motion for a directed verdict, after the jury has disagreed and upon discharge, as provided for in Rule 50 of the new federal rules. This would permit the resolution of the case by the judge, despite a jury disagreement, where only one verdict appears to be reasonable.

8. After the trial of law suit has begun, dismissal without prejudice by the voluntary request of one party should be permitted only in the legally reviewable discretion of the trial judge.

9. In law cases involving complicated issues of fact, there may well be reference to a special master or auditor in advance of a jury trial with the submission of his report for consideration by the jury. In equity and nonjury law cases the report should be accepted by the court as to the facts unless it is clearly in error, but nevertheless the trial judge should have power to adopt or modify or reject the report in whole or in part or, in his discretion, to receive further evidence with regard to th facts found, or to send the report back to the person who prepared it with further instructions. In jury actions the findings of the referee, special master, or auditor should be made admissible as evidence of the matters found and be read to the jury subject to the ruling of the court upon any objection in point of law which may be made to the report.

10. The practice as to issuing preliminary injunctions should be in accordance with that outlined in the new federal Rule 65, which in substance forbids the issuance of preliminary injunctions without a hear-

ing but which permits a temporary restraining order when necessary to prevent irreparable injury.

The first three recommendations above are of the utmost importance, not only for the improvement of trial practice, but for the betterment of the administration of justice as a whole. The functions and authority of the trial judge, his relation to the jury, and his powers in conducting a trial are of particular significance also in the selection of the jury, in the examination of prospective jurors, and in the application of the law of evidence. These three recommendations, however, as well as some of the others, are embodied in the practice of only a minority of states.

Although half of the ten recommendations as to trial practices are followed in a majority of the states, much remains to be done in this direction. The basic common-law concept of the judge as the governor of the trial has not been restored in many of the states in which such power was restricted as a result of fear and distrust of its arbitrary use engendered by the impact of Jacksonian democracy. Consequently, in only a few states does the judge now have the power to comment on the weight of the evidence. Emphasis must be placed on the prime need to accord to the judge his proper place and power in the conduct of a trial, because this is the *sine qua non* of all other improvements in trial practice and, indeed, in the proper administration of justice as a whole.

The law of evidence.—The following fifteen recommendations pertaining to the law of evidence were adopted by the American Bar Association in July, 1938:

1. Error in the admission or rejection of evidence should not itself be grounds for directing a new trial unless the appellate court (the court to which the case is appealed), after an examination of the entire record, is of the opinion that the error has resulted in a miscarriage of justice or has affected the substantial rights of the parties.

2. Where a case is heard by a judge without a jury, a new trial should not be granted because of error in the admission of testimony if there is substantial evidence to support the findings unless it appears that the findings are based on testimony which should have been excluded. A new trial should not be granted for error in the exclusion of testimony unless it appears that the findings were affected by its exclusion.

3. Exceptions (the ritual use of a phrase such as "I except!" in disagreement with a ruling of the court) to the admission or rejection of testimony should not be required for the review of error on appeal. They are now sometimes required to preserve the right of appeal. For all pur-

poses for which the exception has been necessary, it should be sufficient that a party, at the time the ruling or order of the court is made or sought, makes known to the court the action which he desires the court to take or his objection to the action of the court and his grounds for objecting (new federal Rule 46).

4. The rule excluding testimony of an interested party as to transactions with decedents (deceased persons) should be altered by the adoption of a statute like that of Connecticut, which removes the disqualification of the party as a witness and permits the introduction of declarations of the decedent, on a finding by the trial judge that they were made in good faith and on decedent's personal knowledge.

5. Declarations of a deceased or insane person should be received in evidence if the trial judge shall find (*a*) that the person is dead or insane, (*b*) that the declaration was made, and (*c*) that it was made in good faith before commencement of the legal action and upon the personal knowledge of the declarant.

6. The rule of the North Carolina statute—that the trial judge may require the disclosure by a physician of a privileged communication from a patient if in the opinion of the judge such disclosure is necessary for the proper administration of justice—is a good rule and should be adopted in the other states. Privilege (the protection of certain confidential communications against compulsory disclosure) should not be extended to accountants, social workers, or journalists.

7. The rule of the "uniform business records as evidence" act, drafted by the Uniform Laws Conference in 1936 and printed in the appendix to the report of the committee, should be adopted in the several states. This permits the introduction of certain ordinary business records as evidence, in exception to the rules forbidding hearsay.

8. Ordinary witnesses should be allowed to state their conclusions with respect to ordinary matters subject to explanation, thus permitting a witness to state his observation in a natural and nontechnical manner.

9. The principles embodied in the uniform act of 1937 guiding the admissibility as evidence of testimony by experts, and set forth in the appendix to the report of the committee, should be adopted in the several states by appropriate legislation or rules of court.

10. The provision of the new federal Rule 44, permitting the introduction in evidence of certified copies of official records, should be adopted in all states.

11. The uniform act drafted in 1936, requiring that judicial notice be taken of the common law and statutes of other states of this Union and that the law of a foreign country be determined by the court, should be adopted in all the states.

12. Witnesses should be sworn separately, the oath being administered to each witness as he takes the stand to testify; and the judge should see that it is administered in a dignified and understandable way, either by himself or by the clerk.

13. Under the "scintilla" rule now sometimes used, a slight amount of evidence supporting one side of a case would force it to the jury,

despite the overwhelming weight of evidence on the other side; This rule as to the sufficiency of evidence should be abolished.

14. The provisions of new federal Rule 43 (b) should be adopted in the several states; this permits the calling of an adverse party to a suit and his interrogation as if he were under cross-examination and permits impeachment of such a witness.

15. As recommended by the Committee of the Commonwealth Fund a decade ago, a general rule should be adopted in every jurisdiction substantially as follows: "Any rule of evidence need not be enforced if the trial judge, on inquiry made of counsel or otherwise, finds that there is no bona fide dispute between the parties as to the existence or non-existence of the facts which the offered evidence tends to prove, even though such fact may be in issue under the pleadings. No error can be assigned or predicated upon the violation of any rule of evidence, either at law or in equity, when it appears from statements of counsel or from other evidence in the case or is shown in any other lawful way that there is no bona fide dispute between the parties as to the fact sought to be proved or disproved by the offered evidence, even though such fact may be in issue under the pleadings."

The above recommendations, though numerous, are limited in scope, and no attempt was made by the committee to reorganize or rewrite the law of evidence.

Although many of the recommendations are extant in the practice of a majority of jurisdictions, wide acceptance of the minimum standards established in 1938 has not yet been achieved generally. This is particularly evidenced by the degree to which there has been failure to follow the recommendations relating to a survivor's testimony, a deceased person's statements, the limitation on privilege for communication between physician and patient, the opinion rule, expert testimony, and cases in which there is no bona fide dispute of fact. Nor has any jurisdiction other than Missouri attempted to study or to formulate a simplified code of evidence or set of rules refining burden of proof and presumptions. Moreover, little seems to have been done in the matter of studying improved methods of calendar administration or the abuse of continuances.

Appellate practice.—The next group of recommendations, regarding practice in taking appeals to higher courts, was adopted by the American Bar Association in July, 1938:

1. Appeals from inferior courts which involve full retrial of a case in a higher court should be avoided as far as possible by improving the quality of the inferior courts. As a means to this end, the abolition of justice-of-the-peace courts should be seriously considered, sub-

stituting for them municipal courts or courts with wider territorial jurisdiction, properly organized and housed, having trained and salaried judges, competent clerks, office equipment sufficient for keeping proper records, and sitting, so far as practicable, at such times and places as the needs of the community indicate.

2. Under present rules, in certain cases the party against whom judgment has been rendered has the right to bring the case to an appellate court for review, while in others he can get such review only if the appellate court is willing to hear the case. It is recommended that a sum of money be stated for all courts, so that in cases involving judgments in excess of that amount appeal may be had as a matter of right, and in cases involving judgments below that amount review will be at the discretion of the appellate court, on a showing that an important question of law is involved.

3. The filing of a simple notice of appeal, or of an application for leave to appeal, or some simple equivalent of these, should be the only step required to vest jurisdiction in the reviewing court; and defects in the notice or application should not affect the jurisdiction. This notice should preferably be filed in the lower court, in order to serve the convenience of the appellant (person appealing) and to constitute a more easily effective notice to the appellee (person supporting the verdict below), and the clerk should be required to send a notice by mail to the appellee.

4. *Supersedeas* bonds (those suspending the effectiveness of a legal determination pending appeal) should be fixed by the court only at such an amount as will adequately secure to the appellee the full amount of his judgment. The filing of such a bond should be permitted at any time before satisfaction of the judgment; and enforcement of the judgment (from which appeal is made) should not be held up until bond is filed.

5–11. These are a set of recommendations designed to simplify and make less cumbersome and expensive the use and transmission of records, abstracts, and all other papers affecting the case under appeal.

12. A systematic effort should be made by the bar and the appellate bench in each state and federal circuit, through joint committees of lawyers and appellate judges, to examine the causes which limit the effectiveness of oral argument and to adopt measures to restore it to the position of importance which it ought to occupy in our system of jurisprudence.

13. The problem represented by "one-man" decisions on appeal should be made the subject of co-operative studies by the appellate bench and bar in the various jurisdictions.

14. Where no new principle or novel application of law is involved, and the decision is fully and clearly controlled by certain statutes or cases, an effort should be made to limit the opinions to a brief summary of the facts followed by a reference to such statutes or cases.

15. Findings of fact should have the same effect on appeal in all

cases tried by the court without a jury, whether they are cases at law or cases in equity.

16. Appellate courts should have power to enter or order the proper judgment without a new trial when the record of proceedings shows as a matter of law what such judgment should be; when errors affect only a part of a case, the court should only have power to remand for a new trial if such remand will not prejudice the substantial rights of any litigant.

This committee's recommendations are directed primarily at the simplification and general improvement of appellate practice. The most important points of dissatisfaction with the present methods of appellate review are indicated in order to determine the reforms to be prescribed. These general proposals were intended by their draftsmen to be subject to modification appropriate to local needs, since uniformity in these matters was thought to be neither necessary, practical, nor possible.

The recommendations relating to appellate practice are not followed in most states. Thus, pecuniary limits are not set on the right to appeal, papers on file in the trial court are not sent to the appellate court in their original form but copies are commonly required, a systematic effort has not been made by the bench and bar to aid in making oral argument more effective, etc.

The principal criticisms voiced in the various jurisdictions are directed at the existence of the many technicalities of the rules of procedure hampering appellate practice. The continued persistence of such technicalities, it is felt, makes very difficult the attainment of the goal of prompt, effective, and efficient service for the public. There is little evidence of action in the period since 1938 to remedy many of the glaring defects making appellate practice a burden.

In the survey of the situation relating to the adoption of the above minimum practical standards of judicial administration, it was found in 1950 that conformity to them had not been achieved in a single state.

New Jersey, with forty-four highest ratings—the best record of all the states—still had eighteen to go before attaining all standards. Most states had thirty-seven or more to go. New Jersey also took honors for the smallest number of "lowest" ratings, having only nine. The median for all states is twenty-one "lowest" ratings.

California ranks second after New Jersey in the rating based on subtracting the number of lowest ratings from the number of highest ratings. Next come Delaware, Iowa, Wisconsin, Colorado, Minnesota, and New Hampshire. Near the bottom are Kentucky, Nevada, Arkansas, and Mississippi, with Alabama at the very bottom.

THE REFORM OF JUDICIAL ADMINISTRATION

The function of a judicial council is to study and report on the administration of justice and to offer recommendations for improvement. It is a state agency created by the constitution or the legislature. Its powers do not go beyond advice and recommendation to the executive, legislature, and the courts. It serves also to inform the general public on the matters within its scope.

Prior to 1920 there were no judicial councils. As problems in the administration of justice became urgent, commissions were created to study these problems, and it was one of these commissions—in Massachusetts—that first suggested the etablishment of a permanent and continuously functioning body known as the judicial council. The first such council was formed in Ohio in 1921, with Massachusetts following in 1924. There are now some twenty-five.

Personnel of the typical judicial council includes members of the bar, representatives of various branches of the judiciary, sometimes a layman (commonly the chairman of the legislature's judiciary committees), and frequently the attorney-general of the state and a representative of the state law school. Appointment of members is usually made by the governor or the chief justice.

Duties of the council fall into three general categories: (1) collection of statistics on the work of the various courts of the state; (2) study of the problems of procedure with recommendations for necessary changes; and (3) study of the administration of the courts in terms of cost, promptness, and efficiency, with recommendations suggested by the study.

A study of the functioning of judicial councils was made by Maynard E. Pirsig, dean of the University of Minnesota's Law School, and published as a report of the Survey of the Legal Profession in 1952. Making allowances for the necessity of forming value judgments in such a survey and for the "disappointing" amount of response to his inquiries (less than 50 per cent), Dean Pirsig felt justified in concluding that the judicial council movement "has contributed substantially to improvement in the administration of justice." He broke this contribution down into four categories:

1. Many measures of improvement have been adopted as the result of judicial council efforts. These have been in the areas of procedure, court organization, and court administration.

2. They have provided the first substantial body of judicial statistics, particularly with respect to civil litigation, thus furnishing much helpful information about the workings of the judicial system.

3. Their reports have contributed a constantly increasing body of literature relating to the improvement of judicial administration.

4. They have provided an official tribunal to which the citizen can bring his complaint about the administration of justice, although it must be said that there is little evidence that the councils have been used to any substantial extent for this purpose.

The success of the councils has varied greatly from state to state, Pirsig found. In some, the judicial council is an active, going concern, making a sizable impact in the general movement for bringing about an efficient, improved administration of justice. These states include New York, Massachusetts, Washington, Connecticut, Kansas, and Texas. In a number of other states—including Michigan, Ohio, and Indiana—the work of the council has been substantial, but for reasons probably local to the states there has been limited success in adopting their reports. In a third group of states the contributions have been substantial in character but limited in terms of legislation or other change. These include Minnesota, North Dakota, and New Hampshire. Most of the remaining judicial councils appear to have made little contribution and are relatively inactive and ineffective.

Where the judicial councils have failed to measure up to the high hopes with which they were created, that failure can be attributed to such factors as the following:

1. Failure of the legislatures to provide even a minimum of the funds needed for proper functioning. Some of the councils receive no money whatever.

2. In consequence, such "starved" councils have lacked the staff needed for research, investigation, and operating expenses. Council members themselves are almost invariably uncompensated and are

engaged full time in other activity. This makes it essential that they be provided with competent assistance to carry on the necessary work.

3. Failure of the bench and bar to provide the necessary interest, support, and co-operation. There is a widespread ignorance on the part of the bar concerning even the existence of judicial councils. The reported proceedings of bar associations reflect little or no recognition or concern with them.

4. Public apathy and ignorance. The activities and recommendations do not receive much attention from the press or from the public when reported in the press.

5. Appointment of council members whose standing with the bar or community does not command the respect and prestige that are essential if the council's recommendations are to receive serious consideration.

6. Unwise recommendations on the part of the council and, often, mistakes in timing. A premature recommendation may arouse opposition and distrust of the council itself.

7. Substantial failure on the part of court officials and others to supply the council with necessary information.

Experience shows that creation of a judicial council does not of itself mean improvement in the administration of justice. The council must be composed of capable men of reputation, whose opinions and judgment are respected and who can thus muster support for their recommendations. It must have funds, a staff, and facilities with which to make the necessary study and investigation. Essential under any conditions is support both by the public and by the bench and bar.

There is no effective organization to speak the common opinions of the various judicial councils, Pirsig reported, and no uniform system of gathering or reporting statistical information about the courts which would make possible comparisons of litigation of one state with that of another.

The judicial council movement in the states represents a crystallization of public desire for improvement in the administration of justice, says Dean Pirsig. It is a halting and uncertain step, however, which in the majority of states has not been given the public backing, financial support, or bar indorsement needed to achieve its objectives.

In the meantime two major developments have occurred which necessitate a reconsideration of the place of the judicial council. One is the widespread granting of rule-making powers to the courts of the states and the United States, the desirability of which is no longer open to argument. This power has, of necessity, been implemented by the creation of advisory committees which have prepared the original rules and the subsequent modifications for submission to the courts.

The other is the development of administrative responsibility on the part of the courts. Both developments cover areas in which the judicial council was intended to be and has been active. In their respective spheres both these developments have been more successful than the councils. Where both exist, the function of the judicial council as previously conceived has been substantially reduced. Where they do not exist, the council continues to be a vital and necessary agency of reform and possibly a necessary step toward securing the adoption of these other measures.

Even where rule-making and administrative authority have been conferred on the courts, there is need for an agency such as a judicial council, Pirsig holds, for the granting of power is not alone a guaranty of performance. There is still the need for an agency having an official and independent status, representing the interests of the public as well as varied points of view and experience. Its duty would continue to be to study the judicial system, judge its results, and expose, fearlessly and boldly, any failure to conform to expected standards of judicial administration.

Such a body, under these conditions, would be relieved of technical details and could confine itself to the broader and more fundamental aspects of the administration of justice. It would continue to be an advisory body, the success of which would depend on the capacity of its personnel to command respect, on the thoroughness of its studies, and on adequate support from the profession and the public.

"The high purpose of our courts is to administer justice impartially, in accordance with the basic precepts of our democracy and with a minimum of cost and delay," Pirsig concludes. "Experience has shown that . . . each judicial system should contain: 1) a conference of its judges meeting as often as need requires; 2) an administrative office to manage the business and administrative aspects of the system; 3) power in the courts to prescribe the rules of procedure, aided by an advisory committee; and 4) a judicial council ever watchful that the administration of justice is maintained at the highest level."

CHAPTER VI

Legal Education

"Spoon-feeding" versus "sink or swim." Internship versus more university training. Legal theory versus tools-of-the-trade instruction. Strict case method versus emphasis on other lawyer craft skills. Current curriculums versus adoption of new and different approaches to legal learning.

These are some of the controversial questions still plaguing the professionals in the field of legal education. But about four issues there appears to be near-universal agreement: legal training begins at birth and continues until retirement; all knowledge is properly a part of legal education; lawyers are deficient in the things they should know and in the things they need to know; and it is impossible for the law schools to do all that is expected of them.

The fundamental question in any analysis of legal education relates to the objectives of that education. That much is clear. But any attempt at an answer is, at the very least, a hazardous undertaking. For this, the Survey has turned to the experts who have already formulated statements on the subject.

"In the last analysis," said the group which made a 1949 California study, "legal education has two related objectives—the training of lawyers, and the improvement of the law. The latter objective in particular requires not merely that poor law schools be eliminated, but that the best law schools be made better." And said the special committee of Harvard Law School: "A university law school has two purposes, (1) to train men for the legal profession; (2) to provide a center where scholars may contribute to an understanding of law and government and may participate creatively in their growth and improvement."

To these must be added the objectives of training the future legal practitioner to solve not only the problems of individual clients but of the society in which he lives, and of providing many, if not most, public leaders at all levels of authority.

Law-school education by itself is inadequate for the fulfilment of these objectives. Without further tutoring, the training which enables the student to become a member of the bar does not equip him even to meet the needs of his clients, let alone his additional public responsibilities. Law schools can and must be improved, and much can be done in the field of nonuniversity legal education. But there are no rough-and-ready solutions.

FROM THE INNS OF COURT TO THE LAW CENTERS

Summarized in two volumes and nineteen articles, the Survey reports on education were prepared under the direction of Albert J. Harno, dean of the College of Law at the University of Illinois. Harno is also responsible for the principal report on the subject, and his *Legal Education in the United States* bids well to become the landmark work in the field.

"Our English Heritage" is a stock title for the opening chapter of most commentaries on the law and the legal profession, and it is with this theme that Harno's book and the legal education story properly begin. It starts in an England where preparation for the practice of law has been, in the main, either through apprenticeship training or through the Inns of Court. And it begins with a traditional English emphasis on severely practical learning. which has had a profound effect on American legal education, the evolution of our legal institutions, and our outlook on law.

While legal training in the United States, as in Europe, gravitated to the universities, the nature of American legal education has largely met the pattern set in England. In the great Continental centers of legal learning, law has long been taught as a science and analyzed in the setting of its interelationship with the humanities and the social sciences (with extended apprenticeship afterward). But only in recent days has such a program been advocated for the education of the American lawyer.

In 1753 William Blackstone received his appointment as a law lecturer at Oxford and began his lifework of establishing a "system of legal education." In that he failed. However, his failures in England have been equaled by success in the United States, where, from the beginning, legal education has been influenced by his works and ideas.

It did not all happen at once. Under the common law the attention of lawyers is naturally centered on what the judges say and do and, even more important, on how they are likely to decide a case in current dispute. It is this which tended to focus the interest of common-law lawyers on the study of particulars and make them skeptical of the broad training in the law at the universities.

It was not until the 1870's and the initiation of the case method by Harvard's Christopher Columbus Langdell that Blackstone's proposals for law study under full-time law teachers began to be accepted as the best path to the bar. The instruction itself, however, was far different from the broad educational pattern envisioned by Blackstone. It was, in a sense, a return to the system pursued by the Inns of Court; it was a system restricted to the study of judge-made law, isolating the student from all other sources of legal knowledge. There was no question but that it was an improvement over the English scheme, since it was being given at the universities; it was at the same time a system rooted in English methodology and unique to the Anglo-American law.

Even as many of their descendants today, the American colonists looked upon all lawyers with suspicion and distrust. This can be attributed in part to a seemingly natural reaction characteristic of all pioneer societies, but it must also be blamed upon the character of those who called themselves "attorneys." According to one history, they were mostly frauds or minor court officers, such as deputy sheriffs, clerks, and justices, who stirred up litigation for the sake of the petty court fees. Their preparation was desultory, largely through inadequate apprenticeship, and it was not until the 1760's that there was any real development of a profession worthy of the name.

In the late 1700's and early 1800's the profession was in a ferment which was to result in a truly remarkable change in the attitude and outlook of lawyers toward law and legal education. Lawyers became enlightened leaders in public affairs; they wrote the Declaration of Independence and the Constitution; they also started to read books. Lawyer leaders studied Grotius, Pufendorf, Vattel, Hume, Montesquieu, the *Institutes* of Justinian, and—above all —Blackstone's *Commentaries.*

Blackstone's influence, as previously noted, also resulted in the establishment of chairs of law at several American colleges and universities—at William and Mary in 1779 and at the College of Philadelphia in 1790. From 1793 to 1797 and again after 1823, the great James Kent taught law at Columbia College, and in 1815 Chief Justice Isaac Parker of Massachusetts became the first law professor at Harvard. Important as these early teachers were in laying the groundwork for the future, the educational route to the bar was still through office apprenticeships.

But the first American law school was an outgrowth of this apprenticeship training. It was the Litchfield Law School of Connecticut, operated by Tapping Reeve from 1784 to 1833 as a school without any university affiliation. It was the forerunner of several score of so-called "independent" law schools which have had so great an impact on the evolution of legal education. Other, similar law schools soon sprang up, but most of them were short lived, and none achieved the reputation of Litchfield. They were all-important. They bridged the gap between the students who wished to obtain systematized instruction in the law and the colleges that were not as yet prepared to give it.

To Harvard goes the credit for establishing America's first university school of law. When Chief Justice Parker left the Massachusetts bench in 1815 to become the school's first professor, he found that his assignment neither embraced nor envisioned the establishment of a system of legal education. But in his very first lecture he spoke of the importance of teaching legal science in the colleges and proposed that "a school for the instruction of resident graduates in jurisprudence be ingrafted on [his] professorship," and two years later Harvard Law School became a reality. Some years later (by 1826), Yale Law School was in full operation.

Law-school growth and development in the period prior to 1870 was poor—qualitatively and quantitatively. In 1850 there were but fifteen university law schools in the United States; in 1860 the number was only twenty-one; and in 1870 it was only thirty-one. Some of the schools were in operation only a few years; others gave intermittent instruction before achieving permanent status; some, like those at Columbia University and the University of Pennsylvania, grew on the foundations of the old chairs of law which had since ceased to exist. Instruction was "little more than an expanded form of office apprenticeship training."

The lawyers of those days were reluctant to accept the idea of university training. They "clung tenaciously," Harno reported, "to the notion that legal education was nothing more than the mastering of a craft, the skills for which had to be passed on from the practitioner to the novice." Worse than that, the public seemed to have great doubts as to whether the lawyer's trade should even be distinguished as a craft. Jacksonian democracy was the order of the times; there was no respect for formal education or for educational prerequisites for admission to the bar; all male citizens, it would seem, had an inherent right to practice law.

But the seemingly insurmountable obstacles which confronted the university law schools at the threshold of their existence were to be gradually whittled away. And the chief whittler was Associate Justice Joseph Story of the United States Supreme Court, who transformed Harvard Law School into a famous institution of learning and shaped the character of university legal education in America for years to come. Already a distinguished jurist when he was elected Dane Professor of Law in 1829, Story continued his great career on the bench while he taught.

Story scored the narrowness of the legal instruction then being given and pointed up the need for both a knowledge of the principles of law and a broad study "liberalized by philosophy and a large intercourse with the wisdom of ancient and modern times." This did not mean that the Harvard Law School of the 1830's and 1840's was to embark upon a curriculum combining law with liberal arts and social sciences. As much as he believed in the importance of liberal education, Story felt that it must somehow be obtained elsewhere—prior to training in the law.

This was in itself a revolutionary idea and an important one. But Story did far more than merely cite the need for prelegal education. What he did for the training of the lawyer was to define the role to be played by nontechnical studies in legal education and to delineate what should be taught in the law schools. More than that, he put a faltering educational institution on its feet and gave it the impetus which not only was to lead it to distinction but was to make it the nation's law-school model. He made the decisions which were to set the traditional attitudes of university law schools on such matters as local law, legislation, and criminal law. And through the extraordinary productiveness of his scholarship, he set an example which has guided all future generations of teachers of law to do research and publish works in their field.

The year 1870 marks a merger between the past and present of legal education. After nearly a century of training American lawyers in America, said Hurst in *The Growth of American Law,* "events now demanded of the bar knowledge and skills not within the sonorous phrases of the 'constitutional lawyer' of mid-century or the black-letter learning of the conveyancer." The schools now made their first moves toward the establishment of liberal education prerequisites for admission to law study; bar associations were organized for the first time on an other than social basis and were to exert tremendous influence upon the scope of legal learning; and Langdell became Dane Professor of Law at Harvard.

THE CASE METHOD

What Langdell did was to "discover" the case method—a system of teaching legal science through a study of carefully selected judicial decisions, classified and arranged to present both the evolution and the present validity of the essential doctrines of the law. In its principles and outlines it has remained to this day the prevailing system of teaching and learning law, but it has long since ceased to be the all-absorbing educational method conceived by its founder.

Langdell joined the Harvard faculty in January, 1870, and in September of that year was appointed to the newly created office of dean of the Law School, a post which he held for twenty-five years. His basic educational theories were set forth in the Preface of his first casebook, *A Selection of Cases on the Law of Contracts,* published in 1871. Here is what Langdell wrote:

> Law, considered as a science, consists of certain principles or doctrines. To have such mastery of these as to be able to apply them with constant facility and certainty to the ever-tangled skein of human affairs, is what constitutes a true lawyer; and hence to acquire that mastery should be

the business of every earnest student of law. Each of these doctrines has arrived at its present state by slow degrees; in other words, it is a growth, extending in many cases through centuries. This growth is to be traced in the main through a series of cases; and much the shortest and best, if not the only way of mastering the doctrine effectually is by studying the cases in which it is embodied. But the cases which are useful and necessary for this purpose at the present day bear an exceedingly small proportion to all that have been reported. The vast majority are useless, and worse than useless, for any purpose of systematic study. Moreover, the number of fundamental legal doctrines is much less than is commonly supposed; the many different guises in which the same doctrine is constantly making its appearance, and the great extent to which legal treatises are a repetition of each other, being a cause of much misapprehension. If these doctrines could be so classified and arranged that each should be found in its proper place, and nowhere else, they would cease to be formidable from their number.

What the study of law by the case method should do for the student has been summarized by Edmund M. Morgan, formerly of Harvard and now of Vanderbilt University, in another Survey report. The student, he says, becomes acquainted with the characteristic problems that arise in the different fields of the law and with the fundamental principles upon which the courts rely or purport to rely in solving them. He also finds the system valuable as a study of the methods which judges and lawyers use (1) in analyzing a factual situation, separating the legally material elements from the legally immaterial; (2) in eliminating, so far as possible, the emotional and superficially relevant elements; and (3) in reaching such a decision as in their opinion should be reached in any case in the foreseeable future presenting the same problem, regardless of the persons involved or the magnitude of the amount in controversy or the passing prejudices of the community.

However, Morgan goes on to say, "of course, the same objectives could be accomplished by other methods of instruction, and, of course, they could fail of accomplishment under the case method. Much, if not everything, depended and still depends upon the instructor and his capacity to arouse in the student an enthusiasm for the subject and a strong determination to get to the vitals of each problem, and to accept no solution on the mere say-so of the instructor or of a text-writer or of a single judge or of a particular court."

Under the influence of Langdell and his disciples—notably James Barr Ames and William A. Keener—the case system grew to become the basic method of instruction in virtually every law school in the country. But its position of pre-eminence now appears to be on the wane. Reporting to the Survey on legal education in Pennsylvania, Lon Fuller had this to say: "Taking the Pennsylvania schools as a whole, good case-method instruction is a rarity. In this I do not think they are different from other law schools, including our most famous, for I am convinced that there is a decline in the use of the case method over the country as a whole."

Even at its best the case method has been subjected to serious criticisms. One is that the system is highly time-consuming and that thus only a very small proportion of even judge-made law can be covered by a study of the cases themselves. Another is the fact that after the first year at law school there is a distinct lack of interest on the part of students in reading cases.

Most of the criticisms of the case method are not so much directed at its intrinsic merits as against making such study the sole approach to legal education. Compaints are heard that the case programs are lacking in perspective as to the scope and implications of the law and as to the problems the lawyer must solve in practice; that the programs fail to provide a synthesis of the law itself and a synthesis of law with other fields of learning; that they fail to inculcate in students any understanding of professional standards and ideals; and that they neglect training in the practical craft skills which the "practical" lawyer must have to supplement his case skills.

Happily, many of the criticisms have been answered by the developments which have been made in the case method. Langdell believed that a casebook should contain a chosen number of leading or influential cases and, apparently, nothing more. His selections, once they had passed the test of having made a contribution to the growth of essential legal doctrines, were presented chronologically under conceptual headings. The cases were unedited and almost devoid of note citations.

Today, the author of a casebook is a critical editor. The unessentials of selected cases are chopped away; statements of fact in the reports are replaced by shortened restatements; and footnotes amplify and expand the judicial comment in the decisions. But, more than that, there is added to the cases text discussions, legislation, administrative rulings and regulations, excerpts from law-review articles, legal forms, and even nonlegal material having a bearing on the relationship between law and society.

Current stress is pragmatic, and selected cases deal with the contemporary culture in which the student lives and in which he will practice law. The conceptual classifications have been retained but in an expanded form to permit the treatment of such matters as taxation, administrative law, labor law, etc., which were unthought of in Langdell's time. Some are even doing away with present classifications, reorganizing their materials to stress the policy needs of society. And historical, sociological, and even psychological data are now considered in the law-school classrooms as part of the training for the bar.

Despite all the criticisms, there is still no substitute for the case method. To solve the problems which constantly confront him, says Morgan, the lawyer must have "a capacity to think hard and straight, a settled determination to accept the *ipse dixit* of no man or group of men, the ability to make a searching analysis of a complicated state of facts which will disclose the legal problem involved therein, a resourceful imagination to discover possible solutions, the patience to investigate their validity and practicability, and the courage to form and act upon his own considered judgment. No method of instruction," he concludes, "has been or will ever be discovered that will enable any law school in three or four short years to equip him with these qualities and capacities. But experience has shown that the best available method of giving him a sure foundation for the acquisition is the case method."

LIBERAL EDUCATION FOR LAWYERS

While much has been said about the need for liberal education in the training of the lawyer, little attention has been paid to the specific nature of that education. These matters are dealt with in a comprehensive Survey report on "The Materials of Law Study" by Brainerd Currie, formerly of the University of California at Los Angeles, now of the University of Chicago.

Blackstone, it will be remembered, was a strong advocate of

liberal education for the lawyer and believed that, either prior to or concurrently with the study of law, the prospective barrister should acquire "a knowledge of the classics, of logic, of philosophy, of ethics, and of Roman law." Although most educators, confronted by overcrowded curriculums, urged the former approach, Thomas Jefferson propounded the latter. In creating and directing legal training at William and Mary and the University of Virginia, he was outspoken against any general education prerequisites to the privilege of practicing law. Jefferson saw law as a branch of government and the course of legal study as essentially embracing constitutional law, political economy, and legislation. Further, he believed in a law curriculum so organized that legal education could, if desired, be pursued concurrently with other university studies.

Pressure from vocationally minded students and the growing mass of strictly legal materials gradually crowded "political" subjects from the Virginia course of study. By 1851 the process of elimination was substantially complete, and such courses as history and political economy had been definitely committed to the nonprofessional departments of the university. And questions dealing with the concurrent pursuit of liberal and legal studies became largely academic with the establishment of educational requirements for admission to law school.

Recent years, however, have seen a revival of Jeffersonian thinking—though it is certainly not described as such—in the plans to integrate law and the social studies. The primary developments in this direction, Currie says, were at Columbia and Yale in the latter part of the nineteenth century. "Columbia," he says, "restored the identification of law and politics which had characterized the early Virginia establishments, and Yale anticipated the functional course construction and the reliance on social studies which characterize the modern integration movement." Neither law school, however, reorganized its curriculum to permit anything approaching an integrated course of study, and, while quasi-legal subjects were taught, the basic instructional pattern followed traditional lines.

Even the exhaustive studies undertaken by the Columbia law faculty from 1926 to 1928 did little to effect the advocated curriculum reform, but they did accomplish much to clarify thinking on the subject. Characterizing these studies as "the most comprehensive and searching investigation of law-school objectives and methods ever undertaken," Currie sets forth the fundamental thesis which emerged as follows:

> Since law is a means of social control, it ought to be studied as such. Solutions to the problems of a changing social order are not implicit in the rules and principles which are formally elaborated on the basis of past decisions, to be evoked by merely formal logical processes; and effective legal education cannot proceed in disregard of this fact. If men are to be trained for intelligent and effective participation in legal processes, and if law schools are to perform their function of contributing through research to the improvement of law administration, the formalism which confines the understanding and criticism of law within limits fixed by history and authority must be abandoned, and every available resource of knowledge and judgment must be brought to the task.

Satisfying the objectives of such a thesis would require a drastic retooling of the entire program of legal education as presently constituted. This has yet to be done at any school of law. Columbia did proceed almost at once to put its program into practice, reorganizing courses along functional lines, reinforcing the faculty by the appointment of specialists in philosophy, business, and political science, and plunging with prodigious industry into reoriented research and the preparation of new course materials. However, within a very few years, the pace of reform moderated at Columbia, and, while other schools have attempted to put similar programs into operation, the course of development has been decidedly irregular. As Currie puts it: "The main stream of legal education flows on much as before. . . . There are still courses in Contracts, Torts, Property, and Trusts, retaining their old names and shapes; and even in those courses which have been revamped and renamed the appellate decision is the focus of study still. Law and the social sciences remain unintegrated."

As far as the future is concerned, the report to the Survey forecasts the eventual enrichment of law-school curriculums by the infusion of materials other than the traditional cases, statutes, and texts. Notwithstanding the disappointments of the past, there are those who persist in experimentation, and slowly the materials for an integrated approach to the study of law accumulate. More and more courses are being given in "Law and Society." But many questions still face this group of "reformers": Precisely what nonlegal materials are required? How are they to be found and assimilated? Who is to prepare them for classroom use and teach them effectively? And how is room for them to be found in an already overcrowded curriculum?

The Survey of the Legal Profession has no ready answers to these questions. The campaigns for integrated programs have met with jeers as well as applause, and the desirability of integration is far from a settled issue. However, explorations have been made into the subject, and the facts have been reported to the bar and to the public. And, as steps are taken to implement Survey findings and obtain responses to Survey questions, much will eventually be accomplished in determining the appropriate materials for law study.

THE PRESENT STATUS OF THE SCHOOLS OF LAW

One of the basic studies made by the Survey was that of "Law Schools in the United States." It was begun by John G. Hervey (adviser to the American Bar Association's Section of Legal Education and Admissions to the Bar) as assistant to Harno, was carried on by a corps of distinguished lawyers and law teachers who personally inspected the several law schools, and is being completed by Lowell S. Nicholson, formerly dean of Northeastern University Law School. Some of the inspectors' findings are contained in Harno's *Legal Education in the United States* and special reports by Elliott E. Cheatham, of Columbia Law School; Dean Lon L. Fuller, of Harvard Law School; and Dean John W. Morland, of Valparaiso School of Law.

The inspectors found several disappointing factors. One observer went so far as to say that, "of the nine schools I inspected, six showed no impact of the modern world whatsoever." Other commentators were fortunately more kind. Here is one basic observation cited by Harno:

> Law schools fall roughly into three broad categories. One, those which are doing an inadequate job and which do not give value received to the students in exchange for their tuition; two, schools which perform the routine work of basic legal instruction well enough but which are completely orthodox and conventional in their outlook; and three, schools which not only perform their tasks of basic instruction, but which also are constantly alert for new opportunities and are continually attempting to extend the field of their influence.

The schools in the second category are, of course, by far the most numerous.

Most of the advances made in legal education over the last twenty-five years are described in the Hervey Report as "mechanical and pedestrian." They include substantial elimination of the commercial schools of law, run primarily for profit; the increase of prelegal requirements from two to three years; some increase in graduation requirements; and some quantitative improvements in school facilities. But there is much criticism of the progress made through misguided emphasis on such quantitative standards as specified periods of prelaw and law study, size of law libraries, minimum size of law faculties, and the like. Several of the inspectors have pointed out that such standards are presently yielding diminishing returns. The emphasis must now be shifted, they believe, to the criterion of quality. This means the modernizing of old courses, the raising of qualitative standards for admission to and graduation from law schools, and higher requirements for membership in the bar.

One of the first criticisms directed against the law schools was their own failure to work on the problems of legal education. Searching analyses, such as those made by Columbia from 1926 to 1928 and by Harvard in 1947, have been rare undertakings. A minor fraction of the law schools have committees on curriculum, and still fewer have committees on educational aims and objectives.

Another common complaint of the inspectors was that the schools are inadequately financed. One observer expressed the view that the principal difficulties in legal education can all be traced to an insufficiency of funds. Programs involving seminars, legal writing, organized research, etc., must be conducted with small groups of students. Such efforts, therefore, require a higher ratio of faculty members to students than is found in most American law schools. The conclusion is that law schools must eventually come to be heavily subsidized.

Several of the observers also laid stress on the fact that law-school classes are far too large. Size, they claimed, precludes adequate counseling of students, giving profitable written exercises, and proper supervision of individual efforts. This complaint was described by the inspectors as another aspect of inadequate financing, coupled with constant pressure to "mass-produce" lawyers on a low-budget basis.

Overcrowded law-school curriculums provided another basic criticism. Unduly heavy course loads were attributed to (1) the addition of new courses in growing fields of the law, such as taxation, trade regulation, administrative law, and labor law; (2) attempts to broaden the perspective of legal education by offering instruction in law and the economic order, welfare legislation, comparative law, legal history, etc.; and (3) responses to demands that law courses be made more practical by the addition of such subjects as legal writing, legal drafting, legislation, and accounting.

For the student who seeks a comprehensive program of instruction, little or nothing has been accomplished by the addition of new subjects of study. If he takes one particular course, he must forego another. Nothing important has been done toward solving this problem beyond some preliminary progress in course consolidation and in setting up compulsory "core courses" covering the work of the first two years.

Three approaches to a real solution have been advocated. The first is a complete reorganization of current curriculums, involving drastic measures of consolidation and elimination. The second is a fusion of prelegal and legal work in order to make more practical and efficient use of the years spent in study prior to entering law school. The third—and least desirable—is the extension of the period of legal training beyond the orthodox three years. Nine schools (exclusive of several that have introduced four-year programs following only two years of prelegal work) already have lengthened their programs, some to three years and a semester, some to three and one-third years, and some to three years and an eight-week summer session.

Additional and more detailed comments and criticisms appeared in the reports submitted to the Survey by individual inspectors. Cheatham found notable recent progress in the full-time law schools of Tennessee. However, while arguing that there should be good part-time legal education for the able students who are unable to attend full-time schools, he criticized part-time law schools in Tennessee as being "inadequate to the responsibilities they have assumed to prepare men for the bar."

Dean Morland made similar observations following his inspection of the law schools of Georgia. Three schools in that state have been approved by the American Bar Association, and he found that all three not only were well above minimum standards but also were making notable progress. The situation was quite different in the unapproved, part-time schools. While their work was characterized as substantially higher in quality than is presently required for admission to the Georgia bar examination, Dean Morland concluded that the "four schools which require only three nights a week of instruction for twenty or twenty-one months find it impossible to give adequate legal training in that period of time."

The most favorable commentary on the status of legal education appears in Fuller's report on the Pennsylvania law schools. The study points up successes in the elimination of inferior schools, the raising of bar standards in terms both of educational requirements and of moral qualifications, and even a restriction on the number of would-be attorneys admitted to the bar so as to prevent "overcrowding." Fuller concluded that progressive lawyers and the teaching profession in many states would feel that their chief aims had been achieved if they could equal the educational record made in Pennsylvania.

But that state has its own share of educational problems. The severity of bar examinations has led to a predominant orientation of student interest toward the facts of Pennsylvania law and Pennsylvania practice, at the expense of more analytical training, in all the schools except the University of Pennsylvania. Educational costs are high, and there is not adequate aid for talented students lacking means. Despite the general excellence of instruction, Fuller found all too many evidences of poor teaching, largely due to a lack of adequate preparation on the part of the professors. He found good case-method instruction a rarity and criticized the extent of law teaching given by lecture.

THE "PROBLEM CHILDREN" OF LEGAL EDUCATION

The Survey issued two special reports on the "problem children" in the field of legal education. The first is devoted to the metropolitan law schools which offer part-time evening instruction in addition to regular day sessions. The second is concerned with correspondence law schools.

Opinions such as those of Cheatham's that "it is, of course, impossible to have a part-time division do the same kind of work as a full-time division, unless the full-time division is pulled down" are not shared by Dean Lowell S. Nicholson of Boston's Northeastern University School of Law. Admitting that his views are contrary to those of many legal educators, Nicholson contends that schools with both day and evening divisions *try* to apply the same standards and requirements to both sessions—and, in a large measure, achieve their purpose without lowering the quality of the full-time training. Yet he admits that there is some disparity. The solution obviously must be found in raising the standards of the evening divisions.

Part of the disparity is met by the universal requirement that evening students pursue a four-year course rather than the usual three years. In addition, Nicholson observed that "the greater maturity and purposefulness of the students in the evening division have made them, in spite of their lack of time, . . . equal to the full-time students," resulting in the fact that "in a great many instances the evening grades have been higher than the day grades in the same examination."

In a number of statistical studies prepared in conjunction with his report, Nicholson found a "high extent of identity" between the day and evening requirements of the two-division law schools, without any apparent reduction in day standards. Graduation requirements were the same to the extent of 90 per cent, and admission requirements were the same to the extent of 80 per cent. There was an identity quotient of more than 70 per cent in the composition of law faculties, the lists both of required courses and of electives, and grade requirements. Only in the field of legal research was there a serious deficiency in the training offered in the evening divisions, the pressure of time forestalling adequate instruction in legal bibliography, moot court, legal writing, and the like.

This does not mean that part-time legal education at night is an adequate substitute for full-time day training. In the law there is no substitute for work, and evening students unquestionably cannot devote the same amount of alert, concentrated effort to their studies as the more fortunate future attorneys in the day divisions. The reports of Cheatham and Morland—among others—point up deficiencies and call for a concerted effort to raise the standards of the part-time schools.

Criticisms that the bulk of evening training consists of "spoon-fed" information necessary for passing bar examinations must be met by providing effective programs of legal research demanding week-end labors in the library. But this is only the beginning. Evening schools offering instruction only three nights a week must consider the advisability of classes every night and, if necessary, on Saturdays. Assignments must be made more comprehensive and, unfortunately, more difficult. Working students should be encouraged and assisted in attempts to secure quasi-legal employment in law offices, banks, insurance companies, etc., but advised to keep outside work to a minimum. And time must be set aside for extra guidance and counseling for night students, to assist them in getting an integrated picture of the law.

Despite the criticisms, however, the bar is generally agreed that evening legal education should be available, and there is a real hope that, with continued progress in raising part-time standards, the criticisms will disappear.

But the bar has been far more critical in its appraisal and evaluation of the correspondence law schools. In his Survey report, Elbridge B. Pierce, of the Illinois bar, concludes that "the need, the justification, and the value of the correspondence school in the limited field of legal education have definitely ended."

Only twenty-five years ago, thirty-one states and the District of Columbia failed to specify where or how the years of study for admission to the bar should be spent, and three states specifically mentioned correspondence schools as acceptable. Today, only four states—California, Georgia, Mississippi, and Montana—unqualifiedly recognize correspondence courses as suitable legal preparation. Several other states accept this training if pursued in addition to study under a practicing lawyer, but such acceptance differs little from the provisions which still prevail in some states for law-office study.

There are only three correspondence law schools left in the United States, all of which have their headquarters in Chicago.

The American Extension School of Law and the Blackstone College of Law give legal instruction only, while the La Salle Extension University offers courses in many fields. The schools obtain a large proportion of their students through national advertising in newspapers and magazines. The advertising itself has been subjected to much criticism, and the Federal Trade Commission has issued complaints against both Blackstone College and La Salle University for the alleged extravagance of their claims.

Notwithstanding the fact that their texts contain a great deal of good legal material which is undoubtedly absorbed by the students, the correspondence schools suffer badly by comparison with regular day or evening schools in the bar-examination records. Extensive classroom discussions and, perhaps even more important, constant discussions among the students themselves are unavoidably absent in the correspondence courses. In addition, there is necessarily an absence of training in the clear, accurate, and original legal thinking which marks every good—or even adequate—law school. A study of the California bar-examination scores from 1932 to 1949 shows only 13.3 per cent of the correspondence-school alumni passing the bar the first time. This must be compared with the record of 73.8 per cent achieved by graduates of schools approved by the American Bar Association and the 51.7 per cent record of alumni from nonapproved schools. The part-time law schools showed a passing score of 37.2 per cent. Recent statistics are very sketchy for Georgia, Mississippi, and Montana, but what little data are available show nearly 100 per cent failures among correspondence-school students taking the bar examinations for the first time.

THE MODEL LAW CENTER

Jumping from legal education at its worst to legal education at its best is a jump from the correspondence law school to a modern law center. A well-established, recognized, and accredited law school, with a competent faculty and comprehensive library, is the heart of a legal center. But the center is much more. It is a well-supported physical plant, designed to enable law students, professors, and practicing attorneys to eat and work together in an atmosphere of study—striving toward the accomplishment of certain set objectives in the legal world. In short, law centers are "modern Inns of Court," in the best traditions of those sixteenth-century Inns.

New York University and Southern Methodist University completed new buildings to house their study programs in 1950 and 1951. Thirteen additional law schools have reported to the Survey on plans and progress leading toward their own law centers. Their objectives will, of course, vary with local conditions and demands. However, investigations by Dean Robert G. Storey of Southern Methodist University School of Law disclose a number of purposes common to all of them. These include (1) continuing education for the bar; (2) improving the administration of justice; (3) advancing legal research; (4) providing free legal aid and low-cost legal services; and (5) improving the sponsoring law schools.

And, in meeting these objectives, it is significant that the centers are attempting to bridge the gap in approach between the legal educator and the practicing attorney, co-ordinating the efforts of law schools, bar associations, lawyers, and informed laymen to advance the administration of justice.

Some professional educators have criticized the law center for encouraging practicing attorneys to co-operate in training the lawyers-to-be. Practicing lawyers, these critics believe, are too pragmatic in their outlook, and their "practical approach" is a step backward toward the old days of apprenticeship and "training at the expense of learning." There is something to be said for this argument. The history of legal education in the United States is in large measure a record of the development away from law-office instruction under practicing attorneys to comprehensive university training under skilled professional educators. There is no desire to reverse that trend. Further, the professionals are always wary that the addition of "practical" courses like legal drafting might displace instruction in jurisprudence, law and society, and the like.

Actually the professionals need have little worry on this score. Practicing attorneys—especially in recent years—have been aware of the necessary educational requisites for the bar and, through the various bar associations, have exerted pressure for higher standards all along the line.

THE ORGANIZED BAR SETS THE STANDARDS

It is impossible to recount the full influence of the organized bar in the education field. But much can be said about the accomplishments of the acknowledged leader in this field, the American Bar Association. From its very first meeting on August 31, 1878, to sessions which are undoubtedly being held as this book is being read, the ABA has been instrumental in setting the goals to be achieved in training for the bar. Since 1900 the ABA has had a partner—the Association of American Law Schools—and these two professional organizations can even boast of being ahead of the schools themselves in the matter of quantitative standards of legal education.

The word "quantitative" deserves special comment. Inherent in the word are the greatest successes of the ABA and the AALS—and their greatest failure. For the efforts of these professional associations have been largely devoted to achieving measurable standards: required years of prelegal study, years of law study, numbers of books in libraries, numbers of full-time teachers, etc.

When improvements in legal education were first sought, these were probably the only yardsticks that could have been employed. Now, however, the emphasis must be shifted to the *quality* of legal education—quality of content of education and quality, of both mind and character, of individuals admitted to the bar. This qualitative approach is still in its infancy.

Reporting to the Survey on "The Professional Associations and Legal Education," Russell N. Sullivan, of the University of Illinois, laid stress on the development of a progressive attitude of the ABA in the education field. One of the first resolutions presented to the association in 1879 by its newly formed Committee on Legal Education and Admissions to the Bar called upon state and local bar groups to further "the maintenance, by public authority, of schools of law, *provided with faculties of at least four well paid and efficient teachers,* and whose diploma [should], upon being unanimously granted, after a full and fair written examination, be *essential* as a qualification for practicing law." This was supplemented by a resolution requesting the local associations to work toward attendance requirements of three years of law-school study "as a *qualification* for *examination* to be admitted to the bar." Another resolution dealt with recommendations as to law-school curriculums, advocating a course of instruction which would include, among other things, moral and political philosophy, legal history, international law, comparative jurisprudence, and political economy.

Although the three-year course of study was not to become a reality until much later in most of the law schools, the clear statement of the association (which adopted a resolution favoring it in 1881) contributed much toward the development of such a requirement. It is also important to note that the ABA committee recognized in its resolutions that it could not implement the recommendations made and that this could be accomplished only by the state and local bar associations. This principle, Sullivan pointed out, has guided the American Bar Association in all its attempts to aid in the improvement of legal education.

After more than a decade of relative inactivity, the association in 1893 dissolved the committee and created a Section of Legal Education and Admissions to the Bar. This gave educators their own separate forum to consider law-school problems and their own organization for raising educational standards. On the heels of a resolution in 1899 to consider "what action, if any, [should] be taken to bring the reputable law schools of the country into closer relations with each other and with the Section of Legal Education," law-school representatives were invited to attend the annual ABA meeting in 1900. At this meeting the Association of American Law Schools was organized.

Membership in the new association was open to schools which (1) required high-school graduation for admission; (2) owned a library containing the reports of the United States Supreme Court and those of the highest court of its state; and (3) stipulated that its law course extended over at least two academic years of thirty weeks each, with students attending classes at least ten hours per week. These standards were, of course, very low, but they were still sufficiently high to limit membership, and the AALS soon modified the first requirement to provide that, "as a general rule," applicants for admission be high-school graduates. But, by 1905, the AALS demanded that the law course be lengthened to three years as a condition of membership.

One of the most important advances in the cause of legal education occurred in 1921 when the ABA itself took positive steps. It adopted a resolution setting forth standards, which remained substantially the same until 1950. Elihu Root, a former ABA president and former Secretary of State, moved the adoption, and his motion was seconded by the then Chief Justice of the United States, William Howard Taft. The resolution warrants reprinting:

Resolved, (1) The American Bar Association is of the opinion that every candidate for admission to the Bar should give evidence of graduation from a law school complying with the following standards:

(*a*) It shall require as a condition of admission at least two years of study in a college.

(*b*) It shall require its students to pursue a course of three years' duration if they devote substantially all of their working time to their studies, and a longer course, equivalent in the number of working hours, if they devote only part of their working time to their studies.

(*c*) It shall provide an adequate library available for the use of the students.

(*d*) It shall have among its teachers a sufficient number giving their entire time to the school to insure actual personal acquaintance and influence with the whole student body.

(2) The American Bar Association is of the opinion that graduation from a law school should not confer the right of admission to the bar, and that every candidate should be subjected to an examination by public authority to determine his fitness.

(3) The Council on Legal Education and Admissions to the Bar is directed to publish from time to time the names of those law schools which comply with the above standards and of those which do not, and to make such publications available so far as possible to intending law students.

(4) The president of the Association and the Council on Legal Education and Admissions to the Bar are directed to cooperate with the state and local bar associations to urge upon the duly constituted authorities of the several states the adoption of the above requirements for admission to the Bar.

(5) The Council on Legal Education and Admissions to the Bar is directed to call a conference on legal education in the name of the American Bar Association, to which the state and local associations shall be invited to send delegates for the purpose of uniting the bodies represented in an effort to create conditions favorable to the adoption of the principles above set forth.

Further, the AALS, in 1921, amended its articles so that, as a condition of membership, a school had to require, by 1923, one year of prelegal college work—two years by 1925.

In 1923 the ABA published its first list of "approved" law schools. It contained the names of thirty-nine schools then complying with all the association's standards and nine additional schools which were expected to comply in the near future. It is significant to note that, of the thirty-nine approved institutions, twenty-seven had not been complying when the standards were adopted a scant two years before. Subsequent years saw AALS action stipulating numbers of teachers, minimum lawbook collections, and tightened standards in prelegal studies.

Both the ABA Section and the AALS soon realized that it was impossible to act wisely in approving law schools without personal inspections and that such inspections could not be carried on by volunteers. Beginning in 1927, advisers on the ABA staff traveled about the country not only making formal inspections and assisting law schools with their problems but also urging state and local bar associations to seek the adoption of ABA standards for admission to their own state bar examinations.

The roll of states enforcing ABA standards has grown year by year. In 1931 seventeen states required two years of prelegal college work for admission, and the three-year law school had become the rule in thirty-three states. By 1939 forty-one states had incorporated the two-year prelegal training standard. In that year twenty-three states required graduation from an ABA-approved law school before admission to the bar. By 1951, of a total of 164 law schools in the United States, 124 had received ABA approval.

A third nation-wide organization which has contributed much to the development of legal education was organized in 1931 under the leadership of Will Shafroth, then adviser to the ABA Section. This was the National Conference of Bar Examiners, whose work will be discussed in chapter vii.

The Council of the Section has long been disturbed by the fact that the ABA standards have been so largely quantitative in nature, with so little emphasis on quality. Some action in the latter direction was taken in 1938 when the council was given discretion in granting or withholding approval of those schools which enforce only the letter of the quantitative rules. Approval is now limited to the class of schools "which in the judgment of the Council . . .

possesses reasonably adequate facilities and maintains a sound educational policy."

The war years brought the first serious break in the steady progress being made by the ABA and AALS. The strong sentimental appeal to do everything possible for the men about to enter the armed forces threatened to undermine the whole program of minimum educational requirements. Less than a month after Pearl Harbor the AALS approved a resolution authorizing the granting of a law degree to a student who had completed five-sixths of his law course at the time he was called into the service. Further, because of the drastic drop in law-school enrolments, the two associations permitted a reduction in the number of full-time teachers required, consolidation of day and evening schedules, temporary reduction in the amount of money spent on law libraries, and acceleration of the law course by the scheduling of three semesters in a calendar year. However, the ABA and AALS stood firm against the wholesale reduction of standards which threatened, taking the sound position that "a poorly qualified lawyer is still one though he be a soldier."

The end of hostilities brought new problems before the associations. The necessity of helping to re-educate lawyers who had spent as many as six years in military service led the Section, with the approval of the ABA's House of Delegates, to co-operate with the Practicing Law Institute in preparing refresher courses. Since 1948 this function on a national scale has been assumed by the American Law Institute, whose activities are described in detail in chapter ix.

When large numbers of students, mainly veterans, began to swell the law-school ranks once again, the Executive Committee of the AALS ordered the inspection of all law schools which were closed or to which substantial concessions had been made in the war years. The inspections showed that relaxation of requirements had only been temporary and that the quality of work done in the schools was again improving.

The latest important tightening of law-school requirements by the ABA occurred in 1950. Effective in 1952, the two-year rule in prelegal education was abolished. Approved law schools must now "require as a condition to admission at least three years of acceptable college work," with the exception that "a school which requires four years of full-time work or an equivalent of part-time work for the first professional degree in law may admit a student who has successfully completed two years of acceptable college work." Following this action, the AALS also adopted the three-year prelegal rule, but only as a standard and not as a requirement.

TRAINING THE LAWYER BEFORE LAW SCHOOL

The Survey of the Legal Profession appointed a special consultant—Chief Justice Arthur T. Vanderbilt of New Jersey, former president of the American Bar Association—to study prelegal education and to suggest other ways of improving the backgrounds of those who embark upon the study of law. The report is long and informative but not encouraging. For, despite the progress which has been made and the hopes for the future, Vanderbilt is forced to conclude that "our law-school authorities generally are far from satisfied with the intellectual attainments of their incoming students."

All legal educators are agreed that the training of the *full* lawyer must begin long before he enters law school. Virtually nothing can be done about such training, clearly, until the attorney of the future begins his work in the secondary schools, and actually very little concrete action can be taken until he enters college. Much can be done, however, on the college level, and it is this aspect of prelegal education which is emphasized in the Survey report.

When he was named dean of New York University School of Law in 1943, Vanderbilt posed this basic question: "Are the legal and academic requirements for admission to a recognized law school sufficient to enable it to graduate competent lawyers, provided, of course, it performs its task of legal education satisfactorily?" To answer the question, he directed a study, examining the shortcomings of prelegal education and the reasons for their persistence. These researches were buttressed by an analysis of lawyers' work and by the recommendations of lawyer leaders as to the most helpful studies and extracurricular activities.

Following a series of conferences, the Association of American Colleges gave its approval to the American Bar Association report "as an authoritative presentation of what successful lawyers and judges regard as the essentials of prelegal education" and recommended that it be called to the "favorable" attention of the curriculum committees of member-colleges. More than that, steps were taken to advise secondary-school authorities of the conclusions "so that students planning on a prelegal course in college may take in high school subjects that are necessary prerequisites to the college courses, especially in such fields as mathematics and Latin."

There were several significant points raised in the ABA report. Over all, there was the preponderating desire of the bench and bar to move forward in education to meet new conditions in life and, at the same time, unanimous opposition to any prescribed or required courses in prelegal training. The report quoted—and accepted as its guide—the assertion of the late Chief Justice Harlan Fiske Stone that "the emphasis should be on the intellectual discipline which the student derives from courses and by particular teachers, rather than on the selection of particular subjects without reference to the way in which they are taught."

In expanding his researches for the Survey, Vanderbilt enlisted the services of eighty-one law-school deans and faculties to collect and collate data on 24,189 of the 30,190 law students registered in their schools in 1949. He sought information on the students' educational backgrounds, but especially he tried to determine at what stage in their training something was being done to make them better law students and better lawyers.

Seven questions were asked of the students themselves, six of them relating to the times, backgrounds, and interests when decisions were made to study law. The seventh question was, "Are you looking forward to taking an active part in politics?"

Twelve per cent of the American law-school student body had decided to study law before they were fifteen years old; 38 per cent had made their decision between the ages of fifteen and nineteen; 36 per cent between twenty and twenty-four; and 13 per cent at twenty-five and older. (One per cent could not say when the decision was made.) "The fact that one-eighth of all of our prospective lawyers made up their minds to study law before they were fifteen years of age is clear proof that we have been neglecting the most eager section of our constituency in their most impressionable years," says Vanderbilt.

The figures on age are even more impressive when supplemented by statistics as to the stage in education at which the decision to study law was made: Five per cent of the students chose law as their future vocation even before entering high school, and one-third (including the 5 per cent) made up their minds before leaving secondary school. One-fourth more planned a career in law during their first two years at college, and 15 per cent said that they decided to attend law school while in their last two years of undergraduate study. Seventeen per cent made the decision while in military service, and about ten per cent after college or service.

While only 10 per cent of the students stated that they had turned to the law because there was a member of the family or a friend who was a lawyer, actually 30 per cent of the law-school population had close lawyer relatives. Forty-eight per cent of the students had seen the trial of five or more cases, but 18 per cent had yet to observe their first trial.

The analysis of subjects studied was particularly interesting—especially in view of the oft-repeated conclusion that most students are woefully unprepared in the fundamentals of economics, government, and history that are needed in the study of law. More than 20 per cent had majored in economics and business, another 20 per cent in political science and government, and a third 20 per cent in history and social sciences generally. Only 10 per cent had concentrated in English and allied fields; 9 per cent in engineering, mathematics, or the natural sciences; and 3 per cent in philosophy.

Vanderbilt found the answers to Question 7 most significant. Fully 45 per cent of the students expressed an active interest in future political activity, and another 18 per cent were in the "undecided" category. "It follows," he says, "that the college training of this group in government, economics, and history, and in ethics, philosophy, and the humanities is a matter of paramount importance to the body politic. It is equally desirable, too, that in law school they should receive proper training in every branch of public law, as well as in international law, by way of preparation for a career of public life."

Turning to the educational attainments of America's law students, the Survey report condemns them in harsh words. "No instructor in any class in any law school," the report reads, "can make a reference to Plato or Aristotle, to the Bible or Shakespeare, to the *Federalist* or even the Constitution itself with any assurance that he will be understood." But still more acute is the nearly universal criticism that law students are unable to think straight or to write and speak in clear, forceful, attractive English. Coupled with complaints against student deficiencies in English are statements condemning the weakness of student knowledge in the social sciences.

In essence, the complaints of the law schools refer to the colleges' failure to train students to see, to read, to use source material, to assimilate masses of information, to reflect clearly on what they have learned, to use their knowledge in problem-solving—and, in the process, to express themselves, both orally and in writing, in good English. Even more vitally, the complaints are directed to the failure of the colleges to arouse in their students abiding interests in the physical, social, and ethical aspects of the world in which they live and in the best that art and letters have to offer. Above all, according to the law schools, the colleges fail to arouse in their students any personal sense of responsibility for the destiny of the body politic.

Here, again, there is a conspicuous absence of any ready solution to the problem—and every attempt at a solution faces conflicting views as to the aims and objectives of both prelegal and legal education. The law schools themselves give little guidance to those working on these questions at the undergraduate level. Much is said of the necessity of training the law student as the future judge, legislator, and administrator and as the leader of worth-while enterprises in his community. Yet, in actual practice, the law faculties appear to be much concerned with success in law school, less interested in success at the bar, and still less worried about problems of leadership and the good life.

No wonder it is impossible to find a simple answer to the apparently simple question: What should I study before law school? The question brings forth a different response from each group of "experts," and there is nearly unanimous opposition among the bench and bar and the law schools to any requirement of specific courses in the prelegal curriculum.

Colleges, law schools, and leaders of the legal profession do, however, have *ideas* on the subject of curriculum and on extracurricular activities which might be usefully pursued in prelegal years. These opinions are contained in the responses to a questionnaire distributed by the Survey in 1949. Returns were received from three hundred and sixty colleges and a hundred law schools—but in only eighty replies from undergraduate institutions and forty-four from law schools were specific suggestions to be found.

The colleges' recommendations as to suggested curriculums, major fields of study, and specific courses centered on the following: social sciences, including history, economics, political science, sociology, and psychology (various ones being suggested as a prelaw major); philosophy, including ethics and logic; English, including composition, literature, and speech; languages, ancient and modern; mathematics; the sciences; and accounting. As far as extracurricular activities are concerned, it was urged that prelegal students participate in student government and engage in college debating, dramatics, and journalism. Thirteen of the colleges maintain special clubs for prelaw students; these were recommended both for the interchange of ideas among persons with common interests and for their programs of speeches, discussions, forums, and mock trials held in co-operation with members of the profession.

Although few law schools have established any requirements at all as to the substance of prelegal courses, all but twenty of the schools did make recommendations relative to such studies. In thirty-six schools the recommendations were informal; the other forty-four schools publish catalogues and other literature suggesting nonlegal fields for concentration. Only twelve law schools make any recommendations as to extracurricular work, and only two recommended that prelegal students visit the courts to observe the trial of cases. Recommendation of a study of bar-association activities was made by only one school. In general, all these suggestions were similar to those made by the colleges themselves.

Further advice on the subject is found in the opinions of outstanding members of the bench and bar. A questionnaire addressed to justices of the United States Supreme Court, state chief justices, senior federal judges, presidents and past presidents of leading bar associations, and selected authorities in the field of legal education brought forth 118 responses designed to guide those who are looking forward to a study of the law. There was unanimous opposition among the experts to the institution of any required courses in prelegal training; and there was a warning that the prospective lawyer must not concentrate unduly on one subject or in one field or diffuse his efforts in too many directions.

Here are the recommendations of the 118 leaders on specific subjects:

English language and literature received the highest score (72), with government (71), economics (70), and American history (70) following closely. Mathematics (65), English history (63), and Latin (60) came next. Logic scored 56, and, if scientific method (25) be grouped with it, it ranked very high. Philosophy polled 50. Then followed accounting (47), American literature (45), physics (44), modern history (43), and sociology (42). If English language and literature and American literature are regarded as branches of the same subject, its lead is significant.

Next in order were psychology (39), ancient history (38), chemistry (38), medieval history (37), ethics (34), and biology (30). The relatively low place of ethics is doubtless accounted for by the tradition of teaching it as a part of philosophy. Physiology (21) and French and Spanish, each with 20 votes, followed. From this point on the recommendations were scattered: Greek (18), geology (14), Spanish-American history (13), evolution (12), German (8), Hebrew and Bible (6), astronomy (6), botany (6), and Italian (4).

In the field of extracurricular activities it is worth noting that public speaking (60) and debating (57) outranked all their competitors, with writing (56) not far behind. These scores should be compared with individual athletics (25), managerships (20), and membership on teams (16).

Despite the differences of opinion on specific course recommendations, the experts agreed on one vital point: the objectives of prelegal education can be achieved through the medium of *any* courses. Whether the undergraduate learns to reason logically in a class in mathematics or a class in economics will make little or no difference in his future as a law student or a lawyer.

It is not easy to say exactly what the colleges, the law schools, and the bar are doing to raise the standards of prelegal education. Certainly much progress has been made in setting quantitative requirements, and certainly the law schools and the professional associations have accomplished much in advancing prelegal prerequisites to three years of "acceptable college work." But real progress is being made and will be made by giving a valid, qualitative meaning to the word "acceptable." Studies such as those made for the Survey have pointed up deficiencies in prelegal training and have served to guide the undergraduate schools in improving the content of their courses. The main job must be performed by the colleges themselves. It is they who must train the prospective law student in grasping facts, in understanding principles, in reasoning clearly and logically, and in achieving the faculty of self-expression.

THE EDUCATIONAL STATUS OF THE LAWYER

Questions as to the value of quantitative yardsticks arise again in connection with the legal education summaries prepared from the Martindale-Hubbell tabulations, discussed in chapter i. Two extensive and detailed articles, replete with tables and charts, were written for the Survey on the basis of these statistics. Less comprehensive than the other studies based on the Martindale-Hubbell figures, they are nevertheless the only tabulations ever compiled of the number of attorneys who have received college and law-school training, presenting comparative figures on the legal education and practice status of the American lawyer.

Educational data received from 180,774 lawyers (of a total lawyers' listing of 204,111) were gathered together in the 1951 study. They reveal that 170,977 lawyers—or 94.6 per cent of those supplying information—attended some law school prior to admission to the bar. A total of 145,467 lawyers (80.5 per cent) had received law degrees. (Presumably the remainder passed their examination for the bar and were admitted on the basis of some other method of acquiring their skills.) With reference to prelegal education, 149,320 lawyers (82.6 per cent) had records of college attendance, and less than half, 88,938 (49.2 per cent), had received college degrees.

The figures are set forth in Table 14.

Generally speaking, the states with the highest percentages of attorneys trained in law schools are those with the largest populations and highest lawyer-concentration figures. The states with

TABLE 14

EDUCATIONAL DATA FOR 180,774 LAWYERS
(September, 1951)

Education	Lawyer Population	
	No.	Per Cent
Attended college	149,320	82.60
Received college degree	88,938	49.20
Attended law school	170,977	94.58
Received law degree	145,467	80.46
Total data available	180,774	100.00
No data available	23,337	....
Total lawyers' listings	204,111	....

the highest college-attendance records are those in the South Atlantic region, while the college-degree figures are highest along the Atlantic Coast.

The District of Columbia leads the nation in all the statistics for law-school attendance and degrees. A total of 98.3 per cent of the attorneys in Washington, D.C., have obtained formal legal training, and 88.9 per cent of the District bar have been awarded law degrees. Of those who attended law school, 90.3 per cent were subsequently awarded degrees.

Following the District of Columbia on the law-school *attendance* charts are New York, Illinois, and Massachusetts, with percentages of 96.5, 96.3, and 96.2, respectively. States with a relatively small proportion of attorneys trained in law schools are North Dakota, 72.4 per cent; Montana, 76.7 per cent; Vermont, 77.0 per cent; and North Carolina, 79.3 per cent.

In the statistics showing the proportion of the total state bar receiving law *degrees*, Illinois ranks second, with 84.0 per cent, followed by Maryland, 82.8 per cent; Rhode Island, 82.2 per cent; and Massachusetts, 81.8 per cent. New York, second in law-school attendance, ranks sixteenth among the states in the percentage (76.3) of the lawyer population which has been awarded law degrees. States with the smallest proportion of law-school graduates are North Carolina, 42.2 per cent; Maine, 53.4 per cent; Vermon, 54.7 per cent; and Arkansas, 57.6 per cent.

The four states with the highest *college attendance* records are in the South Atlantic region. A total of 93.3 per cent of the lawyers in South Carolina attended college, as compared to 92.3 per cent for Delaware and 90.6 per cent for Virginia and North Carolina. Smallest proportions in this category are in Maryland, 66.5 per cent; New Jersey, 66.7 per cent; Massachusetts, 71.3 per cent; and Missouri, 71.5 per cent. The *college-degree* figures put Delaware on top with 76.6 per cent, followed by Pennsylvania, 70.8 per cent; Rhode Island, 67.8 per cent; and South Carolina, 61.2 per cent. On the low end of the chart listing the percentages of lawyers with undergraduate degrees are South Dakota, 29.6; Arkansas, 30.6; and New Jersey, 30.9.

The 1948 Martindale-Hubbell study contained data on 129,436 lawyers who had records of law-school attendance. A total of 110,211 of these lawyers had attended law schools approved by the American Bar Association; 16,675 attorneys had attended unapproved schools; and 2,550 had been students at "unlisted" schools, that is, schools which had ceased to exist or were now operating under different names.

Statistics on the college records of the American lawyer in 1948, broken down according to the type of law school attended, are set forth in Chart III.

A quick glance at these data reveals a far greater proportion of college-trained alumni among the approved law schools than among those which are unapproved, and certainly the percentage of college degrees received is much higher in the schools which have met the standards set by the American Bar Association. Granting that the approved schools are better than those in the unapproved category, the question is whether these *quantitative* figures on col-

CHART III

College Attendance and College Degrees Received

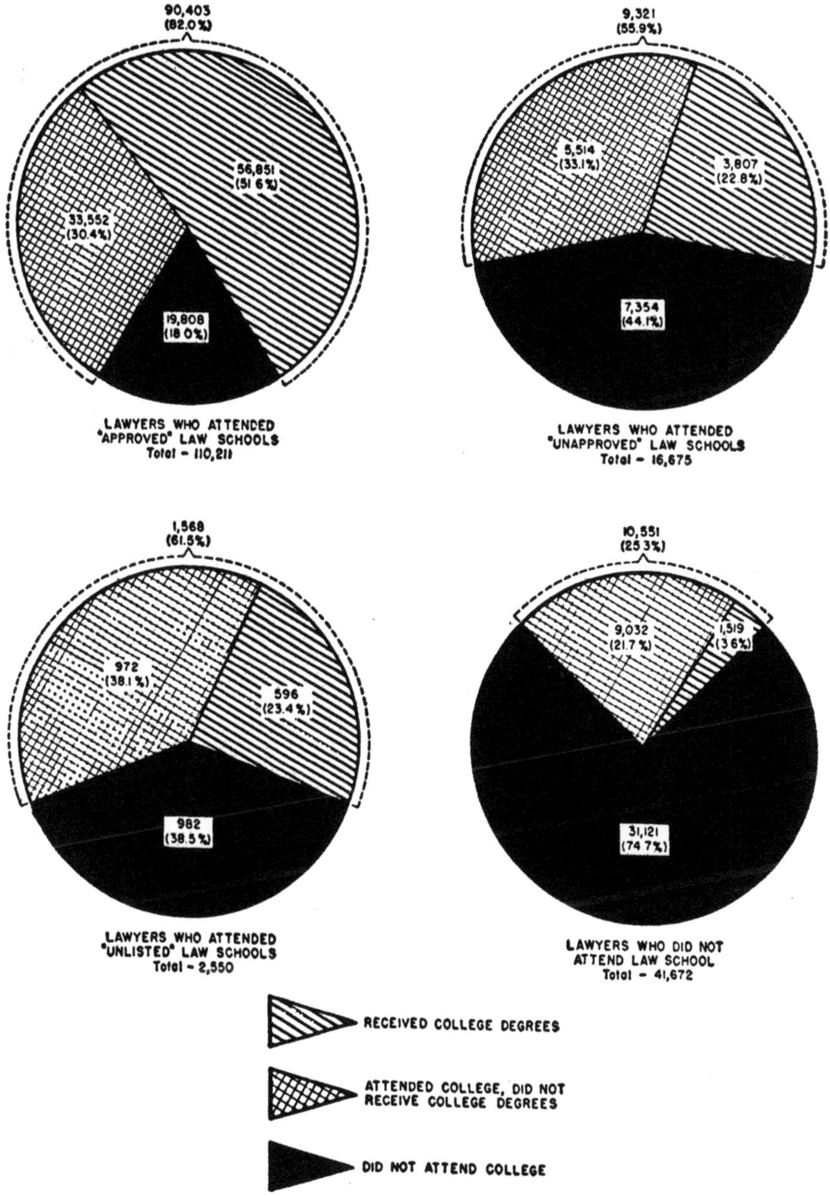

lege training can serve as a guide to the *quality* of the American law school.

Arguments in the affirmative are supported by the statistics on the ten law schools with the highest percentages of college-trained alumni and the ten law schools with the lowest percentages. All the ten top schools have received the approval of the American Bar Association, while only two of the ten schools with the lowest proportion of college-trained alumni are so approved.

But, significant as these figures may be in reaching a *qualitative* evaluation, they certainly cannot provide the sole basis for an accurate rating. No proper analysis can be made of college-education statistics in the absence of a clear understanding of the meaning of the word "college." No distinction was made in the Martindale-Hubbell study between the undergraduate schools of the nation's great universities and those junior colleges which are little more than "advanced high schools." An authoritative rating demands an evaluation of college *quality* and college-degree *quality*.

A second weakness in thee Martindale-Hubbell figures lies in the fact that the college-education data were furnished by attorneys in *all* age groups—including lawyers who attended law school before the days of prelegal requirements as well as more recent graduates. The percentages indicating college attendance and college degrees received are naturally much higher among the more recently established schools, since those schools have enforced ABA prelegal standards during a proportionately greater number of years. Consequently, all these quantitative data must be modified by considering the ages of the law schools being rated.

Finally, the statistics fail to take into account the large number of institutions which in recent years have strengthened their admission standards and requirements. There are many law schools, such as those at California, Cornell, Illinois, Northwestern, and Wisconsin, whose records of college-trained alumni may reflect the quality of those schools prior to reorganization but certainly do not reflect the high standards of those schools today.

Data on the practice status of the American lawyer have also been compiled, relating the percentage of lawyers in active practice and in public service with their educational backgrounds.

Based upon information furnished by 158,207 attorneys, the basic figures are as given in Table 15.

It is interesting to note that the solo-status percentages are much higher for the lawyers without formal legal training than for the members of the bar who attended law school, while the firm, associate, and employed percentages are much higher for attorneys trained in law schools. The Survey also found that the outstanding law schools tend to have the lowest percentages of alumni in the solo category. The solo figures for Harvard and Yale, for example, are 42.5 and 46.3 per cent, respectively, far lower than the percentages for the nation as a whole. On the other hand, the figures for Brooklyn and Fordham law schools—excellent institutions but generally ranked below Harvard and Yale in the *qualitative* ratings—show solo percentages of 78.7 and 69.2.

TABLE 15

ATTENDANCE AND NONATTENDANCE AT LAW SCHOOL BY PRACTICE STATUS

Practice Status	National Totals		Lawyers Who Attended Law School		Lawyers Who Did Not Attend Law School	
	No.	Per Cent	No.	Per Cent	No.	Per Cent
Solo	104,688	66.2	74,335	61.4	30,353	81.7
Firm	40,444	25.6	34,839	28.8	5,605	15.1
Associate	7,520	4.7	7,265	6.0	255	0.7
Employed	5,555	3.5	4,634	3.8	921	2.5
Total	158,207	100.0	121,073	100.0	37,134	100.0

These statistics are certainly not the result of mere coincidence. Status-in-practice figures *do* tend to vary according to the character of law schools. But whether, and to what extent, these percentages can be used in evaluating law schools must await further study.

The most surprising statistics in the Survey's legal education researches are those relating to the percentages of lawyers in public service, especially those in judicial office. Only 10.6 per cent of the lawyers who attended law school are presently in public office, while 18.2 per cent of the lawyers who did not attend law school are in that category. As far as judicial posts are concerned, only 3.0 per cent of the nation's attorneys trained in law schools are judges, as compared to a percentage of 7.9 for lawyers who did not attend law school.

Alumni achievement in public service is one of the factors which adds to the reputation of a school. Since judicial office is definitely a mark of legal achievement, it would seem that the nation's best law schools would have the highest percentages of alumni in judicial office. Yet this is certainly not the case. The percentage of judges among alumni graduating from unapproved schools is higher than the number from approved schools, and such institutions as Harvard and Columbia, which can boast of their many alumni on the United States Supreme Court, have a relatively small number of graduates in judicial posts generally.

These are the statistics. Their value in providing the profession with hitherto unknown data about the law schools of the United States is unquestioned. Much remains to be done, however, in attempting to translate the quantitative figures into significant qualitative information.

FINANCIAL AID TO LAW STUDENTS

Some note should be made of the special loan funds, established or suggested, for the assistance of needy and worthy lawyers-to-be. The need for such funds is great and is growing greater. The cost of education is rising; it is now at least $1,800 a year for three years at Harvard Law School, for example. And many middle-class families are facing difficulties in giving their children a college education, let alone a professional education as well.

Former President James B. Conant of Harvard pointed out that "anyone familiar with education knows that for a very considerable portion of the population it is the family financial status which places a ceiling on the educational ambitions of even the brilliant youth. The oft-repeated statement in certain smug circles that 'any boy who has what it takes can get all the education he wants in the U.S.A.' just is not so; it is contrary to the facts."

In the first of four reports on loans for college and law-school students, Reginald Heber Smith, director of the Survey, observes that the loan plans are intended to supplement and not to take the place of scholarships. If all the law schools had enough scholarship funds, he says, there would be no problem. But it is extremely difficult today to provide enough capital to produce income for scholarships. And, since at least a quarter of the men and women in the law schools need some financial help, plans must be made to assist about ten thousand students in the law schools alone. One happy connection between loan plans and scholarships is that a good student who is given a loan during his first year in law school can devote his time and energy to studying law instead of washing dishes or waiting on tables and may win a scholarship which, without this freedom to concentrate, would have been beyond his reach.

The possibilities of loans for law-school students are outlined in a proposed plan submitted to the Survey by the Conference on Personal Finance Law. Reasons for the plan are set forth as follows: (1) first-class legal education should be made available to all classes of qualified and deserving students without regard to financial status or social standing; (2) most approved schools do not have sufficient funds to furnish the necessary financial assistance to qualified and deserving students (the same can be said for the unapproved schools, of course); and (3) there are too few properly trained lawyers in the United States.

Existence of a loan plan, and public awareness of it, would also tend to increase respect for the schools and the profession and help in the public relations program of the organized bar. This, in turn, would encourage greater public support of higher educational and professional standards, since there would be public recognition that the opportunities of the bar were available to poor as well as rich students with character, ambition, and ability. Finally, a loan plan would help the schools in meeting their ever increasing financial burdens.

Of the twenty approved law schools which presently have student lending plans, the amount available for loans varies from a fund of $330,000 down to an insignificant $150. Only six of the schools have a fund as large as $25,000, and only three have sums in excess of $50,000. One institution charges no interest on loans; at another 6 per cent is demanded; the majority have set the interest rate at 4 per cent.

Recommended limitations on the proposed loan plan are as follows:

1. The first-year law student should not borrow in excess of 50 per cent of his annual expenses, which should not exceed 50 per cent of the annual normal expenses in his law school. (It is estimated that the average normal expenditure of students in approved law schools is $1,600.)

This limitation requires the applicant to show initiative, ability, frugality, and a sense of responsible planning. It is imposed because most scholastic casualties are sustained during the first year. Risk to the loan is greater in the case of law-school freshmen, but any further limitation would be likely to defeat the objective of equal opportunity for all.

2. The second-year student should not borrow in excess of 75 per cent of his annual expenses for that year, which should not exceed 75 per cent of the annual normal expenses in his law school. This amount of indebtedness should be added to that previously incurred, and he should make interest payments on the total indebtedness.

3. The third-year law student should not borrow in excess of 90 per cent of his anual expenses for that year, which should not exceed 90 per cent of the annual normal expenses in his law school.

The third-year law man, having necessarily proved himself capable and industrious, is a good financial risk. But he needs an increased loan backing, for during his senior year he is likely to be fully occupied with extra work on special papers, law reviews, legal aid, and similar worth-while activities. And, at the end of the period, he is confronted with preparing for and passing his bar examinations and locating professional employment.

During the entire period of law-school study the interest rate should not exceed 4 per cent and should be less if possible. It was recommended that this rate of interest be continued during the first year following graduation. After the first postgraduate year, the interest rate should be gradually raised to reach the market rate not later than the time of the formal settlement conference three years after graduation.

It was also recommended that in no case (under current conditions) should the maximum amount of over-all indebtedness for education exceed $6,000. This would allow the student who had to borrow for his college education a limit of about $3,000 before starting his legal training. On the assumption that a college education followed by a law-school education represents an average investment at present of approximately $10,000, this limitation on total possible loans leaves a "margin of safety" of some 40 per cent.

The ideal loan fund, according to the Survey, is one owned by a law school or its designated custodian. Sources of the fund should be law-school alumni, bar associations, philanthropists and philanthropic organizations, large corporate organizations which have come to realize the importance of training competent legal advisers, and commercial banks and insurance companies.

It is impossible to overestimate the importance of student loans. As stated by Smith, "The long-range objective of the loan plans is to carry us one step further toward realizing the American dream of equality of opportunity." Failure on the part of the colleges, the law schools, and the bar to make legal education available to those worthy of it might well lead to government intervention, raising once again the fear of socialization of legal education and, possibly, socialization of the profession.

THE LAWYER AND HIS BOOKS

But even though the lawyer may—with or without financial assistance—receive the quality and quantity of prelegal and law-school training advocated by the experts, it still is not enough. The education of the lawyer is a lifetime undertaking, and law-school "commencement" exercises mark only the beginning of the studies necessary to make the complete lawyer. Not only must the attorney work hard at keeping up with new decisions, legislation, and regulations as they may affect his clients, but he must also continue to train himself to be a better technical craftsman and to have a better grasp of the growing complexities of the legal order.

Most of this post–law-school education comes from reading cases, statutes, treatises, tax and labor services, law reviews, bar-association periodicals, daily legal newspapers, newspapers in general, plus books and magazines of general interest. It is difficult, if not impossible, to determine the specific books read and the amount of time spent by lawyers in keeping up with the law. The Survey of the Legal Profession did not attempt to find the answer. But a study was made of the general reading of the bar which did include some data on professional publications.

Questionnaires on the reading habits of the American lawyer were sent to approximately 1 per cent of the nation's legal population, and replies were received in an almost direct proportion to the number of attorneys in each state. Respondents were asked to report on the thoroughness or casualness of their reading of books, magazines, and newspapers. On technical and semitechnical magazines the figures were as shown in Table 16.

TABLE 16

READING HABITS OF LAWYERS: TECHNICAL AND SEMITECHNICAL PERIODICALS

Publication	Per Cent of Lawyers Reporting Who Read:			
	Regularly and Thoroughly	Regularly but Not Thoroughly	Occasionally	Never
State and/or city bar journals	43	31	8	18
American Bar Association Journal	22	39	21	17
Law reviews	22	31	26	20
United States News	13	8	23	56
Trade and business periodicals	7	11	19	63
Journal of Commerce	3	4	7	86

Most of the report, however, was devoted to outside reading, and, oddly enough, the Survey found more devotees of the western and "whodunit" than readers of popular works about law and the legal profession. More lawyers have read Winston Churchill's *The Gathering Storm* and John Gunther's *Inside U.S.A.* than Plato's *Republic* or *The Federalist,* and such novels as *Raintree County* by Richard Lockridge and *Dinner at Antoine's* by Frances Parkinson Keyes proved more popular among attorneys than Edmund Fuller's *Law in Action* or Alpheus T. Mason's *Brandeis: A Free Man's Life.*

Contemporary histories and political commentaries constitute the favorite literary fare of the American lawyer. They are read frequently by 38 per cent of the bar and occasionally by another 44 per cent. Only 11 per cent of the attorneys are regular readers of books about the legal profession (such as Lloyd Paul Stryker's *For the Defense*), and a scant 8 per cent are regular readers of drama, poetry, and books on art and music.

The figures on selected individual volumes are of considerable interest (Table 17).

Generally speaking, the favorite magazines of the American public are also the favorite magazines of the American lawyer. According to publishers' statements for 1949, the year the reading survey was made, *Reader's Digest* was the nation's leading periodical, with a circulation in excess of nine million. *Life* had a reading public of

TABLE 17

READING HABITS OF LAWYERS: SELECTED INDIVIDUAL BOOKS

Title	Per Cent of Lawyers Reporting Who Read:		
	In Full	Partly	Not at All
The Gathering Storm (Churchill)	44	21	35
The Federalist	33	24	42
Wealth of Nations (Smith)	27	19	53
For the Defense (Stryker)	23	7	69
The Roosevelt Myth (Flynn)	23	14	62
Peace of Mind (Liebman)	21	8	70
The Big Fisherman (Douglas)	16	4	80
The Naked and the Dead (Mailer)	12	4	83
Brandeis: A Free Man's Life (Mason)	12	5	83
The Spirit of the Laws (Montesquieu)	11	13	75
Sexual Behavior of the Human Male (Kinsey)	6	16	77
The Law of the Soviet State (Vishinsky)	3	5	92

5,317,794, while the *Saturday Evening Post* had 3,873,486 sales. *Collier's* had a circulation of 2,984,434, *Look*, 2,891,644, and *Time*, 1,612,587. Table 18 shows the breakdown on lawyer magazine-reading.

Local newspapers, however, constitute far and away the favorite reading matter of the legal profession. They are read regularly and thoroughly by 82 per cent of the bar and regularly but not thoroughly by an additional 12 per cent. In addition to this local readership, no less than 47 per cent of the attorneys are regular readers of newspapers published in large near-by cities. And 24 per cent are regular readers of the *New York Times* and the *New York Herald Tribune.*

TABLE 18

READING HABITS OF LAWYERS: GENERAL MAGAZINES

Magazine	Per Cent of Lawyers Reporting Who Read:			
	Regularly and Thoroughly	Regularly but Not Thoroughly	Occasionally	Never
Time	52	13	17	18
Life	43	22	19	15
Reader's Digest	42	22	21	15
Saturday Evening Post	28	22	28	21
Newsweek	22	10	29	39
Collier's	12	10	31	47
Fortune	6	9	30	54
Look	5	8	26	60
Saturday Review	5	5	11	79
New Republic	1	3	9	86

Newspapers, magazines, and books such as those covered in the Survey report are generally purchased by the attorney-reader, but no individual lawyer and few law firms can hope to own more than a fraction of the volumes which lawyers must read and study in their day-to-day activities. The need is met by law libraries. Of these, 638 were analyzed by William R. Roalfe, librarian at Northwestern University School of Law, in one of the most extensive reports prepared for the Survey.

Touching briefly on the history of the growth of law libraries, Roalfe found that as late as 1876 the largest collection in the United States—that of the New York Law Institute—contained only 20,000 volumes and that in 1892 the largest library was that of the association of the Bar of the City of New York, numbering nearly 40,000 volumes. Table 19 reflects the law-library growth since those early days.

Thus there are now 168 libraries with collections of 30,000 volumes or more, as compared with 53 in 1912. The top 65 libraries, with 75,000 volumes or more, compare strikingly with 9 in 1912. Disregarding the changing minimums required for listing in these data, the combined holdings of all libraries have increased from 5,538,009 volumes in 1912 to 20,932,143 in 1950. The current rate of growth is 574,334 books a year. And it is increasing. So rapidly are the libraries expanding, in fact, that ever increasing complaints are heard as to the inadequacy of facilities to house the books. Numerous methods of photoreproduction have been used to minimize the problem of bulk.

Of the 638 libraries of the legal profession numbering more than 5,000 volumes, 216 are county law libraries and 137 are located in the law schools. There are 53 state law libraries, 25 of which are

TABLE 19

GROWTH OF LAW LIBRARIES

No. of Volumes in Collection	No. of Libraries			
	1912	1930	1940	1950
100,000 or more	6	18	23	31
75,000–99,999	3	10	18	34
50,000–74,999	11	35	40	41
40,000–49,999	11	20	21	18
30,000–39,999	22	22	25	44
20,000–29,999	24	39	55	86
10,000–19,999	73	110	162	196
Less than 10,000	280	316	175	165
Not reported	102	33	0	22
Total	532	603	519	638

under the control of the state court, in addition to 57 state-court libraries. A total of 65 libraries are maintained by the federal courts, federal administrative agencies, and other national governmental departments. Another 57 are in the large law firms, and 25 more are in the legal departments of major corporations. In addition, there are 10 bar-association libraries with collections exceeding 5,000 books and 5 more maintained co-operatively in buildings housing large numbers of law firms.

New York State has the largest number of these law libraries—100, of which 65 are in New York City. There are 61 in California, 58 in the District of Columbia, 52 in Ohio, 46 in Pennsylvania, 28 in Massachusetts, 26 in Texas, and 20 in Illinois. As far as cities are concerned, 15 libraries are located in Chicago, 14 in San Francisco, and 10 each in Los Angeles and Boston.

The largest legal collections in the United States are in the Law Library of Congress (744,442 volumes) and in the Harvard University Law Library (718,666). The top four law-school libraries, starting with Harvard, are: Yale, 326,889 volumes; Columbia, 300,000; and the University of Michigan, 209,810. The Association of the Bar of the City of New York has the biggest bar-association library, with 275,000 volumes. The major state libraries are in New York, 260,000 volumes; Minnesota, 250,000; and Pennsylvania, 200,000. The largest county library is in Los Angeles, with 204,059 volumes.

The major part of Roalfe's report is devoted to the details of maintaining and servicing a law library and of giving service to the judges, lawyers, law students, and members of the general public who seek to do research in the law. The study, which omits law-school libraries, is based on 94 personal inspections of law libraries, plus 178 questionnaire responses.

So many data are contained in this 471-page study that it is impossible to present more than a few brief highlights. The report notes that there are "at least 1,156 persons engaged in law-library work and the number is probably considerably greater"—an estimated 1,700, 54 per cent of whom are women. The average number of staff members per library is 2.65, but the library of the Association of the Bar of the City of New York has 31; the Law Library of Congress, 30; and the Los Angeles County Law Library,. 25. While only 10 chief librarians are both law-school and library-school graduates, 6 law-school alumni in these positions have taken some formal training in library science. Compensation of this group (which includes a number of part-time workers) ranges from $25.00 to $10,750 per year, with the median salary at $4,200.

The report devotes individual chapters to law-office and company law libraries, libraries of counties and states, state and federal courts, federal agencies, and bar associations. This study is supplemented by one on co-operation between libraries, including the work of such groups as the American Association of Law Libraries.

The most significant test that can be applied in evaluating a law library "concerns the quality of the service it provides to those to whom it is responsible," Roalfe points out. He also states that the growing complexity of the law has resulted in the creation of a legal specialist—the law librarian—and stresses the necessity of a professional group especially trained for this field.

Finally, the report emphasizes the responsibilities of the bar to the law libraries. It is important that judges and lawyers gain greater understanding of the role of the libraries and of the quality and type of services they provide. Likewise, the report urges on the bar a greater responsibility for the financial support of the services.

THE CONTINUING EDUCATION OF LAWYERS

Valuable as lawyer reading may be in keeping the practicing lawyer informed as to the law and its changing patterns, it is not sufficient to meet the continuing educational needs of the bar. Lawyer reading tends to be either too general or too specific; the lawyer skims to keep up to date on new developments but pores over a narrow point of law involved in current litigation. The need for continuing comprehensive and analytical legal training is being met by postadmission courses of instruction. These courses are being given by law schools, by bar associations, by the American Law Institute, and by the Practicing Law Institute.

Pioneer in this field for the last twenty years has been the Practicing Law Institute, whose activities are described in a report by one of its former presidents, Arthur A. Ballantine, of the New York bar. Preliminary work by Harold P. Seligson, the institute's founder and guiding spirit, led the Association of the Bar of the City of New York in 1938 to recommend that PLI be chartered as a nonprofit educational corporation. In 1943 the institute conducted a national program on income-tax law under the sponsorship of the American Bar Association's Section on Taxation. And at war's end PLI undertook a national program of refresher courses for lawyer veterans. Since 1948 this program has been carried on by the American Law Institute, leaving PLI free to devote its energies mainly to improving and enlarging its New York courses.

In recent years PLI has served more than ten thousand lawyers annually through evening lecture courses, Saturday forums, summer sessions, home-study programs, and published monographs. The emphasis is on practical aspects of the lawyer's work not dealt with in most law schools. While PLI continues to stress training for recent law-school graduates, designed to bridge the gap between law school and law practice, the majority of attorneys attending the programs have been in practice for some time.

Perhaps the most interesting new development has been the Saturday forum. A recent forum, one on estate planning, was attended by more than seven hundred lawyers, from eighteen states in addition to New York, to hear a panel of twelve specialists. Forum topics have also included current tax legislation, tax planning for corporations, taxation of executive incentive plans, antitrust laws, medical proof, corporate readjustments, defense contracts, and wage and salary stabilization. A more detailed and leisurely consideration of these and similar topics is included in the institute's summer session, held each year in July.

Lawyers unable to attend PLI lectures and forums may enrol in its correspondence courses on general practice, trial practice, fundamentals of federal taxation, and current problems in federal taxation. Enrollees receive monographs and syllabuses for study, and their solutions to typical problems are reviewed by lawyers on the institute's staff. More than 125,000 assignments have been reviewed since the home-study program was developed at the request of the American Bar Association seven years ago.

The PLI also conducts review courses for the New York State bar examinations, especially popular among law-school graduates in other states seeking greater familiarity with New York rules. More than one million copies of some seventy PLI pocket-book monographs have been published and distributed to lawyers throughout the country.

Under the direction of John Mulder, the American Law Institute has generally supervised the postadmission legal education program on the national level. Courses are being conducted for lawyers in many parts of the country, and materials have been provided to serve as the basis of courses offered by state and local bar associations. The educational activities of the ALI and the other agencies of the organized bar are discussed further in chapter ix.

The law schools also are entering this area of legal training. Both the Southwestern Legal Institute and the University of Illinois College of Law are now giving postadmission courses regularly, and

New York University is providing annual courses on taxation and labor law.

Whether the lawyer obtains his postadmission legal training from his own reading or from the many practical and advanced courses being given by the schools and the bar associations is of no importance. What is important is that he continue his legal education to the day of retirement. Limited to three years, the law schools cannot possibly do more than lay a foundation for future study. A list of the basic qualities of a good lawyer compiled by Leach and supplemented by Harno includes: fact consciousness; a sense of relevance; comprehensiveness; foresight; sophistication in using and understanding language; precision and persuasiveness of speech; an attitude of mind that can handle and solve successive problems, untrammeled by preconceptions; "and finally, and pervading all the rest, and possibly the only one that is really basic: *self-discipline in habits of thoroughness,* an abhorrence of superficiality and approximation."

As Harno has pointed out, "It would be too much to assume that legal education, meaning here *law-school* education, can fully endow students with these qualities. The education of a lawyer is a lifetime undertaking. It should, however, be the aim of a law school to plant in the minds of its students the seeds of these qualities and to nurture their growth." The schools can do little more; the rest is up to the lawyer himself.

CHAPTER VII

Admission to the Bar

WHO IS ADMITTED TO THE BAR?

After law school, what? Prior to entering the practice of the law, the attorney-to-be is required to satisfy the profession that he is equipped, by character and education, to join its ranks. This means admission to the bar—a story in itself in the over-all story of the American lawyer.

Admission to the bar in the United States means admission to the bar of a particular state or to the bar of the District of Columbia or admission to the courts in the federal system or specialized administrative agencies.

What do these bodies ask of the neophyte? In no instance is he required to present evidence of the completion of specific legal courses. And, since no bar examination goes beyond the field of law in its questioning, no state requires applicants to have training in specific prelegal courses. What *is* required is that the candidate exhibit an understanding of general substantive law, a detailed knowledge of certain statutes found in that particular jurisdiction, proficiency in pleading and practice, and good character. But the procedures which the applicant must follow as well as the means by which the bar examiners satisfy themselves as to his qualifications vary from state to state.

Some college training is required by the bar examiners of forty-three states and the District of Columbia. Thirty-seven states demand a minimum of two years of college, two demand three years of study, and four (Connecticut, Delaware, Kansas, and Pennsylvania) require a Bachelor's degree. A high-school education will suffice in Louisiana, Mississippi, and South Carolina, and there are no minimum prelegal requirements in Arkansas and Georgia.

In a majority of states, however, the candidate is allowed to substitute an "equivalent" for high-school or college education. There is little uniformity in the methods used to test equivalency. In some states it is determined by the board of bar examiners solely on the basis of the applications and interviews. In other states examinations are given by the board or under its supervision. In still others the university or state department of education gives an examination. A few states leave the matter to the judgment of local law schools.

Bar examiners of twenty-five states require registration prior to entering upon legal studies. This requirement applies to every candidate in only ten states, while the others demand advance registration only for those who prepare for the bar examination through study in a nonapproved school or in a law office. Registration in these circumstances permits an early check on such qualifications as age, citizenship, residence, and prelegal education. It also affords an early opportunity to get information on moral character, providing the candidate with additional time for the correction of amendable faults. Where registration is required of those entering law-office study, the board may also make certain that the study will be done under an attorney who is qualified to guide the novice. Often these attorneys are called upon to make periodic progress reports, and they may also be asked to give examinations to their "apprentices."

Candidates must meet fairly uniform regulations as to age, citizenship, and residence. Forty-five states and the District of Columbia require that the applicant be twenty-one years of age at the time of admission to the bar. Forty-four expressly require their applicants to be citizens of the United States. Two of these states, however, make an exception where the intention to become a citizen has already been filed; one state postpones its requirement on condition that the applicant become a citizen within six months after meeting the procedural requirements of the federal naturalization law.

Residence requirements exist in forty states—with much variation. In four states the applicant need be a resident only at the time he is admitted to practice, in one he must be a resident on the date of the bar examination, and in another eleven he must be a resident at the time he files an application to take the examination. In the remaining twenty-four states different periods of residence are required. Table 20 illustrates the differences among these twenty-four.

Seventeen separate reports were prepared for the Survey on admission to the bar; many of them are contained in the volume edited by James E. Brenner, of Stanford Law School, the Survey's consultant on the subject. An article by Homer D. Crotty, of the California bar, sets the stage for the detailed consideration of the admissions field. Pointing out that "no other profession wields the power in our American life or has assumed greater responsibilities than the legal profession," he emphasizes the public importance of careful selectivity for the bar.

"What then," he asks, "are the actual qualifications which the bar and public are entitled to insist upon before any one shall be called to the bar? The public and the bar have the right to expect that the

TABLE 20

RESIDENCE REQUIREMENTS IN TWENTY-FOUR STATES FOR ADMISSION TO BAR

Months of Residence	Number of States			
	Prior to Application	Prior to Examination	Prior to Admission	Total
2	....	....	1	1
3	3	2	....	5
6	3	5	2	10
9	....	1	....	1
12	2	2	2	6
18	1	....	....	1
Total	9	10	5	24

young lawyer be a person of good character, of ability, and of learning. They also have the right to expect that the recruits to the legal profession will be taken generally from the whole population and will not be confined to the sons of the wealthy or well-to-do."

Good character is cited as the "first and foremost of these qualifications." But it is by no means the only one. For, says Crotty, "the ignorance of a lawyer as to the rights of his client can erode and destroy the client's property just as effectively and as disastrously as if the lawyer had stolen it. So it behooves the bar to overcome [its] apathy and to resist every attempt to lower standards, as well as to be ever on the alert for an opportunity to improve the standards of the profession."

Character standards have been established in all states, and inquiries as to morals, aptitudes, and personality are universal. Here, again, there is uniformity neither as to when the character investigations are made nor in their degree of thoroughness. Depth of inquiry ranges from the rules of Arkansas, Mississippi, and South Carolina, which require only that applicants file certificates of good character; to the informal procedures in such sparsely populated states as New Hampshire and Nevada, where each applicant is almost certain to be known to at least one member of the local bar committee; to the comprehensive systems of the heavily populated states. The extensive and complex procedures of California, New Jersey, New York, and Pennsylvania are discussed below. The California and Pennsylvania systems are of particular importance, since they have been suggested as models for other states.

Reports by John G. Jackson, of the New York bar, and Will Shafroth, the first secretary of the National Conference of Bar Examiners and at present in the Administrative Office of the United States Courts, reveal that only a small number of applicants are refused admission to the bar because of character defects. Yet the fact that the refusal rate is low does not obviate the necessity for careful scrutiny of the backgrounds of those seeking admission. It is relatively easy to discover whether an applicant has violated the criminal code or been guilty of a serious breach of the moral code. If the objective of character inquiry were to weed out only such undesirables, it might be true that most of the examining bodies use an overly cumbersome machinery for the purpose.

The usual character investigation, however, is concerned with such additional matters as reliability and trustworthiness, legal aptitude and interest, habits, avocations, acquaintanceships, memberships in societies and organizations, loyalty, knowledge of legal ethics, and a number of "intangibles." All this is relevant in determining whether an applicant merits admission into the legal fraternity. Bringing the pertinent facts to light and evaluating them intelligently can be done only through the use of affidavits, questionnaires, personal interviews, and, where necessary, field investigations.

California is one of the twenty-five states which requires the student to register his intention to study law. At the time of registration—not later than three months after he enters law school—the student must also file a statement under oath giving his age, residence, addresses, citizenship, occupation, general and legal education, and moral character. He is also fingerprinted. During this period there is a routine examination by the Committee of Bar Examiners.

Following the completion of law-school studies, the candidate is required to make application at least three months in advance for permission to take the bar examination. This involves filling out a detailed questionnaire, to be answered under oath. Confidential questionnaires are then sent to his references, all his employers, and a certificate of character is obtained from his law-school dean. In the meantime his fingerprints have been sent on to the Federal Bureau of Investigation for a routine check.

If nothing of a derogatory nature is developed, the investigation ends at this point. If questions are raised, a complete investigation is made. The applicant and, if necessary, witnesses will be required to appear before the committee for questioning. An adverse decision as to moral character is reviewable by the state supreme court.

Under the new constitution adopted by New Jersey in 1947, the supreme court was given jurisdiction over admissions. Subject to the approval of the court, a board of bar examiners has been appointed, and this body prescribes rules, forms, and procedures. After the prospective applicant has met educational requirements specified in the supreme-court rules, he must file a qualifying certificate, which may be obtained from the State Board of Education. He also submits a "Certificate of Commencement of Clerkship" from the attorney acting as his preceptor, affirming that his nine-month clerkship has begun.

After filing these papers, the candidate files a preliminary statement, setting forth his educational background, citizenship, residence, experience, if any, with admission to other bars, experience, if any, as a litigant or witness, prior occupation, service record, affiliations, etc., and a statement of loyalty to the government. This preliminary statement is submitted to one of the committee members in the candidate's home county. The county committee is required to investigate his character and fitness at this time. The extent of this inquiry depends on local practice. In some counties the custom is to interview the applicant several times in the period of his clerkship.

After the apprenticeship is served, the applicant files with the clerk of the supreme court a written notice of intention to take the bar examination. A list of these candidates is sent to each county clerk for posting, and a list for each county is published twice in a local newspaper. Upon receipt of the notice of intention, the clerk also forwards to the applicant a final statement to be sworn to and filed with the chairman of the committee on character and fitness of his county. This statement brings the candidate's biography up to date and supplies facts relative to his clerkship. The preceptor must vouch for the applicant's character and fitness and also state his opinion as to the truth of statements made in the forms. Another interview with the character committee may take place at this time, but in some counties it is postponed until after the bar exams.

The final statement must be accompanied by a formal application for admission to the examination, certifying certain facts required by the rules. Attached to the application must be letters of recommendation as to moral character, a certificate of residence, age, and clerkship signed by the preceptor, and a law-school certificate showing attendance and completion of courses required for a degree at a school approved by the American Bar Association. After the examination, the candidate must await his license until the county committee has filed a certificate with the supreme court, stating that it is satisfied that the entrant is of good moral character and that his clerkship has been completed satisfactorily.

In New York the law-school graduate files a simple application form requesting examination. Neither registration prior to legal study nor apprenticeship after graduation is required. Character investigation begins only after the bar examination is successfully completed. The applicant then files a sworn questionnaire covering his background and education (including such items as school and college activities, memberships in clubs and societies, and financial condition) and states that he is loyal to, believes in, and will support our form of government. In support of this application, the candidate also submits certificates of successful completion of study through college and law school; character affidavits from all his employers, from an attorney, and from persons who know him well; plus a sponsoring affidavit from an attorney known to a member of the character committee. A birth certificate and a statement of good conduct from the police complete the required papers. After a thorough investigation, the applicant must present himself for an oral examination by a committee member, at which time he is questioned further about his personal background, loyalty, and comprehension of the code of ethics. Presentation before the appellate division of the supreme court and admission follow in due course.

Pensylvania preceded New Jersey in evolving a complex procedure for admission. Here preliminary registration is also necessary. The beginning student must also have a preceptor, acceptable to the county board, who has been in active practice for at least five years. This preceptor must consult with the applicant during his years of law study and make reports on his progress. Generally he takes the applicant into his office after graduation for the required six-month clerkship. The form for registration is an extensive questionnaire. Together with background information, the applicant must state in what county he expects to practice and name at least three citizen sponsors as well as his proposed preceptor. The state board forwards a duplicate of the registration to the county organization with additional questionnaires to be filled out by two members of the local board and, at the same time, forwards other questionnaires to the citizen sponsors and the preceptor.

Thereafter two members of the county board interview the applicant and his preceptor—and sometimes the sponsors. In addition, in some of the larger counties a private investigator will be called in. On the basis of these reports, the county board votes to approve or reject the applicant or the preceptor. Notice of approval —if forthcoming—is forwarded to the state board, and the applicant is then registered if he also meets the prelegal educational requirements. (A careful review procedure is employed if a candidate is turned down by his county board.)

When he applies for admission to the bar after the completion of his law studies, the applicant repeats exactly the same procedure. Further, he must publish a notice of intention to appear for the bar examination, the statement appearing for four consecutive weeks prior to the examination.

The clerking or apprenticeship system, as found in New Jersey and Pennsylvania, is also a part of the procedure for admission to practice in Delaware, Rhode Island, and Vermont, where the period of such service is six months. New Mexico issues a temporary license following successful completion of the bar examination, which becomes final after a year of actual practice.

Despite the advantages of required clerkship reported by the six states using this procedure, some reservations must be made. In his Survey report on state requirements for admission to practice, Marion R. Kirkwood, former president of the Association of American Law Schools, weighs the pros and cons of compulsory clerkship. He notes that many practitioners and educators have urged the adoption of the apprenticeship system in all states, comparing it to the term of internship which must be served by medical-school graduates.

But the situations are not entirely analogous. Unlike the intern, the law apprentice would usually have little opportunity to receive training in the varied aspects of his profession. Another objection to compulsory apprenticeship is raised by those who fear that such a system might lead to exploitation. And there are frequent complaints that the preceptor generally is unable to maintain adequate supervision over the young lawyer's work. However, where it has been utilized, the required clerkship has been of aid to the boards of examiners in providing a further method of passing on an applicant's character and moral qualifications to practice law.

Many of the elements discussed above are included in the uniform system of character investigation proposed by Shafroth:

1. The work of character investigation should be assigned to separate committees in order to relieve the law-examining board of this additional duty.
2. Registration at the beginning of law study should be required of all students studying in the state, and the character examination, including a personal appearance before the committee or a member, should be conducted at the time of registration, as well as before the bar examination.
3. The candidate should be required to file a complete questionnaire, and inquiries should be directed by the committee to all his references and past business connections.
4. The names of candidates should be published.
5. The application and questionnaire should be filed in sufficient time to permit a period of at least ninety days for investigation before examination. At the same time the character interview and investigation should be completed and action taken by the time the examination is held. It is important that the investigation should be made before the examination,

because it is easier to reject a person of doubtful character before the examination than after. The argument that this is wasted effort in the case of those who do not pass is not tenable. The decision on character must be made before anything in the nature of a vested right has accrued. Boards which make the investigation only after the marks are in impose an unnecessary delay on fully qualified applicants.

Singular additional requirements are found in some jurisdictions. In one state a probably unwarranted barrier is set up by the stipulation that applicants file proof of intention to practice or teach law as a career and to devote substantially their full time to such pursuits. The same state also denies admission to any person who, while an alien, has claimed a military exemption on that ground. Another state requires the applicant to furnish a certificate from a state physician to the effect that he is mentally able to engage in the active practice of law. Several states require applicants to furnish their fingerprints.

Of course, every applicant in every state must furnish proof of the completion of law study as required by the state's rules. Some diversity exists as to what is sought in this area. Four methods of studying law are recognized in the different jurisdictions: (1) private, unsupervised study; (2) study in a law office; (3) courses with a correspondence school; and (4) preparation in a resident law school.

Unsupervised study—the first avenue—is acceptable today in only six states (Arkansas, California, Georgia, Massachusetts, Mississippi, and Montana), but it is not commonly used, and there are signs that it may soon be abandoned.

Although the second method was permitted in thirty-five states at the time of the Survey report in 1951, eight states had plans to abolish it in the near future. And there is further evidence that all unformalized study may fall into complete disuse as a means of equipping the young lawyer for the rigors of practice. As of 1951, seventeen of the thirty-five states required a minimum of three years of full-time office study, ten specified four years, and one had a standard of three years of study, of which one year had to be in a law school. Completing the roll, three states asked only two years of law-office training, and the remaining three imposed no minimum standard whatsoever.

Dean Kirkwood criticizes law-office study as a means of preparation for the bar:

> Given a lawyer with ample time to supervise and test the student, and one who possesses not only real learning but capacity to teach, the process should succeed. But how many lawyers of such learning and teaching capacity have the time today to give the student the attention he needs? Furthermore, there is absent the stimulation that comes from studying with a group and being held to competitive testing. Some states have attempted to improve the situation by requiring that the preceptor be approved by the board of examiners, but one wonders whether this effort accomplishes very much other than freeing students of the risk of wasting their time with obvious incompetents. If the board's standard of approval, particularly with reference to the amount of time to be given by the lawyer to instruction, is what it should be, it is doubtful whether enough preceptors, ready, able and willing to perform, can be found.

As noted in chapter vi, correspondence-school graduates ordinarily do quite poorly in their bar examinations, showing a percentage of success even lower than that recorded by those whose preparation was entirely private and unsupervised. Yet correspondence schools continue to be given recognition. In two states (Idaho and New Hampshire) correspondence study is only approved if the applicant is also studying law under the direction of a member of the bar. Both of these states and California require a minimum of four years of such study; Montana and Virginia demand only two years; and Arkansas, Georgia, and Mississippi have established no minimum period at all. In view of the unsatisfactory results shown by the "mailbox" students in the bar examinations, it has often been urged that recognition be denied to correspondence-school study. Such a move, however, does not appear likely in the near future.

Law-school study, of course, is the most common path to the bar today. Forty-three states and the District of Columbia give recognition to both full-time day study and part-time evening study. The other five states, however, refuse to accept any legal training from the night law schools. The vast majority of the states adhere to the American Bar Association standard of three years of full-time law school or its "equivalent" of four years of part-time law-school attendance.

Many states limit their acceptance of law-school study to training in "approved" schools—and their "approved" lists are usually identical with the one prepared by the ABA. In some jurisdictions, however, exceptions are made for the "unapproved" schools within the state. Law-school graduation is demanded in approximately twenty states, and some of the experts believe that this should be made a uniform requirement. Granted that such a step would result in some rise in bar standards, it would have little over-all effect in the absence of a provision eliminating all other modes of preparation.

There has also been advancement in eliminating the "diploma privilege," a practice permitting graduates of certain law schools to be admitted to the bar without examination. The practice has been criticized on several grounds. The privilege might become an inducement to limit the curriculum to the minimal requirements, and it gives the favored schools an unfair advantage in the competition for prospective law students. In many instances the diploma privilege is, in effect, merely an indirect subsidy. In 1921 some twenty-two schools in fifteen states had this privilege, but by 1948 the number had decreased to thirteen schools in nine states. General relaxation of bar standards to assist World War II veterans undoubtedly hindered attempts to revoke this privilege everywhere.

EXAMINATION FOR THE BAR

In the other thirty-nine states and the District of Columbia all applicants must take and pass a bar examination. The great diversity in the form and content of these tests is outlined in the report of Dean Shelden D. Elliott, director of the Institute of Judicial Administration at New York University. Rules as to when, where, and how the bar examination shall be taken also vary somewhat from state to state. Thus, in more than three-quarters of the states the examination is given only in the principal metropolitan center or the state capital, and seven others schedule tests in only two cities. Examinations are normally given twice a year. Three states (Iowa, New York, and Oklahoma) offer examinations three times a year, and in eight other jurisdictions only an annual test is provided for.

Oral questioning is a regular feature of the bar examination in Iowa, Rhode Island, and Vermont. The only other departures from written examinations are found in Indiana and Massachusetts, where oral questions are used solely for applicants whose written answers are on the border line of failure, and in New Mexico, where these additional examinations are given in exceptional cases. Proctoring has been replaced by the honor system in Florida, Nevada, and West Virginia. Eight states make special provision for typewritten examinations.

More significant variations are found in the content of the different examinations.

The report by Dean George Neff Stevens of the Buffalo University School of Law shows the diverse methods used to determine the subject matter of the examination. In twelve states the highest court chooses the topics to be covered; in another five the content is delineated by legislative enactment. Rules of the board of examiners prescribe the subjects in sixteen states, while in five others the highest court and the board collaborate. In Louisiana the board of governors of the state bar association lists the subjects, with the approval of the supreme court.

Surprisingly enough, the survey indicated that eight states try to avoid any references to local law in their questions, and in another seven states credit is given for well-reasoned answers, even though the applicant does not know or does not mention local law.

The number of subjects listed for inclusion range from a minimum of 8 specific fields (plus a miscellaneous group of questions) in Maine to the broad concept of "law and equity" in Georgia. Eleven states list 28 or more topics, and at least 61 distinct subjects are found on one or more of the lists. Contracts, criminal law, and real property are always included; evidence, pleading, and torts appear on 47 lists; constitutional law and corporations on 46; equity on 45; agency and negotiable instruments on 44; personal property on 41; and wills and estates on 39. Fewer than half of the states indicate that questions will be offered on bankruptcy, municipal corporations, taxation, administrative law, bailments, insurance, mortgages, and suretyships. These are detailed in Table 21.

The figures in Table 21 indicate that most bar examinations do include questions on the basic fields of the law. But they also show that there is hesitancy in adding specialized materials and new developments. Because the addition of further subjects is a difficult procedure in some states, requiring the amendment of a statute or court rules, changes must be somewhat slow.

Most of the bar examiners replied in the negative when asked whether the scope of the examinations should be broadened. They expressed the opinion that their tests should continue to deal with the fundamentals, leaving the coverage of new topics to the law schools and the elective system. But the growth of some of these recently opened fields brings its own solution to the problem. Sub-

TABLE 21

SUBJECT MATTER IN STATE BAR EXAMINATIONS

Topic	No. of States	Topic	No. of States
Administrative law	16*	Legal ethics	34*‖
Agency	44*	Legal history	3#
Bailments	19	Local statutes	4
Bankruptcy	12*	Master and servant	2
Carriers	10	Mining law	3
Civil law	1†	Mortgages	21
Common-law pleading	6	Municipal corporations	16
Common-law practice	2	Negotiable instruments	44*
Community property	5	Oil and gas	1* **
Conflict of laws	33	Partnership	35*
Constitutional law	46*	Personal property	41*
Contracts	48*	Personal rights	7
Corporations	46*	Pleading	47*††
Courts	3	Pledges	1‡‡
Creditors' rights	6	Practice	36*
Criminal law	48*	Public utilities	11
Damages	12	Quasi-contracts	3
Domestic relations	36*	Real property	48*
Elementary law	1	Remedies	2
Equity	45*	Sales	27
Equity pleading	7	Statutory construction	5
Executors, administrators	6	Suretyship	23
Extralegal remedies	2*	Taxation	16*
Evidence	47*‡	Torts	47*§§
Federal pleading and practice	12	Trade regulation	3
Future interests	6	Trial and appellate practice	3
Insurance	21	Trusts	29
Judgments	1§	Water rights	3
Labor law	3	Wills, probate, estates	39*
Landlord and tenant	7	Workmen's compensation	2
Legal bibliography	3		

* And the District of Columbia.
† Louisiana.
‡ Omitted in Nevada.
§ Florida.
‖ And in ten states on oral examinations.
And in seven states on oral examinations.
** Montana.
†† Omitted in Nebraska.
‡‡ North Carolina.
§§ Omitted in New Mexico.

jects like taxation, administrative law, and labor relations are rapidly becoming fundamental courses, and the indication is that, as this occurs, bar examinations will be modified to include the new developments.

Most examination questions are derived from actual cases reported in the final appellate courts of the state or its neighbors. Other questions are taken from law-school tests and the bar examinations of other states. Still other sources are such standard lawbooks as *Corpus Juris* and *American Jurisprudence.* Interestingly enough, in California and Connecticut questions are initially submitted by out-of-state law professors. Cases from the individual examiner's own practice or from suggested problems in "law quizzers" and texts are seldom used.

There is no uniformity in grading. The passing mark may be fixed by statute, by the rules of court, or by the examining board. New York has no fixed standard, using an elastic sliding scale which takes numerous factors into account.

Bar-examination results are usually announced between four and six weeks after the tests have been given. In a number of instances, however, the waiting period before notification is extremely brief. Iowa, Nebraska, West Virginia, and Wisconsin make an effort to advise applicants of the results, if possible, by the end of the last day of the examination itself. Results in Kansas, Montana, New Mexico, North Carolina, and North Dakota customarily are announced within twenty-four hours; in Maine and Vermont within forty-eight hours. Uncertainty must linger in the minds of candidates in the remaining states for from one to twelve weeks.

Approximately half the states impose a limitation on the total number of examinations an unsuccessful applicant may take. In three states only two examinations are permitted; in fourteen the limit is three; five states allow up to four tries; and in Illinois five tests may be taken. Even where a limitation has been established, additional examinations may be taken with the special permission of the examining board or the court.

Another limitation sometimes found is that the applicant who fails one examination must wait a certain length of time before being examined again. Usually the minimum period is one year. In Utah, where but one examination is given each year, an unsuccessful applicant after two tries must wait until the second subsequent examination; in Texas the waiting period after three failures is two years. In all but five states an applicant who fails is required to retake the entire examination upon a subsequent attempt; in the five the applicant need retake only the section or part which he has failed.

After this analysis of qualifications for the bar examination, of its preparation and its grading, it is still necessary to arrive at some appraisal of its value as a testing device. In no state is this examination taken lightly, by the applicants, the examiners, or the organized bar. A set of figures compiled for the Survey by Harold Shepherd, of the Stanford University Law School, illustrates this strikingly (Table 22).

THE PROPER CONTENT OF EXAMINATIONS

Purposes and merits of statistical studies in this field are discussed in the article by Brenner, Dean Elliott, and John T. DeGraff, president of the New York State Board of Bar Examiners. Their graphs and charts are of interest to bar examiners in indicating the success of individual questions and can be employed to discover whether questions are being marked by uniform criteria. These statistics enable law schools to determine the relative success of their graduates and whether changes in curriculums or teaching methods may be required. To applicants such studies serve as a valuable guide in deciding which courses to pursue while in law school. And, if statistics can disclose faults and these are remedied, all three groups will profit. Too complex for illustration here, the graphs and tables used by the state board in California have been recommended for use in other states.

As a result of these and other analyses, numerous suggestions have been made for improving the caliber of bar examinations, thus improving the caliber of those who are called to the bar. One of the proposals—a first-year bar examination—is set forth in an article by Eustace Cullinan, chairman of the Advisory and Editorial Committee on Bar Examinations and Admissions to the Bar.

The proposed examination would, of course, be based upon subjects studied during the first two semesters at law school and would be designed to weed out those individuals who are found to be un-

TABLE 22

NUMBER OF QUESTIONS AND TIME INVOLVED IN BAR EXAMINATIONS, BY STATES

State	No. of Questions	No. of Hours per Day	No. of Days	Total Hours	Minutes per Question
Alabama	80–100	8	3	24	14–18
Arizona*	95	8	2	15	9
Arkansas	115–230	8	3	24	6–13
California	24	7	3	21	53
Colorado†	80	7	3	20	15
Connecticut	36	6	2	12	20
Delaware	40	6	2	12	18
District of Columbia	60	6	3	18	18
Florida	48	8	3	24	30
Georgia	50	7	2	....	....
Idaho	50	7	3	....	....
Illinois	50	6	$2\frac{1}{2}$	15	18
Indiana	40	9	....	....	....
Iowa	50	6	$2\frac{1}{2}$	15	18
Kansas	60	6	2	12	12
Kentucky	60–72	8	3	24	20–24
Louisiana	‡	8	3	24	....
Maine	57	6	$1\frac{1}{2}$	9	10
Maryland	60	6	2	12	12
Massachusetts	20	7	1	7	21
Michigan	40	7	$2\frac{1}{2}$	$17\frac{1}{2}$	26
Minnesota	57	8	3	24	25
Mississippi	120	8	3	24	12
Missouri	80	6	$2\frac{1}{2}$	15	10
Montana	100	5	3	15	9
Nebraska	40	6	2	12	18
Nevada	36	6	3	18	30
New Hampshire	90	....	....	....	....
New Jersey	40	6	2	12	18
New York§	313	7	$1\frac{5}{7}$	12	....
North Carolina	67	6	3	18	16
North Dakota‖	....	6	....	....	....
Ohio	100	9	3	27	16
Oklahoma	90–180	8	4	32	11–21
Oregon	32	6	....	....	....
Pennsylvania	32	8	2	16	30
Rhode Island	40	6	2	12	18
South Carolina	60	8	3	24	24
South Dakota	100	8	$2\frac{1}{2}$	20	12
Tennessee	40	6	2	12	18
Texas	50–60	9	2	18	18–22
Utah	36	6	3	18	30
Vermont	80	6	2	....	10
Virginia	40	6	....	....	....
Washington	60	6	....	....	....
West Virginia	57	6	$2\frac{1}{2}$	15	16
Wisconsin	60	6	....	....	....
Wyoming	40	6	2	12	18

* One hour for legal bibliography in Arizona.

† Only six hours on one day in Colorado.

‡ Varies.

§ New York gives thirteen essay and three hundred "Yes-No" questions.

‖ North Dakota asks five questions on each subject.

interested in the law or unfitted for it. This would not only save needless expense but would curtail the disappointment which comes to those who find themselves unsuited to the profession after two or three years of study. Another direct consequence would be tighter admission standards on the part of the state's law schools, as these institutions would naturally seek to avoid unfavorable publicity from having an undue percentage of their students fail on the preliminary bar examination. Both effects have been seen in California, the only state which at present uses a first-year examination. However, the test there is tied up with the accreditation process for schools, and it is only students attending nonaccredited institutions who have to take it. And, as Cullinan points out, the procedure probably is unnecessary in states where only students from accredited law schools may take the bar examinations.

Another suggestion should have wider appeal. Although a nationally administered bar examination has been put forward for several years and presents attractive possibilities, there has as yet been little progress toward it. Drawing upon inconsistencies and variations from state to state as sketched above, Herbert W. Clark, of the San Francisco bar, contends that ineptitudes and deficiencies can best be eliminated by testing candidates for legal practice against a single, national standard. He states four criticisms of the present system whereby, in effect, forty-nine standards of competence to enter the legal profession exist:

1. No uniformity exists in the *quality* of bar examinations given in the different examining and admitting jurisdictions.
2. There is very little uniformity to be found in the *quality* of bar examinations given *within the same examining and admitting jurisdiction.*
3. No uniformity whatsoever appears in the standard of grading answers in the different examining and admitting jurisdictions.
4. As traditionally and currently set, the typical bar examination is not an accurate test of the training that has been and is being offered by the better law schools of the country.

Medical men and certified public accountants, he points out, have been preparing and administering uniform examinations for some years; certificates from both the National Board of Medical Examiners and the American Institute of Accountants are recognized in the vast majority of states and entitle the holders to practice their profession without further examination.

At first glance, it would appear that a national bar examination could screen applicants for legal practice in the same way that other uniform tests screen doctors and certified public accountants. Practical difficulties suggest themselves, however. While substantive law is generally the same in most states, there are significant differences in procedural law. Further, an examination geared to judging the ability of applicants in New York (where the number of candidates each year averages 3,354) might be unsatisfactory for Idaho and South Dakota (where the yearly averages are 7 and 9, respectively). Likewise, a test prepared for the methods and aims of instruction at national law schools like Harvard, Yale, and Columbia might fail to test properly the graduates of the smaller schools, and vice versa.

These objections need not be fatal. Even with a national bar examination, local boards would still have their own standards for educational requirements and character fitness. The differences in state law could be met by having the papers of students from a particular jurisdiction graded according to the law prevailing in that jurisdiction. Objections arising from the number of applicants would become irrelevant if each state board determined for itself what percentage of applicants should be admitted and thus what average was needed to pass the national examination.

As far as different educational methods and approaches are concerned, no new problems are added by substituting a uniform examination for present tests. Most states already have to examine applicants from both national and local schools. It has been suggested as a compromise that the national test deal with core subjects, while local boards add questions on unique local law. But over a period of years this solution might defeat the purpose of universal examinations, as state questions grew in number to crowd out the others.

Whether or not national tests are adopted, the standards of existing bar examinations should be improved, according to another Survey report by Brenner, both in the scope of subjects included and in the amount of freedom of choice given bar examiners and applicants.

Initially, he suggests three categories of subjects which should comprise all bar examinations. The first, a "must" list, has the following basic subjects: contracts, torts, real property, criminal law, evidence, equity, taxation, corporations, trusts, and constitutional law. As assurance that applicants will be well grounded in these topics, it is suggested that the "must" requirement be met by a certificate from a recognized law school that the applicant has satisfactorily completed courses in all of them. And, where candidates are not required to attend law school, an affidavit of completion should be accepted in lieu of the certificate.

A proposed second list—from which at least one subject should be selected for each examination—includes wills, conflict of laws, pleading and practice, and agency and community property. Electives, lending breadth and variety to the test, are found in the third group. Selections from this could also be made each year: administrative law, bills and notes, corporation finance, creditor's rights, domestic relations, federal jurisdiction, future interests, sales, insurance, labor law, legislation, mortgages, municipal corporations, personal property, persons, public uitlities, and government regulation of business.

Although the three categories include some thirty-two subjects, and although a large number of questions are thus included in the examination, it can still be comprehensive and not burdensome if the applicant is given a choice of optional questions. An ideal examination would be one in which the applicant has a choice in all sections of the test and is not required to answer any particular question. Thus, even though the applicant would be confronted with thirty-six questions, he would answer twenty-four, probably covering fifteen-odd subjects. This is less than the number of subjects he will have studied during his three years of law school.

And what should be known about each subject? Since applicants for admission to practice law are not presumed to be experienced practitioners, they should not be examined upon the practical problems with which lawyers should be familiar. They should be examined upon the theory of the law and the application of the theory to specific cases. That is what is taught in law schools. That is what a graduate of a law school should be expected to know. That is what examinations should be geared to test.

WHO PREPARES THE EXAMINATIONS?

Some words should also be devoted to the men behind the bar examinations. To most applicants and to most attorneys, the state board of bar examiners is and remains a shadowy, mysterious organization; and even more nebulous and distant is the National Conference of Bar Examiners. Yet these bodies do not fear publicity, and their organization and activities should also be considered.

In the twenty years between 1930 and 1949 approximately 280,000 applicants took bar examinations. Of the 14,000 candidates to be examined and considered for admission each year, there was an annual average of 3,354 in New York, 986 in the District of Columbia, 962 in Massachusetts, 942 in Illinois, and 881 in California. The burden was far lighter in sixteen states, where the number of candidates was usually under 50—Idaho with a low of 7, and 9 in South Dakota, 11 each in Delaware and Nevada, and 12 in Wyoming. The national "pass" average is 50 per cent—some 7,000 students hurdling the bar examinations each year. Their personal backgrounds and character credentials still must be checked, of course, in most states, and they generally are watched and weighed in the waiting period after their bar examinations are completed.

To take care of this large number of bar candidates, most states have an examining board of five or six members. In fifteen states the force is somewhat larger, ranging up to fifteen in Connecticut. Balancing the states with larger than average boards are the fourteen jurisdictions where the body has only three members. In six states examiners receive no compensation for their services. Another eight states allow only expenses or traveling expenses. Thirteen jurisdictions pay a per diem rate ranging from $8.00 to $50.00, either with or without expenses in addition. Annual compensation of from $100 to $10,300 (New York, with three board members) is found in twelve states. North Carolina pays its examiners $50.00 per examination, plus expenses. The remaining eight states base compensation on an apportionment of the fees paid by applicants.

Twenty-five states rely wholly on their examining boards for the admission process; they have no administrative assistants, either on a part-time or a full-time basis. Assistants for the preparation of bar-examination questions are provided in eight states. Nine states employ readers to aid in the grading of questions. (In California a different reader is assigned to each question.)

The principal source of funds to cover the expenses of bar examinations is in the fees paid by applicants. But in ten states this income is supplemented by legislative appropriation, by an allocation from the annual license fees paid by attorneys, or by disbursements from court or other budgets. In three states (Massachusetts, New York, and West Virginia) the necessary funds are provided solely by legislative appropriations. The average annual expenditure for the bar examination is $9,000 per state, or $30.00 per applicant. However, California spends some $80,000 each year, New York, Pennsylvania, and Michigan pay between $50,000 and $60,000 each, and Illinois and Massachusetts spend in excess of $20,000.

Fees for the character investigation of attorneys who leave one state to seek admission to the bar of another provide the National Conference of Bar Examiners with its revenue. The cost of each character report is $50.00, and from this source the organization realizes enough funds to support an annual budget of about $30,000. At its first regular meeting in 1931 it was stated that the conference was "formed for the purpose of increasing the efficiency of the state boards in admitting to the bar only those candidates who are fully equipped both from a standpoint of knowledge and of character to serve as lawyers, and also to study and co-operate with the other branches of the bar in dealing with problems of legal education." The conference consists of a council, made up of one representative from each state examining board, and an executive committee, composed of the chairman, the immediate past chairman, the chairman-elect, the secretary, and six other members. All serve without compensation. Activities of the organization are discussed in the Survey report by Marjorie Merritt, secretary of the conference.

The *Bar Examiner*, now a bimonthly publication of thirty-two pages or so, was one of the first tangible accomplishments of the conference in furthering its objectives. Copies are distributed free to all members of law examining boards, to character committees, law schools, judges in the courts of last resort, committees on legal education, and to others especially concerned with admissions to the bar. "In this publication," Merritt reports, "may be found articles on such subjects as bar-examination procedure in individual states dealing with the preparation of questions, the giving of the bar examination, the grading of the examination papers, the determination of results and analysis and criticism of bar-examination questions, statistics showing the results of each bar examination in every state, a study of the character examination systems in all states, plans for the investigation of original applicants and of migrant attorneys, new rules for admissions to the bar, lists of approved law schools, decisions covering the inherent power of the court over admissions to the bar, and reports of the meetings of the conference and of other agencies concerned with legal education."

Some of the other accomplishments of the conference are: (1) an exchange system whereby each examining board will receive copies of tests given in other states; (2) the encouragement and promotion of state co-operating committees, composed of the members of the examining board and representatives from the law schools, bar associations, and the courts in a particular jurisdiction; and (3) the collation and publication of admission statistics. Since 1932 the results of each examination have been reported to the conference, which has tabulated the information and made it available nationally.

In 1940, with the financial and editorial assistance of the Section of Legal Education of the American Bar Association and the Association of American Law Schools, *A Manual for Bar Examiners* was printed and distributed. It contains detailed instruction on the preparation, administration, and grading of examinations and materials on the common objectives of state boards and law schools.

TESTING THE MIGRANT ATTORNEY

As of 1948, thirty-three states were using the National Conference of Bar Examiners as the exclusive agency investigating and preparing character reports on all migrant attorneys seeking admission to local bars. In 1947, 1,027 of these migrant attorneys were admitted to practice without the necessity of taking regular bar examinations. However, comprehensive character investigations were required, and 81 per cent of them were made by the conference.

Careful checks are made as to an applicant's reputation and character, involving the questioning of law classmates, associates in practice, past and present employers, lawyers in the same office buildings as those in which the applicant formerly had his office, office-building managers, judges, attorneys specializing in the same type of practice as that of the applicant, credit companies, bonding companies, court officials, etc. If the applicant completed his law course only recently, his high-school, college, and law-school records are also checked. In all cases the conference verifies all dates of admission to the bar and writes all bar associations in the jurisdictions in which the applicant has practiced—state, county, district, or local.

If the applicant is from a small community, inquiries are frequently addressed to the mayor, postmaster, chief of police, or banker, and to lawyers practicing in other towns of the same judicial district or circuit. Sometimes these persons are asked for the names of reliable citizens who may know the applicant. When necessary, court records are obtained on cases in which the applicant was involved; in special instances young attorneys are employed to conduct personal interviews; and a summary of the applicant's history is always sent to the Martindale-Hubbell *Directory* for any possible information.

When it is believed that sufficient information has been gathered, the conference prepares a biographical sketch of the applicant, setting out his age, place of birth, education, and entire experience. Should there have been derogatory reports as to his character or a question as to whether or not he has complied with the educational requirements, the full details are set out, and the reader is referred to particular response letters. No recommendation is made by the conference, nor does it give opinions. It does refer to facts or statements pertinent to the candidate's qualifications, it may sometimes raise questions as to certain points, and frequently it may suggest that the applicant be questioned along certain lines in order to amplify information in the report or to clarify ambiguities. All differences between the applicant's statements and the facts as disclosed by investigation are noted carefully. The report is forwarded to the examining authority, and a copy and tabular data are retained for the conference's files.

While the conference does not keep a record of the ultimate decisions made by state boards upon applicants who have been the subject of a character investigation—and while it does not ask the local body to supply such information—some results have become known:

> A study was made of the first thousand character investigations, and this showed that 104, or 10.4 per cent, of the 1,000 applicants were not admitted to the bar either because they were denied a license or because they withdrew; there were 12 who were told to take the bar examination, 26 who had not appeared or completed their papers, 69 who had failed the examinations, and 23 whose petitions were still pending. Fifty-one applicants were denied admission on character alone, 6 on character and

insufficient practice, 7 withdrew after an interview, 4 with questioned character withdrew for some reason, 4 of those who did not complete their papers were of doubtful character, and 8 applications were pending because of character and practice. Thus, among 104 applications rejected, unsatisfactory character was the cause which eliminated 72 and held up action on 11. The character investigation methods have undoubtedly improved over the years as a result of experience, and it seems safe to assume that there is now a higher percentage of refusal on character grounds than was the case with the first thousand applicants.

Generally, most states provide for the admission of attorneys from other states (and, in a few cases, from foreign countries) without the necessity of their passing a students' bar examination. The usual requirements are that such attorney applicants shall have been admitted to practice before the highest court of another state and shall have been in practice for a substantial period of time—from three to five years. Residence in the admitting state for some months customarily is necessary. Good character must be shown. Some states add the further stipulation that admission of attorneys from other jurisdictions be on a reciprocity basis, extending the privilege of speedy entrance only to lawyer applicants from those states which grant similar privileges to its own migrant attorneys.

Having made these generalizations, the Survey report by Goscoe O. Farley, of the California bar, goes on to show how divergent the state requirements actually are. In most jurisdictions an attorney applicant must be at least twenty-one years old, but in Mississippi and New York the minimum ages are twenty-four and twenty-six years, respectively. In all but nine states the applicant has to be a resident at the time of admission. Where residence is required, it may be for a minimum period prior to admission or even for a period prior to application for admission. North Carolina asks a full year's residence; in the other states the range is from three to six months. In fifteen states the applicant must declare that he intends to maintain an office and actually practice in the admitting state. In one case, the attorney must declare that he intends to become a practitioner of general law and is not seeking admission for the sole purpose of returning to his own state to obtain divorce clients.

The applicant must be a United States citizen in all but eight jurisdictions. In Idaho, Oklahoma, and Oregon it is sufficient that he has declared his intention of becoming a citizen. The great majority of states require the attorney applicant to have been admitted in another state or the District of Columbia. However, in six (California, Colorado, Illinois, New York, Oregon, and Utah) the rules include an attorney who has been admitted in any country where the English common law is the basis of jurisprudence, and in Massachusetts any foreign country at all will do. While almost every state requires the applicant to be able to practice before the highest court of his home state, in a few admission to a designated lower court meets the regulations.

Twenty-one states and the District of Columbia stipulate that attorney applicants must have practiced law for at least five years, while in thirteen states this period is only three years. Florida and Rhode Island stand at an extreme, requiring ten years of previous practice. In Illinois a flexible standard is used—three years of practice if the applicant meets the state's own educational qualifications for student applicants, five years if he had had at least two years of law study, and eight if he has not. The five-year rule does not apply in the District of Columbia and Kentucky if the applicant is a graduate of a law school approved by the American Bar Association or the Association of American Law Schools.

As a further requirement, many jurisdictions state that the necessary term of practice shall have been performed within a certain time immediately before making application. Usually the requirement is three years' practice within the five years next preceding the date of filing. In the great majority of cases the attorney must have been actually and actively engaged in practice. But in half of the jurisdictions service as a judge is considered to be the equivalent of practicing law. Law-school teachers receive the same privilege in twenty-six states, and legal work by government lawyers and officers in the armed forces is treated in the same fashion in others.

Thirty-two states do not ask the applicant to show any prelegal education other than that which he had to possess when first admitted to the bar, but in ten he must have the same prelegal education required of student applicants in the admitting state. In Texas only those who have practiced seven years but less than ten must present the same qualifications as student applicants. Also in Texas, and in Massachusetts, the quality of legal education is left to the discretion of the bar examiners. Seven states specify the legal education required, and five others provide that the applicant must meet the same standard as student candidates in the jurisdiction. Substantially, the same states that require no record of prelegal education by attorney applicants require no record of legal education.

Alabama, Arizona, California, Delaware, Florida, Idaho, Louisiana, Nevada, New Jersey, Washington, and West Virginia require attorney applicants to take an examination in law. This is a special test in California and Washington; it may be one specially prepared in Delaware or that given recent graduates. In the remaining states the examination is identical with that which other applicants must take. South Carolina, Georgia, and the District of Columbia insist upon an examination if the state from which the attorney comes does not extend reciprocity to attorneys from the admitting state. And in Kansas, New York, South Dakota, Texas, and Utah the committee may require a bar examination if it is not satisfied that the attorney has had sufficient legal experience.

Practically all states permit an attorney from another jurisdiction to appear in a particular cause in a specific case. A number, however, require the attorney to become associated with local counsel, and in Idaho and Utah the entire privilege is conditioned on reciprocity.

PRACTICE BEFORE FEDERAL COURTS AND AGENCIES

Two Survey reports give their attention to the rules prevailing for admission of attorneys to the courts and agencies of the federal system. Surprisingly, even within one system, as is shown in the Crotty article on admission to the federal courts, some variations are found. And standards of admission to practice before administrative agencies show wide differences—often without foundation in logic or experience—according to the report by F. Trowbridge vom Baur.

Any attorney who has been in practice or is entitled to practice before the highest court of any state or territory is eligible for admission to the bar of the Supreme Court of the United States. His application must be accompanied by references from two attorneys in his home jurisdiction, affirming that his personal and professional character and standing pass muster.

Different admission rules are found in each of the federal courts of appeals. Attorneys eligible for admission generally fall into one of four categories: (1) those who have been admitted to the Supreme Court; (2) those who have been admitted to the court of appeals in another circuit; (3) those who have been admitted to any United States district court; and (4) those who may practice in the highest courts of their states. One or all of these categories may be required in a particular circuit. Only in the Second Circuit is there the additional requirement that the attorney must maintain an office within its limits. Except in the District of Columbia, there is no formal investigation of an attorney's character.

Procedures in the district courts are likewise far from uniform. Differences may even be found between two district courts in one state. An applicant is always required to be a member of some other court before becoming qualified for admission. In nineteen district courts the applicant must be a resident of the state in which the court is situated. In thirty districts admission to the highest court of any state qualifies an applicant, but in twenty-six other districts it must be the highest court of the state in which the district is located.

Not even the minimal "consistency" that exists in the admissions rules of the United States district courts is found among the federal administrative agencies. The requirements for each agency are somewhat distinctive—if only in phrasing—from the standards set by others. In addition, numerous administrative bodies permit laymen to appear before them and thus further complicate the rules governing admission to practice. Of the forty-six civilian agencies which conduct adversary proceedings, thirty-two permit laymen to serve as trial counsel or to appear in a representative capacity. Agencies which permitted only members of the bar to serve as counsel were: Alien Property Custodian, Federal Communications Commission, Federal Petroleum Board, Federal Trade Commission, Indian Claims Commission, International Claims Commission, Motor Carrier Claims Commission, Appeals Board and Hearing Commissioners of the National Production Authority, Postmaster-General, Secretary of Agriculture (under the Seed and Export Standards for Apples and Pears Acts), Securities and Exchange Commission, Secretary of the Interior (with respect to Indian heirs and wills), Subversive Activities Control Board, and the Wage Stabilization Board. And, of the twenty-seven military agencies which conduct adversary proceedings, only eight require lawyers as trial counsel.

Lay practice is long established in federal law and has received congressional approval in several acts. However, there appears to be no logic behind a procedure which bars laymen from the Federal Communications Commission, the Federal Trade Commission, and the Securities and Exchange Commission and allows them in the Interstate Commerce Commission, the Tax Court, and the National Labor Relations Board. Openings are left in the law even where statutes specify that "attorneys" are to practice before the particular agency, since, oddly enough, the word has been construed to include laymen. This loophole is avoided by use of the word "counsel" instead of "attorney," and this has been done in the acts governing agencies which prohibit appearances by nonlawyers.

Some laws, however, are so drawn that a right to appear "in person or otherwise" is granted. In such instances, rules of construction are of no avail. Although there is certainly no marked trend, there appears to be a movement toward a uniform rule requiring all practitioners before agencies to be lawyers. Some agencies have been able to accomplish this end by prescribing standards of conduct governing laymen—standards which, in effect, impose a code of legal ethics upon them.

Laymen must file formal applications to appear before ten civilian agencies—the Department of the Interior, the Federal Maritime Board, the General Accounting Office, the Interstate Commerce Commission, the Immigration and Naturalization Service, the Patent Office, the Tax Court, the Treasury Department, the Veterans Administration, and the War Claims Commission. The blanks in use require applicants to set forth detailed accounts of background, experience, and references. But only a few agencies appear to require examinations. For special technical reasons, the Patent Office will examine laymen and lawyers alike; and the Treasury Department conducts tests for customs brokers, another unique specialty.

The Interstate Commerce Commission and the Tax Court hold examinations on applicable statutory law, general rules of evidence, and legal ethics.

Lawyers must file applications for admission before thirteen agencies. In the other agencies a notice of appearance or a power of attorney filed in a particular case is enough. But this requirement of filing serves little purpose, since a lawyer qualified to practice law in any state should be qualified to practice before any agency except the Patent Office. In addition, all the agencies except the Patent Office admit lawyers to practice upon substantially the same proof—membership in good standing of a state or federal bar. Insisting upon separate applications, therefore, results in little more than paper work, some loss of time, and additional expense.

While both lawyers and laymen may be "disbarred" from practice before the agencies, records reveal that few ever are. In the case of laymen such action may be difficult, because they are not under the jurisdiction of bar associations and because there are few other supervisory bodies with jurisdiction over ethics. Thus, unless there is a specialty organization of administrative practitioners, in most instances only gross breaches of ethical conduct are punished by disbarment, and the responsibility for that step rests entirely on the agency. A practically exhaustive account shows that the Treasury Department has disbarred two "attorneys" and revoked the licenses of seven customs brokers; the Patent Office has disbarred two; a "quite small" number have been dropped, generally on "uncontested formal grounds," by the Immigration and Naturalization Service. The Interstate Commerce Commission disbarred one lay practitioner in 1937 and suspended four others from practice in 1940, 1941, and 1942.

The disbarment of members of the bar is even less frequent. In the last five or so years the Securities and Exchange Commission has disbarred one, and that appears to be all. In the same length of time the National Labor Relations Board has suspended one lawyer, and the Patent Office has suspended one and reprimanded two. Conflict-of-interest rules, although they do not concern lawyers or lay practitioners, are used by many agencies and are adequately enforced against former employees. Usually the provision is that a former employee is prohibited from practicing before the agency within two years after leaving government service with respect to matters of which he obtained personal knowledge while in the agency. Other statutes prohibit conflicts of interest while the individual is still employed.

Commenting on suggestions for improvement in this area, the Survey report finds that here, too, integration and uniformity of procedure is needed. And, just as the sovereignty of the states makes it difficult to arrive at a consolidated practice, so the large number and functional diversity of the federal agencies raise their own obstacles. What can be done without too much difficulty in the latter field, however, is to adopt the rule that admission to a state or federal bar is carte blanche for admission to any administrative bar, with exceptions for only those agencies where special technical skills are needed. It might also be wise gradually to do away with practice by laymen, or at least to make them adhere to stricter rules than now apply. In contradistinction to state reform, abolition of variations, ambiguities, and obstacles can come overnight in the federal field. There ought to be a law. All Congress has to do is to pass it.

Supplementing Survey researches in this field is the report by Cullinan on requirements for admission to practice in common-law jurisdictions outside the United States. While this study does not deal strictly with the American lawyer, it contains much valuable information and comparative data in its discussion of bar standards in England, Ireland, the Australian states, New Zealand, and the Canadian provinces. Organization for the practice of law in those countries is considerably different from the system found here—so different that it would require that many American traditions be uprooted if the admission procedures of the British Commonwealth were to be adopted. In one important respect, however, the practices of the Commonwealth countries may serve to guide those working in this field in the United States: the American bar must strive to attain the uniformity which characterizes the admission processes in these common-law jurisdictions.

CHAPTER VIII

Ethics of the Law

Standards of conduct in the legal profession, as set forth by the codes, are high. These codes express the ideals of the profession. "They should be the stars that guide our conduct . . . the goals for which we constantly strive," wrote Orie L. Phillips, co-author (with Philbrick McCoy) of "Conduct of Judges and Lawyers," the Survey report in this area.

Writing of the law as a profession, Dean Wigmore said:

> If the law is thus set apart as a profession, it must have traditions and tenets of its own, which are to be mastered and lived up to. This living spirit of the profession, which limits it yet uplifts it as a livelihood, has been customarily known by the vague term "legal ethics." There is much more to it than rules of ethics. There is a whole atmosphere of life's behavior. What is signified is all the learning about the traditions of behavior that mark off and emphasize the legal profession as a guild of public officers. And the apprentice must hope and expect to make full acquaintance with this body of traditions, as his manual of equipment, without which he cannot do his part to keep the law on the level of a profession.

Formal codes of ethics as we know them today are the outgrowth of professional thinking of less than a century. Yet the lawyer's oath and statement of duties, as distinguished from canons of ethics, are nearly as old as the common law itself. The significance of the lawyer's oath is that it stamps him as an officer of the state, with rights, powers, and duties as important as the court judges themselves.

The first formal code in the United States was that approved by the Alabama Bar Association in 1887. The Code of Professional Ethics of the American Bar Association was adopted in 1908, and the Canons of Judicial Ethics in 1924. Both have since been revised and amended.

How widespread among state bar associations are codes of professional ethics? Of the forty-eight states, twenty-five have "integrated" bar associations, which means that all the lawyers are by law members of a state bar association and directly subject to its supervision. All twenty-five of these states have codes, except for two which have "Rules of Professional Conduct" rather than codes or canons. In all cases, the codes or rules have been promulgated by action of the state bar association, by rule or order of the supreme court, or by statute.

Among the twenty-three states which have voluntary bar associations, three have codes adopted by the supreme court of the state, fifteen have codes adopted only by the bar association, and four have no codes at all. Tennessee and the District of Columbia also have codes but did not state (in a 1952 survey) how they were promulgated. The state codes in general are based on the American Bar Association canons, and even in the four states having no codes the canons are apparently recognized as the standards to which the bar should adhere.

Progress in the adoption of canons of ethics for judges has been much less satisfactory. Among the twenty-five states having integrated bar associations, fifteen have no codes of judicial ethics, nor do thirteen of the states in which the bar is organized on a voluntary basis. It cannot be supposed, however, that judges in these states are without some guide to their conduct. In most of them there are certain constitutional or statutory provisions governing the conduct of judges or officeholders generally. And the Canons of Judicial Ethics of the American Bar Association are generally felt to provide standards even where they have not been officially adopted.

The legal profession has made much progress in the first half of this century toward discharging its obligations to society at large through the performance of duties which lawyers owe to the public. Some of this advancement must be attributed to the adoption of canons of ethics. Phillips and McCoy suggest that perhaps the time has come to re-examine these canons to determine whether they adequately define the respective duties which the lawyer and the judge owe to the commonwealth and for a public reaffirmation of the standards of the profession.

HOW STANDARDS ARE TAUGHT

How and how well are young lawyers taught professional standards? *Can* ethics be taught at all? What do young lawyers know of standards as they prepare to start out on their careers?

Law schools.—From a study of the replies of eighty-five law-school deans to a questionnaire in 1950 the following two conclusions were reached:

1. The law schools are in general agreement on the importance of inculcating a strong sense of professional responsibility and on the duty of the schools to promote its development in their students. Dissatisfaction with present methods used by the schools to develop this attitude is widely expressed.

2. There is much variety in what is being done and equally widespread disagreement on what should be done. Many schools have no courses devoted to professional conduct. In the schools which do have such instruction the courses vary in spirit and objective, in method and content, in length and place in the curriculum. There is, however, almost complete agreement that attention should be given to professional standards and obligations in other courses. But this attention seems to vary from conscientious and consistent to sporadic and casual effort.

Two-thirds of the law schools offer course work on the professional functions of the lawyer, though there is much difference in such details as length and content of the courses and percentage of students taking the subject.

From this point on, the diversity of opinion among the law-school deans grows even wider. There is probably a greater variety of views and methods in this field than in any other part of law-school work. This variety stems in part from differences of opinion over the functions of a law school, in part from disagreement as to practicable methods and scope of treatment, and in part from the size of the schools.

Despite their differences as to methods, the deans are agreed on two fundamental matters: that, while guidance in this area must be largely inspirational, "too much preaching" should be avoided and that, regardless of whether there be a course labeled as such, professional responsibility should receive attention in other courses.

On the first point, the deans agree that, while honesty cannot be taught, a course on ethics can perhaps help the student avoid mistakes that are due to ignorance and, second, that the lawyer's place in society should not be ignored by the law school. "I do not advocate a 'school for policy-makers,'" wrote one dean, "but

I do believe that it is possible to show the student how he as a lawyer can move to regain for the profession the role of creator and leader of public opinion that it once had."

The 1950 study revealed a feeling among some law-school heads that responsibility for the inculcation of professional standards rests as much with the bar itself as with the schools, if not to a greater extent. At least two deans were decidedly cynical, saying in effect that law students are discouraged and disillusioned by what they see and hear about their profession. But, without minimizing the responsibility of the bar in the training of young lawyers, Phillips and McCoy hold that, so long as the prospective lawyer is an undergraduate, the direct responsibility of the bar must be secondary to that of the school.

Bar examiners.—For a young lawyer there is a certain temporal "no-man's land" between the time of graduation and admission to practice. During this critical period the burden of responsibility for the young lawyer's career rests chiefly with the bar examiners.

Part of the 1950 survey was designed to ascertain (1) the extent of the powers of the courts and committees of bar examiners to require all applicants to have an understanding of the functions and duties of lawyers; (2) whether questions on this subject are included in bar examinations; and (3) whether law-school deans believe that such questions should be included.

The replies were summarized by Cheatham as follows:

1. The great majority of the deans expressed the view that the courts or bar examiners do have the power to require all applicants to have such understanding.

2. Twenty-one deans said that no questions on this subject were included in the bar examinations; fifty-one said that some were.

3. On the question: "*Should* questions on this subject be in the bar examinations?" fifty-seven deans replied in the affirmative, fourteen in the negative, and six were undecided. The opinion of those opposed was, in general, that character cannot be tested by examination questions and that "the greatest rogue is often the biggest liar."

The principle of examining the prospective lawyer on his ethical concepts as well as his knowledge of law is an ancient one. As early as 1402, in the reign of Henry IV, it was provided by statute that "all attorneys should be examined by the justices, and in their discretion, only those found to be good and virtuous, and of good fame, learned and sworn to do their duty, be allowed to be put upon the roll and all others put out."

The lawyer, upon being admitted to practice, is sworn to perform the duties of his office to the best of his ability. The traditional oath is: "I do swear that I will truly and honestly demean myself in the practice of an attorney or solicitor according to the best of my knowledge and ability. So help me God."

Of what avail, it may be asked, is this oath if the lawyer thus sworn is lacking in adequate knowledge of the nature of these duties? Certainly it cannot be successfully denied that the responsibility rests with the courts, or with the committees of bar examiners acting for the courts, to ascertain the extent of the new lawyer's knowledge on this score before the oath is administered.

Unfortunately, there is much truth in the statement that character cannot be tested by bar examination. There is still, however, a large area which may be called that of professional standards, which seemingly *can* be tested by bar examinations as well as taught by law schools. This distinction is pointed up by one law-school dean who said: "I think it may be conceded that honesty cannot be taught. But two aspects of an ethics course outweigh that argument. Some mistakes are due to ignorance, which a school can prevent; and the lawyer's place in society cannot be ignored by a law school."

If the schools can teach ethics, it follows that the bar examinations can test at least the quantitative measures of that teaching.

The use of preceptors.—The purpose of the preceptor, or apprenticeship, system is to fill the vacuum between a young lawyer's receipt of a law degree and his gaining of sufficient practical competence actually to serve clients. It is at this point that the two problems—practical training for a young lawyer and his training in professional standards—converge.

Many of the older lawyers of today prepared themselves for the bar entirely under the preceptor system. At present, preceptors are used in two ways: (1) in connection with undergraduate training in some law schools (seven of the eighty-five schools queried in the 1950 survey) and (2) in guiding the young lawyer through an apprenticeship period between graduation and admission to the bar.

A. Z. Reed said:

Expertness in legal practice and conduct that is ethically meritorious are, of course, two quite distinct qualities. Either may exist without the other, and the profession contains . . . both too many representatives who unscrupulously use all the tricks of the trade and too many well-meaning but incompetent lawyers. On the other hand, the process by which these two distinct qualities can be developed is the same. Law schools can do a little, but not much, to attain either end. Bar-admission authorities can do a little more, but not much more, so long as it is tacitly assumed that all efforts in either direction, other than disciplinary measures, cease the moment the applicant has been admitted.

Both the sense of mastery over his art that the practiced craftsman possesses, and the sense of obligation to other than one's immediate interests that should pervade the ancient and honorable profession of the law, can be properly developed only after the young lawyer has incurred the responsibilities of genuine legal practice.

It is enough here to recognize the possibilities for good which lie in the preceptor or apprenticeship system. The responsibility for its development and more widespread adoption lies jointly with the law schools and the bar.

The comments of three legal educators are offered as a concluding note on the subject of the inculcation of professional standards:

We think so much of the [professional standards] course that it is not only required, but we would not think of graduating our students without it. The course emphasizes the lawyer's responsibility to his client, the public, and his profession [Robert G. Storey, dean of the School of Law, Southern Methodist University].

There should not be any doubt, I believe, that a course such as this has a contribution to make to the preparation of students for the responsibilities of the profession. It, or something better, should have a place in the professional program of every law school [Albert J. Harno, dean of the College of Law, University of Illinois].

To us it seems futile to educate a man to perform the services of a lawyer without giving him some instruction on the requisites of being a lawyer. If technical competence is all that is required, then we had better confess that practicing law has ceased to be a profession [Whitney R. Harris, Southern Methodist University].

HOW STANDARDS ARE OBSERVED

Just what constitutes unethical or "unprofessional" conduct in a lawyer and how common is it? Or, to put the question another way, what are proper standards of conduct and how well are they maintained?

To what extent does unprofessional conduct indicate infraction of the Code of Professional Ethics and to what extent does it reflect the need for revised or added canons to bring the Code in line with modern conditions or accepted practice? When, if rules are broken, is it time to change the rules?

Should stricter adherence to canons be attempted by education or by disciplinary action?

These are among the questions to be answered in any study of how, in practice, the bar observes professional standards. It is obviously impossible to obtain complete, accurate, and uniform information on the nation-wide conduct of the bar. It is equally impossible to be 100 per cent positive and dogmatic in evaluating the data revealed by even the most careful and thoroughgoing inquiry. The Ten Commandments themselves have been subject to some interpretation, and the bar's canons of professional standards are considerably more complex than the Decalogue.

In connection with the Survey of the Legal Profession, Robert T. McCracken attempted to determine the status of code observance by means of a questionnaire sent to at least three confidential reporters in each state. Replies were received from forty-two states. In the first part of his questionnaire, McCracken described "typical situations" in a lawyer's practice that touch upon various of the canons. He then asked his reporters to state whether the situations described would be considered professional or unprofessional in their respective states and to indicate the degree of prevalence of such conduct in their states. Replies to this latter group of questions were received, however, from only twenty-five of the forty-two states.

It was McCracken's general conclusion that "most of the canons here dealt with seem to be faithfully observed by an overwhelming majority of the lawyers in the United States. A few are departed from for one of two reasons: (*a*) because they are not considered realistic and applicable to business and professional conditions in the modern American world, or (*b*) because some lawyers, for reasons of gain or in their zeal to win cases, see fit to disregard certain canons, departure from the observance of which constitutes clearly unprofessional practice."

No attempt will be made here to present McCracken's findings in detail. Some highlights will be given in order to indicate, first, specifically what is considered to be unprofessional behavior, according to the canons; second, the apparently prevailing attitudes toward such behavior; and, third, its prevalence.

Direct Solicitation of Employment (Canons 27 and 28): "Ambulance chasing" is considered unprofessional in all twenty-five states reporting; it is said to be a common practice in nine states and nonexistent in only two.

Indirect Solicitation (Canon 20): Responses were substantially the same as for direct solicitation.

Employment Which Should Be Declined (Canons 6, 30, 31, 36): It is unprofessional for a lawyer to represent conflicting interests except by consent of all concerned, given after a full disclosure of all the facts. A lawyer must decline to conduct a civil case, or make a defense, that is intended to harass or injure the other party. With minor exceptions, concurrence in all states reporting.

Employment Which Should Be Accepted (Canons 4 and 5): It is part of the lawyer's oath that he "will never reject, from any consideration personal to [himself], the cause of the defenseless or oppressed, or delay any man's cause for lucre or malice." A lawyer assigned as counsel for an indigent person should not excuse himself for a trivial reason and should always exert his best efforts in the person's behalf. Yet rejection of such cases is *not* considered unprofessional in eight states and is reported as common practice in five.

A greater disregard of professional obligations is found in the cases of persons accused of crime than in the civil law area. In thirteen, or more than half of the states reporting, it is not considered unprofessional to reject such cases, and in nine of those states it is common practice to do so. In view of the United States Constitution's guaranty to every person accused of crime the right "to have Assistance of Counsel for his defense," and in view of the lawyer's oath plus every accepted professional standard, this is a startling disclosure.

In England the obligation to represent the indigent as well as other defendants in criminal cases has long been taken for granted. Yet, with a few notable exceptions, it is the rule in this country that the average attorney is unwilling to handle the average criminal case. It is apparent from the McCracken report and from the investigations of Brownell and others (see chap. iii, "Legal Aid") that much work remains to be done by the bar to measure up to its obligations in this phase of professional standards.

Trial Work and Its Incidents (Canons 5, 18, 19, 20, 22, 30, 31, 39, 41): Trial practices considered unprofessional include treating the adverse witness and suitors with lack of fairness and consideration; failure of a lawyer to withdraw from a case after he has appeared as a substantial witness; procuring or facilitating newspaper publicity about pending litigation or making one-sided statements for publication which go beyond the record; lack of candor and fairness in a trial or hearing; interviewing opposing witnesses in a way calculated to induce the witness to deviate from the truth or to remain absent; presentation of an unfounded claim, an unfounded defense, or evidence known to be false; concealing from the court important facts and adverse decisions unknown to the other side; communicating privately with a judge as to the merits of a pending case.

Here there is enough evidence of deviation from standard practice (as high as 20 per cent) to indicate need for grave concern that unprofessional conduct is so widely reported as a "common practice."

Office Work (Canons 9, 16, 41): Practices condemned by the canons include communicating with the adverse party directly instead of through his counsel: failure to seek to restrain a client from unfair action; failure to take appropriate action where fraud or deception is intended or has been perpetrated by the client. The McCracken report indicates generally a wholesome acceptance of these standards. There is, however, evidence of a need for some lawyers to re-examine their own consciences in such matters as seeking to restrain clients from unfair acts.

The Lawyer for the State (Canon 5): The primary duty of the lawyer engaged in public prosecutions, says the code, is "not to convict, but to see that justice is done." Along with this goes the further provision that "the suppression of facts or the secreting of witnesses capable of establishing the innocence of the accused is highly reprehensible." Violation of this canon is generally considered unprofessional, with one state reporting to the contrary and three in doubt or having no opinion. Violations are reported, however, as common practice in three states, rare in fifteen, and nonexistent in only four.

Fees (Canons 12, 13, 34, 38): Unprofessional practices—so considered in the great majority of states reporting—include the charging of excessive fees; overreaching with respect to contingent fees; the acceptance of compensation from others without knowledge of the client; the division of professional fees with laymen. On the other hand, McCracken found that the charging of excessive fees was a common practice in ten states and overreaching on contingent fees commonplace in six. Misconduct of attorneys in fixing fees, says McCracken, "more than anything, is the element which renders the public suspicious and often distrustful of the bar."

Part of the McCracken report was devoted to suggestions for changes in existing canons and the addition of new ones. Among those which various of his reporters singled out as, in their judgment, needing revision were the following representative examples:

Canon 2, which deals with the duties of lawyers toward judges, should be amended so as to cover the duty of the bar to insist on the removal of unfit members of judicial tribunals, as well as to assist in securing good judicial appointments. It should also cover appointments and removal with reference to quasi-judicial bodies such as administrative bureaus.

Canon 10 should be revised so as to demonstrate clearly that it is not considered unethical for a lawyer to take or acquire an interest in the subject matter of the litigation under a contingent arrangement, particularly in states having many suits concerning title to oil, gas, or other minerals. Such arrangements are quite common and are generally felt to be ethical in the area from which this suggestion comes.

Canons 27 and 35 should be modified so as to accommodate "a growing recognition" of the desire of associations, whether for profit or otherwise, to retain the services of an attorney and have him available for representation of individual members of the group. It is a practice often followed and, accordingly, should be frankly recognized and no longer held unethical.

Canon 12, which deals with fees, should be expanded to spell out in greater detail the factors involved in fixing fees.

Other recommendations and questions, dealing both with existing canons and with proposals for new ones, include:

1. A canon should be framed which would warn the lawyer as to his peculiar duty with respect to those offenses to which lawyers are particularly tempted—perjury, bribery, and extortion. This canon might also deal with the bringing of unfounded suits, making of extravagant claims, charging exorbitant fees, and devising ingenious ways of breaking the laws.

2. Because in many instances the lawyer cannot properly advise his clients without the assistance of experts in other fields, a canon should be framed stressing the duty of a lawyer to utilize the services of such experts.

3. A canon should be framed dealing with the problem of whether it is proper for a lawyer, especially in a small community, to engage in other businesses and to have lay partners, especially in accounting and insurance, and whether it is proper for the lay partners to advertise.

4. Since it is frequently necessary for a lawyer to utilize the press, especially where no court or similar tribunal is available, the canon dealing with this subject should be carefully considered with an eye to revision.

5. Should the canons require that a lawyer disclose to his client any interest which might influence the latter, but also disclose to the court or other tribunal before which he practices—and especially to legislatures—the true identity of the party he represents?

6. Should there be a special canon covering negotiations and controversies which do not result in litigation? The present canons lay too much stress on the lawyer's duty as an advocate.

7. The trend is in the direction of more lawyers becoming employees rather than engaging in independent practice. These employees are of two classes: those who never come in contact with the clients and those who do. They might also be classified as those who are strictly office employees and those who appear in

court on behalf of clients of their employers. Although joining labor unions has not become a common practice among lawyers, a canon covering the propriety of joining unions might be adopted.

With reference to all these suggested changes and amendments, McCracken reaches these conclusions:

> These suggestions disclose the alteration in the relations between lawyer and client during the last forty or fifty years. Not only has the bar greatly increased in number during that period but the mounting influence of labor unions and countless other kinds of associations, together with the growing practice of great corporations in installing legal departments, has created a relationship between lawyer and client differing sharply from that of the close personal contact of earlier days.
>
> Lawyers find themselves constantly called upon to represent large groups, such as chambers of commerce and trade associations, the members of which are often in keen competition in their individual businesses. Serious ethical problems are bound to present themselves in these situations—hence the suggestions of so many of these answering the questionnaire that the canons covering these matters, particularly Canon 35, be re-examined.

To this might be added a quotation from a well-known address by Justice Harlan F. Stone on "The Public Influence of the Bar," in 1934:

> We cannot expect the Bar to function as it did in other days and under other conditions. Before it can function at all as the guardian of public interests committed to its care, there must be appraisal and comprehension of the new conditions and the changed relationships of the lawyer to his clients, to his professional brethren and to the public. That appraisal must pass beyond the petty details of form and manners which have been so largely the subject of our codes of ethics, to more fundamental consideration of the way in which our professional activities affect the welfare of society as a whole. Our Canons of Ethics for the most part are generalizations designed for an earlier era. . . .
>
> . . . The very conditions which have caused specialization, which have drawn so heavily on the technical proficiency of the Bar, have likewise placed it in a position where the possibilities of its influence are almost beyond calculation. The intricacies of business organization are built upon a legal framework which the current growth of administrative law is still further elaborating. Without the constant advice and guidance of lawyers, business would come to an abrupt halt. And whatever standards of conduct in the performance of its functions the Bar consciously adopts must be reflected at once in the character of the world of business and finance. Given a measure of self-conscious and cohesive professional unity, the Bar may exert a power more beneficent and far-reaching than it or any other non-governmental group has wielded in the past.

EDUCATION OR DISCIPLINE

Assuming that a stricter adherence to the canons is desirable, the question arises: Should attempts to bring it about be through educational processes or through disciplinary action?

To judge by the comments of the respondents in the McCracken study, the answer would be "Both."

Collectively the views of the bar throughout the country, as determined by the survey, may be summarized in the following quotations:

> . . . especially by educational processes. Disciplinary action is more or less futile. Only the most brazen violations are questioned, and grievance committee members are always too lenient with offenders.
>
> A more widespread understanding of all the canons . . . should be attempted by educational processes, which should be constant in order to keep the new members of the profession fully advised of the moral obligations . . . with such disciplinary action as will assure keeping the profession in the proper light before the lay public.
>
> There is a need for greater publicity. The general public is not aware that there is any such thing as a set standard for the bar, and there is seldom any effective disciplinary action taken, for the reason that most violations are secretive and evidence is hard to get.
>
> The courts could help greatly. They could be more active and mete out real discipline in the actual cases brought to them instead of withholding the record from the public and the newspapers. There are quite a few open violations of the canons in the capital district of New York State, but there is very little interest and practically no support for housecleaning by the courts or the newspapers and less by the profession.
>
> The more a brother errs, the more grace the courts give him. We wish the courts would quit condoling and excusing. Mercy is a great temptation to power, as vicarious benevolence is to all of us.

These excerpts are enough to illustrate the strong feeling that a greater adherence to stated professional standards should be sought through extended educational work as well as through the imposition of swift and sure discipline in appropriate cases. Here again is shown the need for education, not only of the student lawyer, his practicing brother, and the courts, but of the general public as well. Here again is a challenge to the law schools and to the organized bar.

What is this business of discipline and disbarment? Is it of any real value to the public? What is its relation to the courts and to the legal profession? These are some of the questions that are basic to a consideration of disciplinary procedures in use throughout the country.

The court in a California disbarment case not many years ago said:

> The license to practice as an attorney and counselor is a certificate of good moral character. It is a representation by the court, speaking as of the date of the license, that the licensee is a trustworthy person who reasonably may be expected to act fairly and honestly in the practice of his profession. Thereafter, in the absence of proof to the contrary, the original representation exists as a continuing presumption. . . . But when the charges of misconduct have been made and proved in a disbarment proceeding, the original representation has fallen, and with it the presumption becomes dust and ashes.

It needs to be emphasized that suspension or disbarment of a lawyer is not *punishment*. The purpose of discipline is to protect the courts from the official ministrations of persons unfit to practice in them. From this it follows that it is equally the purpose of discipline to protect the public and the legal profession itself from the ministration of these unfit persons.

The power of the courts to investigate and to control the membership of the bar through disciplinary proceedings is as old as the profession itself. It is coequal with the power to regulate admissions to the practice of law and includes the power to determine the good character and fitness of all those who seek admission to practice. If this power were not fully recognized and fully exercised by the courts, with the support and assistance of the organized bar, the law could not be thought of as a learned profession.

A nation-wide study of disciplinary procedures was undertaken in 1948, when questionnaires were sent out to bar presidents, county clerks, and other appropriate officials in all the states. Information from this and other sources is insufficient to permit making a general comparison between states in which the bar is integrated by statute, rule of court, or court decision (twenty-five, as of 1950) and those in which the bar is organized on a voluntary basis. In the latter states, discipline remains primarily the responsibility of the courts.

Regardless of the type of bar organization that may exist, two conditions are essentially involved in efficient disciplinary action.

First, there must be the *will* to rid the profession of unethical lawyers. Second, there must be an effective *procedure* by which this can be accomplished.

As an example of each type of organization, lawyer discipline in California (integrated) and Illinois (voluntary) will be examined in some detail. California and Illinois are generally comparable in total population and lawyer population. (*The Second Statistical Report of Lawyers in the United States*—January, 1952—lists 16,858 lawyers in California and 16,365 in Illinois.) The bar of California was incorporated in 1927; that of Illinois is still voluntary. For the period 1928–48 California reported a total of 1,993 formal disciplinary proceedings, and Illinois, for the same period, a total of 1,291. Since the history of the integrated bar as a going concern roughly parallels the period under review, the record in California might be taken as a fair reflection of the effect of integration.

In 1900 there were 114,703 attorneys in the United States, and in 1910 the number had increased by only one. In California, during the same period, the number increased from 4,278 to 4,908, or 14 per cent. From 1910 to 1920 the number in the whole country increased 7 per cent, whereas in California the increase was 30 per cent. In the next decade, from 1920 to 1930, the increase in the United States was 31 per cent, and in California 50 per cent. By 1950 there were 13,655 lawyers in the state; in 1952, 16,858.

Integration of the bar in 1927 brought with it the power of the board of governors and local committees appointed by it to try lawyers for professional misconduct, to reprimand publicly or privately, and to recommend discipline by the supreme court. Of more importance, the State Bar Act provided for the use of subpoenas to compel the production of evidence. Even more important was the act's provision for an informal preliminary investigation, again with the use of subpoenas, of any charges brought against a lawyer by any person desiring to make such a complaint.

From 1927 to 1939 there had been 8,335 complaints brought against lawyers. There had been 7,965 preliminary investigations and 1,425 notices to show cause. In 278 cases recommendations for discipline had been made to the supreme court. In 1939 the president of the state bar reported that the number of disciplinary proceedings was constantly decreasing (see Table 23). Commenting on this, he said: "I believe it is due to the fact that any lawyer who might be inclined to forget his oath and his professional obligations realizes that he cannot get away with it. I think another cause has been the fact that the type of men and women admitted to the bar in the last several years has much higher standards than formerly."

There is much evidence in the California records to support the complaint of the bar that the courts show too much leniency toward attorneys against whom disciplinary steps have been taken. On many occasions of disagreement with the state bar's board of governors, the supreme court of California has imposed a *lesser* degree of discipline, but there is no case on record in which the court has even considered imposing a *greater* degree of discipline, even though it has the power to do so.

A state bar president said of the California procedure for investigating complaints against lawyers:

> Each of these complaints evidenced a grievance against some member of the legal profession. Practically all of them evidenced a grievance against the whole profession . . . grievances that were shared by relatives, neighbors and friends.
>
> We have recognized the simple truth that there is no sure and permanent way to secure more respect than by deserving more respect. . . . By personal and painstaking work we have removed the causes of grievances; we have made friends of those who were our most severe critics. . . .
>
> By this process the bar is serving the public by raising the moral standards of the bar; and it is serving the legal profession by making the legal profession more worthy of respect, and therefore more respected.

Rule 59 of the supreme court of Illinois establishes the machinery for the legal profession's disciplining of its own members. It was not until 1909 that the court officially recognized the organized bar's duty in this regard. Rule 59 dates from 1933, when a prior rule was amended to set up the procedure now followed in that state.

In numerous instances the supreme court has shown that it is clearly its intention to vest the initiation of disciplinary proceedings in the state's two bar organizations, the Chicago Bar Association and the Illinois State Bar Association. Thus the methods by which

TABLE 23

STATISTICAL DATA CONCERNING DISCIPLINARY WORK IN THE STATE BAR OF CALIFORNIA

	1928	1929	1930	1931	1932	1933	1934	1935	1936	1937	1938	1939	1940	1941	1942	1943	1944	1945	1946	1947	1948
Preliminary investigations	1072	1531	960	941	750	490	394	444	626	247	160	287	382	302	158	190	122	128	171	181	148
Notices to show cause	367	132	178	84	75	77	123	101	77	85	73	86	105	57	37	51	27	26	30	48	19
Action of the board of governors:																					
Dismissed	337	90	125	58	45	36	76	55	42	51	37	54	66	30	7	26	12	7	21	33	10
Privately reproved	0	3	14	8	7	10	6	7	5	6	6	7	3	3	2	6	1	4	3	0	1
Publicly reproved	12	20	11	4	3	3	8	7	8	5	3	5	7	3	4	2	3	5	2	5	1
Suspension recommended	7	7	15	10	13	17	20	19	14	11	12	8	17	8	17	9	10	8	2	3	7
Disbarment recommended	11	12	13	4	7	11	13	13	8	12	15	12	12	13	7	8	1	2	2	2	0
Action of supreme court:																					
Dismissed	0	0	0	4	0	1	1	2	2	1	2	1	0	7	1	0	1	1	1	0	1
Reproved	0	0	0	1	1	1	0	0	0	0	0	0	0	0	0	0	1	0	0	0	0
Suspended	0	15	16	18	12	13	23	19	15	12	11	11	12	12	12	10	9	8	5	4	7
Disbarred	0	14	8	5	3	8	9	9	14	10	5	13	5	16	5	8	4	2	0	3	0
Resignations:																					
Voluntary	1	2	7	2	7	9	6	6	11	10	6	1	6	5	4	4	2	2	0	0	2
With prejudice*	0	0	0	0	0	0	4	3	1	4	2	5	3	5	2	0	0	1	0	0	0
Conviction of crime:																					
Disbarred or suspended until further order of supreme court	3	4	2	5	7	9	8	3	10	8	14	8	5	9	6	0	1	3	0	0	5

* The decision in November, 1946, in Jonesi v. State Bar, 29 Calif. 2d 181, probably put an end to this type of resignation in California.

these associations operate determine to a large extent the effectiveness of legal disciplinary measures in Illinois.

In general, both bar organizations operate in the same fashion in this area. The committee on grievances serves the respondent with a formal complaint, and a hearing is held in which regular trial practice is observed. After the evidence has been taken, a report of findings of fact and conclusions of law is prepared. To this report the respondent may file objections, and the board of governors, sitting as commissioners, reviews the record and passes on the objections. If a recommendation for disciplinary action is agreed upon, the report and the recommendation are sent to the court. The complained-against attorney may file exceptions before the court, which then holds the final hearing.

TABLE 24

COMPLAINTS RECEIVED BY THE TWO ILLINOIS BAR ASSOCIATIONS

Area	Complaints per 100,000 Population	Complaints per 1,000 Lawyers
Chicago	27.85	97.43
Rest of Illinois	1.17	15.21

A very striking difference exists between the number of complaints received by the two associations: approximately 1,000 per year in Chicago, as contrasted with an average of 59 per year for the state association. Adjusted to population and the number of lawyers, the difference is shown in Table 24.

It would be easy to conclude that the incidence of unethical practice is far greater in the metropolitan area. However, a number of other possible factors must be considered, and the easy conclusion is to be accepted—if at all—with great caution.

The Chicago Bar Association serves a compact and densely populated area. Publicity concerning the work of the organization and individual cases reaches a large segment of the public. Again, in a city it is easy for an aggrieved person to call individually at the association office, while the downstate association serves many communities over a wide area. Moreover, in the case of the Illinois

State Bar Association, there is in each county a local bar association which, in a sense, stands between the state organization and the public. It is possible, too, that metropolitan living conditions give rise to more complaints without real basis than is true in the rural districts.

The record in Illinois reveals what appears to be a definite correlation between economic conditions and complaints of unethical practices. During the period 1922–29 an annual average of 375 complaints was investigated by the Chicago Bar Association. In 1930–31 the figure was 550; in 1931–32, 767; in 1932–33, 864; in 1933–34, 952. Thereafter the average dropped substantially, and the average for the years 1942–48 was 174.

COMPLAINTS AND CONSEQUENCES

A valuable understanding of the nature of complaints against lawyers can be gained from a look at the cases that have come before the Illinois State Bar Association. From 1928 to 1948 a total of 566 complaints were received. Of this number, 531 were dismissed as unwarranted. A breakdown of these dismissed cases affords an interesting insight into the kinds of behavior that inspire demands for disciplinary action, whether those demands ultimately be deemed justified or not.

Cases that were dismissed fall into seven main classifications:

1. *Complaints arising essentially from failure of the lawyer to conduct his practice in a business-like way* (150 cases). This group includes complaints of failure to keep the client informed of action taken in handling the particular situation and neglecting to answer correspondence of a client asking what action, if any, has been taken. A great many of these cases involve collection agencies as the complainant. Also included in this group are seemingly honest mistakes made in sending out statements of fees or failing to take action which has been promised by a certain date and neglecting to give the client an explanation. The client's complaint is a method of prodding the lawyer into action or at least into giving him some satisfaction. In some instances the client evinces a feeling that the delay is due to the fact that he is being defrauded.

2. *Complaints arising from disputes over fees* (104 cases). Again due to unbusiness-like practices, these complaints in many cases

arise out of the fact that no fee has been agreed upon and that, upon completion of the work, the client feels he has been overcharged. Most numerous in this group are those cases in which the lawyer accepts a retainer. The client believes this to be the entire fee, and, when more is asked, he complains to the bar association. Also in this group are those complaints that arise when collections are to be made and the collection fee is not stipulated in advance. The supreme court has stated that such complaints are properly the subject of a civil action and do not involve the imposition of discipline. The committee on inquiry must, nevertheless, investigate the facts set forth.

3. *Complaints involving charges by the unsuccessful litigant that his lawyer "sold him out" or "fixed" the case or that the opposing counsel was guilty of unethical practices* (55 cases). Investigation reveals that such cases are usually the result of the litigant's bitterness seeking an outlet and are generally unfounded in fact.

4. *Complaints involving charges that the lawyer defrauded or overreached the client* (54 cases). Some of these complaints pass the preliminary investigation stage.

5. *Complaints arising out of criminal cases* (34 cases). These complaints, very similar to those in the third class, are generally the result of dissatisfaction with the outcome of the litigation. Thus convicted parties complain that their lawyer "sold them out" or that the prosecuting attorney had witnesses perjure themselves, that the judge was unfair, or that promises of leniency had been made and not fulfilled.

6. *Complaints arising from situations which were obviously headed for disaster from the beginning* (41 cases). In numerous cases these complaints are due to the personality of the client. Included are cases in which the client told the lawyer how to handle the case, but the lawyer substituted his own judgment; complaints that a lawyer had given bad advice on a business deal, accompanied by accusations of fraud; and complaints from clients who are obviously emotionally unstable or mentally ill.

7. *Miscellaneous complaints* (83 cases). These are a group of general complaints which call the lawyer a "crook" or a "shyster" but which fail to produce specific charges or evidence. In this group also are complaints that a lawyer has failed to pay his debts, mali-

cious attacks by unknown complainants, complaints in which the lawyer has predeceased the investigation, and a few in which the gist of the complaint cannot be ascertained at all.

The great number of complaints falling in the first two classifications is significant despite the fact that they are not proper subjects for the institution of disciplinary action. Most of them could have been avoided. Each of them detracted from the prestige of the legal profession and extended beyond the original complainant to the many persons to whom he told his story. The lawyer often operates in the atmosphere of strife and bitterness which naturally accompanies litigation. In this atmosphere the client may easily transfer his ill feeling to the lawyer. While this cannot always be avoided, complaints of the types in these two classifications could be reduced by taking the right precautions.

Cases in which complaints resulted in disciplinary action fall into four main groups:

1. *Complaints in which the lawyer is charged with conversion, fraud, or overreaching the client.* Only this group involves the taking of action on the basis of *complaints* received from the general public. The other three groups are cases which receive their impetus either through the activities of public officials or through investigation by the bar associations themselves.

2. *Moral turpitude.* These are cases in which a lawyer has been convicted of a crime involving moral turpitude and in which the supreme court refuses to look behind the record of conviction.

3. *Graft.* These are cases in which a lawyer has become involved in graft, political or otherwise, such as padded payroll schemes and "kickbacks" of fees.

4. *Solicitation cases, or "ambulance-chasing."* This type of complaint presents such a serious problem in metropolitan Chicago that the Chicago Bar Association created a special committee to deal with it. For years it has been trying to get legislation passed which would outlaw the practice, both for lawyers over whom the association has control and for lay helpers over whom the bar has no jurisdiction. Progress has been made, but the problem remains. One official of the disciplinary committee has said that "ambulance-chasing" remains prevalent for many reasons, not the least of which

is an apathy on the part of the state supreme court toward vigorous punishment of offenders against whom action has been taken.

By comparison with the twenty-year record of disciplinary cases in the Illinois State Bar Association (566 complaints, 531 dismissals), the Chicago Bar Association in the same period received a total of 18,000 complaints. Less than half of the complaints (8,600) were referred to the Committee on Inquiry, and, of these, 7,344 were dismissed.

TABLE 25

DISPOSITION OF DISCIPLINARY CASES BY THE ILLINOIS SUPREME COURT, 1928–48

	Chicago	State	Total
Disbarment	214	17	231
Suspension (maximum 3 years)	45	9	54
Dismissal	53	2	55

TABLE 26

ACTION RECOMMENDED BY BAR ASSOCIATION AND ACTION FOLLOWED BY ILLINOIS SUPREME COURT IN CONTESTED CASES, 1928–48

	Disbarment	Suspension	Dismissal or Censure	Total
Action recommended	75	6	....	81
Action by court	35	18	28	81

A total of 312 complaints for Chicago and 28 for the state association resulted in recommendations of disciplinary action. The disposition by the supreme court of these cases (still for the 1928–48 period) was as shown in Table 25.

It frequently happens that a lawyer against whom disciplinary proceedings are instituted will petition the court to have his name stricken. This is tantamount to a plea of guilty and has the effect of halting the proceedings and the attendant publicity. Eliminating these cases and including only those which were contested before the supreme court of Illinois during the period under study, the figures given in Table 26 result.

The court has thus followed the recommendations of disbarment in about 50 per cent of the cases. Remembering that the complaint has passed through three levels of investigation by fellow-members of the bar prior to the recommendation, it appears that the court has been lenient with those who see fit to contest the recommendation. This is truly significant in view of the thoroughness of the investigations conducted by the prosecuting bar associations.

The appearance of court leniency becomes even more pronounced when it is remembered that all expenses of the proceedings, from start to finish, are borne by the bar associations. They are therefore reluctant to recommend discipline unless the prospect of success is at least probable.

At present no showing of rehabilitation is required in Illinois of a suspended lawyer who has "sat out" the period of suspension and re-enters practice. A lawyer who has been disbarred, however, must prove character rehabilitation in order to have his application for reinstatement approved. In the 1928–48 period twelve disbarred and reinstated lawyers became the subject of further disciplinary action in Illinois, a fact which may raise a question as to the effectiveness of proof of character rehabilitation in any case.

In California reinstatement of disbarred lawyers is governed by rigid rules. The supreme court, which alone has power to admit lawyers to practice in the first place, likewise has exclusive jurisdiction to reinstate a disbarred attorney. Neither the legislature nor the governor has any power in this field. Petitions for reinstatement must be filed in the first instance with the board of governors of the state bar.

Throughout the years many lawyers have resigned from the bar. It is impossible to tell from available information how many have done so in order to avoid discipline or disbarment and how many for other reasons.

The problem of the "repeater"—the disciplined lawyer who is reinstated only to become involved again in disciplinary action—is an important one for the bar and the courts. The answer lies partly in the field of discipline and partly in the field of reinstatement. California furnishes a good example of the anomalous conditions which may prevail in other parts of the country as well.

A lawyer who has been disbarred, upon applying for reinstatement, must make a detailed statement concerning his activities since his disbarment. Extensive hearings are held in which the burden of proof rests with the applicant. If his showing is adequate, he may again practice law. The purpose of such investigation is obviously to determine whether the disbarred lawyer still has the professional qualifications and is again of such good moral character as will make him a trustworthy and honorable member of the bar.

The contrast between the reinstatement cases applying these rigid requirements and the total lack of investigation in the case of suspended lawyers upon their resumption of practice is both enlightening and startling. A case in 1948 involving a "repeater" in California is in point. The board of governors found the lawyer guilty of a violation of his oath in having made certain false representations to the court to his financial advantage. Taking into consideration the fact that the lawyer had previously been suspended on two occasions based on four different complaints, the board recommended his disbarment. Nevertheless, the court without explanation suspended the lawyer for three years, with one member of the court voting to dismiss the proceedings on the ground that the attorney had been guilty only of an error in judgment for which he should not have been disciplined.

The vice inherent in such a decision in relation to the problem under discussion is apparent. The lawyer so suspended for a third time was, with leave of the supreme court, thus authorized to resume practice again at the end of three years, without any inquiry as to his qualifications or character.

The remedy in such cases is patent. If, with propriety, the courts are willing to grant yet another chance to a lawyer who so far forgets his oath as to warrant suspension from practice for three years—and in this case suspension for the third time!—then the courts should certainly condition this grant upon his submitting to an investigation of his fitness.

Where the line should be drawn in any case is but a question of degree. The fact remains that the courts *must* be more stringent in the discipline of repeating offenders in order that the public may have the protection to which it is entitled.

ELECTION AND CONDUCT OF JUDGES

Regardless of whatever claim to fame he may have, or whatever his qualifications may be, as fixed by constitution or statute, a judge is in essence simply a lawyer, clothed for the time being with the powers of his office, subject to the obligations he voluntarily assumed when he took his oath.

It is a far cry from the Colonial days when the courts were controlled by the crown and the judges were noted for their ignorance and their lack of legal education. With the establishment of state governments, lawyers gradually assumed all judicial offices, and it is now customary to find in the constitutions or statutes provisions concerning the qualifications of judges, including, for most courts, the requirement that they be members of the bar. (A notable exception is that with respect to the Supreme Court of the United States.)

It has been said that the lawyer has three obligations: to his client, to the court, and to society. These obligations may conflict. They may, indeed, be in some cases irreconcilable. When a lawyer becomes a judge, he is relieved of any obligations to client, retaining only those to the court and to society. These obligations should never be in conflict. Canon 2 of the Canons of Judicial Ethics declares that "courts exist to promote justice, and thus to serve the public interest."

The lawyer who is unwilling to forego private obligations that might interfere with the proper performance of his judicial duties should not become a judge. A judge who administers his office for the purpose of advancing his personal ambitions or increasing his popularity at the expense of public interest should resign or be retired by the people.

But few states appear to be free of political influence in the selection of judges, whether the system is basically appointive or elective. Assuming nonpartisan elections in a given state, which may and frequently do assure virtual life-tenure, the fact remains that even in such a state a vacancy on the bench is filled in the first instance by the governor, who is normally far from being nonpartisan. Yet Roscoe Pound of Harvard has written, "In spite of the very general subjection of the bench to politics involved in an elective, short-term judiciary and direct primary in many states, the bench, upon the whole, has been the soundest of our institutions."

The comments of observers throughout the nation, on whose information the Survey's study of this subject is based, generally echo Pound's observation. At the same time a great many of the correspondents expressed the hope that some method might be adopted in their respective states to take judges out of politics, with respect both to their selection and to their conduct while on the bench.

The appointive system of selecting judges prevails in only six states. In addition, in at least twenty-four others vacancies are filled by the governor without any restriction on his appointments. In several of those states the so-called "Missouri Plan," or some similar plan for the nonpartisan selection of judges, is under serious consideration. Missouri's experience seems to show that the selection of judges *can* be effectively taken out of politics, to the benefit of all parties interested in the efficient and honest administration of justice.

Inquiry was made by the Survey as to judicial conduct as predicated on certain of the Canons of Judicial Ethics, specifically Canons 12, 13, 14, 17, 25, and 26. The first four of these are, substantially, a declaration of the obviously sound principle that a judge should not utilize the power or prestige of his office to enhance his own position, politically or otherwise. The findings show that throughout the country some judges depart from one or more of these canons but that generally the canons are more honored than ignored.

Specifically, the comments and criticisms of correspondents indicated ways which might lead to a more complete adherence to this group of canons. The actions, of course, would not eliminate the continuing need for judicial integrity and for a broader public education in the requirements and implications of the canons. The course suggested would simply be to adopt everywhere more adequate statutes stating the causes for removal of judges and to enforce these statutes more rigorously.

For example, Canons 12 and 13 deal, respectively, with nepotism and the acting of judges in controversies where a near-relative is a party. Any departure from the principles stated in these canons is clear evidence of a lack of judicial integrity. These, along with a number of other causes for disqualification, should be included in the statutes of every state.

Said Mr. Justice Roberts:

> When a man goes on the court, he ought not to have to depend on the strength and robustness of his own character to resist the temptation to shade a view in order to put an umbrella up in case it should rain. He ought to be free to say his say, knowing, as the founding fathers meant he should know, that nothing could reach him and that his conscience was as free as could be. . . . He ought not to have to make a vow to himself that ambition shall not color his opinions. It should be impossible for that to happen.

Canon 28 flatly prohibits partisan political activity on the part of judges. To an alarming degree this canon is disregarded throughout the country, largely as a result of the constant need of judges for political support in order to retain their positions. Yet it is difficult to awaken the public, the bar, and the judges themselves to the need for reform in methods of judicial selection as well as in matters relating to the tenure and compensation.

The matter of political activity by judges is governed by constitutional provisions in many jurisdictions. A flagrant departure was the case of a justice of the Oklahoma supreme court who, in 1948, abortively attempted to get his name on the ballot as a candidate for election to the United States Senate at the same time that he appeared as a candidate to succeed himself.

That such things can and do happen can be attributed only to the indifference and apathy of the electorate or to the people's lack of understanding of the bad effect of the practice on the administration of justice. Here again the need for education is obvious.

With the possible exception of those in the state of Maine, judges of courts of review and trial courts of general jurisdiction do not engage in the practice of law. Usually this is prohibited by statutory or constitutional provision. In fifteen states, even judges of trial courts of limited jurisdiction are not to practice law. Judges of the probate courts in Maine, Massachusetts, New Hampshire, Connecticut, Michigan, Indiana, Wisconsin, and New Mexico engage in private practice, as they do also in New York to a very limited extent. It is difficult to understand why matters of such substantial importance are placed under the jurisdiction of courts presided over by part-time judges. This is no reflection on the judges of those courts; it is, rather, an indictment of the judicial system of those states in which the condition exists.

It is doubtful if the practice of law by lawyers who preside in justice, police, or city courts, or those of similar jurisdiction, will ever be entirely eliminated, however much that may be desired. New Jersey and California have led the way in this regard. Until the public is educated to the importance of these courts as a vital part of the judicial branch of the government, present conditions will continue to exist.

Proceedings for the removal of a judge from office are essentially political in nature and ordinarily do not deprive him of the right to return to the private practice of law if he so desires. In most states, judges of appellate courts and courts of general jurisdiction are subject to discipline or removal from office by impeachment at the hands of the legislature, pursuant to constitutional provisions similar to those applicable to the federal judiciary. Such proceedings are seldom instituted. In the 1928–48 period there were only three. And, in all three, the defense prevailed.

"A vital element in the usual constitutional provision for impeachment," says Judge Frederic M. Miller in his preliminary report for the Survey, "is the rule of law that, where the constitution of the state sets forth the grounds for discipline of a judge and the procedure to be invoked therefor, the legislature has no other power to provide other grounds for discipline or other methods of trial."

The effectiveness of the impeachment process is open to question. Miller reports the opinion in a goodly number of states that "the judges have been uniformly of such high character and integrity that there has been no occasion to invoke disciplinary proceedings, so there is no need for change." On the other hand, in some jurisdictions it appears that the constitutional provisions are too cumbersome. In some the legislature is in session for only a relatively short time—once in two years. An impeachment trial would unduly interrupt the session and, therefore, would be undertaken only in the most flagrant cases. But there are also those who champion the very cumbersomeness of impeachment proceedings as a necessary brake on ill-advised and unwarranted attacks upon the judiciary for personal or political reasons.

Miller observes that any change in the power to discipline such judges would require constitutional amendments. Perhaps in recognition of the inadequacy of impeachment, the people of several states have amended their constitutions to provide somewhat smoother procedures. These states include Arkansas, California, Louisiana, Maryland, Massachusetts, Michigan, New Hampshire, New York, Oregon, Rhode Island, Utah, Washington, and Wisconsin. In them no judge was removed from office during the 1928–48 period.

In virtually every state there are trial courts of limited jurisdiction to which the provisions for removal from office by impeachment do not apply. Ordinarily the legislature has constitutional power to provide for the removal of judges of such courts, and the judges are subject to discipline and disbarment by the usual proceedings.

Canon 2 of the Canons of Judicial Ethics declares:

> Courts exist to promote justice, and thus to serve the public interest. Their administration should be speedy and careful. Every judge should at all times be alert in his rulings and in the conduct of the business of the court, so far as he can, to make it useful to litigants and to the community. He should avoid unconsciously falling into the attitude of mind that litigants are made for the courts instead of the courts for litigants.

Supervision of courts and judges is not regarded as synonymous with the discipline of judges. Many state constitutions provide for general supervision of the work of trial courts and judges by the court of last resort and its chief justice. Undoubtedly much criticism of the courts could be prevented if these constitutional powers of supervision were interpreted as including discipline and exercised more effectively than they are.

One of the most common criticisms is directed at the delays that postpone final decisions of controversies between litigants. It is often said that "justice delayed is justice denied." Responsibility for such delays often belongs as much to the lawyers as it does to the courts, in Miller's view. "A reasonably satisfactory solution," he believes, "lies in the newly promulgated federal rules of civil and criminal procedure and in the creation of the Administrative Office of the United States Courts. The states have power to follow the example thus set."

McCoy wrote in conclusion as a result of his analysis of the Survey's questionnaire:

> The answers [to the questionnaire] as a whole and the general comments in particular indicate the healthy condition of the bench throughout the nation. Judges are human, and it is perhaps to be expected that there should be some deviations [from the Canons] in every state. While the committee did not take a judicial census, the impression is strong that, in proportion to the total number of judges in all states, there are relatively few who fail to adhere to their oaths of office or to faithfully discharge their judicial obligations.
>
> On the other hand, we cannot read of conditions such as those prevailing in Cook County, Illinois, and to a lesser degree in other states where the disregard of the Canons is said to be "flagrant" in too many particulars, without realizing the need for improvement. Somehow the political pressures which seem to motivate most of the judges who depart from the requirements of the Canons must be removed. To a lesser degree, the judges themselves must be brought to a fuller realization of the nature of their responsibilities as judicial officers.
>
> It is not enough that they stay within the letter of the law or conduct themselves as some of them do because of the absence of some constitutional or statutory prohibition. To quote a distinguished judge. . . . "That which is ethical is necessarily legal; that which is legal is not necessarily ethical."
>
> The Survey shows the imperative need for improvement in the matter of judicial conduct. Reform in methods of selection of judges in order to remove them from political pressure should be a first step toward this end. The desired conditions can be attained through the force of enlightened public opinion, brought to bear equally on the legislative, executive, and judicial branches of our state governments.
>
> The responsibility for enlightened public opinion rests not only with the bar but with the bench as well, whose members too often display a lack of a proper sense of individual responsibility as leaders of public opinion. . . .
>
> We submit that, when all the members of the bar and of the bench assume their full responsibilities as leaders of public opinion, the desired end will be attained. That end is well expressed by John W. Davis: "While we are hoping for peace and praying, somewhat vainly I fear, for easy taxes, let us, lawyers and laymen alike, see to it that we have an administration of justice not merely tolerable but approaching in purity and wisdom as near to the standard of the divine as feeble human nature can attain."

Finally, it is Miller's considered judgment that the remedy for complaints now made against judges lies, not in reform of the methods of discipline of judges, but rather in reforms along the line of supervising their work. In this field the complaints appear to be well grounded. Corrective measures are urgently needed. The challenge to lawyers is quite obvious. The judges may help a great deal, but the real impetus for reforms must come primarily from the lawyers.

THE CHALLENGE OF THE PRESS

For more than half a century the bar has been discussing one of the most spectacular problems in the field of legal ethics: the problem of trial by newspaper. But virtually nothing has been done to eliminate the real cause of this evil.

What is "trial by newspaper," and why does it constitute what might be called "the challenge of the press"? "Trial by newspaper" is the term commonly applied to the familiar practice of newspapers in reporting—and often in commenting on—details of a trial prematurely. While the term was originally applied to newspapers, it now extends to similar practices via radio, television, and other forms of mass communication.

It is a challenge to the legal profession, because the fault does not rest solely with the press. To quote from the *Journal of the American Judicature Society:* "Except for the slush and gush of the sob artists, there is very little offense chargeable against the press in which it is not led or abetted by lawyers, judges and other public officers." This summation is corroborated by the statements of many lawyers "and by the experience of every newspaper reporter and editor in the United States," said a Michigan newspaper publisher and member of the bar some years ago. The courts have broad power to control their officers, from judge to jailer, but with a few notable exceptions they have failed to meet this challenge.

The problem has existed for at least two centuries. One of the early monumental statements on the evil was delivered in 1742 by the Lord High Chancellor of England. Two hundred years later, Justice Jackson of the United States Supreme Court found it necessary to write:

> But neither counsel nor court can control the admission of evidence if unproven, and probably unprovable, "confessions" are put before the jury by newspapers and radio. Rights of the defendant to be confronted by witnesses against him and to cross-examine them are thereby circumvented. It is hard to imagine a more prejudicial influence than a press

release by an officer of the court charged with the defendants' custody stating they had confessed, and here just such a statement—unsworn to, unseen, un-cross-examined, and uncontradicted—was conveyed by the press to the jury.

. . . Newspapers, in the enjoyment of their constitutional rights, may not deprive accused persons of their right to a fair trial. These convictions, accompanied by such events, do not meet any civilized concept of due process of law.

The indictment of the courts and its officers is still on the docket. The challenge of the press cannot be met until the legal profession cleans its own house. The conduct of lawyers who have failed to observe the accepted standards of the profession and of judges unwilling to discharge their judicial obligations materially lowers public respect for the bar as a whole.

In recent years the bar has done a great deal in improving the caliber of our judges and in removing their selection from politics. Through integration, the bar has made great strides with respect to the discipline and disbarment of lawyers. On at least one occasion (in Baltimore) appropriate action was taken against a police officer who overstepped the bounds of propriety in discussing with the newspapers matters relating to a pending case. But there is no record of a single case in which such action has been taken against an offending judge or lawyer in the United States.

Both the Code of Professional Ethics and the Canons of Judicial Ethics deal explicitly and implicitly with the matter of trial by newspaper. Canon 20 of the former says:

Newspaper publications by a lawyer as to a pending or anticipated litigation may interfere with a fair trial in the courts and otherwise prejudice the due administration of justice. Generally they are to be condemned. If the extreme circumstances of a particular case justify a statement to the public, it is unprofessional to make it anonymously. An *ex parte* reference to the facts should not go beyond the records or papers on file in the court; but even in extreme cases it is better to avoid any *ex parte* statement.

There are at least three canons in the judicial code which have a bearing:

Courts exist to promote justice, and thus to serve the public interest [Canon 2].

[The judge] should utilize his opportunities to criticize and correct unprofessional conduct of attorneys and counselors, brought to his attention; and, if adverse comment is not a sufficient corrective, should send the matter at once to the proper investigative and disciplinary authorities [Canon 11].

In every particular his conduct should be above reproach. . . . He should administer justice according to law . . . [and should not] administer the office for the purpose of advancing his personal ambitions or increasing his popularity [Canon 34].

It is of the first importance to ask whether Canon 20 of the professional code is an adequate statement with respect to the practices of lawyers, including prosecuting attorneys, which result in trial by newspaper. In this connection the language of Canon 5 is pertinent: "The primary duty of the lawyer engaged in public prosecution is not to convict, but to see that justice is done."

To ascertain the state of opinion among responsible representatives of both fields, press and law, a carefully selected list of editors, lawyers, and judges was prepared in connection with this aspect of the Survey and a series of questions put to these men. The first was: "Do you believe that adherence to Canon 20 by all lawyers, including those in public office, is desirable?" Almost unanimously, the correspondents replied in the affirmative. But one reason for any possible doubt on this point is suggested by a public prosecutor who, agreeing that adherence is desirable, said that he "believed that it is impracticable because of the demands by the press for information concerning litigation, particularly in the public field."

The editor of a large metropolitan newspaper pointed out that the canon affects two of the basic rights granted to all Americans, "namely, freedom of the press and a fair and impartial trial by jury." (It hardly need be explained that these two basic rights seldom, if ever, come into conflict with respect to a single individual. It is usually a matter of the public's right to know versus the individual's right to a fair trial.) "I do not believe either the legal profession or the press can solve this vexatious problem through any code of ethics or canons," the editor wrote. "It can be solved only by a sense of fair play and responsibility on the part of both professions."

Still another editor said that he thought Canon 20 is actually framed "in such a manner as to invite violations." This may be what a former United States district attorney had in mind when he advised that the word "generally" be stricken from the canon's sentence reading, "Generally they are to be condemned." When the correspondents were asked directly if they thought Canon 20 in its present form is an adequate statement, their answers were about evenly divided between yes and no. But the forcefulness of those who answered in the negative clearly indicated that the language of the Canon needs substantial revision.

One judge said that radio and television broadcasts should be included along with newspaper publications. A prominent attorney who is not unfamiliar with the legal problems of the press offered this straightforward comment: "I think that the newspapers are far more responsible than the bar and that lawyers have a positive duty to co-operate with the courts to stop the gallivantings of a drunken press."

Another lawyer put a somewhat different slant on the need for change:

> Since it is impossible for the bar to muzzle the press, why should the bar seek to muzzle the only authentic source of information of the press? Canon 20 was adopted to remedy certain abuses which I cannot help but feel were given exaggerated importance by attorneys.
>
> Unfortunately, it frequently happens that prospective jurors are influenced by what has been published in the press. This almost invariably happens in criminal cases where the police have been eager to release damaging evidence against a suspect in order to prove to the public the efficiency of the police. This cannot be helped by the bar. The only way it can be stopped is by a campaign of education, enlisting the editorial co-operation of the press.

While admitting that pretrial statements sometimes impair the opportunity for an unprejudiced trial and "may even be uttered with such intent," a distinguished eastern attorney said that he would not care to see Canon 20 made more drastic.

> I realize that many times public interest in litigation is so intense as to make it difficult, even for lawyers of integrity, not to make some statement, frequently at the insistence of newspaper reporters, who are driven in turn by an awareness of extreme public interest in the case. Nevertheless I cannot help feeling that when the public interest on the one hand and the right of an individual to a fair trial on the other hand come into conflict, the right of the individual to a fair trial should be paramount.

However much the Canon may be considered as a "counsel of perfection," as a prominent West Coast lawyer described it, the responses to the questionnaire leave no doubt of the widespread feeling that in principle Canon 20 should be observed by the bar. Approximately two out of three respondents stated their belief that lack of observance has lessened the confidence of the public in the integrity and impartiality of the administration of justice in both state and federal courts.

It must be kept in mind that integrity and impartiality are relative qualities. Realistically, it is perhaps unreasonable to expect the bar to live up to high standards of morals and justice when the communities they serve expect them to convert trials into circuses and move them from the courtroom into the stadium. Pertinent here is an observation made many years ago by a president of the California Bar Association on retiring from that office: "The moral elevation and social education of our people are the chief source from which we must expect better judicial service. We must not expect courts to reflect much higher standards of morals and justice than the communities which select them. Nor must we fear that the officials chosen from the body of a society will fall far short of representing its actual character." This point of view must be considered, however, in context with the widely acknowledged responsibilities of moral leadership that repose in the legal profession.

A question was also asked on the effect of publication "of press releases given out by counsel [for the United States or for a state] purporting to state the facts with respect to a case about to be presented to the grand jury, or about to be tried in a trial court." With but few qualifications and no categorical dissents, those who replied were of the opinion that such press releases interfere with the administration of justice. Among those who most strongly condemned the practice was a trial lawyer in a large city. "If an indictment is returned or a complaint filed by the United States or the state, such information within the limits provided by law is available for publication. That should be sufficient until the trial itself actually takes place," he declared.

The editor of a well-known newspaper declined to answer flatly one way or the other:

> There are too many elements to be considered, [such as] importance of the issue, impact on the community, etc. For instance, announcement by a prosecutor that a defendant in a crime, which we assume has shocked the community, will be brought to speedy indictment and trial: this implies that the case is complete, that conviction is fairly certain.

Surely, it prejudices a fair trial. On the other hand, such a statement, in more than one instance, has been used successfully to thwart mob violence.

Two public prosecutors defended the release of such statements on the ground that "the public has a right to expect proper information from its public officials." Said one: "It is my belief that such press releases cannot be prevented and should not be, [even though] they may interfere with a fair trial or otherwise prejudice the due administration of justice."

In contrast, a former United States attorney replied: "Often counsel for the prosecution are the worst violators of the canon. Too frequently our appellate tribunals have drawn attention to the fact that our prosecutors are too enthusiastic in winning cases rather than in promoting justice in the public offices which they hold."

THE PUBLIC INTEREST IN INFORMATION

It is well recognized that wide publicity of trials is desirable, that those who administer justice should always act under the sense of public responsibility, and that every citizen should be able to satisfy himself with his own eyes as to the way in which a public duty is performed.

Notwithstanding, it is hardly surprising that the judges, lawyers, and editors who gave direct answers to the Survey questions were unanimous in agreeing that it is *not* in the public interest that lawyers make, or newspapers print, statements relating to litigation that create a public demand for a particular judgment in such a case. "A judgment should be that which the law and the evidence demand, not what the public may demand," one distinguished trial judge said bluntly.

The managing editor of an old and highly respected newspaper declined to answer the question:

> I could never give an answer to a question . . . which raises the issue of public interest on such broad and vague grounds and confuses two wholly unrelated factors—the professional standards of lawyers and the editorial judgment of editors.
>
> Assuming that some extremely high court were capable of determining exactly the "public interest," it might be wise to have a bar association forbid lawyers to impair it. I doubt it, but it might be wise and practical. However, I do not see how we can preserve the Bill of Rights and the

basic concept of our society if we give to any group or court the right to dictate to the press what is in the public interest.

Here is a statement that reflects a widely held viewpoint among the members of the Fourth Estate, namely, general and sincere agreement with the principle involved but skepticism as to the means of actually applying the principle. Such editors seem to forget for the moment that the Fifth and Fourteenth amendments, which guarantee to every individual a fair trial, are of equal dignity with the First Amendment, which guarantees freedom of speech and of the press. Obviously, the problem cannot be solved by considering the rights of a free press separate and apart from the right of an accused to a fair trial under due process of law. The view is worth repeating that, "when the public interest, on the one hand, and the right of an individual to a fair trial, on the other, come into conflict, the right of the individual to such a trial should be paramount."

A second question in this phase of the Survey was whether it is in the public interest that lawyers should make, or newspapers print, statements during a trial as to evidence they *intend* to offer, before the offer has been made, and before the court has ruled on its admissibility. Here again there is substantial unanimity among those giving categorical answers.

"I think that there is little excuse in the ordinary case for statements or intimations as to what the evidenc will be until it is offered and accepted by the court," said a distinguished jurist. "No good can come of it as far as the trial is concerned and, if the promised evidence fails to materialize or is rejected by the court, the presentation of it to the jury by the indirect methods of publicity is certainly prejudicial."

An editor thoroughly familiar with the problem added: "This would seem to be most undesirable and possibly a flat evasion of the court's authority. Surely such acts should be held in contempt." And a well-known southern attorney said: "This practice makes a mere mockery of the actual trial and cheapens the public opinion of the integrity and effectiveness of the courts."

There were only two replies indicating approval of such statements.

A third question was whether the publication in newspapers of lawyers' statements as to pending or anticipated litigation, including criminal cases, is necessary or desirable to the legitimate function and purpose of newspapers in disseminating news. Only one lawyer answered this question in the affirmative. The comments of those who qualified their answers suggest the need for clarification of the canon itself and for greater adherence to the principle stated in the canon as well.

"If lawyers, particularly public officials, make statements, I do not think we can blame the newspapers for printing them," observed a judge. In the opinion of one editor, the answer "depends on the statement. The area of fair comment should be more carefully defined." One lawyer observed: "Prior to litigation the 'news' is contained in the official files of the case. It may also be contained in original investigation made by the newspapers themselves. Statements by the attorneys prior to litigation must be viewed as representing one side or the other in the litigation."

One of the replies made a case for more and better publicity:

> As matters stand today, the lawyers have withdrawn the process of justice from the public, and the public has withdrawn its confidence in the lawyers.
>
> It is the highest duty of an attorney to his client, to the judge, and to his profession to see that any inquiring reporter who plans to publish anything about a case gets his facts right. An attorney should no more misrepresent a fact to the press than he should to the court . . . .
>
> . . . I think attorneys make an enormous mistake in regarding the press and the power of publicity with suspicion. Newspapers have as high a standard of ethics as do attorneys, and if the bar would only co-operate with the press and thereby reach the public with a sympathetic presentation of the problems involved in getting justice for the citizens of this country, we will find we are all better off.

What is it that the bar seeks to achieve by preventing trial by newspaper? The answer is relatively simple, however difficult it may be to gain the desired end.

Due process of law in America is based on a concept as old as the Magna Carta. That concept is an integral part of our Constitution and governs the trial of every case in every court. The spirit of the practice under the common law dictates that the parties must have notice, an opportunity to appear and present their cases, an impartial tribunal, and a trial before a court of competent jurisdiction.

It is in the public interest that every person shall have a fair trial unchallenged by outside influences as to the result. It is in the public interest that the bar shall insist that its members adhere to those standards of professional conduct which alone will insure due process of law. And it is in the public interest that the bar whose members are officers of the court shall insist that the courts take every action necessary to prevent any departure from this fundamental concept.

If we accept these things as the legitimate purpose of the bar, what is it that prevents the accomplishment of that purpose? One answer to that question is trial by newspaper. With the development of modern means of communication, a vice which has plagued the administration of justice for more than two centuries could well be the vice which will destroy due process of law.

It must be said to the credit of the bar that, although to some extent it has endured the vice of trial by newspaper, it has not embraced it—nor does it intend to. Fortunately, the vast majority of lawyers, including those in public office as prosecutors, respect the fact that they are members of a profession engaged in rendering a public service and adhere to the principle declared in Canon 20.

But, unfortunately, in our times as in the past, there are those members of the bar who so far forget their trust as to believe that trial by newspaper is not wrong. If they do not actually seek publicity for their clients' affairs and for themselves—and many do—they at least succumb to that segment of the press which caters to sensationalism for commercial gain. This is a marriage of the worst and most irresponsible elements of two basically responsible and high-principled institutions.

Trial by newspaper, as we know it in this country, is virtually unknown in England. The public there has long accepted the control of the press by the courts in such matters. The English law of constructive contempt of court has been successful in preventing all attempts to prejudice the trial of either civil or criminal cases. In no case in England has it been suggested that a party has been prejudiced by his inability to appeal for public sympathy before his case is heard in court, nor is there any real hardship on either the newspapers or the public. As the trial must be open to the public, and as it can always be fully reported, there is no danger that the doctrine of contempt of court can interfere with the fundamental principle of open justice, openly administered.

Why is it that we have not achieved the same result in the United States? The newspaper editor answers, "Freedom of the press," a constitutional guaranty unknown in England. Have not our senses been dulled to the true meaning of freedom of the press? "The liberty of the press," said Chancellor Kent, "consists in the right to publish with impunity, truth, with good motives, and for justifiable ends, whether it respects government, magistracy, or individuals." Even the right of a newspaper to report the trial of a case in open court is not absolute; certainly neither a newspaper nor an individual has a right to prejudice a case, to misstate it, or to hold any party to it up to scorn or ridicule.

Justice Felix Frankfurter wrote:

> Freedom of the press, properly conceived, is basic to our constitutional system. Safeguards for the fair administration of criminal justice are enshrined in our Bill of Rights. Respect for both these indispensable elements of our constitutional system presents some of the most difficult and delicate problems for adjudication when they are before the Court for adjudication. It has taken centuries of struggle to evolve our system for bringing the guilty to book, protecting the innocent, and maintaining the interests of our society consonant with our democratic professions. One of the demands of a democratic society is that the public should know what goes on in the courts by being told by the press what happens there, to the end that the public may judge whether our system of criminal justice is fair and right. On the other hand, our society has set apart court and jury as the tribunal for determining guilt or innocence on the basis of evidence adduced in court, so far as it is humanly possible.

The conflict between the right of free speech and the right of every litigant to a fair trial by due process is not insoluble. The issues have not yet been adjudicated by the Supreme Court of the United States, but it can be hoped that the day will come soon when that will happen. Meanwhile, the bar has done its share of talking about trial by newspaper but so far has done little to abate the evil. It is not without power to act while waiting for the Supreme Court to reach some conclusion on the power of the states, and Congress, to safeguard the fair administration of justice.

Through co-operation of the press with the bar, the public must come to see that there is no basic conflict between the rights of the press under the First Amendment and those of litigants to trial by jury and due process of law; that the constitutional guaranty of a fair and public trial is for the benefit of the litigant and not to give entertainment to the public. There must be a change in the climate of public opinion with respect to the administration of justice. Through adherence to its own high standards of professional conduct and through a sustained program of education, the bar must create a public demand for evenhanded justice for all litigants, unobstructed by trial by newspaper.

CHAPTER IX

Organization of the Legal Profession

THE BAR AS A PROFESSION

The legal profession is found in every civilized country. It has always been organized in bar associations—except in that young nation, the United States, where the history of the organized bar is checkered and still partly unknown.

As an illustration of the lack of data on this subject, and the difficulty of obtaining it, the experience of the Survey of the Legal Profession may be cited. In 1950 the Survey sent a questionnaire to the twelve-hundred-odd state and local bar associations in the United States, requesting such simple information as name, date of founding, chief promoters, and reasons for founding. Less than 12 per cent of the associations replied.

No one could write the history of legal associations with more authority than Roscoe Pound, dean emeritus of the Harvard Law School, yet with all his vast knowledge, in his report for the Survey, Pound admits that the basic data about the origins of early bar associations have never been sufficiently assembled. Again, for example, until recently there had been every reason to believe that the Association of the Bar of the City of New York, organized in 1870, was the oldest lawyer group in the United States; yet Director of the Survey Smith found positive evidence that the Columbus (Ohio) Bar Association was founded on April 20, 1869, and the Survey turned up seven local associations claiming to antedate the New York association as continuous groups!

Dean Pound reminds us that throughout history there have been abortive attempts to set up or to maintain a policy without law. "Every Utopia that has been pictured has been designed to dispense with lawyers," he says in the Preface to his *The Lawyer from Antiquity to Modern Times*. Following the French Revolution, and again after the Russian Revolution, the organized legal profession was abolished, but in each case the attempt proved vain. Marx believed that the real function of the lawyer was to hold one class in subjection to another, and hence, as social classes disappeared, the law would "wither away." Nevertheless, the Soviet lawbooks today make up an impressive library, and organized groups of lawyers are established institutions in Russia.

Colonial America had visions of a New World society without law and without lawyers. New England sought an administration of justice by the clergy according to "the word of God." The Quakers sought to set up a regime of amicable adjustment of relations by friendly neighbors. Yet, by the time of the American Revolution, Boston and Philadelphia both had notable bodies of well-trained lawyers practicing in the courts.

Law and hence lawyers are the enemies of autocracy, says Pound. In consequence, American states, as constitutional democracies, are characteristically legal bodies in which the Constitution is the "supreme law of the land." An American state constitution is not merely a frame of government. It is also a body of law to be interpreted and applied by the courts as the highest law of the land. In our polity many political questions are likewise legal, and many legal questions also political.

"Thus," he writes, "our constitutional polity is so legal as to be dependent upon lawyers for interpretation, application, and maintenance against official absolutism and legislative encroachment."

Yet, having developed a strong profession and having set up a legal constitutional government, the people, at two points in our history, all but destroyed the profession while permitting the calling. The first such time came early in our history. In an era of emergent frontier democracy, with its leveling zeal, its faith in the ability of any man to do anything, and its jealous regard for unrestrained individual liberty, men sought to do away with a profession pursuing a learned art, substituting, instead, an uneducated, untrained trade pursuing money-making in the spirit of business.

The second threat to professionalism is seen by Pound in the present day in two distinct forms. One is the rise of the "service state and tendency of government to take over every form of public service and substitute bureaus for professions." The second consists of the appearance of other callings claiming to be professions, "which should result in raising them to the level of a spirit of public service, not in lowering the level of the spirit of the recognized professions."

At this point it might be well to ask: What *is* a profession? Much more than merely a traditionally dignified calling, a profession, says Pound, is "a group of men pursuing a learned art as a common calling in the spirit of a public service—no less a public service because it may incidentally be a means of livelihood. Pursuit of the learned art in the spirit of public service is the primary purpose. Gaining a livelihood is incidental, whereas in a business or a trade it is the entire purpose."

Historically there are three ideas involved in a profession: organization, learning, and a spirit of public service. These are essential. A further idea, that of gaining a livelihood, is involved in all callings. It is the main, if not the only, purpose in the money-making callings. In a profession it is incidental.

Both in concept and as a matter of history, a profession is a *learned* profession. The earlier threat to professionalism in the law noted by Pound may be illustrated by quoting from the constitution of Indiana in 1851, which expresses the frontier idea toward such matters: "Every person of good moral character, being a voter, shall be entitled to admission to law practice in all courts of justice." Experience has since taught the impracticability of this attitude. To carry on their tasks effectively, professional men must be learned men. Hence, the court in Indiana decided only a few years ago that a man could not have a "good moral character" if he tried to practice without an education.

It is the third idea, however, that is of chief importance. It is of the essence of a profession that it be practiced in the spirit of public service. The other two elements—organization and pursuit of a learned art—have their justification in that they secure and maintain that spirit.

THE ORGANIZATION OF THE BAR

Turning to the first of these elements, it is clear that the bar association as an organization of those practicing the profession is an essential element of professional life. It is only through organization, Pound declares, that the spirit of public service can be developed and maintained and crucial types of public service be rendered effectively.

> It is the bar association, not the individual lawyer, that can maintain high educational standards insuring a learned profession, that can maintain high standards of character as a prerequisite of admission to practice, that can formulate and maintain high standards of ethical conduct in relations both with clients and with courts. The public has a deep interest in having a well-organized bar as part of the machinery of administering justice in a complex social and economic order.

A bar association, then, is an organization of lawyers to promote and maintain the practice of law as a profession, in the spirit of furthering the administration of justice through law. The declared purposes of a bar association generally are (1) to advance the science of jurisprudence; (2) to promote the administration of justice in the jurisdiction in which the association exists; (3) to uphold the honor of the profession of the law; and (4) to establish cordial intercourse among members of the bar of the jurisdiction.

These are set forth in the constitution of the American Bar Association (1878), which adds to the second a further purpose: "to promote uniformity of legislation throughout the Union."

Pound shows that, beginning with ancient Greece and Rome, three main functions of the lawyer have always existed: the lawyer as agent for litigation, as advocate, and as counselor. To the last named is often added the function of law-teaching and law-writing. These three functions were well developed in Rome. Here, as elsewhere in the legal order, the Romans laid well the foundations on which the Middle Ages and the modern world have built.

In the early development of the legal profession in the modern world, the practice of law was largely in the hands of the clergy, for a long time the only educated element in society. But, as the law developed, so did lawyers, and by the twelfth century they were prominent in the courts. In the thirteenth century they became dominant, and presently the church forbade the clergy to practice in the courts. At that time the lay lawyer obtained the monopoly he has held ever since.

In the medieval era of the old mechanical trials of Anglo-Saxon law there was no need of advocacy. Germanic law divided all litigation into an "issue term" and a "trial term." At the issue term the parties stated their contentions, all very formally and with the purpose of reducing the case to a simple, narrow issue. The issue having been settled, the mode of trial was directed, the burden of the issue assigned, and the case proceeded to the trial term. The trial itself was not an investigation of the facts. Rather it was a mechanical and arbitrary device expected to reveal the judgment of God, or predicated on fear of ill consequences from a false oath, or presupposing the unchallengeable verity of certain records and the undoubted authority of charters. He who had the burden of the issue had no need of legal assistance, although a litigant could have need of a lawyer at the issue term in order to help him bring about as favorable a setting for the trial term as possible. There could, however, be no development of a legal profession until a system of courts had grown up and a body of law, as distinguished from laws, had begun to be developed by judicial decision.

By the time of Edward I the common-law courts had become well established, and the legal profession was definitely in the process of formation. But representation in litigation was regarded, in the early development of English law, as something exceptional, as it was in the beginnings of all legal systems. And in English law, as in all systems, it appeared slowly. As late as Blackstone's day it was "a settled rule at common law that no counsel shall be allowed a prisoner upon his trial upon the general issue in any capital crime, unless some point of law shall arise proper to be debated."

Almost since the very beginnings of the common law, the education and admission of members to the upper branch of the profession in England have been—and still are—in the hands of the four societies of barristers, or Inns of Court. The medieval education in the Inns of Court was, for its time, an admirable system, Pound states. In contrast to the Continental training, it was not academic. The teachers were not professors teaching from books or jurists writing commentaries as authoritative texts and seeking to organize and systematize the learning which had grown up about them in the universities. Instead they were practicing lawyers, in touch with the law in action, seeking to develop the common law of England as a workable system for meeting concrete problems of adjusting human relations and ordering conduct. This gave a color to the common law that it has retained. Teaching in the Inns of Court was tied to the work of the courts, and this bond between legal education and the work of the courts had much to do with enabling judges to develop the common law through judicial decision.

But what is significant to the history of legal organization, Pound concludes, is that the English lawyers at the end of the Middle Ages had become a well-developed, well-organized profession, maintaining a system of societies or associations promoting a professional tradition, providing adequate training of those who were to enter the profession, and actively furthering the development of the law.

Professional attorneys begin under Edward I. As late as the fifteenth century, however, apprentices at law might be professional attorneys, and attorneys still might be members of the Inns of Court. Later, the Inns and the judges came to discourage calling the apprentices to the bar, and by the seventeenth century these apprentice attorneys had become a wholly separate branch of the profession. They were not members of the Inns, nor had they studied there. Neither were they organized in any other way. They were simply admitted to practice in and were borne on the rolls of the common-law courts. Thus it developed that while the *barristers* of England were well organized, had a fine professional tradition, and were subject to effective discipline, the *attorneys*-at-law and *solicitors* in chancery, from the fifteenth almost to the middle of the nineteenth century, had no organization, had come to lose much of the professional tradition, and were under no effective discipline.

The sharp lines which developed early in the English legal profession are still present today with little modification. The attorney, rather than the barrister, came to be the model for the organization of the profession in America. After independence, American students ceased to go to the Inns of Court for study of law. American lawyers looked to their books, which told of the English institutions of the eighteenth century, and to the traditions which they had inherited from the profession as it was in seventeenth-century England.

Law depends upon lawyers, and lawyers are little needed in a new community until there has been a considerable economic development. Hence there was comparatively little in the way of law in the American colonies during the greater part of the seventeenth century. Among the factors hindering legal development were the

Puritan distrust of the common law, which had been hard on dissenters, and the Puritan dislike of lawyers themselves; the scarcity of lawbooks; the supremacy of the clergy as secular as well as sacred guides; the administration of justice on a personal rather than legal basis by the royal governors; and the greater familiarity of the colonists as a class with local courts rather than with the common-law courts at the seat of government.

Summing up developments in America, Pound distinguishes four stages which in a general way followed each other in the one hundred and seventy-five years from the first settlement to the Declaration of Independence. He calls them (1) the attempt to get on without lawyers; (2) the stage of irresponsible filling-out of writs by court officials and pettifoggers; (3) the era of admitted practitioners in permanent judicial organizations; and (4) the era of trained lawyers—the bar of the eve of the Revolution.

At no time did this evolution move with uniform progress through all the colonies. In some, organization was far advanced, while it was wholly wanting in others. Two conditions seem to have made for a consciousness of the bar as an entity and for action of the bar as a unit. First and most important was the vesting of control of admission, and hence of qualification and training, in the local bar, through the system of admission by the local court. This seems to explain the general custom of bar meetings in New England, says Pound. Second, controversies with royal governors called for united action in New York, New Jersey, and Maryland.

On the other hand, two conditions operated to hold back and even prevent organization. One was jealousy on the part of a dominant class, such as the landed proprietors in Virginia, of a profession which might challenge their power. The other was the fact that in Pennsylvania, Virginia, and South Carolina a large and probably most influential element in the profession had been admitted by the Inns of Court and practiced by virtue of this, not by virtue of admission by the local court. Hence they did not think of themselves as members of a local bar but as members of their respective Inns. Of these two factors, Pound regards the latter as decisive.

The Revolution itself had a disintegrative effect on the legal profession in America. The conservatism which is characteristic of lawyers led some of the strongest to take the royalist side, with the result that in several colonies the Revolution left a huge gap in what had become a great body of lawyers. But both for American law and legal institutions and for the legal profession, the formative era is the period from the Revolution to the Civil War. Reshaping of English common law into a law of America and the development of a legal profession were well begun at the time of the Revolution.

After the war a reaction set in. Among the reasons for this was the general economic depression, which gave rise to dissatisfaction with law and distrust of lawyers. Another was a political climate of hostility toward English law and lawyers trained in the common law. Social conditions, third, were such as to discourage professionalization in all callings as "undemocratic." Finally, geographical conditions gave rise to an extreme decentralizing of the administration of justice and so of the bar.

There is another side to this gloomy picture, however. The period from the Revolution to the Civil War was, in another sense, "the golden age of American law." The creative legal achievements of that period will compare favorably with those of any period of growth and adjustment in legal history. In seventy-five years at the most, the seventeenth-century legal materials of the English common law were made over into a common law for America. This was the work of great judges and great lawyers practicing before them, for there was a high type at the upper level of the profession throughout this period. Of ten outstanding names in the judicial history of the United States, six belong to this formative era: James Kent, John Marshall, Joseph Story, Lemuel Shaw, John Bannister Gibson, and Thomas Ruffin.

The only early organizations were local bar groups, but toward the end of the period the locally organized bar was disappearing, and there were small beginnings of what were to become the bar associations of a later generation. The professional idea had gone through a cycle from growing recognition to gradual loss and then virtual abandonment. But after this low point the idea again slowly regained ground, proceeding toward the highly integrated bar of today. The great rise begins in the 1870's, with the present-day type of bar association, and the contemporary high point was attained after 1921.

In 1849 an attempt to organize a Massachusetts state bar association came to naught. Between 1836 and the Civil War the times were not ripe for such associations. If lawyer organizations could have succeeded in maintaining themselves anywhere, it would have been in New England, where there was a long tradition of *local* bars. But even here there was no tradition of a state bar.

Bar associations as social organizations kept a certain degree of professional organization alive in some communities until the revival in the last quarter of the nineteenth century. In some states, too, county bars concluded occasional dinners with an address, or were called to special meetings to adopt resolutions on the death of a judge, or when some scandal of jury-fixing or flagrant misconduct called for exceptional action. "That this is the most that can be said testifies to the thorough de-professionalizing of the bar in the era of decadence," Pound says. "There had come to be, not a bar, but so many hundred or so many thousand lawyers, each a law unto himself, accountable only to God and his conscience—if any."

It is advisable at this point to differentiate three related terms: "bar," "bar meeting," and "bar association." Except where the *integrated* bar is meant, the term "bar" in a strict sense can mean only the aggregate of lawyers admitted to practice in a given jurisdiction or before a given court. "Bar meeting" in Colonial New England meant a meeting of the lawyers admitted to practice in a county or district, without formal organization but considering themselves a unit for maintaining and promoting the standards of the profession. In the era of decadence it came to refer to any meeting of the lawyers in a given locality for whatever reason. The term "bar association" means a definite and permanent organization of lawyers for purposes of the profession.

A principal result of the organization of the Association of the Bar of the City of New York in 1870 was to awaken lawyers generally to the need for effective professional organization. In its endeavor to improve the administration of justice, the New York organization at once came in conflict with the Tweed ring, then dominant in New York politics. And in the struggle which ultimately brought about the ring's downfall, the association played an important part. The impeachment of two judges and the resignation of a third as a result of an investigation it had recommended established it in public confidence.

Widespread organization of state bar associations began also in the 1870's. The founding of twenty-five state associations in the first decade of the American Bar Association was notable testimony to the effect of that organization. But, of these twenty-five, only fourteen survived the decade. Of the remaining eleven, two were reorganized by 1907. It was not until 1923 that there was an active state bar association in every state or territory.

By the time state associations had become active in nearly every state, the movement for integration of the bar of the state as a whole began in North Dakota (in 1921). A model form of statute for integration of a state bar had been published in 1918 through the activities of the American Judicature Society and the American Bar Association.

Following is a list of the states and territories with active bar associations, with the date of first organization and date of the present organization in case of breach of continuity. Where the bar is integrated (all-inclusive, with all lawyers in the state required to be members and to pay dues), that is noted in each case. The list is from Dean Pound's book, which was published in 1953.

New Hampshire, 1873; reorganized 1899
Iowa, 1874; reorganized 1895
District of Columbia, 1874; reorganized 1891
New York, 1876 (December)
Illinois, 1877 (January)
Alabama, 1878; integrated 1923
Vermont, 1878
Wisconsin, 1878
New Jersey, 1878; reorganized 1899
Nebraska, 1878; reorganized 1900; integrated 1937
Missouri, 1880; integrated 1944
Ohio, 1880
Tennessee, 1881
Indiana, 1881; reorganized 1886
Texas, 1882; integrated 1939
Maine, 1882; reorganized 1891.
Arkansas, 1882; reorganized 1899; integrated 1938
Colorado, 1882; reorganized 1897
Kentucky, 1882; reorganized 1901; integrated 1934
Georgia, 1883
Kansas, 1883
Minnesota, 1884; reorganized 1904
Montana, 1885
New Mexico, 1886; integrated 1925
West Virginia, 1886; integrated 1945
South Carolina, 1887; reorganized 1901

Virginia, 1888; integrated 1938
Washington, 1888; integrated 1933
California, 1889; reorganized 1909; integrated 1927
Florida, 1889; reorganized 1907; integrated 1949
Michigan, 1890; integrated 1935
Oklahoma, 1890; integrated 1939
Oregon, 1890; integrated 1935
Mississippi, 1892; reorganized 1906; integrated 1930
Utah, 1894; integrated 1931
Nevada, 1894; reorganized 1911; integrated 1929
Pennsylvania; 1895
Alaska, 1896
Maryland, 1896
South Dakota, 1897; integrated 1931
Louisiana, 1898; integrated 1940
Rhode Island, 1898
Hawaii, 1898
North Carolina, 1899; integrated 1933
North Dakota, 1899; integrated 1921
Delaware, 1901; reorganized 1923
Idaho, 1901; reorganized 1909; integrated 1923
Arizona, 1906; renewed activity 1912; integrated 1933
Massachusetts, 1909
Wyoming, 1915; integrated 1939
Puerto Rico, integrated 1932

THE AMERICAN BAR ASSOCIATION

According to the Survey report, "History of the American Bar Association and Its Work," by Edson R. Sunderland, it was a Yale law professor, Simeon E. Baldwin, who first proposed the organization of a nation-wide bar association. At a meeting of the Connecticut State Bar Association in January, 1878, he introduced a motion that "a committee of three be appointed to consider the propriety of organizing an association of American lawyers."

Prompt and cordial response greeted the committee's overtures to leading lawyers, and a circular letter, dated July 1, 1878, was sent out calling for "an informal meeting" at Saratoga Springs, New York, on August 21, 1878, "to consider the feasibility and expediency of establishing an American Bar Association." About a hundred persons attended the Saratoga meeting. Organizational work went forward rapidly and smoothly. A constitution was adopted (Professor Baldwin had previously prepared a draft), and the Saratoga session was formally held to be the first annual meeting.

Key articles of the constitution include:

ARTICLE I. *Name and Object.* This Association shall be known as "The American Bar Association." Its object shall be to advance the science of jurisprudence, promote the administration of justice and uniformity of legislation throughout the union, uphold the honor of the profession of the law, and encourage cordial intercourse among the members of the American Bar.

ARTICLE II. *Qualifications for Membership.* Any person shall be eligible to membership of this association who shall be, and shall, for five years next preceding, have been, a member in good standing of the bar in any state, and who shall be nominated as hereinafter provided.

ARTICLE III. *Officers and Committees.* The following officers shall be elected at each annual meeting for the year ensuing:—A President (the same person shall not be elected President two years in succession); one Vice-President from each State; a Secretary; a Treasurer; a Council, consisting of one member from each state; the Council shall be a standing committee on nominations for office; an Executive Committee, to be composed of the Secretary and Treasurer, together with three members (of the Council) to be chosen by the Association, one of whom shall be chairman of the committee.

The following committees shall be annually appointed by the President for the year ensuing, and shall consist of five members each:

On Jurisprudence and Law Reform;
On Judicial Administration and Remedial Procedure;
On Legal Education and Admission to the Bar;
On Commercial Law;
On International Law;
On Publications;
On Grievances.

The history of the American Bar Association covers nearly three-quarters of a century. It may be divided into three periods.

First period (1878–1902).—During this twenty-five-year period the association met annually, or every other year, at Saratoga Springs, New York. It was the period in which the association was establishing itself as a national organization, was attracting and building up a distinguished personnel, and was determining the policies to be followed in developing a position of leadership in the American bar. This, the "Saratoga period," was a time of conservative and leisurely activity.

Second period (1902–36).—This period covers the thirty-three years from the abandoning of Saratoga Springs as a meeting place to the reorganization of the association in 1936. During that time it moved from city to city throughout the country, making its regional appeals for the support of the bar in its rapidly expanding program for better laws and a better administration of justice. It was a period of tremendous growth, both in membership and in the variety of its activities. Membership grew from 1,718 to 29,008. This may be called the "Era of National Expansion."

Third period (since 1936).—In 1936 the association completely changed its plan of organization from that of a fully autonomous association of individuals to an association of limited autonomy under the almost complete control of a directing and supervisory body called the House of Delegates. This body consists of delegates representing state and local bar associations and juridical groups throughout the country, including the incumbents of various important juridical offices. Under this arrangement the association, in its ordinary operations, was no longer expected to reflect the views of its members but the views of the delegates who represented the organized units of the legal profession. This period may be called the "Era of Federation."

In the Saratoga era the number of standing committees was increased from seven to eleven (by 1899). In the second period, seventeen additional standing committees were created and survived, briefly or for some time. Meanwhile, seven of the eleven standing committees existing in 1903 had disappeared by 1935, leaving a net of thirteen in operation at the close of the expansion era. During this era more than seventy new special committees were created.

Membership in the American Bar Association increased very slowly during the Saratoga era and for a number of years thereafter. In 1912 a standing committee on increase of membership was set up, and by 1916 membership had grown from 5,584 to 10,636. By the end of the expansion era, membership was at the previously quoted 29,008 figure.

In view of the fact that the American Bar Association depends, in the last analysis, upon public opinion for the success of its efforts to improve the administration of justice, it is surprising that for thirty-seven years after its organization no systematic steps were taken to keep the public informed regarding the nature and extent of the work it was carrying on in the public interest. In 1912 the president was authorized to appoint a standing committee on publicity, the chairman of which was Charles A. Boston. Since that time the publicity machinery of the association has expanded greatly in the dissemination of information both to the public at large through press and radio and internally to the members of the profession.

The reorganization of 1936 put the American Bar Association on a federalized basis. The new plan of organization enabled it to speak with an authoritative voice as the representative of the various organized units of the legal profession throughout the country. Further, the co-operation of those units in a nation-wide organization was expected to increase their efficiency and give them a broader sense of professional solidarity and responsibility. These objects of federalization were stated in Article I of the new constitution by adding to the original wording: "to correlate the activities of the Bar organizations of the respective states on a representative basis in the interest of the legal profession throughout United States."

In 1949 this article was amended by adding two new objectives: (1) "to uphold and defend the constitution of the United States and maintain representative government" and (2) "to apply its knowledge and experience in the field of law to the promotion of the public good." The amendment also omitted the words "on a representative basis" in the 1936 provision and rewrote them as "and to correlate and promote such activities of the bar organizations in the nation and in the respective states as are within these objects, in the interest of the legal profession and the public."

Membership in the House of Delegates, under the reorganized plan, was carefully designed to give the broadest practicable representation of the groups and agencies actively interested in maintaining and developing high standards for the administration of justice in the country. There were originally fifteen classes or types of representatives, as follows:

1. State delegates. These were to be chosen, one from each state, by the ABA members residing in each state.

2. State bar association delegates. One such delegate was to be chosen by each state bar association, and an additional delegate in states having in excess of 2,000 lawyers, one for each 1,000 lawyers above that number, but not more than four such delegates. When a state bar association was entitled to additional delegates, the number of such additional state bar association delegates was to be reduced by the number of delegates elected by local bar associations within such state.

3. Local bar association delegates. Such delegates were to be chosen by and from local bar associations having 800 or more members, 25 per cent of whom were members of the ABA.

4. Five delegates chosen by the assembly. The assembly consisted of such members of the ABA as were registered as attendants at any annual meeting.

5. The delegates of such membership organizations of the legal profession as might be affiliated pursuant to Section 7 of Article V. That section provided that "the American Law Institute, the American Judicature Society, and any other national organization in the legal profession having individual membership and having 25 per cent of its members who are members of the American Bar Association, and which shall be approved by the House of Delegates as an organization to be represented in the House of Delegates through affiliation with the American Bar Association, may, upon such approval, select in such manner as such organization shall determine, one delegate, who shall thereupon become a member of the House of Delegates for a term of one year and until his successor shall have been certified."

6. The president of the National Conference of Commissioners on Uniform State Laws.

7. The chairman of the National Conference of Bar Examiners.

8. The chairman of the National Conference of Judicial Councils.

9. The president of the Association of American Law Schools.

10. The Attorney-General of the United States.

11. The Solicitor-General of the United States.

12. The president of the National Association of Attorneys-General.

13. The chairman, or, in his absence, the vice-chairman, of each section of the association.

14. The president, secretary, and treasurer of the association.

15. The members of the Board of Governors.

Two additional membership designations were subsequently added:

16. The director of the Administrative Office of the United States Courts.

17. Former presidents of the ABA and former chairmen of the House of Delegates who register as attendants at any annual meeting of the association by twelve o'clock noon on the opening day thereof.

The first House of Delegates organized under the new federalized constitution contained 164 members. In 1950 the House of Delegates had 213 members.

When invoked by a majority vote of its entire membership, the House of Delegates is authorized to refer to the members of the association, or to membership of the state and participating local bar associations, "defined questions affecting the substance or the administration of the law or affecting the policy or recommendation of this Association, which in the opinion of the House of Delegates are of immediate, practical consequence to the legal

TABLE 27

SECTIONS AND MEMBERSHIP OF THE AMERICAN BAR ASSOCIATION

Bar Organization Activities	457
Commercial Law	937
Criminal Law	1,274
Insurance Law	2,656
International and Comparative Law	1,563
Judicial Administration	826
Junior Bar Conference	6,306
Legal Education and Admission to the Bar	1,261
Mineral Law	578
Municipal Law	701
Patent, Trade-Mark, and Copyright Law	1,076
Public Utility Law	918
Real Property, Probate, and Trust Law	3,306
Taxation	890
Total enrolment	22,749

profession and the public throughout the United States." Referendum results control the action of the association and its officers.

The Board of Governors was established to perform all the acts and functions of the House of Delegates during the intervals between meetings of the latter body. Its members are the president, the chairman of the House of Delegates, last retiring president, the secretary, the treasurer, and the editor-in-chief of the *American Bar Association Journal,* all ex officio, together with one member chosen from each federal judicial circuit.

Various sections, each largely autonomous and with its own by-laws, make up the association. Any member of the association may enrol himself in any section or any number of sections. As of January, 1941, the sections and their membership were as shown in Table 27.

The strong financial condition of the American Bar Association is indicated by highlights of recent financial statements. In 1936, the year of reorganization, the ABA showed an income from all sources totaling $191,587.83 and expenses totaling $187,222.60. Net income for the year (including $2,704.34 income over expense for the *American Bar Association Journal*) was $7,069.57. In that year net income from memberships was $158,934.82. Comparatively, in 1950 the total income was $356,736.24 and expenses were $354,-236.24. Net income (including the *Journal*) was $18,058.47. Of the 1950 income, $351,364.38 (net) was from membership dues.

Of the several annual awards made by the American Bar Association, the oldest and best known is the medal of the American Bar Association, which is awarded each year "to a member of the bar of the United States who shall have rendered conspicuous service in the cause of American Jurisprudence." The first recipient of this medal was Samuel Williston, to whom it was awarded in 1929. Through 1951 the medal had been awarded seventeen times in twenty-three years.

In 1947 the Committee on Scope and Correlation of Work was created in the interest of "the better correlation of the work of the Association and the better utilization of its resources." The committee's powers were limited to studying the work of the association and making recommendations to the House of Delegates and Board of Governors.

The most important function of the Committee on Scope and Correlation of Work has been the planning of a continuing long-range program of objectives and activities. After having worked on correlation, the committee selected certain activities as deserving special emphasis. Originally there were four such activities: legal aid, American citizenship, lawyer-referral service, and the promotion of minimum standards of judicial administration.

In 1951, however, upon the committee's recommendation, the House of Delegates adopted the following as long-range objectives of the association:

1. The preservation of representative government in the United States through a program of public education and understanding of the privileges and responsibilities of American citizenship.

2. The promotion and establishment within the legal profession

of organized facilities for the furnishing of legal services to all citizens at a cost within their means.

3. The improvement of the administration of justice through the selection of qualified judges and adherence to effective standards of judicial administration and administrative procedure.

4. The maintenance of high standards of legal education and professional conduct to the end that only those properly qualified to do so shall undertake to perform legal service.

5. The promotion of peace through the development of a system of international law consistent with the rights and liberties of American citizens under the Constitution of the United States.

6. The co-ordination and correlation of the activities of the entire organized bar of the United States.

It was the considered opinion of the Committee on Scope and Correlation that these objectives embrace a major part of the present program of the association in so far as it relates to public responsibilities. No attempt was made to incorporate activities designed to serve purely professional interest.

The current activities of the American Bar Association embraced by each of the six objectives may be subdivided as follows:

Under No. 1: American Citizenship, Bill of Rights, Communist Tactics, Investigation of Organized Crime.

Under No. 2: Legal Aid, Lawyer-Referral Service, Legal Service to the Armed Forces.

Under No. 3: Judicial Administration, Administrative Law, Criminal Law, Federal Judiciary, Judicial Selection, Tenure and Compensation, Jurisprudence and Law Reform, Military Justice, Traffic-Court Program.

Under No. 4: Legal Education and Admissions to the Bar, Continuing Legal Education, Professional Ethics and Grievances, Law Lists, Unauthorized Practice of Law.

Under No. 5: International and Comparative Law, Peace and Law through United Nations.

Under No. 6: House of Delegates, Bar Activities, Conference of Bar Association Presidents, Co-ordination, Director of Activities, Public Relations, Regional Meetings, Scope and Correlation.

For the future, writes William J. Jameson in the final chapter of

Sunderland's report to the Survey, the implementation of the work of the Survey of the Legal Profession should constitute a major function of the ABA's Committee on Scope and Correlation of Work. The Survey director has furnished the members of the committee with the reports as they have been issued, including this volume. Many of these reports have assisted the committee in formulating long-range objectives. The committee may assist in determining whether the subject matter of other reports should be handled by the American Bar Association and, if so, to which section it should be assigned. In some instances the subject matter of Survey reports might properly be undertaken by other existing agencies or by agencies newly created.

"It is essential that the work of the Survey be properly implemented," Jameson concludes. "The co-operation of the Committee on Scope and Correlation and other agencies of the Association with the Council of the Survey in this important task will assure a more effective discharge of the responsibility of the organized bar to the public."

ORGANIZATIONS FOR NEW LAWYERS

Creation in 1934 of the Junior Bar Conference, a section of the American Bar Association composed of all its members under thirty-six years of age, marked an important milestone in the history of the junior bar movement. "One of the most profound of all influences affecting our law and judicial administration in this century was the awakening and organizing of the younger practitioners," says James D. Fellers in a Survey report on the Junior Bar Conference.

Junior bar groups had been forming in several cities for a considerable period prior to the actual organization of the Junior Bar Conference. In 1923 the original Barristers Club was organized in Washington, D.C., with a membership limited to thirty-five outstanding younger members of the bar under thirty-five. Subsequently, comparable groups sprang up in Los Angeles, Denver, Milwaukee, and other centers. The first call to those interested in a national organization went out in 1932, and two years later, at the ABA convention in Milwaukee, approximately 125 lawyers under the age of thirty-six, representing twenty-seven states, convened and organized the Junior Bar Conference.

Despite the difficulties of perfecting a national organization during the first years, the conference was able to render effective aid to the United States Attorney-General in his anticrime drive by conducting a nation-wide speaking campaign, addressing service clubs, citizens' groups, and schools. In several communities effective work was accomplished in restricting unauthorized practice of law, and in some states members of the conference lent important support to the integrated bar movement.

"It was not long before the doubts of the elder statesmen as to the capacity of the younger attorneys to share in bar councils were beginning to look comical," Fellers writes. It must be borne in mind, too, that, for the most part, the men who devoted their time to the work of the conference were just getting their own practices started. Unlike their seniors in the association, these young men were not in a position to delegate their usual daily professional duties to associates. Their conference work was in many cases done at a sacrifice of personal business.

The chief purposes of the Junior Bar Conference are (1) to increase membership of younger men in the American Bar Association and to increase their attendance at the ABA annual meetings; (2) to stimulate cordial relationships among young practitioners throughout the country; (3) to co-ordinate the work of all local junior associations or groups on mutual problems; and (4) to instil in the young practitioner a deeper, more enlightened appreciation of his professional conduct, ethics, and obligations.

The Junior Bar Conference of the American Bar Association is fundamentally a treble organization, Fellers points out. On the one hand, it is a *congress* of state-wide and local bar associations of young lawyers, autonomous and self-governing but affiliated with the Junior Bar Conference. Second, it is an *association* of members of the American Bar Association in good standing not over the age of thirty-five years. Finally, it functions as a *section* of the American Bar Association.

By the time of its second session, at the annual meeting of the ABA in Los Angeles in 1935, the Junior Bar Conference's membership had grown from 125 to more than 2,000.

At first there was strong agitation by a few enthusiastic young lawyers who insisted upon an independent national junior association parallel to the ABA. But those in favor of co-operating with the American Bar Association prevailed. Administratively, the chain of command proceeds from the national officers through circuit councilmen to state chairmen. Substantively, it proceeds from national officers through the national committee chairmen to the members of the committee. Each state chairman is responsible, however, for the substantive accomplishments, or lack of them, within his state. Each councilman is similarly responsible for his circuit.

The ultimate success of the Junior Bar Conference will be dependent upon the effectiveness of the organization at the state and local levels, for on those groups inevitably falls the burden of carrying out the plans made by the conference as the national policy-making and co-ordinating unit. As of January, 1951, there were approximately thirty-three state and thirty-two local junior bar groups affiliated with the conference.

In his evaluation of the Junior Bar Conference, Fellers terms it a "natural and desirable process" that the younger members of the bar should band together.

> They have a common point of view as to the more serious problems confronting the bar. It is mainly their battle, and they must fight it. They have more time to devote to the cause. They enjoy a discussion of legal developments and do not mind the epithet "academic," whether used deservedly or not.
>
> An organization of their own makes for an esprit de corps and provides a flexible agency for getting things done. It affords training for later leadership in bar work. It presents opportunities to a great number of young lawyers to work on committees, in sections, and in research—an opening granted to but few young men in the older associations.

Today, former juniors are already serving as officers of the American Bar Association, as chairmen of a number of its important sections and committees, and as representatives in the House of Delegates. Not a few of them have been selected as presidents of their local and state associations. But for their earlier work in the conference, their talents might not have developed for years. The legal profession is stronger today to an appreciable degree, Fellers believes, because training in the Junior Bar Conference made many of its leaders bar-minded. This training imbued them with an appreciation of the necessity for supporting the program of the organized bar in developing a sense of public and professional responsibility.

A recent successful development in the direction of giving practical training to law students has been the creation, acceptance, and growth of the American Law Student Association. "A young giant has arisen among the bar associations of the United States," says James M. Spiro in a Survey report on the student organization.

Organized at St. Louis on September 5, 1949, under the sponsorship of the American Bar Association, the American Law Student Association now has a membership of more than thirty thousand law students. It represents the student bar associations of ninety-four law schools. Its members gather at yearly regional and national meetings, work on problems which concern both their legal education and their later professional life, and in general follow a program similar to those of the most effective regular bar associations.

The student association was set up with an executive staff of five national officers—a president, an executive vice-president, a secretary, a treasurer, and a sergeant-at-arms. They were assigned the duty of planning and guiding the organization's activities. Since many of those activities were to be on the local level, the country was divided into regions to be supervised by circuit vice-presidents. As the federal judicial circuits were followed in establishing these areas, there were eleven such offices. Legislatively, a bicameral structure was set up, one branch called the House of Delegates and the other the Board of Governors. Some fifteen standing committees were established.

Because of the relatively rapid turnover of law students, it was obvious that something should be done to provide continuity. To this end, the American Bar Association established the office of Director of the Law Student Program, to be filled by a young lawyer having a vital interest in the work. (Spiro himself was first director of the program.)

Approval and support of the new organization was forthcoming from many leaders in the legal profession, though not without exception. There were those who pointed to similar past attempts; others questioned the value of the activity, either to the law student or to the profession. Having successfully passed through a test period of several years, the American Law Student Association already has survived the first, and often critical, test.

The variety and the extent of the association's activities program give rise to the question of whether they will result in permanent good for the legal profession and for the individuals who participate in them. To this question Spiro says:

> The answer must be in the affirmative, for here is a national student bar association which is a training ground for the development of character and leadership so sorely needed by the profession and the general public. It initiates the student, at the very outset of his legal career, in the value and importance of group work and the obligations which are incurred in becoming part of his chosen profession. It leads him after graduation to similar participation in national, state, and local bar association activities, without which the legal profession would founder.

Do the students agree with this view? Again the answer is "Yes," says Spiro, if judgment is based on the rapid growth of the American Law Student Association. A total of forty-six student bar associations immediately affiliated when the organization was founded in 1949. In slightly more than two years the membership had more than doubled to ninety-four member groups, representing more than 75 per cent of the nation's approved law schools, with a total enrolment of more than thirty thousand law students. Even the ABA has less than 25 per cent of the eligible lawyers as members after three-quarters of a century.

Spiro sounds a warning, however:

> Unless nourishment and care is provided, the organization will wither away or else take some misshapen form. . . . Perhaps no other program the bar has inaugurated is so important to the profession presently and in the future. It is to be hoped that the bar will fully recognize this fact and, in the years ahead, not only will continue but will also increase its financial and physical support of the American Law Student Association. If the bar does this, the legal profession and the public will be the permanent beneficiaries.

STATE BAR ASSOCIATIONS

For purposes of illustration, two bar associations, Massachusetts and North Carolina, will be described briefly.

The approximately 9,200 practicing lawyers in Massachusetts have more than ninety professional organizations to which they can belong and through which they can work as organized groups. Massachusetts does not have an integrated bar organization. Approximately 65 per cent of the lawyers are voluntary members of some association or professional group. Approximately 20 per cent belong to more than one organization.

Probably more than three-fourths of the organized professional groups perform most of their work in or from Boston, in the metropolitan area of which are located almost two-thirds of the state's lawyers. About 75 per cent of Massachusetts' lawyers are in practice for themselves, as compared to the national average of 61 per cent. Boston is the location of six law schools, having approximately four thousand undergraduate students.

The five largest and most active bar associations in the Boston metropolitan area are:

1. Massachusetts Bar Association, founded in 1909; membership (in 1952) of 4,300.
2. Massachusetts Association of Women Lawyers, founded 1905; membership, 300. It covers the entire state.
3. Boston Bar Association (the county association for Suffolk County), founded 1876; membership, 3,200.
4. Middlesex County Bar Association, founded 1899; membership, 720.
5. Norfolk County Bar Association, founded 1886; membership, 475.

Of the approximately 9,200 lawyers in the state, probably 10 per cent of them, or from 800 to 900 different lawyers, participate currently in various activities sponsored by the organized groups. This percentage of participation would rank among the highest in the country.

Concerning weaknesses of the organized bar in Massachusetts, Dean Lowell S. Nicholson of Northeastern University School of Law itemized them as follows in a Survey report: Dues are "extremely low" and should be substantially increased. The associations are too conservative. ("The attitude of undue caution appears too frequently in bar circles in Massachusetts.") There is a need for more paid workers and for greater co-operation among local groups and with national groups.

The matter of integration of the bar in Massachusetts—that is, making it all-inclusive so that every lawyer must be a member and pay dues—is a dead issue, at least for some time, according to Nicholson.

North Carolina has approximately 2,500 lawyers. It has two state bar associations, the North Carolina Bar Association (voluntary) and the North Carolina State Bar (integrated). In addition, there are twenty-one district bar associations, a number of county and city associations, and one active Junior Bar Association.

The North Carolina Bar Association was founded in 1899, with 157 charter members. Active membership was restricted to persons of the white race who were members of the state bar in good standing. Honorary members were judges of the state supreme, superior, and criminal courts and judges of the federal courts in the state, so long as they remained in office. In 1947 the provision for honorary membership was dropped, and, at present, memberships are either "active" or "sustaining."

Association activities have found expression in the work of committees and officers rather than in any organized efforts on the part of the membership. Particularly active have been the committees on legislation and law reform, on justices of the peace (which has labored for twenty-five years without success to secure passage of legislation to remedy defects in the present system), on courts and court procedure, on uniform laws (which has played an important part in securing the adoption of eighteen uniform acts), on legal aid, on public relations, and on rule-making power. Generally, the efforts of the association in securing passage of legislation has not been marked with success, according to the Survey report of Edwin C. Bryson, of Duke University.

The North Carolina State Bar was created by an act of the 1933 General Assembly entitled, "An Act To Provide for the Organization as an Agency of the State of North Carolina of the North Carolina State Bar, and for Its Regulation, Powers, and Government, Including the Admission of Lawyers to Practice and Their Discipline and Disbarment." The challenge to the profession by the passage of this act was voiced by the North Carolina Bar Association president, Kemp D. Battle, who declared: "[It] means only that the public is restive under present conditions and is willing to try the experiment of permitting the lawyers to put their house in order and to regulate their professional destinies in harmony with the general welfare."

Perhaps the primary task which faced the state bar upon organization was the matter of discipline. Owing to inadequate laws and lack of effective machinery, a backlog of complaints against lawyers had accumulated to such an extent that some 122 were filed with the grievance committee in its first year of existence. (In several instances a single attorney was responsible for a large number of complaints, thirty-five in one case and sixteen in another.) In 1935 a full-time investigator was employed, and, with the employment by the council of a full-time secretary in 1938, the job of making investigations was assigned to that office.

An evaluation of bar-association activity at the local level in North Carolina is difficult to make. Many counties have less than a dozen resident lawyers, and in them no attempt has been made to set up an association. Most of the organized county associations meet only before each term of civil court to arrange a calendar for trial of civil cases, and at this time such business as needs attention is disposed of.

With the incorporation of the North Carolina State Bar in 1933, imposing compulsory membership for every lawyer in the state engaged in the practice of law, the question immediately arose as to whether there was any need for two bar associations on a statewide basis and whether the lawyers could and would support both. Some argued that the newer organization should supplant the voluntary one and assume all the obligations of the bar, both to its members and to the public. Others argued that the State Bar was purely a state administrative agency which belonged to the public and not to the lawyers themselves and which had no power to deal with problems not covered in the act creating it. Thus, they argued, there was still need for a voluntary bar association to supplement and implement the work of the State Bar.

"The members of the North Carolina State Bar can point with pride to the work of that organization and the manner in which it has raised the standards of the legal profession in North Carolina," says Bryson. "It has clearly demonstrated that the bar is willing and able to protect itself and the public against erring members of the profession." But he agrees that there is need for the voluntary association to continue in operation because much necessary work falls outside the scope of the State Bar. There is also need for improvement in the older organization, he says.

The average member of the North Carolina Bar Association now has but two assured points of contact with the association: he pays his dues and he receives a copy of the reports of the annual meetings. He does not participate in any program. . . . There is no publication to keep the membership informed, and attendance at meetings is very poor. Therefore, the business of the association reaches only a small part of the membership and is carried on by the faithful few who do attend meetings and serve on committees.

Improvement can best be achieved, Bryson believes, by carrying the business of the association to the membership at local levels.

CITY BAR ORGANIZATIONS

Bar associations in four principal American cities—Chicago, New York, Philadelphia, and Los Angeles—will be dealt with in this section as examples of bar organizations at the local level in metropolitan centers. The information comes from reports for the Survey of the Legal Profession by George W. Gale, Albert P. Blaustein, Meredith Hanna, and Clinton Clad and Harned Pettus Hoose for the respective cities.

It is estimated that more than 75 per cent of the active practicing lawyers in Chicago are members of the Chicago Bar Association, the principal one in the city. Included are almost every local, federal, state, and city judge.

The corporate charter for the Chicago Bar Association was issued on May 27, 1874, the climax of organizational activities which had begun the preceding November under the instigation of Colonel John S. Cooper, a young lawyer. The *Chicago Legal News* hailed the movement with a ringing editorial that foresaw such an organization driving out "those disreputable shysters who now disgrace the profession." Among the charter members were many prominent Chicago attorneys, including Robert Todd Lincoln.

The original by-laws provided for four standing committees: Amendment of Law, Judiciary, Grievances, and Legal Education. Meetings were held every Saturday, and, at first, membership increased rapidly. Advertising to secure divorces was one of the early evils which the association tried to suppress. Several lawyers were presented to the supreme court for disbarment for so advertising, but the Grievance Committee was not, on the whole, successful. Jury-bribing appears to have been rampant at the time, and this was another grave problem about which much was said but little done. Efforts to raise the standards of education likewise met with little success.

The association was very nearly dormant until 1886. It moved several times, each time into cheaper quarters, and finally in 1882 to a room in the courthouse donated by the county commissioners. The renaissance seems to have begun in 1886, when, after a six-year lapse, annual dinners were resumed. Had the association succumbed to the lassitude of the early 1880's, it could easily be explained by saying that it ate itself to death, Gale remarks. Veterans of the tough-beef-and-cold-potatoes afflictions of latter-day banqueting may read in disbelief the following menu for the seventh annual Chicago Bar Association dinner:

OYSTERS ON HALF SHELL

GREEN TURTLE SOUP

SMALL PATTIES À LA FINANCIÈRE

BOILED SALMON, WITH SMALL POTATOES

FILLET OF BEEF, LARDED, WITH MUSHROOMS
ASPARAGUS BAKED MASHED POTATOES

ROAST TURKEY, STUFFED CRANBERRY SAUCE
GREEN PEAS STEWED TOMATOES

CUTLETS OF PARTRIDGE, À LA VILLEROY
ESCALLOPED OYSTERS, BAKED IN SHELL

PUNCH, À LA ROMAINE

SADDLE OF VENISON, LARDED AND BRAISED
GAME SAUCE
ROAST QUAIL ON TOAST, WITH JELLY

BONED TURKEY, WITH JELLY
CHICKEN À LA MAYONNAISE
LETTUCE

DESSERT
FRUIT COFFEE

EDAM CHEESE CRACKERS

ROQUEFORT CHEESE

"That anyone could listen to a speech after such an orgy seems incredible," writes Gale in obvious awe, "but that anyone could make a speech worth listening to after indulging in such a repast seems even more surprising. Not only did the guests listen to four or five speakers, but the excerpts from the speeches . . . make interesting reading even today."

A major accomplishment of the association, as it emerged from the doldrums, was its eventual success in stamping out jury-bribing. All efforts for years had been futile, but at last the bribers went too far, and the public elected an attorney-general who welcomed the association's help and really meant business. After 1899 jury-bribing was no longer profitable in Cook County.

Throughout its history one of the chief activities of the Chicago Bar Association has been in the field of improving the administration of justice by improving the judiciary. Perhaps its greatest single accomplishment in this area was its success in 1906, after nearly twenty years of sustained effort, in establishing the Municipal Court of Chicago to replace the notoriously corrupt justices of the peace. They had been a disgrace to the legal profession in Chicago for many years.

Unquestionably the association's most important and valuable activity in the last fifteen years has been its lawyer-reference plan, begun in January, 1940. The purpose of the plan was to furnish counsel to clients who for some reason were without counsel. Progress is shown by the increase in number of referrals from 345 in the first year to 2,041 in 1949. This does not include the total number of persons who have utilized the service and have been assisted in ironing out their difficulties, some of which did not involve legal problems. In 1950 there were 535 members of the Chicago Bar Association on the lawyer-reference plan roster.

As to membership, any lawyer of good character may join the association. There are many women and a few Negroes among the more than six thousand members. While the bulk of the membership is composed of active practitioners, many lawyers who are engaged in business, particularly those engaged in trust-company work, maintain their memberships, and a few of these members are active in committee work. Most of the law-school professors in the city belong to the organization.

The association is continuously widening the sphere of its activities. It was organized "to maintain the honor and dignity of the profession of law, . . . to promote the administration of justice," and in this it has succeeded far beyond the dreams of its founders, Gale declares. "Its six thousand members look to the future, confident that the Chicago Bar Association will continue to be of increasing benefit to the bar, the bench, and the community."

Other bar organizations serving Chicago include the Illinois State Bar Association, to which many Chicago lawyers belong; the Cook County Bar Association, formed in 1914 to give Negro lawyers an organization whose primary objective would be the solution of their special problems; the Women's Bar Association of Illinois, founded in 1914; the Patent Law Association of Chicago, founded in 1884 and the oldest of its kind in the country; the Decalogue Society of Lawyers, organized in 1934 by Jewish lawyers to combat discrimination; the Bohemian Lawyers Association of Chicago, founded in 1911; the Advocates Society, originally organized in 1932 as the Polish Lawyer Association; the Justinian Society of Advocates, for lawyers of Italian birth; the Lithuanian American Lawyers Association, founded in 1927; the Nordic Law Club of Chicago, formed in 1932 by lawyers of Scandinavian descent; the South Side Lawyers Association, a small group organized in 1928; and the West Suburban Bar Association, organized in 1942.

The first meeting of the Association of the Bar of the City of New York was held on the evening of February 1, 1870. One after another, the legal giants of the day ascended the rostrum to assert the needs of organization and association. Thunderous applause greeted the statement of Samuel J. Tilden, soon to be a presidential candidate, that the bar "must be bold in defense and, if need be, in aggression." Relatively little attention was given the remarks of one leader, Dorman B. Eaton. Twelve days later, Eaton, a severe and outspoken critic of the political conditions of the day, was assaulted and left close to death. Reaction was swift. At a meeting three days later the Association of the Bar of the City of New York posted a $5,000 reward for the apprehension and conviction of the assailants.

Actually little came of the incident, and it was soon forgotten.

What has been remembered is the adoption at that time of the association's constitution, which reads in part: "The Association is established to maintain the honor and dignity of the profession of the law, to cultivate social intercourse among its members, and to increase its usefulness in promoting the due administration of justice." Behind this broad statement of principle and purpose, as later events were to show, lay a determination on the part of the bar leaders in New York City to carry to a finish the fight against political corruption as epitomized in the notorious Tweed ring. Success for the bar and allied forces came within the next two years with the defeat of the Tweed machine at the polls.

William D. Guthrie has called the New York association "the premier association of its kind in every sense of the term," and Philip J. Wickser termed it "the model for the others." But the fight for improvement in the administration of justice did not always result in victory. In 1873 the association was soundly beaten when voters turned down a proposed amendment to the state constitution for the appointment of all judges by the governor, with the advice and consent of the senate. Other defeats, along with some victories, marked the next decade or so of the association's history. Some of the efforts in behalf of a better judiciary were preventive as well as curative, as in the blocking of President Grant's first choice for chief justice of the United States Supreme Court upon the death of Salmon P. Chase.

With the most "exclusive" membership provisions of any bar association in New York City, the association has less than five thousand members. The organization is unique in having a committee on admissions as well as a traditional committee on increase of membership. Admission to the bar is only one of the requirements for membership. Every applicant must be proposed and seconded by existing members who "recommend the candidate on the basis of their personal knowledge of his character and qualifications as a desirable member of the Association." Two letters of recommendation must be submitted, and the candidate must be interviewed and approved by members of the committee on admissions. Dues are high.

An outstanding feature of the Association of the Bar of the City of New York is its library, which now numbers nearly 280,000 volumes and is one of the largest law libraries in the United States. The association's largest expenditure in 1947–48 was the sum of $108,594.37 for maintenance of the library. A distinguished periodical on the shelves is the association's own publication, *The Record.*

One noteworthy episode in the history of the association is the story of the five Socialists who were elected to the New York state assembly in 1920 and who were arbitrarily deprived of their legislative seats. While the vast majority of the bar has little sympathy with the principles set forth in the Socialist platform, many members of the association "saw a foul blow to representative government in the attempt to expel from the Legislature, because of their political opinions, duly elected representatives of the people," in the words of Harlan Fiske Stone.

A special meeting was called, the issue was debated, and the following resolution was adopted:

> *Resolved,* That this Association is unalterably opposed to any action of the Assembly excluding from its membership because of affiliation with any political party, when seeking by constitutional and legal methods to bring about any change in our Constitution and law, and person duly elected to its membership. . . .

Heading the list of the thirty-five lawyers who signed the resolution were Charles Evans Hughes, Henry L. Stimson, and Stone. Justice Hughes led the fight for the reinstatement of the five legislators in the debates before the assembly's judiciary committee, but the assembly eventually sustained its earlier decision, and the Socialists were denied their parliamentary privileges.

Summing up the record of the Association of the Bar of the City of New York, Chief Justice Stone had this to say:

> Recognizing that life itself is change, and that law is rooted in life, the Association has been wisely progressive in meeting the manifold changes which, through the years, have affected the law, the courts and the Bar. With it all, the Association has had no selfish aim. It has sought to promote no individual or Association interest which was not calculated to advance the best interests of the profession and the public.

Like the Association of the Bar of the City of New York, the New York County Lawyers' Association has opened its active membership rolls to attorneys practicing or residing anywhere in New York City. The County Lawyers' Association also has established committees which run the alphabetical gamut from "Administrative

Law" to "Unlawful Practice of the Law." And, similarly, it is devoted to maintaining the honor of the profession and the due administration of justice.

But why two general bar associations in one city—two general bar associations with similar organizations, similar functions, and similar objectives—two general bar associations located in one borough, a scant eight-minute subway ride apart?

The Association of the Bar of the City of New York was founded in 1870; the New York County Lawyers' Association was formed in 1908, at a time when the Association of the Bar was highly rated and well considered by both the legal profession and the general public. And local bar organizations had already been established in Brooklyn, Queens, and the Bronx, supplementing the activities of the "premier" association.

Several theories have been advanced to explain the formation of this new lawyers' group. One was the belief that the Association of the Bar was largely controlled by lawyers active in the Republican party and sympathetic to Republican candidates for the judiciary; another was the contention that the association was too exclusive and discriminatory in matters of race, religion, and so-called "social status."

But these reasons—reasons which would indicate conflict and contention between the two bar associations—cannot be substantiated. In fact, the 133 attorneys who comprised the first Committee on Organization of the County Lawyers Association, in January, 1908, included 75 members of the Association of the Bar. This circumstance, according to a legal periodical of that day, should be "sufficient to dispel the notion which first prevailed in some quarters that the new organization was conceived in some sort of spirit of rivalry with or antagonism to the old."

The general principle of "selective membership"—a basic tenet of the City Association today, as well as in 1908—was undoubtedly the main reason for the formation of the new organization. The founders were convinced that admission to the bar should be the only requirement for active membership—that any attorney "who had met the rigid standards set up by law for admission to the bar should, by virtue of that circumstance, be eligible for admission to any bar association." There were to be no special committees on admissions, no special intreviews, and no letters of recommendation. Thus it was that forty years later David W. Peck, presiding justice of the Appellate Division, First Department, was able to state that the County Lawyers had "struck root deep down into the great body of the bar of New York, and that [it is] becoming more and more truly representative of the great democratic mass of the bar of the City of New York."

The story of the County Lawyers is the story of a tremendous growth and development. Within a year of its organization it had become the largest bar association in the country, even larger than the American Bar Association. Approximately 2,500 applications for membership were submitted two months prior to the issuance of the organization's certificate of incorporation! There were 1,500 organizing members, and by 1909 the membership had more than doubled. And this was at a time when the ABA, after nearly thirty years of existence, had only about 2,700 members, and the New York State Bar Association and the Association of the Bar of the City of New York had less than 2,000 members each. By 1928 the membership exceeded 5,000, and the official count as of January 1, 1950, was 7,166.

The history of the New York County Lawyers' Association is one of service and accomplishment as well as of growth and development. The purposes for which the organization was formed were "the cultivation of the science of jurisprudence; the promotion of reforms in the law; the facilitation of the administration of justice; the elevation of the standards of integrity, honor and courtesy in the legal profession; [and] the cherishing of the spirit of brotherhood among the members of said Association." The County Lawyers' Association has not failed in the accomplishment of its many missions.

Despite the great work of the Association of the Bar, there was much for the new organization to do. The older group had devoted its primary efforts toward improvement of the judiciary and supervision of state legislation. The County Lawyers was to put its immediate emphasis upon the systematic instruction of the bar in professional ethics and the prosecution of those engaged in the unauthorized practice of the law.

There was plenty of work, too, to be done in the way of legal reform. Committees of lawyers, it was said, "should parcel out the Civil Code between them, with a view of correcting at least its most flagrant shortcomings. . . . Representatives of the County Bar should be in the forefront of every public movement. They should be quick to detect dereliction on the part of the public officials or members of the bar, and vigorous to prosecute, and see that fit punishment is meted out."

Target number one was the unauthorized practice of the law, then the province of the Committee on Discipline, which used a large part of the budget expense for its purposes to rid the profession of interlopers. The committee initiated surveys into the "legal" services performed by banks, insurance companies, and real estate brokers.

The struggle against "lay lawyers" has continued to be one of the most important functions of the County Lawyers and of its new Committee on the Unlawful Practice of the Law. The highlight of its activities has been the celebrated Bercu case, initiated early in 1946, in which the organization sought to enjoin a so-called "tax consultant" from giving legal advice. Bercu, a C.P.A., contended that his services as a taxation specialist were within the scope of his duties as an accountant. The case attracted nation-wide attention. Various accountants' associations joined forces with Bercu to prevent the issuance of the injunction. The American Bar Association, the New York State Bar Association, and the Association of the Bar of the City of New York filed briefs on behalf of the County Lawyers as petitioner. The issue came before the New York Court of Appeals in 1949. The decision: for the plaintiff, the New York County Lawyers' Association.

Meanwhile, the Committe on Discipline has devoted its efforts to enforcing high standards of professional conduct among the members of the New York bar. While it is by no means as active as the Committee on Grievances of the Association of the Bar, the Committee on Discipline nonetheless has performed important services in investigating complaints against local attorneys made by both the bar and the general public. In recent years the committee has also taken action against attorneys who have advertised their services in foreign-language newspapers.

A special courts committee was appointed in 1948 to work out a plan to solve the calendar problem of the supreme court in New York County. This committee did much to encourage the disposition of general tort claims—the main reason for calendar congestion—and to discourage other actions which more properly belong in the lower courts. The committee also made various important recommendations, many accepted by the 1951 state legislature, with respect to reorganization and simplification of the New York court structure.

Despite its many contributions to the public in general and to the bench and bar, the County Lawyers' Association is probably proudest of its efforts in support of the national war effort during World War II. Early in 1942 a dozen local bar associations united to form the War Committee of the Bar of the City of New York, which organized the many activities of the profession in the war effort. Association and nonassociation members alike rallied to the committee's banner, and every attorney in the city was given the opportunity of rendering legal services to the armed forces, legislative bodies, war committees, the Civilian Defense Administration, and to the men in uniform and their families. The County Lawyers group was authorized to appoint more committee members than any other constituent group; it supplied the chairmen of five of the nine chief subcommittees; and a former president, Charles E. Hughes, Jr., served as general chairman.

In 1950 Archibald R. Watson, editor of the *New York Law Journal*, clerk of the Supreme Court of New York and of the County of New York, the sole survivor of the thirty directors named in the certificate of incorporation (and chairman of the Incorporation Committee), summed up the County Lawyers' record in these words:

> It is gratifying to realize that the plans and purposes conceived and initiated by our small group more than forty years ago have in so great a part been realized. But the main credit for this record of accomplishment must be given to the outstanding members of the bar who have labored so faithfully to keep the County Lawyers' Association in the highest brackets of professional honor and services.
>
> No association in the country has had so much influence upon the opinion of the American bar as the County Lawyers. The prophetic paragraphs of bench and bar in 1908 well warranted another prophecy —that the history and development of New York State will continue to be beneficially affected by the organization and activities of the New York County Lawyers' Association.

Beginnings of the organized bar in Philadelphia go back to 1802, when a charter was granted for "The Law Library Company of the City of Philadelphia." The charter directed that the library shall permanently remain in some convenient place in the city and be open during the sitting of the courts to all members of the company and that the books shall be furnished to them and to any judge for their use in court. Twenty years later a separate organization of the legal profession was evolved under the name "The Associated Members of the Bar of Philadelphia Practicing before the Supreme Court." Six years later, on March 29, 1827, the company and the association merged under the charter of 1802 and became "The Law Association of Philadelphia." In 1930 the name was changed to the Philadelphia Bar Association.

Membership in the association as of January 1, 1950, was 2,260, or somewhat more than half of the 4,029 members of the bar in the county. The library, believed to be the first law library established in this country, contains more than 110,000 bound volumes. Another claim for distinction is the library's possession of the only complete series of *Transcripts of Records of the United States Supreme Court.*

An appraisal of the Philadelphia Law Association in 1906 by the late Chief Justice Mitchell may stand today as a characterization of the spirit and dedication to principle that has marked the organization throughout its long history:

> A review of its work redounds to the credit of the Association. From the day of small things, through difficulties and discouragements, it has fostered a library, now a noble responsibility of learning in every branch of the law, for scholars as well as for the daily toilers of the profession. It has interested itself in the morals and conduct of the Bar with moderation and discretion; has exerted its influence on legislation as well as on litigation, and always for patriotic and beneficial ends. It has maintained the tone of professional ethics, and has been recognized as doing so with courageous and undeviating fidelity, so that, though it has never had the membership of the majority of the whole Bar, it has always had the best, and has been the recognized organ of the highest professional opinion.

Among other organizations of note in Philadelphia is the Law Academy of Philadelphia, the oldest legal society in America. It traces its beginning to a law student's group which was formed in 1783 under the name "The Law Society." The original purpose of the Law Academy was that of a law school, but this function changed with the development of law schools in the universities. The academy continued to function regularly until World War II as a center for moot courts and arguments and trials under actual court conditions. Annual addresses were delivered by eminent statesmen, renowned judges, and lawyers, usually followed by a reception.

Other organized groups include the Philadelphia chapter of the Federal Bar Association, established in 1936; the Lawyers Club of Philadelphia, organized in 1892; the Constitutional Club, 1916; and the Juristic Society, 1925. The Lawyers Guild, a national organization, has members among the Philadelphia bar, but no regular meetings are held in the city.

The county of Los Angeles, larger in area than many states and larger in population than over half of them, has a total of twenty-eight organized bar associations, plus numerous social organizations composed primarily or entirely of lawyers. The first effort at organizing in the Los Angeles area was made in the spring of 1888, when the Los Angeles Bar Association came into existence.

In the early days the association devoted most of its attention to its Grievance Committee. There was then no other organization in a position to make any attempt to discipline lawyers. California adopted the integrated bar concept in 1927, making the State Bar of California actually a part of the state government. Practically all functions of a grievance committee have been taken over by it. Membership in the State Bar of California, mandatory under the act of 1927, consisted in 1951 of 15,297 active and 1,427 inactive members. The maintenance of uniform state-wide standards of admission has eliminated local differences which might have been important in former days. In connection with disciplinary matters, it has been the experience in California that this function can be carried out far more efficiently by the integrated State Bar, which possesses official powers to act and to make recommendations to the supreme court, than by local voluntary associations.

Even though the State Bar superseded the voluntary organization known as the California Bar Association, its creation by no means resulted in the discontinuance of local bar groups. The latter have increased in number, membership, and activities, substantially as a result of the stimulation provided by the State Bar. The latter, in turn, leans heavily on the local associations in carrying out its programs. The integrated bar is not equipped to cope with purely local problems. Oldest and by far the largest in the area (and fourth largest local bar group in the entire country), the Los Angeles Bar Association offers convincing evidence of this. Its membership consists of approximately 2,800 of the more than 7,000 practicing lawyers in Los Angeles.

Perhaps two of the most successful innovations of the Los Angeles Bar Association are the Lawyer Reference Service and the Junior Barristers Committee, both of which appear to have had their first development in Los Angeles. The Junior Barristers Committee was started in 1928 upon the suggestion of Hugh Morrow, then president of the Los Angeles Bar Association. It is composed of lawyers under thirty-six years of age who have not practiced more than seven years. The work of the Junior Barristers has been of great importance in integrating the young lawyer with the bar association. It has tended to improve the caliber of legal practitioners through early responsibility in bar administration and joint study. The senior members of the association have been co-operative in permitting the Junior Barristers to participate in, and sometimes control, various functions of the parent-organization.

Guiding spirit in the development of the Lawyer Reference Service was William C. Mathes, now a United States district court judge. The plan originated in 1937. Any lawyer in Los Angeles county who is in active practice and in good standing with the State Bar may register in the service; he need not be a member of the Los Angeles Bar Association. As many as eighteen hundred referrals have been made in one year.

Among the twenty-seven other professional organizations serving the Los Angeles area is the Lawyers' Club, which started in 1931 as a splinter group of the Los Angeles Bar Association and which felt that the latter should not confine itself exclusively to questions of legal significance to its members but should cover a wider field and make an effort to bring the legal profession closer to the public. Membership in the two organizations is not mutually exclusive, and many lawyers belong to both. The general emphasis of the Lawyers' Club is upon somewhat broader social and economic problems than that of the Los Angeles Bar Association.

There are two chapters of the National Lawyers Guild in Los Angeles, with a membership of approximately 120. The Lawyers Guild is less concerned with internal organization of the profession than with the guild's announced purpose to protect civil liberties generally. The guild is also active against any form of attempted coercion of lawyers who are engaged in defending persons accused of unpopular thoughts or who advocate unpopular modes of political organization. It opposes loyalty oaths and congressional hearings which it deems unconstitutional or unwise.

Other legal professional organizations include the Southern California Women Lawyers, organized in 1929; the Women Lawyers' Club, incorporated in 1928; the Patent Law Association of Los Angeles, formed in 1934; and many suburban bar associations.

THE AMERICAN LAW INSTITUTE

"The two chief defects in the American law are its uncertainty and its complexity." The legal profession was told this in 1920 by a group of prominent judges, lawyers, and law teachers organized as the Committee on Establishment of a Permanent Organization for the Improvement of the Law. Elihu Root, then known as the "dean of the American bar," was chairman of the committee. Other members included George Woodward Wickersham, former attorney-general of the United States; Harlan Fiske Stone, later chief justice of the Supreme Court; Benjamin N. Cardozo, later a Supreme Court justice; Judge Learned Hand; Cuthbert W. Pound; and other distinguished men.

The committee proposed the formation of a lawyers' organization to improve the law and its administration. Such an organization should concern itself with the form in which public law should be expressed, the details of private law, procedure or administration of the law, and judicial organization. It should neither promote nor obstruct political, social, or economic changes. It should pursue that patient, legal scientific and scholastic work which had to precede all real improvements of substantive and procedural law. As a result of the committee's recommendations, the American Law Institute was organized at a meeting in Washington, D.C., in 1923. Its accomplishments are related in "The Story of the American Law Institute," a Survey report by Herbert F. Goodrich.

An initial project for the institute, as suggested by the committee, was an effort to help overcome the uncertainty of the law, one of the two chief defects underscored in 1920. In the United States each of the forty-eight states has its own system of courts making law every day. In addition, there are the federal courts. Decisions of these courts are the precedents for future cases. Together with the statutory law, they make up the framework of the law. A lawyer working on a case must not only find, read, and digest the cases, past and present, of all the courts in his state, but, where the proposition he wants to urge is without firm precedent there, he must research the law of all the other states and the federal courts. Even after all this work, he may not find a clear-cut authority. Textbooks and encyclopedias might be of help, but their quality is always questionable, and with rare exceptions they lack status as authority for a court opinion.

The committee accordingly suggested that the new organization should produce a restatement of certain phases of the law which would tell judges and lawyers what the law was. Such a work would dispel uncertainty if it had "an authority greater than that now accorded to any legal treatise, an authority more nearly on a par with that accorded the decisions of the courts." A judge, a lawyer, or a law teacher could then go to that one source, find what the law in point was, and with confidence state it to be so.

Funds for work were secured from the Carnegie Corporation, and the institute worked at restating the law of the subjects selected from 1923 to 1944. The men engaged in it were strong men with strong opinions, and the work did not always proceed smoothly. At one time the differences between Professor Joseph H. Beale, reporter for conflict of laws, and James Byrne, vice-president of the institute, produced such a violent controversy that the whole of the material on this subject was held for two years' additional time and re-examined by the institute's executive committee. But the work went on. Over the span of two decades, nine broad phases of the law were studied and restated.

With the index materials and the institute's special tools for use of the restatements, the twenty-year period of work producd twenty-two volumes consisting of over sixteen thousand pages. In addition, programs were undertaken in co-operation with state bar associations to research the law of each state and find whether it agreed or disagreed with the propositions carried in a particular restatement. This state work was labeled "annotation," and annotations have been produced in many, if not most, of the states.

The first restatement appeared in 1932 and the last one in 1944. From 1932 to 1950 the Restatement of the Law had been cited by appellate courts 17,951 times. The Restatement has become authoritative to a far greater extent than those who organized the institute ever anticipated. That very fact is evidence that it has served the purpose of dispelling some of the uncertainty of the law which led to the formation of the American Law Institute.

The founders of the institute recognized the urgent necessity for continued learning by lawyers, even though they were members of the bar with formal legal training. The need was sharpened with the end of World War II, which had called many lawyers from their practice with a consequent loss of contact with developments in their profession. An organization in New York City known as the Practicing Law Institute became a leader in the task of meeting the demand for in-practice education.

Formal inauguration of continuing legal education as a project of the American Law Institute came in 1948. Since then the institute has encouraged and assisted in the creation upon a national scale of permanent agencies, state-wide and local, to conduct regularly planned educational projects for members of the bar. Meetings have been attended by more than nine thousand lawyers in thirty states. Another phase of the program has been the publication of lecture outlines and complete texts useful not only for courses and institutes but having a permanent value in a lawyer's library.

Continuing legal education on a nation-wide basis is still in the infant stage. As of today, the institute's committee is in a position (1) to aid in the creation of permanent state organizations to sponsor continuing legal education programs; (2) to prepare and furnish appropriate literature for use by such organizations and by individuals; and (3) to supply panels of experienced and competent lecturers.

No report on the American Law Institute would be complete without mention of the "model laws" which it has prepared. These are drafts of statutes which have the force of law when state legislatures adopt them. In connection with this work, a 1925 institute survey of criminal procedure in the United States found a remarkable degree of uniformity among the forty-eight states. But it also found remarkably little change in the methods of enforcing the criminal law in the last one hundred years. Many old technical rules abandoned in England and Canada were still in force in a majority of the states. Many such rules did not make for justice either for the state or for the defendant.

The institute undertook the preparation of a code of criminal procedure, and five years later, in 1930, the final product was adopted. It consisted of some 470 rules, with complete notes on each rule. Arizona has adopted the code in its entirety, and several other states have included a very substantial number of its sections in their laws of criminal procedure. Still others have taken over code provisions on a smaller scale. The code also served as an important point of reference in the drafting of the Federal Rules of Criminal Procedure.

Another phase of criminal law with which the institute is concerned and has acted is the handling of youthful offenders. A Model Youth Correction Authority Act, aimed at the rehabilitation of young offenders, was produced as a result of a 1940 study of juvenile crime. California, Minnesota, Wisconsin, Massachusetts, and Texas have adopted it, and in 1951 Congress enacted a version of it.

Other accomplishments of the institute in the field of "model laws" include the model code of evidence and the uniform commercial code; the latter covers an aspect of the law of vital concern not only to merchants but to every person who writes a check or makes a purchase of equipment or consumable goods. The institute is also engaged in a major project in the field of federal income-tax statutes, one of the "hottest potatoes" in the entire fiscal and political scene. The main object of this project is to improve the technical provisions of the income-tax laws, not to write a complete income-tax code. To do so would be to enter upon problems of a kind the institute was not meant to solve.

For the purpose of helping to improve the law, institute members and officers are required to pay their dues annually, incur the expense of traveling to institute meetings, and spend many hours doing their homework in preparation for such meetings. "Their purpose must be an entirely unselfish one," says Goodrich, "for, so far as anyone has ever been able to discover, membership in the institute is not a means for obtaining wealthy clients, nor do its meetings offer the customary inducements for fun and riotous living that are part and parcel of most conventions. In the final analysis, the institute is an organization where the members participate in the fulfilment of a sense of public obligation and duty to help in the realization of the sole purpose and reason for the institute's existence—to improve the law under which men live."

OTHER GROUPS OF LAWYERS

Federal Bar Association.—The Federal Bar Association was organized and chartered on January 5, 1920, in the District of Columbia. It was the outgrowth of a previous meeting of a group of federal attorneys who gathered to exchange views relative to the movement which culminated in the Classification Act of 1923 regarding federal employees. Out of this discussion came the idea that it would be a wholesome thing to form an association of government attorneys for discussion of problems of mutual interest.

Throughout its history the national character of the Federal Bar Association has been based on the interest taken in it by United States attorneys and their staffs. Before many years had passed, the social aspects of the organization became prominent and have continued to be so until the present time. While social affairs do not dominate, they form an important function as a medium through which the attorneys, judges, and legislators can get to know one another.

Dominated and controlled by government attorneys, the association nevertheless encourages the membership of attorneys in private practice who were formerly with the government. A unique feature of the association for the private practitioner is that it permits him to participate in its various functions and thereby renew old acquaintances among government officials themselves and to make new ones which may be of value to him in his law practice.

The tendency of the Federal Bar Association recently has been to sponsor a greater feeling of liaison with other bar associations. For several years it has held membership in the Inter-American Bar Association and has maintained a delegate to the American Bar Association—by custom, the retiring national president.

Patent Law Associations.—Patent law is a specialty. As would be expected, those who practice patent law find association with each other on the basis of their specialty to be desirable. From this urge arose local and regional patent-law associations. The first one, which is typical of all the others, was the Patent Law Association of Chicago, established in 1884. The Chicago association was the first local patent-law group to restrict its membership to members of the bar. Until 1944 it had two classes of membership: (1) those who were attorneys-at-law admitted to practice in the United States courts and (2) solicitors of patents and experts.

There are two branches of patent law, and thus two types of patent attorneys. One branch is the purely statutory law of the procedure of securing the grant of a patent. The other is the general substantive law of persons and property and the adjective law of court procedures as it relates to rights in the patent property. The two corresponding types of patent lawyers are (1) those who work within the narrow confines of the patent statutes and the Patent Office rules to create the property that is the patent and (2) those who cover the fields of use, conveyancing, and enjoyment of the patent as a form of the general law of persons and property and the conduct of litigation involved. "While this functional classification is accurate and factual, it becomes confused by the tendency of the first group, namely, the patent agents, to invade the field of the second group, namely, members of the bar," explains John A. Dienner in his Survey report on patent-law associations.

Because of the nature of inventions—originating as they do in the out-of-the-way corners as well as in the population center—early patent lawyers in this country found themselves in a position comparable to that of a businessman confronted with customers scattered over a wide area. The natural impulse would be to advertise, and it was thus for the patent attorneys.

The success stories which had begun to gather about the patent system after the Civil War captured the national imagination. The rate of filing patent applications began to rise rapidly, both because of the merits of the system and because of the artificial stimulus of advertisements of the Washington patent attorneys with their booklets on *What To Invent, Millions in Patents,* etc. The Patent Office allowed the situation to grow unbelievably foul before it finally decided to act. At last, in 1887, it cracked down on John Wedderburn.

Wedderburn, an extensive advertiser, conducted a lucrative practice of representing (and misrepresenting) applicants before the Patent Office. His advertising was startling in volume, extent, and audacity. Each year he held a banquet for his inventors, at which he awarded the grand prize of a silver medal and scroll for achievement. These awards were rigged and constituted merely advertising stunts. Having evidence that his work was inadequate and performed by incompetent personnel, the Patent Office finally took steps to remove his name from the register of qualified practitioners admitted to practice before it.

Wedderburn was debarred from further practice before the Patent Office. But he was by no means the only offender. The depth to which the practice before the Patent Office had fallen was incredibly low. "The noxious odor which this practice developed about the name of 'patent attorney' has been a stench in the nostrils of the Patent Office and the members of the bar who conducted their business on an ethical basis," says Dienner.

Then began the long upward climb. Progress was slow and has been achieved only in the face of intrenched opposition, on the one hand, and lack of support, on the other. Along with improvement, and lending itself thereto, came the spreading of the association idea. Following the example of the Chicago association, groups of lawyers in various other centers of invention and development founded similar associations. At present there are twenty-one throughout the country, all patterned after the original Chicago organization.

The nation-wide organization grew out of the Patent Law Association of Washington (D.C.), which was formed in 1897. Some years later this group began to take on a national character, and in 1914 the name was changed to the American Patent Law Association. It had by then become a truly national organization and a watchdog of the patent system. The chief functions of the organization are (1) to maintain social contacts at frequent meetings between members and officialdom and the judiciary; (2) to study subjects of interest to patent lawyers, including pending or proposed legislation and rules relating to patents; (3) to make appearances before committees of Congress at hearings on patent bills and the like; (4) to co-operate with the Commissioner of Patents in respect to any problems arising in connection with the Patent Office practice, such as might be involved in a proposed rule change and so on; (5) to maintain a standard of propriety of its members' actions through a code of ethics; and (6) to publish a periodical, *The Bulletin.*

The American Patent Law Association differs in function from the patents section of the American Bar Association, the latter being more deliberative and more concerned with long-range policies, tendencies, and actions.

National Association of Claimants' Compensation Attorneys.—Founded in Portland, Oregon, in 1946, the National Association of Claimants' Compensation Attorneys consists of more than fifteen hundred lawyers specializing in workmen's compensation, railroad, admiralty, and allied personal injury cases. There are members in each state, in the territories, and abroad.

By the year 1946 the number of injuries in industry had reached 2,000,000 annually. Of these, 18,000 resulted in death and 103,000 in loss of arms, legs, or eyes or other serious injury. There was and is need for persons injured in the employer-employee relationship to obtain adequate representation, not only before the industrial accident commissioners, but before the courts.

Functions of the NACCA can be summarized briefly as follows:

1. To publish the *NACCA Law Journal* for educational purposes in the direction of judges, lawyers generally, and the public, as well as the members themselves. Roscoe Pound, dean emeritus of Harvard Law School, is now editor.

2. To hold an annual national convention for men doing the same work to meet and discuss mutual problems and to encourage legislation improving the rights of injured workers in workmen's compensation, railroad, admiralty, and allied tort law.

3. To encourage the organization of branches throughout the country for the same purposes.

4. To develop a library—now one of the largest of its kind—on the rights of injured workers. The library and home office in Boston will be, it is hoped, the clearing-house for all lawyers who are trying to help injured persons.

5. To encourage the teaching of workmen's compensation, railroad, admiralty, and personal injury (tort) law. The NACCA has established lectureships throughout the country, and more than forty law schools have applied for them.

Legal fraternities.—No exact computation of the number of practicing attorneys who are members of legal fraternities is available. It is known, however, that well over 120,000 law students in the last eighty years have affiliated with them, not counting the purely local societies.

In 1869—by which time the Greek-letter society was already a recognized phenomenon of American college undergraduate life—a group of students at the University of Michigan Law School formed a secret society along the lines of the conventional collegiate fraternity for the candidly avowed purpose of "controlling politics." This group became Phi Delta Phi, the first and for thirty years the only undergraduate legal fraternity. Today there are nine national fraternities and three sororities.

While retaining the Greek-letter designations and much of the essentially social characteristics of the undergraduate societies, the legal fraternities aim at such professional decorum as might be possible on the part of the American law student and have consequently dropped the horseplay and secrecy trappings of the nonprofessional campus fraternal organizations. Each, by constitutional preamble, or otherwise, has adopted a statement of purpose involving promotion of ethical standards of personal conduct and furtherance of justice. All maintain a varied program of professional activities which generally center about speakers' programs, orientation for new students, scholarship stimulation, placement help, student loan funds, housing, veterans' assistance, legal aid, and publications.

Apart from the considerable pleasures of association with others of like background, training, and inclination, the greatest advantage attributable to membership in a national legal fraternity is generally supposed to be the professional one of wider contacts and possible exchange of business. It is fair to observe that the criterion for exchange and referral of legal business rarely is that the other man belongs to this or that fraternity.

Despite numerous criticisms—partly from critics of fraternities and sororities generally—it appears certain that the legal fraternities will continue to be an adjunct of the present system of legal education and a sideline of the legal profession. "On the whole, they have performed well a function which they do not pretend is monumental," says Kenneth H. York in reporting on the subject for the Survey of the Legal Profession.

THE ORGANIZED BAR ABROAD

For purposes of comparison, the legal profession and the organized bar in other countries will be briefly reviewed here. England, Italy, and Russia will be used as examples.

England.—The legal profession in England and Wales is divided into two branches: solicitors and barristers. The judiciary are recruited primarily from the ranks of the practicing barristers. Appointments to all higher judicial posts are permanent.

In the earliest days of the English courts all litigants had to appear in person. Gradually two types of lawyers began to appear—the pleader before the bar and the attorney or solicitor. The latter superintends the legal affairs of others but does not have the right of audience in the superior courts. The four great Inns of Court, which developed as the seats of legal education, have since the beginning of the nineteenth century excluded all attorneys and solicitors from membership in their societies, which now consist exclusively of barristers. Control of this branch of the profession is still vested exclusively in the four Inns.

No person can be a member of both branches at once, but it is possible to change from one to the other, and such a course is by no means rare. The exchange is small but steady, and perhaps the trend for barristers to become solicitors is slightly greater than the reverse, according to Thomas G. Lund, secretary of the Law Society of England and author of a Survey of the Legal Profession report on the profession in his country.

Barristers have a monopoly of the right of audience in the superior courts. The right is extended to solicitors in other courts, such as county and magistrate. Barristers' work is not entirely limited to advocacy. In addition, they are often consulted as experts by solicitors, much in the same way as a general practitioner in medicine may call a specialist into consultation. The other fundamental difference between the two branches is that the bar, by convention, has no right of direct access to the client. The latter can only approach, consult, or instruct a barrister through a solicitor. A barrister, furthermore, must work as an individual and may not practice in partnership, whereas a solicitor not only may do so but generally does. Solicitors do nine-tenths of the work performed by members of the bar in the United States, says Lund.

The right to practice as a barrister is limited to those who have been called to the bar by one of the four Inns of Court. These are voluntary, unincorporated societies of equal rank and status independent of the state and of each other. They are outside the jurisdiction of the courts, though subject to the visitorial jurisdiction of the judges. They have similar constitutions and are bound by the same rules. The Inns of Court have delegated the education and examination of students to the Council of Legal Education, which organizes courses of lectures. The bar student is under no obligation to attend any classes or to receive any practical training, although the majority of those who intend to practice "undoubtedly remedy these defects." In contradistinction to solicitors, who must be British subjects, barristers may be of any nationality.

A career at the bar is highly speculative, says Lund. All a barrister's work must come to him from solicitors, and he must accordingly acquire a reputation with them. Clearly this takes time. The system tends to concentrate work in the hands of a comparatively limited number of "fashionable" barristers who are able to earn large incomes. In the whole of England there are between a thousand and twelve hundred members of the bar who earn their living exclusively from their profession, Lund says. A barrister's fee is regarded as an honorarium, and he may not sue either the solicitor or the lay client for it. The solicitor, however, is primarily responsible, and the Law Society (the governing body of the solicitors' profession) will bring pressure upon him, if necessary, to insure the barrister's payment.

The Law Society was formed in 1823, the outgrowth of an early eighteenth-century "Society of Gentlemen Practicers in the Courts of Law and Equity." In 1951, of 22,000 English solicitors engaged in the practice of law, about 16,000 were members. However, the actual number of practicing solicitors (those who take out an annual certificate) that year was 17,000. "With taxation at its present high rate, it is really remarkable that we have as many voluntary members as we do," says Lund.

Management and control of examinations for solicitors have been placed by Parliament in the hands of the Law Society, which is empowered to make regulations governing the syllabus, the appointment of examiners, and other kindred matters. Notwithstanding that a solicitor may have duly qualified, Parliament does not permit him to practice as such unless he takes out an annual practicing certificate or license.

Disciplinary procedures are provided for any breach of the Law Society's rules. A permanent committee of nine past or present members of the Council of the Law Society hears complaints of any sort of unprofessional conduct against solicitors and has power to strike a solicitor's name off the roll, to suspend him from practice, to fine him up to £500, and to order the payment of costs.

Perhaps the most important duty intrusted by Parliament to the Law Society is the administration of the Legal Aid and Advice Act of 1949. At present, for financial reasons, only part of the scheme relating to legal aid has been introduced. This is a system whereby those of moderate means can, on payment of a proportion of the costs calculated on their ability to pay, receive legal aid and assistance in litigation. The balance, up to 85 per cent, of the lawyer's normal fee is met by the state. Administrative details of the service are embodied in a scheme drawn up by the Law Society on the authority of Parliament. The scheme, therefore, is that of a largely state-financed plan drawn up and operated by a voluntary organization representative of the profession itself, subject only to ultimate government consent. This, says Lund, "is a far cry from nationalization of the legal profession."

There is one important matter where control of the solicitor's profession is not vested in the Law Society: the matter of compensation. The remuneration of a solicitor in noncontentious business (which includes by far the greater part of his work) is governed by scales laid down by a committee consisting of the Lord Chancellor, the Master of the Rolls, the Lord Chief Justice, the president of the Law Society, and one provincial solicitor. There are two systems of charging, one based on each item of work performed by the solicitor, the other based on the amount of the consideration involved. Rules prescribe which system is to be used in a particular case. Neither system takes into account the skill, ability, and knowledge of the individual solicitor. A solicitor may make an agreement with his client to charge more than the prescribed fee, but the solicitor's bill is always open to review at the instance of the client, and an official of the court may review it and disallow or reduce certain items. The Law Society is striving to obtain a further increase in the scale of charges and also to place remuneration of solicitors on a more realistic basis. The newly qualified solicitor can hope to earn £450–£550 per annum immediately, but after two or three years' experience he should be able to command a salary of £700 (about $2,000 per year at 1954 rates of exchange but worth perhaps $3,000 in purchasing power in England).

No account of the legal profession in England and Wales would be complete, says Lund, without reference to the recent tendency for the two branches of the profession—barristers and solicitors—to work much more closely in co-operation. Not only are many members of the bar serving on committees the Law Society set up to administer the Legal Aid and Service Act, but since World War II there has been a standing joint committee representing the Law Society Council and the General Council of the Bar. This committee meets once a month during term time and considers matters of common interest to both branches of the profession.

Italy.—The Survey report on the legal profession in Italy was written by Angelo Piero Sereni, professor of law at the University of Ferrara and a member of the Italian bar and the New York bar.

In most cities and towns of central and southern Italy, he writes, a lawyer's office consists of two or three rooms set aside in his own home. The family maid opens the door to the client and ushers him into the foyer to wait; often the conference is held in the living-room. The lawyer is assisted merely by a secretary and perhaps one or two law clerks. This rather simple arrangement is typical of the many contrasts between the practice of law in Italy and that in the United States. But, says Sereni, "while some of these contrasts are a natural outgrowth of the widely divergent economic structures of the two countries, others have no such foundations, and a study of Italian practice suggests profitable lessons for the American bar."

As in most civil law countries, lawyers in Italy are divided into two classes: *avvocati* and *procuratori.* (This distinction does not correspond to either the barrister-solicitor division of the English legal profession or the French *avocat-avoué* division.) The distinction is important chiefly in civil litigation. The *procuratore* subscribes all pleadings and other papers submitted to the court. He is present at the taking of all depositions and must sign the briefs. With few exceptions, all papers during litigation are served on him rather than on his client. The *avvocato* in general performs broader and more responsible functions: he advises the client, drafts all papers and briefs, and argues the case. In practice, however, the distinction between the two classes tends to disappear, since a single individual may serve in both capacities. Most Italian practitioners find it advisable to qualify for both positions. Moreover, practice for a certain number of years as a *procuratore* entitles one automatically to become an *avvocato.*

Candidates for admission to the bar must pass an examination consisting of written and oral parts. Most unfortunately, Sereni adds, it has became a frequent practice in the last fifteen years to reduce the period of apprenticeship or to waive it altogether, and even to waive the examination requirements for certain classes of applicants—first Fascists, then veterans, and more recently those who could not find places as clerks or take the examination because of Italy's troubled conditions.

Relations between judges and lawyers are on a more formal basis than in the United States. There is, in fact, a sharp separation between the two. It is quite unusual for a judge to resign and become a lawyer or for a lawyer to be called to the bench. Judges are never elected, and their tenure is protected; so they need never curry the political favor of lawyers. Theirs is a lifelong career which usually starts almost immediately after graduation from law school and ends upon retirement, usually at seventy. New judges are chosen from law graduates by competitive examinations and go through a period of apprenticeship, either in a court or with the Department of Justice. Appointments to position on higher courts are open only to judges of lower courts and are made on the basis of seniority coupled with competitive examinations.

On the theory that the lawyer's relation to his client should be one of individual and personal trust, the practice of law in partnership is not permitted in Italy. Usually a busy lawyer has one or more "substitutes" to assist him and to whom he delegates duties under authorization of the client. However, the fee is paid to the one who was retained, and he alone is directly responsible to the client. Italy has witnessed in the last few years the well-known phenomenon of concentration of the better and larger part of the legal practice in the hands of a few lawyers. Yet most Italian practitioners, even the busiest, practice alone or with one or two assistants. "Without being disrespectful or critical, it may be said that Italian lawyers are still organized like artisans rather than entrepreneurs," says Sereni.

Lawyers' fees, both in litigation and in other matters, are controlled by statutory schedules and are subject to court supervision. Generally, fees in litigated matters are much smaller than in this country, while fees for matters outside of court, such as drafting contracts, organizing corporations, and handling real estate transactions, are much higher. Persons who are unable to pay a lawyer's fee are permitted to sue or defend as paupers. Representing paupers is considered an honor and a duty for the legal profession. There is need to extend the system to provide legal assistance outside of court, says Sereni.

The organization of the Italian legal profession is typical of a country where a highly developed economy does not yet prevail, where lawyers generally belong to the middle and upper middle class, and where the separation between lawyers and businessmen is much sharper, at least in principle, than in the United States. Among the strengths of the Italian profession, Professor Sereni proposes, are the systems of determining fees and of assistance to paupers. Most serious of the several weaknesses, on the other hand, is the fact that in recent years too many applicants have been admitted who lack either the legal training or the moral qualities and financial strength which are basic requirements to a successful practice. Some other changes are necessary, Sereni declares. "Law schools must develop from dignified finishing schools into true professional schools. The number of law graduates must be reduced by ruthlessly eliminating unworthy students. . . . Law clerkships must be better organized. Finally, the fee schedule must be amended to conform to the increase in the cost of living."

Russia.—The Survey's report on the organized bar in the U.S.S.R. was written by John N. Hazard, of the Columbia University School of Law, long a student of Soviet law, who has served as an adviser to the United States government on the subject in several capacities.

The organized bar of imperial Russia was abolished by decree on November 22, 1917. The practice of law, as it had developed prior to the Revolution, was over, but it was not the last day for lawyers. Soviet jurists recognized at the outset that ordinary citizens required assistance in presenting their cases. The decree provided, therefore, that attorneys or agents would be permitted to appear in criminal court or at preliminary examination, either as accusers or as defenders, and could also appear as representatives of the parties to civil suits. The only requirement placed on individuals wishing to appear in this capacity was that they be blameless persons, of either sex, having the rights of citizens. Former members of the imperial bar were not excluded and many continued to practice.

Difficulty was soon discovered in the fact that none of the persons practicing law was subject to the controls and restraints characteristic of a formally constituted bar. The beginnings of a new organized bar were created by a second decree of February 22, 1918, which required that persons wishing to appear as attorneys for a fee had to apply for membership in a college created in each local administrative unit. This college was little more than a panel of persons licensed to practice for a fee.

Next came experimentation with a professional salaried bar on the payroll of the state. By the People's Court Act of November 30, 1918, the newly created bar was reorganized as a state organization of "defenders." The experiment met with objections. Service as a defense attorney was made a labor duty, somewhat comparable to jury duty in the United States. This resulted in the practice of law by persons who had no continuing experience in the law, and the low point in the history of law practice in the Soviet state was soon reached.

Soviet law in its present-day sense dates from 1922. The first criminal code was adopted in May of that year, followed by a civil code patterned largely on the Swiss and French codes. The change reflected a new approach to the Soviet lawyer. He became an important instrumentality of the judicial process.

The activity of the lawyer was directed in several channels. On the one hand, he had to deal with the state enterprises. Lawyers skilled in administrative regulations became essential to their operation. On the other hand, lawyers had to deal with the small industries, artisans' shops, and one-family homes, which remained privately owned and concerning which legal problems arose similar to those familiar to the American bar. Between the state-owned industries and the private sector were the co-operative societies, with millions of members. These co-operatives also required the services of lawyers.

A reorganization of the bar accompanied the introduction of the new codes. The principle of a "college of defenders" was restored. There was a college in each province, governed by a executive committee (presidium) elected from its own membership by all members. Funds of the college were subject to control of the presidium. Each lawyer collected his own fees, but he was required to pay a percentage, in an amount established by the People's Commissariat of Justice, into the general account of the college.

The pattern of organization established in 1922 has come to be the established system of today in Russia, with some notable changes, says Hazard. Control of the bar has passed from the several provincial courts to the central Ministry of Justice. All regulations concerning the bar are issued by a central authority. The bar is organized in "colleges of advocates," which are essentially the same as the "colleges of defenders" established in 1922. The task of the bar is set in the statute as the providing of legal assistance to individuals, organizations, enterprises, and governmental corporations by giving advice in response to questions, by preparing affidavits, protests, and other legal documents, and by participating in civil and criminal actions on behalf of any interested party.

Admission to the bar is governed by standards set by the Ministry of Justice. Three classes of persons are deemed qualified professionally: (1) those who have been granted a law degree following satisfactory completion of the four-year law course; (2) those who have completed satisfactorily the two-year course in the junior law schools and who have also had practical experience for not less than one year as a judge, prosecutor, court investigator, or counsel to a government corporation or office; and (3) those who have had no formal education but who have a record of not less than three years' experience as judge, prosecutor, court investigator, or counsel to a government corporation or office. Those candidâtes for admission to the bar who present themselves on the basis of legal experience alone are required to pass bar examinations which parallel the examinations given by the law schools at the end of the four-year course.

"Consultation points," or what would be recognized by Americans as law offices, are established in number and at locations selected by the presidium in accordance with a plan approved by the Ministry of Justice. The chief of each consultation point is a manager named by the presidium and responsible to it. The manager distributes the work of the office among the members and sets the fee which each client is to pay.

Office rules indicate the routine in the consultation points. They provide that the manager's orders are compulsory for all lawyers and clerks in the office. The manager sets the hours of work and the lunch periods. Hours must be published in the public press. Every lawyer must appear at the office in accordance with a program arranged with the manager so as to permit him to keep court appointments and do research. Other rules govern every detail of the office work.

Under the Soviet Code of Criminal Procedure a defendant has an absolute right to counsel in every case in which a prosecutor appears. In consequence, if a lawyer is not provided to a defendant, the case may not be heard at all if the defendant refuses to consent to trial without a lawyer.

It would seem that the position of the lawyer has been much improved in the U.S.S.R. socially, politically, and economically since the days of the Revolution, Hazard observes. The outsider cannot help but be struck, however, with the small number of lawyers and the limitations upon legal assistance rendered to the population because of this fact. The Communist party has indicated its concern, and the reason is apparent. A program of mass legal assistance such as that devised in Russia requires many trained men and women, and they do not yet exist. Legal periodicals and the Ministry of Justice are urging the preparation of more and better lawyers.

In a society organized like the U.S.S.R. the primary burden of increasing the number and quality of lawyers rests upon the state itself. No private law schools exist to aid in training. Students are admitted to legal education in accordance with a plan prepared by the Ministry of Justice. Young men and women are not drafted into the profession; they have to be attracted by what is offered. The inducements have been important ones for the legal profession only since the late 1930's, and there has not yet been sufficient time to determine their effect, particularly in view of the recent war years when the amount of law training was at a minimum.

Lawyers in Russia are aware of their relationship to the state at all times. They are taught Soviet political theory in all their schools. They are taught that the court and lawyers are agents of political power and that the interests of the state must always be paramount. A lawyer cannot conduct a campaign against the state in a spirit of hostility. Yet this fact, which is appreciated by every Soviet lawyer, does not mean that his duties are only those of a rubber stamp, Hazard says.

STRENGTHENING THE ORGANIZED BAR

The presence of an organized bar results from two problems. First, the individual lawyer has neither the time nor the facilities for performing the public services which are rightfully expected of the legal profession. Second, he is likewise unequipped by himself to take care of his own interests in matters such as keeping abreast of new developments in the law, protecting himself against other persons who may attempt to invade his field, and developing an opportunity to compare notes and experiences with other lawyers doing similar work. He solves both these problems—his public duties and his personal interests—by banding together with his fellows in what he calls a "bar association."

In order to consider the possibilities of increased future service to the public and to the individual lawyer, an attempt to explore methods by which bar organizations may be strengthened was made by Howard L. Barkdull as a phase of the Survey of the Legal Profession.

At the outset of his examination, Barkdull seeks to find what the reason may be for the "immediate threat of socialized medicine in the United States" as contrasted with the absence of any serious demand for socialization in the case of the legal profession. The doctors are more completely organized than are the lawyers, yet the fact remains that, as a profession, they are in deep trouble. What have the doctors done or left undone? Where does their fault lie? Scientifically and professionally, their accomplishments are outstanding, and their competence is beyond question. They lead the world in research, new developments, and discoveries. The question is frequently raised, says Barkdull, whether the present threat of socialization would be confronting the medical profession if during the last two or three decades its members had displayed the same solicitude for persons of limited means which is being shown at the present time.

The fees charged by lawyers are determined largely by the cost of doing business, and they are not exorbitant. Nevertheless, fees for legal services are beyond the paying ability of many members of the public. The greatest difficulty rests with those who are between the two economic extremes—the great middle class, neither well-to-do nor indigent. There are large numbers of earnest, respectable, hard-working Americans who at times are in need of legal advice but who lack all contact with lawyers. Knowing no lawyers, they are frequently suspicious and, as a result of rumors they have heard, fear excessive charges.

Here is where the American Bar Association steps in with what is now known as the lawyer-reference plan. A description of this movement is found in chapter iii and need not be repeated here. Suffice it to say that the lawyer-reference plan, legal aid, and other similarly motivated movements constitute, in Barkdull's judgment, the best avenue of approach to the question of strengthening bar associations. "The most important single factor in strengthening bar associations is the taking of further steps to care for the interests of the man of modest means who has too long been a complete stranger to the lawyer," he declares.

Another approach lies in the problems of the judiciary. The selection of judges is a field in which the public places a natural reliance on the legal profession, Barkdull notes. Continued concern of the organized bar with this subject is of vital importance.

Policing of its own ranks is also a matter of importance for the legal profession. Bar organizations may be strengthened in this respect by further emphasis on the present policy of raising entrance requirements, in the effort to remove at the source the type of person who is likely to go astray. The associations also must prevail upon courts to resist pressure, political and otherwise, for the premature reinstatement of those who have for good cause been disbarred.

The integrated bar movement offers a strengthening device in that it puts the organized bar in a position to speak with a unanimous voice for all members of the profession, rather than for a limited fraction, and because it makes for greater financial strength. On the latter point Barkdull shows that the average annual income of the integrated state bars is $11,000 greater than that of the voluntary organizations. The integrated bar has been adopted in twenty-five of the forty-eight states, most of them in the West and Southeast. The voluntary form prevails in the Middle East and Central sections. The integrated states contain only about one-third of the total number of lawyers.

Membership of the organized bar in the national field is a matter bearing upon the subject at hand and on which there are two conflicting views. One school of thought favors a continual increase of numbers, thus enabling the organized bar to speak with a voice as nearly unanimous as possible. The other view favors giving emphasis to quality rather than quantity, with election to membership to be looked upon as a mark of distinction, bestowed upon those most likely to contribute time and money to the support of their demonstrated interest in improving the administration of justice and the profession generally. Present membership in the American Bar Association is approximately 43,000 out of an estimated 190,000 practicing lawyers in the country. Barkdull declares that the key is to be found in the matter of *service*.

"When the point is reached at which the organized bar is performing so many valuable functions on behalf of the lawyers that no one can afford not to belong, the support will be near-unanimous, and the financial status of the profession will be similar to that of our medical brethren. Service is one of the important secrets of strengthening bar organization."

A distinct point of weakness among bar organizations is in their executive and administrative work, Barkdull states. This weakness, he says, is characteristic of lawyers, not only in their professional associations, but in their own legal practice as well. Another point of weakness, he feels, has been the idea, which prevailed so long, that association work was something set aside for the elder statesmen in the profession. Barkdull applauds the junior-bar movement as having accomplished much to overcome this misconception and calls for its continued encouragement and support as an important means of strengthening the associations.

Barkdull deals with additional factors, such as the importance of publications, the vital role of committees, and the desirability of paid secretaries. In his conclusion he comes back to the concept of service as the basic answer to the question, and he writes: "It is this underlying principle which, more than any other one factor, will strengthen the organization and produce the leadership of the organized bar."

Bibliography

GENERAL REPORTS

BEAR, JOSEPH. "Survey of the Legal Profession," *Journal of the Law Society of Massachusetts,* November, 1948.

BROSMAN, PAUL. "Survey of the Legal Profession—an Effort at Objective Appraisal," *Tulane Law Review,* June, 1949.

HARNO, ALBERT J. "Survey of the Legal Profession: The Legal Education Phase," *Journal of Legal Education,* Summer, 1949.

NICHOLSON, LOWELL S. "The Survey of the Legal Profession," *Bar Bulletin* (Boston), March, 1948.

PORTER, CHARLES O. "Exorcising the Socialization Spectre," *Lawyers Guild Review,* Vol. X, No. 1 (Winter, 1950).

———. "Models, Media and Men," *Journal of the American Judicature Society,* February, 1950.

———. "Surveying the Legal Profession: In Whose Interest, How, and To Test What Hypotheses?" *Journal of the American Judicature Society,* February, 1949.

"Survey of the Legal Profession," *U.S. Law Week,* October 19, 1948.

"Survey of the Legal Profession: Council and Director Announce Definite Plans," *ABA Journal,* November, 1947.

"Survey of the Legal Profession: Second Progress Report," *ABA Journal,* September, 1949.

"Survey of the Legal Profession: Third Progress Report," *ABA Journal,* September, 1950.

"Survey of the Legal Profession: Final Progress Report," *ABA Journal,* September, 1951.

"Survey of Our Profession: 'Progress Report' as to Organization and Work," *ABA Journal,* September, 1948.

VANDERBILT, ARTHUR T. "Survey of the Legal Profession," *ABA Reports,* LXXII (1947), 349–52.

CHAPTER I

ARMSTRONG, BARBARA L. "Women in the Law," *Harvard Law School Record,* Part I, December 6, 1951; Part II, December 13, 1951.

BLAUSTEIN, ALBERT P. "Lawyers at Work," *Journal of the American Judicature Society,* Vol. XXXIII, No. 6 (April, 1950). (Reprinted in REDDEN, *Career Planning in the Law* [1951].)

———. "The Legal Profession in the United States: A 1952 Statistical Analysis," *ABA Journal,* Vol. XXXVIII (December, 1952). (Reprinted in *Law Review Digest,* March–April, 1953.)

———. "The 1949 Lawyer Count: A Preliminary Statement," *ibid.,* Vol. XXXVI (May, 1950).

BLAUSTEIN, ALBERT P. "The 1949 'Lawyer Count'—the New York Report," *New York State Bar Association Bulletin*, Vol. XXII, No. 1 (February, 1950).

BLAUSTEIN, ALBERT P., and KAPLAN, HOWARD S. "America's Women Lawyers—the 1949 'Lawyer Count,'" *Women Lawyers Journal*, Vol. XXXVII, No. 2 (Spring, 1951).

———. "New York City Lawyer Statistics," *New York County Lawyers Bar Bulletin*, Vol. VIII, No. 1 (May, 1950).

GERHART, EUGENE C. "Organization for the Practice of Law," *The Brief*, Vol. XLVI, No. 3 (Spring, 1951). (Reprinted in *ABA Journal*, October, 1951; *New Jersey Law Journal*, Vol. LXXV, No. 4 [January 24, 1952]; *Law Review Digest*, Vol. II, No. 1 [November, 1951].)

KUNZIG, ROBERT L. "Report of the Committee on the Survey of the Legal Profession for Pennsylvania," *Pennsylvania Bar Association Quarterly*, Vol. XXIII, No. 4 (June, 1952).

LOVE, HAROLD O. "Social Security and Retirement Plan for Lawyers: It Need Not Mean Socialism," *ABA Journal*, Vol. XXXVII (June, 1952).

MARTINDALE, JAMES V.; NOFER, EDWARD J.; and HILDEBRAND, WILLIAM, JR. *Second Statistical Report on the Lawyers of the United States*. February, 1952. Based on data in the 1952 *Martindale-Hubbell Law Directory*.

———. *Statistical Report on the Lawyers of the United States*. July, 1949. Based on data in the 1949 *Martindale-Hubbell Law Directory*.

———. *Statistical Report on the Lawyers of the United States, Special Abridged Edition*. August, 1949.

———. *Statistical Report on the Lawyers of the United States: Law Schools*. December, 1949.

MORRIS, GEORGE MAURICE. "Public Relations Programs of the Bar: An Analysis of the Problem and the Solution," *ABA Journal*, Vol. XXXVIII (1952). (Reprinted in *New York State Bar Bulletin*, Vol. XXIV [1952].)

PORTER, CHARLES O. "Lawyer Bankruptcies," *Journal of the National Association of Referees in Bankruptcies*, Vol. XXIV, No. 3 (July, 1950). (Reprinted in *Case and Comment*, Vol. LVI, No. 4 [July–August, 1951].)

SEGAL, ROBERT M. "The Economics of the Legal Profession in Massachusetts," *Bar Bulletin* (Boston), Vol. XXIII, No. 3 (March, 1952).

SEGAL, ROBERT M., and FEI, JOHN. "The Economics of the Legal Profession: An Analysis by States," *ABA Journal*, Part I, Vol. XXXIX (February, 1953); Part II, Vol XXXIX (March, 1953).

SMITH, REGINALD HEBER. "Complaints against Lawyers." 1st ed. February, 1949. (Mimeographed.) (2d rev. ed. to be published for the Survey of the Legal Profession by Little, Brown & Co.)

TOEPFER, LOUIS A. "Placement in the Legal Profession: A Responsibility of the Organized Bar," *ABA Journal*, Vol. XXXVII (July, 1951).

WEINFELD, WILLIAM. "Income of Lawyers, 1929–48," *Survey of Current Business*, Vol. XXIX (August, 1949).

CHAPTER II

BEAR, JOSEPH. "Workmen's Compensation and the Lawyer," *Columbia Law Review*, Vol. LI (December, 1951). (Reprinted in *Law Review Digest*, March–April, 1952.)

CHAFEE, ZECHARIAH, JR. "Changes in the Law during Forty Years," *Boston Law Review*, Vol. XXXII, No. 1 (January, 1952).

FORD, PEYTON; PALMER, CLIVE W.; and REICH, DAVID. *The Government Lawyer*. Published for the Survey of the Legal Profession by Prentice-Hall, Inc., 1952.

KOOS, EARL LOMON. "The Family and the Law." 1948. (Mimeographed.)

MADDOCK, CHARLES S. *Corporate Legal Departments*. ("Studies in Business Policy," No. 39.) National Industrial Conference Board, Inc., January, 1950.

———. "The Corporation Law Department," *Harvard Business Review*, Vol. XXX, No. 2 (March–April, 1952).

RHYNE, CHARLES S. "Salaried Services by Lawyers in Local Government," in *Municipalities and the Law in Action*. Published by National Institution of Municipal Law Officers, 1952.

SEGAL, ROBERT M. "Labor Union Lawyers," *Industrial and Labor Relations Review*, Vol. V, No. 3 (April, 1952).

SMITH, REGINALD HEBER. "The Legal Profession Takes Stock," *Church Militant*, Vol. LII, No. 10 (January, 1950).

CHAPTER III

ABRAHAMS, ROBERT D. "The English Legal Assistance Plan: A Description of Its Machinery," *ABA Journal*, Vol. XXXVI, No. 1 (January, 1950).

———. "The Neighborhood Law Office Plan," *Wisconsin Law Review*, July, 1949.

———. "The New Philadelphia Lawyer," *Atlantic Monthly*, April, 1950. (A revision of the above.)

BRADWAY, JOHN S. "Extension of Legal Aid into Smaller Communities," *Tennessee Law Review*, Vol. XXII, No. 4 (June, 1952).

BROWNELL, EMERY A. *Legal Aid in the United States*. Published for the Survey of the Legal Profession by Lawyers Cooperative Publishing Co., 1951.

CALLAGY, MARTIN V. "Legal Aid in Criminal Cases," *Journal of Criminal Law, Criminology and Police Science*, Vol. XLII, No. 5 (January–February, 1952).

DWYER, FRANCES C. "The Development of Legal Aid Movement in the Southeast," *Tennessee Law Review*, Vol. XXII, No. 4 (June, 1952).

FISHER, ALLAN, and WOODS, EDWIN M. "A Standard of Measurement for Determining the Need of Legal Aid Service in Urban Areas." 1948. (Mimeographed.)

GARDINER, RAYNOR M. "Defects in Present Legal Aid Service and the Remedies," *Tennessee Law Review*, Vol. XXII, No. 4 (June, 1952).

GARIEPY, MARGUERITE R. "Legal Aid and Social Work." 1948. (Mimeographed.)

IREY, PAUL F. "Development of Legal Aid, Tenth Federal Judicial Circuit." 1948. (Mimeographed.)

JOHNSTONE, QUINTIN. "Law School Legal Aid Clinics," *Journal of Legal Education,* Vol. III, No. 4 (Summer, 1951).

———. "Legal Aid Clinic Reports." 1951. (Mimeographed.)

MONSMAN, GERALD. "Memorandum on the Relation between Legal Aid and Lawyer Reference Plans." 1948. (Mimeographed.)

PORTER, CHARLES O. "Answers to Objections to Lawyer Reference Service," *Oregon Law Review,* Vol. XXIX (December, 1949).

———. *Lawyer Reference Plans: A Manual for Local Bar Associations.* Published for the Survey of the Legal Profession by Poole Bros., Inc., 1949.

SILVERMAN, GEORGE H. "Legal Aid as Watchdog for the Poor." 1948. (Mimeographed.)

SMITH, REGINALD HEBER. *The Cost of Legal Aid in a Metropolitan Area.* Published for the Survey of the Legal Profession by the American Bar Association's Committee on Legal Aid Work, 1951. (Originally printed in *Collected Addresses of Lawyers' Week* by Southwestern Legal Center, Dallas, Texas, 1951.)

———. "The English Legal Assistance Plan: Its Significance for American Legal Institutions," *ABA Journal,* Vol. XXXV (June, 1949). (Reprinted in *Law Society Gazette* [England].)

———. "Legal Service Offices for Persons of Moderate Means," *Wisconsin Law Review,* May, 1949. Revised and published in pamphlet form for the Survey of the Legal Profession by Court Square Press, Inc., Boston, 1950.

STOREY, ROBERT G. "Law School Legal Aid Clinics: Foreword," *Journal of Legal Education,* Vol. III, No. 4 (Summer, 1951).

CHAPTER IV

ALEXANDER, PAUL W. "Public Service by Lawyers in the Field of Divorce," *Ohio State Law Journal,* Vol. XIII (Winter, 1952).

BLAKE, MILTON J. *Legal Assistance for Servicemen.* Published for the Survey of the Legal Profession by Lord Baltimore Press, 1951.

BROWNELL, GEORGE A. "Lawyers and National Defense," *Harvard Law School Bulletin,* December, 1951.

DENFELD, LOUIS E. "Wartime Work by Lawyers for the Navy: A Tribute to Lawyers-at-Arms," *ABA Journal,* Vol. XXXVII (April, 1951).

JONES, HARRY. "Lawyers and the Legislative Development of the Law." (In three parts.) Part I (condensed), "Lawyers as Elected Legislators," *ABA Journal,* Vol. XXXVII (July, 1951); Part II (together with portions of Part I), *The Brief,* Winter, 1952; Part III, "Bill Drafting Services in Congress and the State Legislatures," *Harvard Law Review,* Vol. LXV (January, 1952).

KAPLAN, H. ELIOT. "The Lawyers' Contribution to the Merit System," *Good Government,* July–August, 1951.

KELLOR, FRANCES. *Arbitration and the Legal Profession.* Published for the Survey of the Legal Profession by the American Arbitration Association in a special pamphlet (undated). See also *Case and Comment*, Vol. LVII, No. 5 (September–October, 1952).

LEACH, W. BARTON. "Lawyers as Operations Analysts in the Army Air Forces in World War II," *Boston University Law Review*, Vol. XXXII, No. 4 (November, 1952). See also *Law Review Digest*, Vol. I, No. 1 (November–December, 1952).

NEALE, J. HENRY. "Naval Procurement during World War II: Its Legal Aspects," *ABA Journal*, Vol. XXXVIII (March, 1952).

OTTERBOURG, EDWIN M. "A Study of Unauthorized Practice." Published for the Survey of the Legal Profession by *Unauthorized Practice News*, September, 1951 (special issue).

RHYNE, CHARLES S. *Salaried Services by Lawyers in Local Government*. Boston, Mass.: Survey of the Legal Profession.

ROYALL, KENNETH C. "Lawyers in War: They Serve in the Pentagon and at the Front," *ABA Journal*, Vol. XXXVII (July, 1951).

SEASONGOOD, MURRAY. "Public Service by Lawyers in Local Government," *Syracuse Law Review*, Vol. II (Spring, 1951).

CHAPTER V

NIMS, HARRY D. "The Cost of Justice," *ABA Journal*, Vol. XXXIX (June, 1953).

PIRSIG, MAYNARD E. "A Survey of Judicial Councils, Judicial Conferences and Administrative Directors," *The Brief*, Vol. XLVII, No. 3 (Spring, 1952).

PORTER, CHARLES O. "Minimum Standards of Judicial Administration: The Extent of Acceptance," *ABA Journal*, Vol. XXXVI (August, 1950).

VANDERBILT, ARTHUR T. *Cases and Materials on Modern Procedure and Judicial Administration*. New York: Washington Square Publishing Corp., 1952.

——. (ed.). *Minimum Standards of Judicial Administration*. New York: Law Center of New York University, 1950.

CHAPTER VI

BALLANTINE, ARTHUR A. "The Work of the Practicing Law Institute: A Lawyer's Education Never Stops," *ABA Journal*, Vol. XXXVIII (October, 1952).

BLAUSTEIN, ALBERT P. "College and Law School Education of the American Lawyer. Part I," *Journal of Legal Education*, Vol. III, No. 3 (Spring, 1951).

——. "College and Law School Education of the American Lawyer. Part II," *ibid.*, Vol. IV, No. 3 (Spring, 1952).

——. "What Lawyers Read," *New York State Bar Association Bulletin*, Vol. XXII, No. 5 (October, 1950). (Reprinted in *Journal of Bar Association of State of Kansas*, Vol. XIX [February, 1951].)

CHEATHAM, ELLIOTT E. "The Law Schools of Tennessee," *Tennessee Law Review*, Vol. XXI (April, 1950). (Reprinted in *Vanderbilt Law Review*, April, 1950.)

CURRIE, BRAINERD. "The Materials of Law Study," *Journal of Legal Education,* Vol. III, No. 3 (Spring, 1951).

FULLER, LON L. "Legal Education and Admissions to the Bar of Pennsylvania," *Temple Law Quarterly,* Vol. XXV, No. 25 (January, 1952).

HARNO, ALBERT J. *Legal Education in the United States.* Published for the Survey of the Legal Profession by Bancroft-Whitney Co., 1952.

———. "Survey of the Legal Profession: The Legal Education Phase," *Journal of Legal Education,* Vol. I (1949).

"Loans for Law School Students," *Quarterly Report of the Conference on Personal Finance Law,* Vol. VI (Fall, 1952). A summary of the report of the Conference on Personal Finance Law Loan Plan Committee.

"Loans for Law Students," *Journal of Legal Education,* Vol. V, No. 3 (1953). A report to the Survey of the Legal Profession by a Committee of the Conference on Personal Finance Law.

MONRO, JOHN U. "Loans to College Students," *Quarterly Report of the Conference on Personal Finance Law,* Vol. VI (Winter, 1951–52).

MORGAN, EDMUND M. "The Case Method," *Journal of Legal Education,* Vol. IV (1952).

MORLAND, JOHN W. "Legal Education in Georgia," *Mercer Law Review,* Vol. II, No. 2 (Spring, 1951).

NICHOLSON, LOWELL S. "Some Problems of Metropolitan Law Schools Having Day and Night Divisions," *Journal of Legal Education,* Vol. IV, No. 2 (Winter, 1951).

PIERCE, ELBRIDGE B. "Correspondence Law Schools," *Journal of Legal Education,* Vol. IV, No. 2 (Winter, 1951).

ROALFE, WILLIAM R. *The Libraries of the Legal Profession.* Published for the Survey of the Legal Profession by the West Publishing Co., 1953.

SMITH, REGINALD HEBER. "Loan Plan for Law Students," *Quarterly Report of the Conference on Personal Finance Law,* Vol. V (Spring, 1951).

STOREY, ROBERT G. "The Modern Law Center," *Southwestern Law Journal,* Vol. IV (Fall, 1950).

SULLIVAN, RUSSELL N. "The Professional Associations and Legal Education," *Journal of Legal Education,* Vol. IV, No. 4 (Summer, 1952).

VANDERBILT, ARTHUR T. "A Report on Prelegal Education," *New York University Law Review,* Vol. XXV (April, 1950).

CHAPTER VII

BAUR, F. TROWBRIDGE VOM. *Standards of Admission for Practice before Federal Administrative Agencies.* Published for the Survey of the Legal Profession by Prentice-Hall, Inc., 1953.

BRENNER, JAMES E. *Bar Examinations and Requirements for Admission to the Bar.* Published for the Survey of the Legal Profession by Shepard's Citations, 1952.

———. "Improving Bar Examinations," *ABA Journal,* Vol. XXXVI (1950).

BRENNER, JAMES E.; DE GRAFF, JOHN T.; and ELLIOT, SHELDON D. "Statistical Studies of Bar Examination Results," *Bar Examinations and Re-*

quirements for Admissions to the Bar and *A Manual for Bar Examiners,* Part IV. 1951.

CLARK, HERBERT W. "Bar Examinations: Should They Be Nationally Administered?" *ABA Journal,* December, 1950.

CROTTY, HOMER D. "The Accreditation of Law Schools," *Bar Examiner,* Vol. XIX, No. 4 (July, 1950).

———. "Requirements for Admission to Practice in the Federal Courts," *ibid.,* No. 5 (September, 1950).

———. "Who Should Be Called to the Bar," *Los Angeles Bar Bulletin,* Vol. XXVI, No. 9 (May, 1951) (abridged). See also *Bar Examiner,* Vol. XX, No. 4 (July, 1951).

CULLINAN, EUSTACE. "First Year Bar Examination," *Bar Examiner,* Vol. XX (March, 1951).

———. "Requirements for Admission to Practice in England, Ireland, the Australian States, New Zealand and the Canadian Provinces," *Bar Examiner,* Part I, Vol. XIX, No. 1 (January, 1950); Part II, Vol. XIX, No. 2 (March, 1950).

ELLIOT, SHELDON D. "Administration, Preparation, and Grading of Bar Examinations," *Bar Examiner,* Vol. XIX, No. 3 (May, 1950).

FARLEY, GOSCOE O. "Admission of Attorneys from Other Jurisdictions," *Bar Examiner,* Vol. XIX, No. 5 (September, 1950).

JACKSON, JOHN G. "Character Requirements for Admission to the Bar," *Fordham Law Review,* Vol. XX (December, 1951). See also *Bar Examiner,* Vol. XXI, No. 4 (July, 1952).

KIRKWOOD, MARION R. "Requirements for Admission to Practice Law—Statutes, Rules, Regulations, and Correspondence Schools, Law Office Study, Private Study," *Bar Examiner,* Vol. XX, No. 1 (January, 1951).

MERRITT, MARJORIE. "The National Conference of Bar Examiners," *Bar Examiner,* Vol. XVIII, No. 5 (August, 1949).

SHAFROTH, WILL. "Character Investigation—an Essential Element of the Bar Admission Process," *Bar Examiner,* Vol. XVIII, No. 6 (October, 1949).

SHEPHERD, HAROLD. "Bar Examinations as Testing Devices," *Bar Examiner,* Vol. XIX, No. 2 (March, 1950).

STEVENS, GEORGE NEFF. "Scope and Subject Content of Bar Examinations," *Bar Examiner,* Vol. XIX, No. 3 (May, 1950).

CHAPTER VIII

CHEATHAM, ELLIOTT E. "The Inculcation of Professional Standards and the Functions of the Lawyer," *Tennessee Law Review,* Vol. XXI (June, 1951). See also *Bar Examiner,* Vol. XXI, No. 2 (March, 1952).

DRINKER, HENRY S. "Laymen on the Competency and Integrity of Lawyers," *Tennessee Law Review,* Vol. XXII, No. 3 (April, 1952).

HARNO, ALBERT J. "Professional Ethics at the University of Illinois," *Tennessee Law Review,* Vol. XXI (June, 1951). See also *Bar Examiner,* Vol. XXI, No. 2 (March, 1952).

HARRIS, WHITNEY ROBSON. "The Inculcation of Professional Standards at Southern Methodist University School of Law," *Tennessee Law*

Review, Vol. XXI (June, 1951). See also *Bar Examiner,* Vol. XXI, No. 2 (March, 1952).

McCoy, Philbrick. "Judicial Conduct and Judicial Selection," *Southern California Law Review,* Vol. XXIV, No. 1 (December, 1950).

McCracken, Robert T. "Report on Observance by the Bar of Stated Professional Standards," *Virginia Law Review,* Vol. XXXVII (April, 1951).

Miller, Frederic M. "Discipline of Judges," *Michigan Law Review,* Vol. L, No. 4 (March, 1952).

Phillips, Orie L., and McCoy, Philbrick. *Conduct of Lawyers and Judges.* Published for the Survey of the Legal Profession by Parker & Co., 1953.

CHAPTER IX

Barkdull, Howard L. "Methods of Strengthening Bar Associations," *Journal of the American Judicature Society,* Vol. XXXV, No. 1 (June, 1951).

Blaustein, Albert P. "The Association of the Bar of the City of New York, 1870–1951," *The Record,* Vol. VI, No. 6 (June, 1951).

———. "New York Bar Associations prior to 1870," *New York Law Journal,* Vol. CXXV (April 3 and 4, 1951).

———. "NYCLA–Giant of Bar Associations," *New York County Lawyers Association Bar Bulletin,* Vol. IX, No. 1 (May, 1951).

Bryson, Edwin C. "The Organized Bar in North Carolina," *North Carolina Law Review,* Vol. XXX, No. 4 (June, 1952).

Clad, Clinton, and Hoose, Harned Pettus. "The Organized Bar in Los Angeles," *Los Angeles Bar Bulletin,* Vol. XXVIII, No. 1 (October, 1952).

Dienner, John A. "Patent Law Associations: The American Patent Law Association, National Council of Patent Law Associations," *Journal of the Patent Office Society,* Vol. XXXII, No. 11 (November, 1950).

Fellers, James D. "The Junior Bar," *Rocky Mountain Law Review,* Vol. XXV, No. 3 (1953).

Gale, George W. "The Organized Bar in Chicago," *Chicago Bar Record,* September, 1950.

Gauer, Charlotte E. "National Association of Women Lawyers," *Women Lawyers Journal,* Vol. XXXV, No. 4 (Fall, 1949).

Goodrich, Herbert F. "The Story of the American Law Institute," *Washington University Law Quarterly,* Vol. 1951, No. 3 (June, 1951). See also *Law Review Digest,* November, 1951.

Hanna, Meredith. "The Organized Bar in Philadelphia," *Temple Law Quarterly,* Vol. XXV, No. 3 (January, 1952).

Hazard, John N. "Law Practice in Russia: The Organized Bar in the U.S.S.R.," *ABA Journal,* March, 1949. See also *Lawyers Guild Review,* Summer, 1949.

Horovitz, Samual B. "National Association of Claimants' Compensation Attorneys," *NACCA Law Journal,* Vol. VIII (November, 1951).

LACHENAL, PAUL. "The Organized Bar in Switzerland," *ABA Journal*, February, 1953.

LEPAULLE, PIERRE GEORGES. "Law Practice in France," *Columbia Law Review*, Vol. L (November, 1950).

LUND, THOMAS G. "The Legal Profession in England and Wales," *Journal of the American Judicature Society*, Vol. XXXV, No. 5 (February, 1952).

MORRIS, EARL F. "The Organized Bar in Columbus," *Ohio Bar*, Vol. XXIV, No. 32 (August 6, 1951).

NICHOLSON, LOWELL S. *The Organized Bar in Massachusetts*. Published for the Survey of the Legal Profession by the Standard Diary Co., 1952.

PALMER, JAMES E., JR., "Report on the Federal Bar Association," *Federal Bar Journal*, Vol. XI, No. 2 (January, 1951).

PORTER, CHARLES O. "Dean Pound and Bar Association Beginnings: A Survey Request for Primary Data," *ABA Journal*, April, 1951.

POUND, ROSCOE. *The Lawyer from Antiquity to Modern Times*. Published for the Survey of the Legal Profession by West Publishing Co., 1953.

SERENI, ANGELO PIERO. "The Legal Profession in Italy," *Harvard Law Review*, Vol. LXIII, No. 6 (April, 1950). See also *Case and Comment*, Vol. LVI, No. 6 (November–December, 1951).

SPIRO, JAMES M. "The American Law Student Association: Developing Future Leaders of the Bar," *ABA Journal*, May, 1952.

SUNDERLAND, EDSON R. *History of the American Bar Association and Its Work*. With a concluding chapter on "The Committee on Scope and Correlation of Work and Its Program," by WILLIAM J. JAMESON. Published for the Survey of the Legal Profession by Lord Baltimore Press, 1953.

WINTERS, GLENN R. *Bar Association Organization and Activities*. Published for the Survey of the Legal Profession and the Conference of Bar Association Presidents by the American Judicature Society, 1954.

YORK, KENNETH H. "Legal Fraternities," *Michigan Law Review*, Vol. L, No. 7 (May, 1952).

Index

The authors wish to express their thanks to Rudolph Heimanson and Mathew Foner for their generous assistance in research and indexing.

www.ingramcontent.com/pod-product-compliance
Ingram Content Group UK Ltd.
Pitfield, Milton Keynes, MK11 3LW, UK
UKHW020204290926
15470UKWH00001B/10

9 780837 164380